Women at the Well

Women at the Well
Meditations on Healing and Wholeness

Edited by Mary L. Mild

Judson Press ® Valley Forge

Women at the Well: Meditations on Healing and Wholeness
© 1996 Judson Press, Valley Forge, PA 19482-0851

Unless otherwise noted, Bible quotations in this volume are from the New Revised Standard Version of the Bible (NRSV), copyright © 1989 by the Division of Christian Education of the National Council of the Churches of Christ in the United States of America. Used by permission. All rights reserved. *The Holy Bible*, King James Version (KJV). *The Living Bible* (TLB), copyright © 1971. Used by permission of Tyndale House Publishers, Inc., Wheaton, IL, 60189. HOLY BIBLE: *New International Version* (NIV), copyright © 1973, 1978, 1984. Used by permission of Zondervan Bible Publishers. The New King James Version (NKJV). Copyright © 1972, 1984 by Thomas Nelson, Inc. The New American Standard Bible (NASB), © 1960, 1962, 1963, 1968, 1971, 1972, 1973, 1975, 1977 by The Lockman Foundation. Used by permission. *The Jerusalem Bible*, copyright © 1966 by Darton, Longman & Todd, Ltd. and Doubleday and Company, Inc. Used by permission of the publisher.

Words to "Be Not Afraid," © 1975, 1978, Robert J. Dufford, SJ and New Dawn Music, 5536 NE Hassalo, Portland, OR 97213. All rights reserved. Used with permission.

Library of Congress Cataloging-in-Publication Data
Women at the well : meditations on healing and wholeness / edited by Mary L. Mild.
   p. cm.
  ISBN 0-8170-1245-1 (pbk. : alk. paper)
  1. Women—Prayer—books and devotions—English. 2. Spiritual healing—Meditations. 3. Health—Religious aspects—Christianity—Meditations. 4. Devotional calendars. I. Mild, Mary L., 1944-.
BV4844.W654 1996
242'.643—dc20   96-29296

Printed in the U.S.A.
05 04 03 02 01 00 99 98 97
10 9 8 7 6 5 4 3 2 1

To my partner in life and love,
William H. Mild III

A Samaritan woman came to draw
water, and Jesus said to her,
"Give me a drink." .... Jesus answered her,
"If you knew the gift of God, and who
it is that is saying to you,
'Give me a drink,' you would have
asked him, and he would have
given you living water." ...
"Everyone who drinks of this water
will be thirsty again, but those who
drink of the water that I will give
them will never be thirsty.
The water that I will give
will become in them a spring of
water gushing up to eternal life."
—John 4:7, 10, 13-14

Foreword

Healing metaphors work at many levels, conscious and unconscious. They are most effective if we make them part of a daily practice, as simple as walking and breathing and prayer. Each meditation works with a central scriptural image or metaphor. With intent, focus, and imagination we can meet Christ at the well ourselves.

Like the Samaritan woman who came to the well alone, we have physical connections with water that are mostly solitary: drinking at a fountain, taking a shower, rinsing dishes. I encourage you to find some prayer anchors to remind you of these meditations throughout the day so that they are tangible reminders of God's "living water." Water would be a wonderful place to start!

The communal aspect of being at the well is more difficult to find. A place where we meet regularly with other people, even casually, could be a reminder that we celebrate God in the quality of our relationships. A carpool, family meal, lunchtime at work, or even a business meeting could be a prayer reminder for the possibility of deeper connection. When the Samaritan woman acknowledged the social taboos that separated her from Jesus, he simply invited her to a larger loyalty and purpose. And she responded. We can do that too.

The Samaritan woman "set down her jar" in order to run back to the village. The heavy jar can be a symbol for those things we may need to set down in order to make space for these meditations. It's not just the reading time (they're comfortably short) but the reflecting time we need. Most of us fill every waking moment with sound and light. Something as simple as leaving the car radio *off* would be a way to let these meditations take root in our souls.

Maybe the sound of a bell (or phone) ringing could be an invitation to breathe and center first before answering. Make space for the miraculous!

The Samaritan woman invited others to come and "meet this man." It's a natural kind of evangelism—to share what's helpful or exciting. The depth and variety of these meditations remind us that ordinary people do have the power to share the words of hope and new life when they find it for themselves. May you discover living water here!

—*Marjory Zoet Bankson*

Marjory Zoet Bankson is president of *Faith at Work*, a magazine for ministry in daily life and resource for relational Christianity in Falls Church, Virginia. She is the author of *Braided Streams, Seasons of Friendship,* and *This Is My Body.*

Acknowledgments

Eleven years ago when I began to work on women's issues at National Ministries (ABC/USA), I met two groups of women who were my ecumenical counterparts in other denominations and faith groups. They were the women from the Justice for Women Working Group of the National Council of Churches and the Religious Network for the Equality of Women. The mission of the Working Group is to focus and enrich the church's social justice ministry through advocacy for women in church and society. The mission of the Religious Network is "to build and strengthen religious communities of women through interreligious dialog among women of faith leading to actions for equality." These two groups of women were my guiding lights for eleven years of ministry in women's work. Together we worked on such issues as women and economic justice, women in prison, prostitution, women's changing role in the church, women's health, and many other timely issues.

The idea for this book of devotional articles grew out of this collaborative work in the area of women's health. These two groups of women found the wonderful women writers whom you are about to meet. This book would not have been possible without the dedicated work of the following women: Karen Hessel, Peggy Halsey, Ann Smith, Faith Johnson, Hazel Staats-Westover, Frances Unsell, Jane Kamp, Patricia Rumer, Carol Q. Cosby, Tee Garlington, Marge Christie, Joan Pope, Mary Cooper, Judith Hertz, and Mary Rehmann.

In addition, this project was brought to completion by the fine editorial work of Mary Lovett, who worked as a seminary intern at National Ministries during the year that this book was in progress. Her sense of humor and her attention to detail made working together a real blessing.

Both of us are deeply grateful for the day-to-day secretarial support of Ruth Ann Glover. Ruth Ann's skills and dedication were immeasurable and deeply appreciated.

Introduction

Two thousand years ago a woman of Samaria went to Jacob's well to draw water. Like each one of our lives, her life was complicated. Then one day she met a man at the well "who told her everything she had ever done." That encounter changed her entire life.

These devotional thoughts were composed by women who have gone to the well and have encountered the One who understands everything they have ever done. You are privileged to hear and to learn from their experiences. These writers are women who have learned, often through very difficult experiences, lessons on health, healing, and wholeness. They are women of faith who have experienced health and wholeness in wonderful ways. Many have been health-care professionals, survivors of health crises, and caregivers. Others have learned holistic living through years of experience. Each day as you read one of these devotionals, you will find yourself once again at the Well. Jesus said, "Those who drink of the water that I will give will never be thirsty. The water that I will give will become in them a spring of water gushing up to eternal life." Drink ye all of it.

January

Sharing Living Water

Jesus answered her, "If you knew the gift of God, and who it is that is saying to you, 'Give me a drink,' you would have asked him, and he would have given you living water." . . . Jesus said to her, "Everyone who drinks of this water will be thirsty again, but those who drink of the water that I will give them will never be thirsty. The water that I will give will become in them a spring of water gushing up to eternal life."

John 4:10, 13-14

Whoever gives even a cup of cold water to one of these little ones in the name of a disciple—truly I tell you, none of these will lose their reward. Matthew 10:42

There is still Living Water to be shared.
We cup it in our hands
And drink, refreshed.
Sometimes it comes as words
that heal
and hold Good News to tell,
the broken quieted,
scattered in lines of type,
or sounds we hear,
words that include us all,
the quiet coolness
of the fresh blessed moments.
Sometimes it comes as touch
in handshakes and in hugs,
a laying on of hands, a healing touch
to bring us in from loneliness.
Acceptance sealed with love and care
and Living Water ours to share.

God of steadfastness and encouragement, help us to accept your living water and to share it with those around us. Amen.

Carolyn Hall Felger

Bread of Life

*One does not live by bread alone, but by every word
that comes from the mouth of God.   Matthew 4:4b*

I thought of Jesus' words during the Blizzard of '96 because
that week (January 7–12) most people paid a great deal of
attention to bread. In my house it seemed as if we did little besides
eat, clean up, shovel, eat, clean up, eat, eat, eat. On TV, we saw
long lines at the grocery stores and heard stories about people
waylaying bread delivery trucks and snatching rolls and loaves
from the shelves and from each other. In person, we drove
frantically to stores and loaded our carts with necessities and
nonessentials as soon as we could after the snow stopped. During
the blizzard, we acted as if we do live by bread alone. For a while
we got our priorities confused. For a week we panicked and
focused mostly on physical survival. During the blizzard, we
thought of bread in nutritional, biological terms. But we are called
to be the church, God's people in the world. We are challenged to
follow Jesus—born at Christmastime, worshiped, consecrated,
and baptized, set his face toward Jerusalem, crucified on Good
Friday, rose from the dead on Easter Sunday, and living on
through the Christian church. To us Jesus says, "I am the bread of
life. Whoever comes to me will never be hungry." (John 6:35).

There is a lesson in the Blizzard of '96. As God's people, we
need to think less about physical survival—less about food,
shelter, heat, light, and travel. We need to focus more on God's
gracious gifts to us, God's love for us, our need for God, and our
relationship to God. Our spiritual survival is much more important
than our physical comfort.

*Gracious and giving God, thank you for earthly bread that
nourishes and sustains our bodies. Thank you for the bread of
heaven that feeds our souls and spirits. Help us not to be so
worried about our physical well-being that we are unmindful of
our spiritual needs. Amen.*

Janet K. Hess

It's All in the Making

And the one who was seated on the throne said, "See, I am making all things new."   *Revelation 21:5a*

As a writer, I enjoy the story of the brain surgeon who approached a well-known novelist at a writer's conference. The surgeon stated that having become established in her practice and having more control of her time, she was going to take six months off and write a novel.

The novelist replied, "That's a great idea! I think I'll follow your example. I'm going to take six months off and do brain surgery. Now that I'm an established writer, I just might have the time to heal a few brain wounds."

The novelist may have overstated his case. But we do tend, in our culture, to overlook the importance of the process, of the making. I want to write without laboring over grammar and readability. I want to lead a balanced life without having to develop it. I want to have healthy relationships without struggling with conflict.

Most of us harbor a fantasy, born in our youth, that someday we will have *made it*. But as we grow older, we begin to realize, rather, that we always will be *making it*. Acknowledging our apprenticeship as human beings allows us freedom to grow throughout our lives. And it is in this process—however wonderful or painful it may be—that we experience God's making of our lives.

Mover and Maker God, thank you for allowing us to cocreate our lives with you. Allow us to appreciate our failures as well as our triumphs. And, above all, help us to honor our apprenticeship. Amen.

Laura Alden

✨Waiting

But those who wait for the LORD shall renew their
strength, they shall mount up with wings like eagles,
they shall run and not be weary, they shall walk and
not faint.   *Isaiah 40:31*

It's the new year, which generally means making resolutions for action in some area of life. The media is full of ads for fitness centers that promise stronger bodies and healthier lifestyles. "Do it today!" one ad says. "Don't wait another minute," another warns. They directly appeal to the guilt in all of us, and we make resolutions to train for the marathon we will never run. Our Scripture from Isaiah seems to run counter to this line of thinking. The action takes a different tempo, the discipline a different tone. Strength and endurance require waiting. This is a concept that is difficult to practice. It takes patience and discipline to wait for the Lord.

I experienced this last spring. I didn't feel well; I was emotionally exhausted, and our family's financial situation looked bleak. Life seemed to be taking a turn for the worse, and I could feel depression creeping into my being. On the way to campus one morning, I saw eagles in a grove of trees. Apparently they were making a pit stop on their migratory path. One took flight as my car approached the grove, and suddenly I was reminded of the words in Isaiah. The realization came that our family's needs will be met if we are patient and faithful to the task that God has called us to do. I made a resolution to claim the promise in this Scripture, and my spirits lifted.

Giver of all, thank you for the promise of your steadfast love.
Give me the patience I need to lean on you and to wait for your
movement. Amen.

Sally Olsen

From Strength to Strength

As they go through the valley of Baca they [those who praise you and whose strength is in you] make it a place of springs; the early rain also covers it with pools. They go from strength to strength; the God of gods will be seen in Zion. Psalm 84:6-7

So this is the journey. This is the way of those who love you—passing through the Baca valley (no detours, no stalling, no getting stuck, no wearing *cement boots,* no moaning). This valley, called the Valley of the Weeper in one edition of *The Jerusalem Bible* is remembered as a place of refreshment, nourishment, growth, even delight, once it is passed through. There are many Baca valleys for me—periodic oral surgeries, loss of dear ones, family splintering, financial destruction. Yet I have learned that each experience strengthens us for the next one, if we are willing.

We go from strength to strength. Not weakness, not sniveling, not blaming, not cursing. In God's strength we find strength to keep going. Whatever it is, strength to strength, energy to energy, power to power. Circumstances appear deadly *fraught with drought,* yet this dry spell of brokenness becomes watered not only with our tears but with the refreshing springs of God's living waters and wholeness. On we go until, oh glorious hope, oh glorious promise, oh glorious moment, we appear before God in Zion! The journey complete, we are embraced, enveloped in the very light of the Zion God, where there are no more Baca valleys and never again brokenness.

God who is our strength, in the worst as in the best of times on this earthly journey, remind us of your unending love, your presence and your power, through Christ. Amen.

Grace T. Lawrence

Planted in God's Love

I pray that, according to the riches of his glory, he may grant that you may be strengthened in your inner being with power through his Spirit, and that Christ may dwell in your hearts through faith, as you are rooted and grounded in love. Ephesians 3:16-17

This is one of my favorite Scriptures because too often I find myself not being very well grounded. This happens when I am caught up in the business of work, church, and home. I find that I need to stop and reassess the involvements that may be obstructing my inner being. This tension between doing and being is especially a struggle for us, women who spend much of our time serving others in some capacity. I know that I am not alone in falling into the unhealthy habit of neglecting my own needs for restoration and grounding.

Paul's prayer, that we be rooted and grounded in God's love, brings to my mind the wonderful image of a tree. The qualities of trees, among which are their beauty and tranquility, have always been a great source of awe and inspiration for me. When I first moved to New York I thought, "I can survive here, there are trees!"

As an image of healing, the tree is rooted deep in the earth so that the winds of change and transition will not topple it. A tree needs room for its roots to grow in good soil so that it will flourish and grow, bearing fruit that nurtures and provides nourishment. We hear about such a healing tree in Revelation 22:2, the tree of life whose leaves are for the healing of the nations. These images of well-rooted trees evoke qualities that I want to practice in my daily encounters. I know that in order to be a source of healing for others, I need to make room for my own roots to become grounded in God's Word.

God of all being, be my helper and healer that I may discern the things that will keep me rooted in your love and the ways to strengthen my inner being, guided by your Holy Spirit. Amen.

Kolya M. Braun

God's Canvas

*Then God said to Noah, "Go out of the ark. . . . Bring
out with you every living thing that is with you of all
flesh—birds and animals and every creeping thing that
creeps on the earth—so that they may abound on the
earth, and be fruitful and multiply on the earth."*
Genesis 8:15-17

We are making her an easel. She is a painter who has been
struggling along, trying to work on the top of a table—the only
surface available for her work. Eleven years ago she had a stroke,
ending her career as a nurse, immobilizing most of her body,
silencing her speech. But with astonishing persistence, she has
continued to paint.

The easel will have a wide base. The far-apart legs will straddle
her own legs where they stick out from the wheelchair. She will
be able to roll her chair under the easel frame so that the canvas
can sit at waist level a few inches from her body. She cannot reach
far. Only one hand is flexible enough to hold a brush. That hand
is swollen, so her brushwork is awkward. But what a playful spirit
makes its way to the canvas!

She painted *Noah's Flood* several years ago. The picture swirls
and dances. Whimsical, Thurberesque elephants, rhinos, and gi-
raffes leap against a royal blue sky. Lions poke their heads from
the roof of a chocolate brown ark. A black dog chases a white cat
chasing a gray mouse out of the ark; white birds flurry up in
their path. Two camels look down their snouts disdainfully as
varicolored sea creatures swim through their legs. In the middle, holding two doves, stands a befuddled, wide-eyed Noah—
praying for peace? Praying for respite? Praying for a short
voyage?

The easel will help. But the paintings will continue, no matter
what. As *Noah's Flood* attests, there is more than enough life to
begin again.

*God of life and health, may we bring forth all the playful,
vibrant, leaping life within us. Amen.*

Penny Sarvis

God's Healing Power

Bless the LORD, O my soul, and do not forget all his benefits—who forgives all your iniquity, who heals all your diseases, who redeems your life from the Pit, who crowns you with steadfast love and mercy, who satisfies you with good as long as you live so that your youth is renewed like the eagle's.   Psalm 103:2-5

I am continually awed by the power and influence of God in my life. No matter what my fears may be, God always removes them. God turns my rocks into cotton.

A few years ago I was told that I had enlarged facial features, suggesting the presence of a tumor. Not only was there a rather large tumor situated on my pituitary gland, but treatment was complicated by the presence of a cerebral aneurysm (a swollen blood vessel near the brain). Could the tumor be safely removed without causing the aneurysm to rupture (which would mean certain death), or should the surgeon repair the aneurysm first? As God would have it, the aneurysm was not a factor, and the tumor was successfully removed.

The day of the surgery was followed by an afternoon and evening of snow in the form of a blizzard. The magnitude of the blizzard prevented staff persons from reporting to work at the hospital, including the surgeon who operated on me. By the second day, roads were opened, and I was visited early that morning by the surgeon. He had advised me that my recovery would require at least five days in the hospital. But God made my recovery move very rapidly. When the surgeon examined me on that second day, he said that he was amazed by my progress, and I was released from the hospital. The doctor may have been surprised, but I expected no less from God.

I still have the aneurysm, and I have been advised to take notice of any problematic symptoms. I do that, but I also know who causes me to take notice and who heals.

God, our healer and our comforter, I praise you and thank you for opening my eyes to your miracles and my mind to your wonder and power. I thank you for never forsaking me, and I pray for all who know neither you nor your power and love. Amen.

Ruth M. Lawson

Must Be Born Again

*Nicodemus said to him, "How can anyone be born
after having grown old? Can one enter a second time
into the mother's womb and be born?" Jesus
answered, "Very truly, I tell you, no one can enter the
kingdom of God without being born of water and
Spirit."*   John 3:4-5

Cheryl is one of the women in prison I visit regularly. Her life
has been a nightmare of poverty, drug abuse, prostitution, exotic
dancing in the Combat Zone in Boston, battering, rape, and
intermittent suicide attempts. Recently, the abuse that she has
survived, the drugs she has taken, the stress of trying to provide
for her two daughters—the sheer frustration of her situation—
caught up with Cheryl. She lashed out at a man she had met while
working the streets as a prostitute. He was seriously injured.

A few hours later, Cheryl turned herself in to the police. She
freely admitted what she had done, and she was remorseful.
Nothing could be said in her defense.

Months later, the fateful trial day came. I went to the courtroom
a few minutes early, hoping to leave a word of encouragement
with Cheryl, but she was guarded by a sheriff's officer who
wouldn't let us talk.

There was only one other person in the room, a worn, tired
woman who sat stiffly, clutching her handbag on her lap. I soon
discovered that she was Cheryl's mother, Colleen. We talked for
a while about what Cheryl was like as a child. How she enjoyed
math at school. How she loved animals and the outdoors. How
she had always liked to be alone. Gradually, we lapsed into
silence. Colleen seemed lost in her memories. You could have
heard a pin drop.

Finally Colleen turned to me with tears in her eyes and said,
"Sometimes I look at Cheryl, and I just want to put her back in
the womb and start over." In that instant, I saw God in this tired,
patient, frustrated, longing, sorrowful, enduring woman. I could
see just how God must feel about us. Knowing both the good and
the evil in us. Loving us, despite our shortcomings and mistakes.
Hoping for the best. Longing to take us back to a place where we

were loved and cared for. Longing to embrace us with tender arms. Offering us, again and again, the chance to be born anew.

Giver of every new beginning, hold us in the waters of healing. Birth us once again through the waters of grace. Cleanse us with the waters of wholeness. Refresh us with the waters of peace. Amen.

Ann Marie Hunter

January 10

Daily Refreshment

As for those who in the present age are rich, command them not to be haughty, or to set their hopes on the uncertainty of riches, but rather on God who richly provides us with everything for our enjoyment.

1 Timothy 6:17

I was in the middle of a three-month sabbatical when I realized that I had taken very little time to do anything but complete the class assignments of readings, papers, and class presentations. When I finally stopped to think about the purpose of being away from routine responsibilities, I knew I could not do all that I had committed to do if I did not take time to enjoy life in the midst of the more serious pursuits.

As I look back, I realize that I did find ways to give myself the opportunity to be refreshed daily. While taking seminary classes, I also took a beginning sign language class. I found refreshment in learning a totally different language. I truly enjoyed the class and the fellowship with my seven classmates. The inevitable mistake that I would make with at least one of the signs would bring a smile to my instructor's face. As she corrected me, I knew she understood how hard I was trying to do it *right*. But her smile reminded me that it was okay to do it incorrectly and that learning could be enjoyable.

I experienced joy each day as I lunched with my friends. We had begun having lunch together during the first week of class and continued through the summer. We sat under a tree by Lake Michigan and talked about serious and not-so-serious subjects, as well as laughed and just enjoyed the fresh (though muggy) air, the brilliant blue of the lake, and the occasional cool lake breezes. We were being refreshed and reminded of the richness of friendship and the beauty of God's world.

God of light and darkness, it is easy to lose ourselves in routine. As we break from our established patterns, please give us joy and refreshment through events that may seem ordinary. Thank you for your constant presence as we seek to enjoy all that you have provided. Amen.

Cecelia M. Long

Resting in God

Blessed be the God and Father of our Lord Jesus Christ, the Father of mercies and the God of all consolation, who consoles us in all our affliction, so that we may be able to console those who are in any affliction with the consolation with which we ourselves are consoled by God.   2 Corinthians 1:3-4*

Eight months after a simple pancreatic attack, I developed a rare form of pancreatitis that stymied the doctors. After twenty-five days of hospitalization, tests, and consultants, a fine surgeon removed 85 percent of my pancreas, eliminating the enzyme leakage and leaving me free of diabetes. I felt very blessed and grateful to God and to all who helped in so many ways.

The Lord enabled me to rest through the whole six weeks, and I was able to focus my energy on learning how to cooperate with God in the rewarding experience of being a partner with him in my healing.

Centering in God's peace and being concerned without being worried were vital. God could heal faster if I simply relaxed in his care, leaning on the everlasting arms, while he worked for me.

My healing involved choosing to do everything in my power to help. I regularly asked questions and took careful notes of doctors' answers and comments. The doctors and nurses responded to my interest and participation with strong support. Having maintained general health and strength helped me cope with the first hard steps, the severe initial pain I felt each time my feet touched the floor. In just minutes, the pain eased, and I walked miles through the hospital corridors each day.

The cards, visits, calls, gifts, and prayers of family, friends, and prayer chains made a huge difference. I learned the value of repeated contacts, like weekly cards or notes. Concern for my various roommates' needs helped. Today, as I write or talk or pray with someone who is suffering or struggling with a problem, my first concern is for the person's inner peace—the relaxation and freedom that let healing and ideas for solutions come from God.

God of forgiveness and understanding, we seek your peace, love, and joy as we face the troubled people and world around us, rejoicing with grateful hearts as you walk beside us. Amen.

Anabel Moseley

January 12

I Will Not Fear

For I, the LORD your God, hold your right hand; it is I who say to you, "Do not fear, I will help you."
Isaiah 41:13

After two days of Xrays, blood tests, more Xrays, and biopsies, the doctor told me calmly that I had a cancerous tumor that needed to be removed as soon as possible. Cancer! I felt as if I had been kicked in the stomach. I couldn't breathe. The possibility of cancer had never entered my mind. I was stunned. Had there been signs, symptoms, anything? I'm a registered nurse, for heaven's sake. Icy cold fear twisted the pit of my stomach.

Cancer was a *new* old word for me to assimilate. Of course I'd heard it many times before and knew its effects intimately from my work in pediatric and surgical nursing, but it had never applied to me before. When cancer becomes personalized, it takes on a whole new meaning. It's easy to tell other folks to have faith, to be strong, not to be afraid, and all the other clichés that go along with a serious illness. It is quite another thing to heed those clichés when the patient is you.

After coming to terms with what had to be done, I knew I

couldn't do it alone. I began to pray in earnest that I would be able to face up to whatever came my way. The day of surgery finally arrived. I turned all my fears and worries over to the Lord. I took him at his word, and he did not fail me. He never has. I came through surgery without a colostomy, but since the cancer had metastasized into the lymph nodes, I knew the road ahead was not going to be easy. I also knew that I was not alone. The Lord has allowed me to live in victory over cancer one day at a time. To live is my goal, but if I don't, I'll still go home to heaven. Either way, I win!

Thank you, wondrous Fashioner and Sustainer of life, for holding our hands and helping us through our times of despair, heartache, and illnesses. Amen.

Bonnie Scherer

January 13

Soar Like an Eagle

But those who wait for the LORD shall renew their strength, they shall mount up with wings like eagles, they will run and not be weary, they will walk and not faint.   Isaiah 40:31

Hope in the Lord . . . what do you think of when you hear the word "hope"? What does it mean to you? If you've been struggling with an illness, you, like me, may be hoping in the Lord for that strength to walk and run again. Hoping for good health so your spirit can soar like an eagle!

Is your hoping a form of worrying? Do you get impatient because God isn't answering your prayers when and how you would like? We must trust God, just as the eagle trusts the air currents to lift those powerful wings so it can glide and soar.

I don't get to see any eagles flying over the Carquinez Straits near my home, but I do see other birds at my backyard feeder. I also have a hummingbird feeder, and it's always a special treat to see one come zooming in, its wings moving so fast that they are just a blur. The hummingbird is so different from an eagle that glides effortlessly on the wind. We're sometimes like the little hummingbird *beating our wings*, using so much energy, darting here and there, so busy, so caught up in the hurry and worry of life's problems and stress that finding time to be still seems to escape us.

Inner rightness is a gift of God. The changes within me are God's work. I can try and try and beat my wings like the hummingbird, but until I place my self before God in prayer, quiet time, meditation, and Bible study, the changes won't come.

Lord of eagles and hummingbirds, renew our strength. Help us to put our hope and trust in you. Amen.

Donna Authelet

January 14

Power of Prayer

Are any among you suffering? They should pray. Are any cheerful? They should sing songs of praise. Are any among you sick? They should call for the elders of the church and have them pray over them, anointing them with oil in the name of the Lord. The prayer of faith will save the sick, and the Lord will raise them up; and anyone who has committed sins will be forgiven.　　　　　　　　　　*James 5:13-15*

I had traveled 750 miles away from family, friends, and loved ones to attend graduate school at Howard University School of Divinity. During my very first year, I noticed a nagging sense of discomfort in my lower abdomen, centered immediately below my navel, and feelings of nausea. As time passed, this discomfort persisted, growing in intensity, my abdomen becoming distended. I consulted with a physician at the student health-care center. He found nothing wrong, but prescribed medication to relieve the feelings of discomfort and the nausea. I became increasingly alarmed, since there was no medical explanation for my feelings. I knew that I was not pregnant.

I traveled home and found that the sensations remained with me. I decided to attend a healing service at my home church, Trinity UCC, in Chicago. I went there and sat in the front pew as those in charge led the service. When a deacon approached me, I asked for prayer for my condition. She seemed to know that it had been bothering me for some time, and she placed her hand on my abdomen and began to pray for me. I was very self-conscious about her touching my abdomen, but I knew that I needed help. She prayed, and as she did so, something happened. I left that service feeling different. A few days later, I noticed that I was no longer in discomfort and my nausea was gone. I had been healed by the power of prayer.

Ever-present, all-powerful, loving God, I stand humbly before you thanking you for all the blessings that you have bestowed upon me. For your power, mercy, and grace, I praise your name. Because you have loved me and allowed me to be under your care, I bless you. Thank you, Lord, for hearing the prayers of your people and coming to our aid. Amen.

Melbalenia D. Evans

January 15

There's an Alcoholic in the Family

But Zion said, "The LORD has forsaken me, my Lord has forgotten me." [So the Lord answers] Can a woman forget her nursing child, or show no compassion for the child of her womb? Even these may forget, yet I will not forget you. See, I have inscribed you on the palms of my hands.   *Isaiah 49:14-16a*

My best friend, Eileen, found healing and renewal of faith in the biblical story of Noah. Eileen's husband has been an alcoholic and drug abuser for eighteen years (fortunately, for the past eight years he has been sober). As can be expected, their patterns of family dynamics were typical for such long-term abuse. Eileen's husband couldn't keep a job, and he sold household items for his drugs and liquor. He went out at night and slept during the day. The window shades were drawn closed, and for years the house was dark inside when his two children left for school and when they came home in the afternoon.

Eileen took on the financial responsibility of the family by always working, borrowing money from her parents, and asking other family members for loans. Through all of these times, she never disclosed their feelings, pain, fear, or sorrow. Denial, cover-up, and codependence were the tools Eileen, her husband, and their two children learned to use to make sense out of family life. Despite those long, long years of personal suffering and family confusion, God's mercy led to healing in a most unexpected form—Bible study. I can still remember Eileen's astonishment when she learned that the biblical Noah was an alcoholic and that his family suffered under the same patterns of blaming, denial, and cover-up. With surprise she asked, "How could it be that an honored Bible family could have the same problems as my family?" She read the Scripture over and over to get the storyline right: an alcoholic father, unpredictable behavior, one son breaking the silence and naming his father's condition. The sons take care of the father. Denial continues. Noah blames the youngest son for causing trouble and punishes him for generations to come. The patterns of behavior in Noah's family were no different from her family.

For the first time in her life, she felt the Spirit of God. For her the God of the Bible is no longer a God of long ago, a Sunday morning God, or a God who shows favor to well-behaved and *perfect* people only.

Eileen experienced healing in her heart when she realized that neither Noah and his family nor she and her family were ever abandoned by God. In fact, she learned just the opposite: even at our worst we are held in the palms of God's loving hands.

Dear Spirit of the family, do you love us when we are broken, dysfunctional, unemployed, and abusive? Do you leave us when we are mean to each other, when we are sarcastic and blaming? Do you hear us when we have cried so long that there are no more tears? How long, O Lord, must we suffer? Amen.

Gini King

Mental Wholeness

*If you continue in my word . . . you will know the truth
and the truth will make you free.   John 8:31-32*

We who follow Christ need to be in the forefront of advocating
for healthful healing attitudes for persons with brain illness, just
as Jesus did in his healing ministry. This has become clear to me
since the time sixteen years ago when two members of my family
became mentally ill, as it was then called. Since then more truth
has been discovered about that marvelous organ of the human
body known as the brain. It contains ten billion or so cells spitting
chemicals at each other across synapses (gaps). These chemicals
are known as neurotransmitters. Each second of life the brain
performs about five million chemical operations. "In the human
head," concludes Nobel laureate Roger Sperry, "there are forces
within forces within forces as in no other cubic half-foot of the
universe we know. There is nothing on earth so wonderful."

It is this kind of truth that is helping to set me and millions like
me free from the stigma of so-called mental illness. As doctors
gain a better understanding of the brain and its illnesses, people
are being freed from the suffering (often caused by society's
reaction) of having a brain illness. With the development of new
medications that affect the minute chemical imbalances that can
occur in such a complex organ as the brain, people are being freed
to experience a new health and wholeness. By combining up-to-
date knowledge with Christ's compassion and understanding, we
can speed the healing process.

*Creating, saving, and sustaining God, we thank you for creat-
ing us in your image with our marvelous brains that enable us to
relate, think, feel, learn, taste, see, and hear. May we be sensitive
and helpful to one another in our areas of need as we seek to live
healthfully and abundantly as you intend for your creation. Amen.*
                                        Norma S. Mengel

Family Forgiveness

*For you, O LORD, are good and forgiving, abounding in
steadfast love to all who call on you.   Psalm 86:5*

*Do not judge, and you will not be judged; do not
condemn, and you will not be condemned. Forgive,
and you will be forgiven; give, and it will be given to
you. A good measure, pressed down, shaken together,
running over, will be put into your lap; for the measure
you give will be the measure you get back.*
                                            Luke 6:37-38

The mere mention of AIDS strikes fear and dread in the hearts
of all who know the devastation of this disease. This was also true
for Gentral. He had been sick on and off for a few months when
he found out, inadvertently, that he had AIDS—full-blown AIDS.
He came to our facility to spend his last months, and he lived with
us for almost three years. He reached out to God and found the
strength, comfort, and love that he needed. And most importantly
he found the gift of forgiveness. His initial fear and dread of the
disease and of dying gave way to anger, and anger gave way to
forgiveness—forgiveness for his family who could not understand his illness. They had abandoned him, and, to a certain
degree, each other. He forgave the one who intentionally infected
him with AIDS, and he forgave those who shrank back from him
because of AIDS. He reached out and touched the lives of many
people: old, young; male, female; gay, straight; staff, residents;
sick, well; black, white; Christian or not. He reached out to his
family so often that they quit saying no. Then they reached out to
each other. During the last week of his life—contrary to all the
studies showing a lack of attention being given to those who are
dying—people lined the halls waiting to say good-bye to him. In
his farewell to them, he gave words of reassurance and encouragement. He no longer raged against AIDS and against those who
had rejected him. Rather, he acknowledged that AIDS helped
bring his family back together, and in the end he was at peace with
AIDS.

*Creator and Preserver of all humankind, who knows our every
need, who hears our cries of anger and pain, who gives us strength*

to meet life's trials, we give you thanks for delivering us from all of life's horrors and for showing us love that lifts us up and shows us your face. We thank you for the gift of forgiveness that makes it all possible. Amen.

Jacqueline Sullivan

January 18

Stillness

Be still, and know that I am God!   Psalm 46:10a

My rocking chair on my front porch—where I sit in the early morning looking down the hill and across the road to the pond and the old house on the hill beyond—is the place I become most keenly aware of the grounding of that statement in my being. The phrase from another psalm, "the cattle on a thousand hills," also echoes in my mind as I drink in that pastoral scene.

As I search that verse in situations that I confront in mission and ministry, it leads me to examine my motives in situations that I often face as a pastor.

The temptation to us all is to be God:

in confrontations with others (*you had better respect this office I hold*),

in making decisions (*church law supports me*),

in conducting meetings (*I am in charge, don't mess with me*),

in relationships (*God has called me; I can't be wrong*),

in teaching (*my opinion is the right one; there is no room for discussion*),

in preaching (*this is the word that has come to me*).

To be sure, we are reinforced in our idolatry. A small boy in my first pastoral appointment was convinced that I was Jesus and lived inside the church building. Thus, we become guilty of putting something or someone (ourselves) in the place of God.

As long as I can keep in my mind that God is God, I am able to remember that I am not the one in charge. *God is.* It helps me keep things in perspective.

It is easier, perhaps, to sense God's presence in situations of danger, particularly those situations that I know I cannot control.

In times of tension and when confronting justice issues, it is not always as easy. I find it necessary again and again to mentally retreat to my rocking chair on my front porch to hear God say to me, "Be still and know that I am God!"

God of the stillness, we thank you that you are here. Keep us ever mindful of your presence with us as we live out the moments of our lives. Assure us and love us. Amen.

Juanita Bass Wright

January 19

Focus on God

Therefore I tell you, do not worry about your life, what you will eat or what you will drink, or about your body, what you will wear. Is not life more than food, and the body more than clothing?   Matthew 6:25

Worry, stress, anxiety—great destroyers of health. My stomach tightens, my blood pressure rises, I toss and turn all night, I snap at loved ones, my productivity decreases. I know all the symptoms. And I know they're not good. I know not to worry. I know how destructive and useless anxiety is. Surely you understand . . .

I need new tires for the car, but Sarah's thirteenth birthday party is so important to her. My father's dementia is destroying my mother. How can I not worry? How can I let go?

I know you tell me the answer: Strive first for the kingdom of God, and God's righteousness, and all these things will be given to you as well. (See Matthew 6:33.)

I sit and meditate. For just that five minutes you are right. No room for thoughts about balding tires, Dad's silly but dangerous antics, or the undulating temperament of a teenager to crowd my mind. Calm and peace sweep over me.

I say yes to you, God. I may not be able to heal my father or buy new tires right now, but I will try to set aside time each day to seek your peace and let these problems be what they are—temporary obstacles on life's path. I trust that in trusting you I will surmount these barriers.

Source of deliverance and help, quiet my anxious mind. Lead me in your peace. Amen.

Adele K. Wilcox

Small Work

When Jesus came to the place, he looked up and said to him, "Zacchaeus, hurry and come down." Luke 19:5

When I moved to the new Continuing Care Retirement Community two years ago, I certainly never planned to spend so much time "volunteering" in the health center! Three weeks after I moved in, I stubbed my toe on a city sidewalk, broke my right elbow, and ended up in the health center for three months.

So, I was there to participate in the first armchair exercises. And—I could play the melody section of music with my left hand on the piano. And—I had done work as a church secretary for over forty years and called on shut-ins before and after retirement. I'm no leader, but I did assist with a musical group at the Cleveland Sight Center.

As organizations grow, they do need volunteers, so, reluctantly, I do my best in three exercise sessions and one sing-along each week (not as the piano player, as the leader!).

Three questions still remain for me. How long does it take for these little coincidences to happen? Do we need to be in prayer to respond? How often have I been in the right place at the right time, without realizing it, and said no?

Lord of all creatures, great and small, thank you for all the blessings and serendipities of my life. Help me to keep in more constant prayer that I may be aware of the direction of my life and the times when I should be the one to be helping others. I pray for a sense of your presence, love, and guidance for all of us, your children, especially those who need it most at this time. Amen.

Alice Cotabish

God's Creation

Open my eyes, so that I may behold wondrous things.
Psalm 119:18a

I have always been a visual person, one who responds to color and shape and beauty. I have always loved flowers and have always been awed by nature's vistas and changing seasons. So I find myself surprised that I am suddenly *seeing* a whole new way. Where I used to walk down the street in springtime past a garden and say, "Isn't that lovely!" I now am likely to be stopped in my tracks by a single flower. I stare at it, examine it, try to memorize the color and the way the petals overlap each other and whether the leaves are staggered on the stem or grow opposite each other. I look at a scene out the car window now and am struck by the hundreds of shades of green; I catch myself mentally cataloguing which ones contain an extra touch of blue, which ones have more yellow.

The difference is that several years ago I began to paint. My watercolor classes are held at a botanical garden in my neighborhood, so most of my subjects are flowers and plants, as well as fruits and vegetables. For the first months, I was so thrilled with the feel of the brush and the finished painting that I didn't realize what was happening in my relationship to the things I was painting. Then I noticed that I was *beholding wondrous things—* ordinary things. Things that had always been there but of which I had never fully appreciated the intricacy and complexity. Recently, I have noticed another outcome of the creative process: I value those things of beauty in a new way. You cannot stare at a peony blossom or a red onion or a croton leaf for hours, attempting to capture its line and texture and color on paper, without developing a sense of reverence for it. I find it hard now to throw away a dead flower or a dried-up pomegranate; their beauty, even when it has faded, has become a part of me.

I knew the creative process would bring me satisfaction, and it has. When I paint, the stress goes out of my body; I imagine that I literally feel my blood pressure dropping. I suspected that I would enjoy the product, and I have. I love looking at what I have created, and I love giving paintings away, replacing them periodically as my skills increase. What I did not expect was that I would develop such a passionate love affair with God's creation, with weeds and wildflowers, with pine cones and eggplants and berry vines. It has not only enriched my life with beauty; it has given me a new sense of perspective and balance, a new twist on the meaning of wholeness.

High and Holy One, thank you for being Creator and for sharing the gift of creation with each of us. Thank you for creating such a marvelous world; remind us to give it the respect and attention it deserves. Amen.

Peggy Halsey

January 22

Do Not Be Afraid

Even though I walk through the darkest valley, I fear no evil; for you are with me.   Psalms 23:4a

She was young and distraught. Her first chemotherapy treatment was about to begin. Skilled oncology nurses explained procedures as they performed them. A pharmacist checked solutions and spoke supportively. The patient's mother sat nearby, obviously fearful, an open Bible in her lap. Mother and daughter didn't speak. When all was ready, the treatment began.

She sat with her head bowed and her eyes closed, nervously swinging her crossed legs. The room was eerily quiet as the nurses kept close, but not too close. I wanted to go to her and give her a hug, but I could not. My own formula of chemotherapy drugs was dripping slowly into my body. Even though I was a veteran of these procedures and knew that the drugs were effective, I felt uneasy about them, too.

In another hour my treatment was over. The nurses disconnected me from the chemotherapy apparatus, and I prepared to leave. I walked over to the young woman, touched her, and whispered, "Don't be afraid. These people and these drugs are your friends. God is with you." She opened her eyes. I saw worry and sadness, then a faint smile. I turned and left.

As I walked down the long hall of the medical center toward

the parking exit, I pondered the human emotions that run rampant in the treatment room. I recognized them as my own.

I was scheduled to return in one week to play the leading role in my own personal drama. I repeated my lines, "Don't be afraid. These people and these drugs are my friends. God is with me." Suddenly, the moment danced, and I flew!

Gentle, knowing Spirit, thank you for your presence at all times! Amen.

Jean Triplett

January 23

Only God Is Good

"Good Teacher, what must I do to inherit eternal life?"
Jesus said to him, "Why do you call me good? No one
is good but God alone."   Luke 18:18-19

I intended to study the story of the rich ruler, but this simple opening statement captured my complete attention. A sudden flood of relief went through me! All my life I had struggled to be *good.* Here the Scripture seemed to be giving me permission to let go of the never-ending battle to meet some impossible standard of perfection. As the middle child in a large family, I found that being good won me affection and approval at home. This tactic worked well at school too. Even as an adult, I recognized hard work, flexibility, and self-giving as sure means of earning favor. The whole package was then wrapped up in my biblical understanding that being Christian not only allowed me, but expected me, to reflect the perfect love of God.

Problems emerged, even erupted, from this constant battle to figure out what the *right* thing was and do it. But my efforts to meet my own unreal expectations left me frustrated, angry, and often physically ill. Life was a never-ending succession of *shoulds* that left me constantly feeling like an unacceptable failure. There was an intellectual understanding that I was acceptable, forgiven and loved by God. Yet deep down I ached with the need to just relax and know that I was okay.

Jesus' uncomplicated statement, "No one is good but God

alone," opened the door to a whole new way of being for me. I began to try to give myself permission to work less, to think about my own needs, and to risk being wrong. Of course, I had been wrong often. The real difference came as I released the feelings of guilt and unworthiness that being wrong had always caused in the past. Breaking free from the *good trap* is slow. It is difficult to let go of something that in some ways has served one well. However, each time I am blessed with something or someone who affirms me—warts and all—I am encouraged to continue growing. The goodness of God warms my imperfect spirit with the assurance of unconditional love.

God of goodness and grace, fill me with the warmth of your unconditional love, so that I may live boldly and courageously, secure in your love. Amen.

Siegrid Belden

January 24

Learning to Receive

In everything do to others as you would have them do to you.   Matthew 7:12a

For many years, I was blessed with relatively good health. Then I experienced a fainting spell, fell, and broke four of my ribs. I was admitted to the coronary unit of the hospital for observation and monitoring because my doctor thought I had suffered a heart attack.

Through the course of the hospital stay and my subsequent recovery, I found that I had friends who wanted to stay in close contact with me. Herein lies the dilemma that I encountered. I was torn between wanting to take care of myself and living my regular solitary life and staying on the telephone with friends who asked many questions and the ultimate question, "What can I do to help?" I found myself becoming irritated with those who offered assistance. After all, I had only broken a few ribs. I wasn't helpless or anything. I had to hold back my quick responses as I thought of how my words would have been received by those who care very much for me.

I find it fairly easy to do for others. I like the feeling of doing—of being the active one. But I found, for the first time in my adult life, that I had to learn to receive graciously. I found myself thinking that I would have preferred being alone until my healing had occurred rather than having to receive from others.

As one who lives alone, I found that I had to open myself up to receive assistance from my friends. This was a difficult lesson for me. I hope that others who are independent learn to be open to the love and concern of others. For it is truly when we learn to receive graciously from others that we experience the fullness of love and concern that God intends for us to know.

Loving and caring God, thank you for daily acts of kindness. When we are least able to care for ourselves, help us to be gracious and open to your love. Amen.

Cecelia M. Long

January 25

To Forgive

And forgive us our trespasses, as we forgive those who trespass against us.

It is hard to forgive. When a sense of betrayal and anger tell me rightfully that my boundaries have been trespassed, I feel hurt. By replaying the scenes in my mind, I reassure myself that I was right. And I feel entitled to nurse my wounds. Over time, however, my relationship with the world becomes subtly shaped by these wounds as I continue to pick at the skin and refuse to allow scabs to form. Eventually these wounds shape the person I become.

I need to forgive, just as I hope to be forgiven. Forgiveness is the only thing that is conditional in the Lord's Prayer. Forgiveness is also part of healing and becoming whole.

The much-touted goodness of coming to consciousness, enlightenment, transformation, and newness of life is actually a scary thing. I may not know myself in my new and tender skin. If I give up my personality quirks, I may not know who I am.

Forgiveness is the willingness to let go of parts of me that belong to the past, the parts that are dead, and heavy, unnecessary burdens.

God of unchangeable power, remind me that it takes an act of will to throw the hurts, as well as the times I was right, into the cosmic crucible. Only then, can the mystery of grace recycle them into blessings for me and for others. Then I can grow into a new creation, one defined not by wounds, but by blessings. Amen.

Amelia Chua

January 26

Need for Rest

The apostles gathered around Jesus, and told him all they had done and taught. He said to them, "Come away to a deserted place all by yourselves and rest a while." For many were coming and going, and they had no leisure even to eat. Mark 6:30-31

Jesus recognized the need for relaxation and rest. He knew that his disciples had poured themselves out for him and for others, and that they needed to be renewed. Even though the work was important, even though he may have urgently needed to train them for ministry, he knew that what they needed most was time to relax, to rest, to reflect and evaluate. In order to be effective disciples, they needed time to listen quietly for God's voice.

Stress is a fact of life. People die. Arguments erupt among family, friends, and coworkers. There are deadlines to meet. Someone always needs to be visited. Stress is no respecter of race, class, age, occupation, or faith. We live with it daily. Prolonged stress can lead to major health problems. We need to learn to deal with stress in positive ways. Some simple guidelines have been shown to help. I found the following hints among those on a list posted in my doctor's office:

"Seek tasks that you are capable of accomplishing, that you enjoy, that other people appreciate.

"Work off your stress through exercise.

"Learn to accept what you cannot change.

"Get enough sleep.

"Do something for others.

"Talk about your worries.

"Renew old friendships and hobbies that once gave you pleasure.

"Be flexible.

"Laugh out loud.

"Keep your sense of humor.

"Teach a child to fly a kite.

"Practice breathing deeply.

"Try not to sulk, pout, or whine for one full day. Then try again the next day.

"Gaze at the stars."

But my favorite advice for coping with stress is found in Jesus' words to his disciples. It is a few days after Jesus first sent his disciples out to preach and teach. They have returned exhausted and hungry. The crowds have been pressing in on them; they have barely had time to eat or sleep. They need a break; they need reassurance and encouragement. And Jesus, the Great Physician, responds to their need and says, "Come away to a deserted place all by yourselves and rest a while."

A deserted place? Where in our world are the deserted places? They are the places that bring us peace. They are the places of quiet restoration where we can hear the voice of God, who sometimes speaks to us in a whisper.

God of stillness and calm, come to me with your still, small voice. Refresh and renew me for the work you call me to do. Amen.
Katherine Halsey Bostrom

January 27

It Is Not My Battle

" 'Do not fear or be dismayed at this great multitude; for the battle is not yours but God's. . . . This battle is not for you to fight; take your position, stand still, and see the victory of the LORD on your behalf, O Judah and Jerusalem.' Do not fear or be dismayed; tomorrow go out against them, and the LORD will be with you."
2 Chronicles 20:15-17

Over and over in the Scriptures the message that the writers give us is that the Lord can be trusted—trusted to care about the personal battles in our lives, the battles with ourselves, the battles with others. Sometimes I think that if we really believed this, we would never need to go to war to protect ourselves. We would trust God enough to do what those in the Philippines did when they simply showed up and stood in front of the soldiers and faced them unarmed. The power of that story lives with me daily as I ask myself, "Do I trust God enough to lay down all forms of self-protection, to become defenseless save for the Lord?" It would seem to me to be the call of Christ.

God of all things great and small, help me see and refuse to pick up war as defense of myself, whether that war be with words or deeds. Amen.

Anne H. Brady

Seeing Jesus

" 'Lord, when was it that we saw you hungry or thirsty or a stranger or naked or sick or in prison, and did not take care of you?' Then he will answer them, 'Truly I tell you, just as you did not do it to one of the least of these, you did not do it to me.' " Matthew 25:44-45

As a chaplain, I have seen a lot of pain—physical, mental, and spiritual. I believe that the most persistent is the mental and spiritual pain. Physical pain goes away or can be controlled by medicine. What happens when a person suffers pain from being rejected by family, friends, or the church? How do you take that kind of pain away? In a long-term care facility, many residents are simply abandoned. Parents who have raised children and sometimes grandchildren are placed in a home or hospital because their care becomes too demanding. Even though family members may fully intend to visit regularly, the visits become farther and farther apart until they stop altogether.

There are some people who lose their ability to communicate as a result of stroke or disease. These people lose their visitors because others don't know what to say to them. Still other people have diseases that cause muscle spasms or constant movements, and some people are embarrassed to be around them. Then there are people who have AIDS. Family members are ashamed that a member of their family would get that disease, even refusing to call the disease by name. And the church . . . well, I am sorry to say that the church is no different from the people who make up the church. They use all of these excuses and more. Despite Jesus' statements to the contrary, many still believe that lifestyle choice or sin caused the disabling condition. We all need to remember that we are called to show the love of Christ to all, especially to "the least of these."

Lord of all creation, remind us that you created each one of us and that we are all your children. Remind us also that Jesus is in each one of us. Help us to see him in the beggar on the street, in the runaway child, in that person with a mental illness, and in those with AIDS. Help us to reach out and touch as Jesus touched and to love as Jesus loved. Amen.

Jacqueline Sullivan

January 29

Made Well

When Jesus saw him lying there and knew that he had been there a long time, he said to him, "Do you want to be made well?"   John 5:6

Do you want to made well? It sounds like such a rhetorical question that Jesus is asking. Who would choose to be sick?

Do we choose our sickness or our wellness? I wonder.

I was living at a frantic pace. Work. Child care. Household duties. Volunteer projects. There was no time for friends. No time for tennis. No time to garden.

Then I got cancer. I had to give up my volunteer responsibilities and had a good reason to say no. My husband showed genuine care and concern for me. I was inundated by expressions of support. I had to stop working to have an operation and chemotherapy. I could imagine a huge funeral with lots of people saying what a great person I had been.

And Jesus asked, "Do you want to be made well?"

I have a friend who believes that some people make a decision to live or to die. And if they have an overwhelming desire to live, if they are passionate about their goals and dreams, they will indeed live. He asked me, "Why do you want to live? What are your hopes and your visions?"

I was stopped short. I was spending so much time worrying about other persons' needs, supporting their dreams, that I had not even considered my own.

And Jesus asked, "Do you want to be made well?"

My answer is now an emphatic *yes!* My personal experience supports the growing scientific evidence that there is indeed a connection between how we think and feel and how our bodies respond.

Help us to know, loving God, that we are your children. As a loving parent, you desire for us wholeness, wellness, and the pursuit of meaningful dreams. Amen.

Jean DeGraff Tischler

January 30

God's Mules

A certain woman named Lydia, a worshiper of God . . . was from the city of Thyatira and a dealer in purple cloth. The Lord opened her heart to listen eagerly to what was said by Paul. When she and her household were baptized, she urged us, saying, "If you have judged me to be faithful to the Lord, come and stay at my home." And she prevailed upon us.

Acts 16:14-15

Lydia is a woman of confidence, a confidence that she uses to persuade Paul and the others to stay at her house. She is a strong woman of faith.

My sister has strong hands with no-nonsense fingernails. She can put up wallboard, replace a toilet, gut a hog, and do counted cross-stitch so fine that it makes my eyes smart. She is a single parent raising two young sons.

When we are together, we laugh and tell stories and do crafts and build things, and we sing "How Great Thou Art" for our mom. It always makes us cry.

Once a woman has developed a self, she can use that self to serve others. The gift of self-giving love is perhaps the greatest gift of the middle-aged woman. She has the energy and the know-how to transform the world with her love. And when she does this *she looks a lot like God.*

Florence volunteered each Tuesday afternoon at the soup kitchen. At first, she paid all her attention to cooking the food, and she avoided the eyes of the homeless folks who stood in line to get a meal. But then she began to learn their names, to recognize their faces. As they passed her way, to those homeless persons, Florence looked a lot like God.

The gifts of the middle-aged woman are many. But there are risks for the kind of self-giving love that she dispenses with such generosity and perseverance. Women in their middle years can get used up by not taking good enough care of themselves.

In a ride on a canal boat, a young guide told us about Dixie and Daisy, the two mules who pulled the boat up and down the canal. "Mules get a lot of bad press," she said, "because they have the reputation for being stubborn. But the real truth is that mules stop when something is wrong. If they are tired or do not feel well or are afraid, they just refuse to go any farther."

If women could be that careful! In a culture and an age that challenges women with more and more years of care, such truth could save our lives. We are taking care of our children and our parents or grandparents, all at the same time. We must make ourselves recipients of the same self-giving love that we offer so freely to others.

Power-giving God, we are torn apart by so much need in the world. Help us to see in ourselves the gifts of self-giving love that can feed and help and heal. Be our replenisher when we are weary. Be our protector when we do not protect ourselves enough. And give us peace. Amen.

Kay Ward

January 31

Perfect Love

There is no fear in love, but perfect love casts out fear.
1 John 4:18a

At twilight, a nurse brought my day-old son into my hospital room for me to hold. In the gathering darkness I contemplated his face and tried to sort through the rush of events that had overwhelmed my world in one day.

Just a few hours after his birth, bad news had come: There's a problem with the baby. Down's syndrome. Holding hands, my husband David and I posed our brave questions. The professional answers, a host of possible negatives, filled the room. They hovered there: ominous dark clouds on our horizon. All the next day we worked hard toward acquiring information and finding acceptance. Late in the afternoon, David went to spend time with our three-year-old daughter. I was alone for the next blow: in the morning our baby would be transported to Denver for emergency surgery at Children's Hospital.

Holding him now, I thought about the pain he was escaping through sleep and about the future we faced. I was trying hard to love him, but my heart was overwhelmed with fears. Would he make it through the night? Would he survive the trip? Would the surgery succeed?

Still more fears crowded in. Assuming he survived, what then? Would he grow and learn? Would we be able to help him? Would I be able to love him enough?

Hearing a tentative step, I looked up to see the familiar face of an older woman from our church. As soon as Edna sat down, I blurted out my troubles. She was quiet for awhile.

"Can I hold him? What's his name?" she asked. "Michael," I said, handing him into her arms. She gazed at him a long time, then with a little sigh she smiled and said, "He's beautiful!" Such power in a simple, natural gesture! Her delight was so genuine and true, I had to believe her. He's beautiful! This gentle truth broke through like sunlight. Love—proud mother love—rose in my heart as fear retreated in its path.

Since then, in situations when the best I can offer is a simple ministry of presence, this memory has helped me to believe that, by God's grace, it is enough.

Thank you, gracious God, for the mature, kind, and true people you keep sending into my life. Be present to me today. Fill me with your perfect love so that fear and doubt must stand aside. If it be possible, let me carry your love where it is needed. Amen.

Rhonda Cushman

February

Longing for God

*As a deer longs for flowing streams, so my soul longs
for you, O God.*   Psalm 42:1

Instinctively, the deer takes slow, deliberate steps through the forest in search of that which will sustain its life. Catching the scent of clean water and turning toward the sound of it rushing over rocks, she carefully picks her way toward survival.

In contrast, we are all too often out of touch with that which nurtures life. The instincts have been dulled—by desire coaxed through advertising, by obligation, or by exhaustion. Sometimes I can hardly respond to my body's most basic needs. Is it time to sleep? What food would best nourish and satisfy at this particular moment? Why am I staring at the television? Sometimes I may not even know. We need not satisfy all our longings. However, the wise among us will practice noticing them.

If we cannot read even these most basic signals, how will we recognize our deeper longings? How will we perceive the call of the Spirit through matter? For that is how the Spirit makes its presence known. It is a small, constant flame that beckons us deeper as we attend to what is on the surface. Moses was doing his everyday job of herding sheep as the bush caught unearthly fire, and Ruth found her destiny as she coped with the lifestyle decisions following a husband's death.

As we follow the Christian path, let us be aware of all the cues: the rumbling stomach, the parched throat, the need for movement or rest, the desire for companionship. The presence of the sacred can be better noticed as we pay attention to the commonplace. We can turn off the noise of the marketplace. To recognize our own hunger and thirst is to move closer to God.

O flowing Stream for which I thirst, guide my steps as I make my way toward you. Sharpen my senses and focus my awareness, that I may recognize my own needs and my desire to bring them to you. I want to be strong in my resolve to find you and to drink deeply from your waters. Amen.

Marie Roberts

What Does the Lord Require?

*To act justly and to love mercy and to walk humbly
with your God.* Micah 6:8 (NIV)

Major crises often create a sense of numbness and of losing
control over one's destiny. Concentrating on these crises destroys
all usefulness and sense of accomplishment. In searching for a
way to more positive living, I saw a small child desperately trying
to create a toy from a lump of clay. Many failures resulted before
a small round ball appeared. A smile of triumph lit his face!

How easy it is for us to give up when the ball does not emerge
quickly from the clay. God seems far away. It's easy to feel that
we have nothing more to give. The smallest triumph in trying to
be positive may be a major breakthrough in becoming useful
again.

There was a time when I could move nothing but my head. Life
seemed pretty much over. Then one day, two friends came into
my room. They asked when I was going to finish an article I
promised to write. My first reaction was anger, but as I thought
about it, I realized that God had left my mind intact. Mercy and
humbleness needed to replace some of the arrogance and
smugness that had crept into my life. When I realized that I was
no longer the center of the universe, and centered myself in the
love of God, life became easy! How many things there were to
do and how little time in which to do them. Twenty-four hours
was a short time, and many worthwhile endeavors filled the hours.
The depth of meaning, the joy of service, the appreciation of
friends, and the depth of goodness surrounding me was awesome.

*Merciful God, help us to realize our opportunities, minimize
our shortcomings, and be ever grateful for your loving care and
concern. Amen.*

Betty Blue

Healing the Wounds of Vietnam

*But love your enemies, do good, and lend, expecting
nothing in return.*   Luke 6:35

How vividly I remember my first trip to Vietnam. As the Thai
flight approached Hanoi, my heart pounded like a calypso drum.
When I stepped off the plane, I looked directly into the eyes of a
young Vietnamese soldier. In the center of his cap blazed a bright
gold star. Our eyes briefly locked, and I felt the blood rush from
my face. Then, quite unexpectedly, he smiled at me.

That brief exchange was the start of a healing connection and
a realization that I needed to make peace with Vietnam—a need
lying dormant in the hidden corners of my soul. Perhaps this need
dwells in the heart of every American old enough to remember
the war.

From that first encounter, the healing processes multiplied like
circles rippling out from a stone thrown in a quiet pond. One day,
walking in the streets of Hanoi, I realized that I was searching for
someone: I was looking for *an enemy*. Sometimes I'd look at a
man and imagine him as a Vietcong searching for the enemy who
was bombing his country. On my many visits I learned that the
Vietnamese wanted Americans and Vietnamese to work together
to heal the scars of war.

One day, as we returned to Hanoi from a village with our guide,
Mr. Nhu, his family joined us in our already crowded car. I can
still feel Mrs. Nhu squeezed tightly beside me, her sleeping
daughter on her lap with her black hair falling across my sweaty
arm. Mr. Nhu was in the front, tightly hugging his small, carsick
son. As I looked out the car window, I watched the spectacular
scenery of Vietnam pass by: green rice paddies, tiny women in
bamboo hats knee-deep in muddy water, little boys on the backs
of water buffalos, distant misty mountains. From the car's tape
deck came the voice of Willie Nelson singing "Amazing Grace."

In that moment of amazing grace, a healing power took over.
Vietnam was no longer a place on the map where soldiers had
fought and died in a war. It became a place where people like me

loved their children and worked hard to make a peaceful future
for them.

*Loving God, you promise that if we forgive, we will be forgiven.
Help us to forgive so that we may be given the gift of healing.
Amen.*

Joy Carol

ʻNever Alone

I will not leave you orphaned; I am coming to you.
John 14:18

Somewhere hidden within me is an anger I can't describe. I
don't even know at whom it is aimed. It's just there and keeps
rearing its ugly head when I least expect it. I do know it isn't
directed against God. I honestly don't blame God for all that has
happened. Feeling the presence of the Holy Spirit in my emotional
bouts has helped me to put the anger aside. Psychologists say that
anger is a form of grieving.

My son died from AIDS at the age of thirty-six. Death has been
a reality we have lived with for five years beyond Joel Kith's initial
diagnosis. Having chosen to live the gay lifestyle, he was one of
many who were infected before the disease became newsworthy.
Being a clergy family and coping with the issue of homosexuality
wasn't earth-shattering for us. That is not to say that there weren't
tense moments in all of our lives when he finally revealed to us what
we had suspected. But he was loved. Unconditionally. He died
knowing our love and commitment to him. We fulfilled our
promise to be his final caregivers and to let him remain at home
to die. Isn't that the way God loves?

My grief, I'm told, will subside to a dull ache to which I'll
adjust. However, moments come when even a hymn or chorus in
church can trigger the loss and emptiness. One author I've read
calls them *ambushes of grief.* Whatever. They are enabling me to
go further in my understanding of grief. They are preparing me
to reach out in situations where others are following in my path
of grief. For me, the priceless gift was a physical presence of

someone who cared. Their embrace gave me a feeling of release and peace. They removed the aloneness that I felt.

Jesus comes to me in my aloneness, in my anger. He promises never to leave me alone. I place my confidence in this promise.

O God of all compassion, help me in my ambushes of grief. Make your presence known to me. Touch my life in such a way that I'm more attuned to others, less self-serving. Walk through the valley of sorrow and grief with me until time eases the reality of death and the pain subsides. Amen.

Mary Jo Ferreira

February 5

Come Follow Me

The words to a song called "Be Not Afraid" came alive for me a few years ago. The words recall Jesus' promise to go before us always and to "come, follow me," and I recalled them when I met Jack, a gentle man in his sixties, husband to Rose, father of five, and victim of Alzheimer's disease. Walking with him and his caregivers has helped me understand the power of fear and the strength of fearless women.

Jack came to the nursing home after being hospitalized for violent behavior. The nursing staff was willing to try to work with him, but they were afraid. Would they be a victim of his violence? How would they manage his behavior? His family was afraid that this nursing home would reject him, as so many others had done.

Fear was everywhere. No one was surprised when Jack took his first swing during a trip to the bathroom, and everyone mobilized in a defensive pattern. Nurses appeared out of nowhere to help. Jack became more aggressive. The staff responded with more fear until someone heard Jack whisper, *"I'm afraid."*

And at that moment, the staff let go of their own fear and began to look for ways to relieve Jack's fear. They began to think how it must *feel* to be Jack. Like a raft adrift in a stormy ocean, Jack moves through life with no direction. For a person without memory, nothing is predictable and everything is a possible threat. He was looking for someone to follow. And the nursing staff learned to communicate the security that comes from living the words of Jesus: I go before you always. Come follow me.

And Jack does find rest, even to this day.

God of all generations, open our ears so that we may hear the words spoken in fear.

Gracious Giver of knowledge, open our hearts so that we may understand your call.

God who art perfect love, open our hands so that we may comfort those you love. Amen.

Maureen Matthews

February 6

I Am Woman

Physician, heal yourself!   Luke 4:23 (RSV)

We women spend much of our lives taking care of others. We constantly give of our time and ourselves. We give to our partners. We nurture our friends. We care for our children and for the children of others. We come to the aid of our extended families. Our efforts hold our churches and synagogues together. Our leadership moves our organizations forward. Our labors provide the backbone of productivity in our workplaces. So much depends on us, and we give it our all.

Just thinking of all we have to do is enough to make us tired. The slogan "I am woman, I am invincible, I am tired!" hits a little too close to home. Too often, we are so busy taking care of everyone and everything that we get lost in the process. We expend so much energy making sure everything gets done (and gets done well) that we have no energy left for ourselves. We give so much that sometimes we end up feeling empty.

Perhaps before we get to this point, we could remember, "Physician, heal yourself." For we do have a great physician inside ourselves, one that we so willingly share with others. It would do us good to remember that we are just as worthy of this healing. We need and deserve our own time: time for prayer and contemplation, time for exercise and recreation, time just for rest and relaxation. Our wholeness comes when we take care of ourselves, when we nurture ourselves, when we allow ourselves to be who we are and celebrate the life within us! Our wholeness comes when we allow the Spirit to tickle our hearts and minds, fill us with laughter, sprinkle us with joy, and envelop us with peace. Our wholeness comes when we are able to stop defining ourselves in terms of what we do and are able to shout with God, *I Am!*

O Great Physician, remind me today that I too am in need of and worthy of your healing. As I give of myself to others, let me also remember to give to myself. Rest your healing touch on me that I may remember who I am, who you are, and who we are together, and then I will be whole. Amen.

Betsy L. Halsey

February 7

Sweet Fragrance

Mary took a pound of costly perfume made of pure nard, anointed Jesus' feet, and wiped them with her hair. The house was filled with the fragrance of the perfume.   John 12:3

I'm standing at my kitchen sink, cleaning up the dishes after dinner. I can smell the food that we just cooked for dinner, and the dish detergent that is sudsing around my hands, and the Windex I used to clean the kitchen table. All the usual after-dinner smells.

Suddenly a heavenly and exotic scent wafts into the kitchen, cutting through the ordinary evening smells. My husband has just opened a *New Yorker* magazine, which always includes a center-fold ad for some expensive perfume or another. The moment the page turns the smell of the perfume fills the house with a bewitching scent. The ordinary smells of everyday living are transformed into something surprising and magical.

Just so, the followers of Jesus gathered in the evening, surrounded by the hustle and bustle, the ordinary noises and smells of everyday life: dusty afternoon streets, tired bodies, goat meat and olive oil from the evening meal.

And then Mary broke open her jar of nard and anointed Jesus' feet. And the house was filled with the fragrance of the perfume.

The fragrance pushed back the smell of the goats and the sweat and the dust, transforming the moment. Startled, the disciples looked up from their business as usual.

And suddenly, in the anointing, Jesus was no longer just an itinerant rabbi. He was the Messiah. Suddenly, in the anointing, Jesus was no longer just wandering about, preaching here and there. He was on his way to Jerusalem. Suddenly, in the anointing, Jesus was preparing to die in his confrontation with the entrenched and self-righteous powers of his day.

All this, in the moment of anointing, as the nard was broken open and Mary poured out at Jesus' feet the most precious gift that she had to give. All this, in a moment that transformed the ordinary into the extraordinary, as the house was filled with the fragrance of the perfume. All this, in a moment that changed Jesus's life and human history. All this, in a moment drenched with insight and significance. All this, in a moment that transformed Mary too.

And then the smell of the perfume faded, and the disciples began to quibble about the cost. And Jesus headed to Jerusalem. And I am once more at my kitchen sink—but there is still a lingering whiff of perfume in the air.

O transforming God, give us the insight and the strength to act upon our dreams. Amen.

Ann Marie Hunter

February 8

Power to Serve

Whoever speaks must do so as one speaking the very words of God; whoever serves must do so with the strength that God supplies, so that God may be glorified in all things through Jesus Christ.

1 Peter 4:11

On a recent Sunday I visited a church in Atlanta. A young woman named Phyllis told the story of being asked to serve as chair of the Hospitality Committee soon after she became a member. She gladly accepted the responsibility only to be told by an older member of the congregation that she had done the worst job this older member had ever seen. Beset by disappointment and feelings of inadequacy, Phyllis believed that she was incapable of serving and that she would never again make the mistake of believing that she could serve in any capacity.

These feelings spilled over into all her relationships, and she faced serious problems of self-esteem. But then something happened. She enrolled in the Bible study and learned about the power of the Holy Spirit. She likened herself to a shiny, brand-new automobile at the time she joined the church—new in every capacity—new body, new paint, new parts, new sound system, new exhaust system, new engine. But something was missing, even though the parts were in perfect working condition.

Through the Bible study, Phyllis became aware that the missing element was the fuel. She needed fuel to start the engine and to keep it running. That fuel was Jesus. Once her *engine* was fueled with the power of the Holy Spirit, she began to understand and her life began to change. She accepted responsibilities in the church with a new energy; her relationships took on new meaning and new strength; she became more creative in her work. The brand new, shiny automobile was now in service.

It is the power of the Holy Spirit that gives us the strength, the wisdom, and the understanding to face the responsibilities of our living. That power may be revealed to us in many ways. For Phyllis, it was through Bible study; for others it may be in the comment of a child, the support of a friend or colleague, or a parent's advice. We are assured that when we are fueled by the power of God, we are ready and able to serve.

God of all knowledge and holiness, who brings fuel and energy to our everyday living, may we be made strong with all the strength that comes from your glorious power. Amen.

Ruth M. Lawson

Needless Worry

But the Lord answered her, "Martha, Martha, you are
worried and distracted by many things; there is need of
only one thing. Mary has chosen the better part, which
will not be taken away from her."   Luke 10:41-42

Many of us were taught how to worry by our mothers. We come by it honestly. And truly, we often have a lot to worry about. We may have problems in our relationships and in our families. We may be concerned about our health or the health of a loved one. We may struggle financially, sometimes facing problems of unemployment, underemployment, and almost certainly, underpayment. We may labor to get ahead professionally and face choices that could mean sacrificing our values, since the rules of the game were written by men, not women. And if surviving in the present does not have enough concerns, we can always worry about the unknowns of the future.

To the worries and concerns in our minds, we add a host of other distractions. Our to-do list is endless—for every one thing we cross off, another two or three are added. Everybody seems to want some of our time. We face the needs of our families, the demands of our employers, the needs of our employees, and the desires of our coworkers and friends. The church needs our service; there's always a plea to lend a helping hand to our neighbors or others we know of who need help. It's no wonder we are so often anxious and distracted. But God comes to us in the midst of our troubles and anxieties. God calls us to remember the better part of our lives—that part of ourselves that emerges when we take time to be still and listen. To the ragings of our minds, God issues the command "Peace. Be still." And in the stillness, we remember who we are; we remember what's most important; we remember the gentle familiarity of the Spirit's caress. And when the peace of the Presence is united with the faithfulness of our service, we are whole.

Gentle Spirit, fall afresh on me now. Quiet the clamorings of
my mind that I may be filled with your peace. Free me with your
assurance that all shall be well, that I may go forth to serve you
in peace and joy. Amen.

Betsy L. Halsey

Women Ways

Do not fear, for I have redeemed you; I have called you by name, you are mine.　　　　　　*Isaiah 43:1b*

It comes to us women—our way of looking at the world—with our bodies. Our way of seeing time compacted, willing the future to take a certain shape, like a child unborn.

I sit at home working. And I hear the world weeping.

My chair is soft—I don't strain over a desk. Papers rest on my lap. A blue pencil is in my hand.

My work is very low tech (thank you, God; I would not have it otherwise).

Words on paper make sense to me, and not because they obey grammatical rules. In the written word inheres the breath of God. Sound. Meaning. Communication. Relationship.

I proof each word and try to protect its small perfection, its geometry of letters, its meaning and its place among others.

Word warrior. Word surfer.

Each word lives on its own; yet in community it plants its root, its meaning, and the world takes shape.

Prayer, too, is a verbal event. In silence, in expectation, the word waits for utterance. Needing humankind to give it birth, entrance to this plane.

Most precious Spirit, Mother of life, help us to birth children and words and release them to a clean world. The dark seems so immense. Amen.

Diane Bonner Zarowin

Spiritual Nutrition

O taste and see that the LORD is good. Psalm 34:8a

One aspect of life that many of us consider to be less than ideal is our physical condition or shape. There are books, videos, and businesses that cater to our perceived or real concerns. Nutritional data must be displayed on food packages to keep us informed and help us make wise choices. We can alter our eating habits and exercise routines to build up or trim down our bodies.

Our daily spiritual, as well as physical, nutrition is important for our overall health and growth. Just as we nourish our bodies daily, we need daily nutrition to maintain and enhance our spiritual health. Spiritual nutrients are referenced in the Scriptures. Jesus Christ states, *I am the Bread of Life. No one coming to me will ever be hungry again* (John 6:35 TLB). The B vitamins that are found in bread and grains are responsible for helping our bodies grow at a normal rate, preventing certain anemias, and building and maintaining body tissue. Partaking of our daily bread of life from God's Word is one way to prevent spiritual anemia.

Galatians 5:22-23 lists the fruits of the Spirit: love, joy, peace, long suffering, gentleness, goodness, faith, meekness, temperance. Vitamin C, which is found in citrus fruits and juices, provides our bodies with nutrients that help us resist infections as well as form proteins that help to support our body structure. The fruits of the Spirit help us to support and build up the body of Christ. The important D vitamins that help to build healthy bones are found in milk and dairy products. The corresponding spiritual nutrient is referred to in 1 Peter 2:2: Like newborn babes, long for the pure spiritual milk, that you may grow up to salvation.

Water is the nutrient that is essential to life, and the lack of it is very evident in everyday life. A wilted plant, brown grass, and dehydrated skin are vivid evidence of the effects that the lack of water has on individuals and nature. John 4:10 states, If only you knew what a wonderful gift God has for you, and who I am, you would ask me for some living water! (TLB).

Bread, fruit, milk, and water are just four foods that are essential for the support of our physical well-being. Our spiritual food is available to us through Jesus Christ when we partake daily from God's Word—our spiritual storehouse—and through fellowship with other Christians.

Source of health and strength, you have prepared a table before us. Help us to nourish our souls as well as our bodies every day so that we can serve you. Amen.

Marilyn D. Harris

February 12

The Transplant

No one has greater love than this, to lay down one's life for one's friends. John 15:13

After twenty-one years of diabetes, in the spring of 1983 I became very ill and discovered that both of my kidneys had failed. God worked multiple miracles in order to restore me to complete wholeness. God used brilliant doctors, compassionate nurses, prayerful Christians, committed family members, my devoted husband, my special, hopeful mother, and many others to bring healing to me.

I was placed on dialysis for three months. The cleansing of my blood through a dialysis machine reminded me of God's plan for my salvation and eternal life. Jesus shed his blood to cleanse me of my sin.

My youngest brother volunteered to donate a kidney if our blood types were compatible. We matched identically. My mother shared that she had only wanted two children, one girl and one boy. She saw God's divine wisdom as she realized her fourth child was able to donate a kidney to save her firstborn. Another miracle from God!

God showed me the meaning of true love when my husband assisted a private duty nurse in taking care of me the night after the transplant. The world would like to convince us that true love is roses and romance, but love took on an entirely different meaning that night.

Our family has had its share of conflicts, and sometimes I have wondered about our commitment to one another. Family love was confirmed when all three of my siblings were willing to donate a kidney to me to save my life.

On May 23, 1995, I celebrated twelve years with my transplanted kidney. I am well and working full-time. My life is devoted to Christ, and I have many things to thank him for daily.

God of ages past, thank you for the health you give me daily. Thank you for the miracles you work on my behalf. Help me to trust you even when things seem dark. Thank you for friends, family, doctors, nurses, caregivers, and guardian angels! Amen.

Brenda Marinaro

February 13

Transformation

But we have this treasure in clay jars. . . . We are afflicted in every way, but not crushed; perplexed, but not driven to despair; persecuted, but not forsaken; struck down, but not destroyed. . . . For while we live, we are always being given up to death for Jesus' sake, so that the life of Jesus may be made visible in our mortal flesh. So death is at work in us, but life in you.
2 Corinthians 4:7-12

Growing up as a minority in the United States, even in California, has never been easy. I remember being aware early in my life that I was *different*. I never saw anybody who even looked slightly like me on television. People not only looked different; they acted differently and ate differently. When I started elementary school, I knew I was different. I was called names like chink, ching chong chinaman, slanted eyes, yellow face, pig nose. As I grew older, these taunts changed to: "I can't tell you people apart." "You all look alike." "Where did you learn to speak English so well?" "Why don't you people go back where you came from?" I would reply, "But I was born here—so you go back!" But there was something even worse than the comments, outward displays of prejudice, stereotyping, and racism. It was being invisible.

Invisibility—not being noticed, not being recognized, seeing through me, ignoring me, not seeing the treasure in my earthen vessel, was probably the worst. Even if I was taunted, teased, spat upon, trampled on, I existed. But when I was now acknowledged at all, I became a nonperson, a no-name, someone excluded from God's created kingdom.

The stress of living in this country, where I often was not accepted or was considered a nonentity, acted upon my life as a disease, an illness, and began to eat into my spirit, my self-esteem, and probably my physical body. For many years I was ashamed of who I was and hated myself. Although I didn't go to the extremes pursued by some of my Asian American brothers and sisters in mutilating their bodies (breast enlargements, cosmetic surgery, dyed hair), I did go through a period of my life when I tried *to look more white.*

The passage from 2 Corinthians speaks to how my faith has helped me through this period of my life. It was God, through Jesus, who made me feel loved, appreciated, and valued.

We have this treasure in clay jars, in our earthen vessels, that even though we are afflicted, crushed, perplexed, struck down, persecuted, and driven to despair, we are not forsaken, not abandoned because God is always with us and dwells in us.

Guide and inspiration of humanity, thank you for teaching me that I am not alone. My soul is at peace and I am in joy, because someone knows my name. I am who I am and that's all that counts. No matter what the world throws at me, I have this treasure. I am created and valued by my Lord and Savior. Amen.

Kathryn Choy-Wong

February 14

Childlike Faith

People were bringing little children to him in order that he might touch them; and the disciples spoke sternly to them. But when Jesus saw this, he was indignant and said to them, "Let the little children come to me; do not stop them; for it is to such as these that the kingdom of God belongs. Truly I tell you, whoever does not receive the kingdom of God as a little child will never enter it." And he took them up in

his arms, laid his hands on them, and blessed them.
Mark 10:13-16

It is a new experience for me, being a grandmother. Jesse has come into our lives, creating all of the wonder and joy that any eighteen-month-old does for her grandparents. During a recent visit with her and her parents, it did not take me long to rediscover, through her eyes, the delights of God's extravagant world. The pebbles at the edge of the road were collected into one tiny fist—what an accomplishment! We stood very still in the night's darkness in order to hear the riotous sounds that surrounded us, and she smiled—at the insistent noises of tree frogs and crickets and all those other invisible creatures of the night. The squirrels had a heyday for a week after she left—we had collected every hickory nut in sight and had left them in a huge (for her and them) pile, a too-easy breakfast, lunch, or dinner.

What a relief this respite of a weekend was. Bosnia, the Middle East, AIDS, and hunger in the U.S. had been bombarding my mind. This time with Jesse was not an answer to the tragedies of our world, and I returned soon enough to the news of the day. But she is a word of hope for me. She reminds me that the God who creates and who has chosen to reveal Godself uniquely in the life of Jesus of Nazareth is a God who births us as helpless infants. Our God does not overpower us and chooses not to be a tyrant. Rather, Divine Mystery comes to us in wonder, love, beauty, and truth, and chooses the way of the cross.

And so my life has two pulls, and I would answer both: to rejoice and wonder, as does a child, in God's love, truth, and beauty; and to stand alongside a loving God with compassion for my neighbor.

Righteous One of all generations, although peace and love are always in us, being and working, we are not always in peace and love. Help us to become more like you. Amen.

Velma McGee Ferrell

Understanding God's Way

Peace I leave with you; my peace I give to you. I do not give to you as the world gives. Do not let your hearts be troubled, and do not let them be afraid.
John 14:27

Rarely does the average woman consider that one day she may be faced with a life-changing illness or disability, or may bear a child who has a disability. Cancer, stroke, or some other malady may touch other lives, we reason, but not ours. When and if such an event occurs, we are shocked and at first cannot believe this has happened to us.

Many may ask, Why me? If God is good, how could God allow this to happen to me? No one can fully answer such a question. A partial reply may be that God has set in motion laws of the universe for the good of all. When these are broken, evil, pain, and suffering result. For example, the law of gravity pulls all things toward the earth. When, however, an individual leans too far out of a window, gravity will pull that person to the earth, resulting in disability or death.

How then can we live triumphant lives in the face of pain, suffering, and/or disability? As Christ was about to leave his disciples, he had little to give them other than the legacy of peace. Peace I leave with you, he said, my peace I give to you. What did this mean then, and what does it mean for us today? Does it not mean that as we are able to commit our lives, our illnesses or disabilities, or even our will and whole bodies, minds, and spirits to God, holding nothing back, that God will lead us and use us in ways we never believed possible? Then we will know true inner peace, no matter what life may bring.

God of earth and air, height and depth, help me to surrender myself and all that I am to you. Let me know the peace that comes through our Lord Christ, and let me be a blessing to all those around me. Amen.

Virginia Kreyer

God's Glory Revealed

*I consider that the sufferings of this present time are
not worth comparing with the glory about to be
revealed to us. . . . What then are we to say about
these things? If God is for us, who is against us? . . . I
am convinced that neither death, nor life, nor angels,
nor rulers, nor things present, nor things to come, nor
powers, nor height, nor depth, nor anything else in all
creation, will be able to separate us from the love of
God in Christ Jesus our Lord.*

Romans 8:18, 31, 38-39

A sign stands on my desk that reads, "Troubles are often the
tools by which God fashions us for better things" (H. W. Beecher).
I recall several events of the past twenty years that qualify as
troubles. First, I lost my ability to walk, the result of a very painful
neurological syndrome called reflex sympathetic dystrophy. It
was treated by benign neglect, then by numerous hospitalizations
and surgeries. Then, successively, there was the death of my
husband from a brain tumor; my breast cancer, and scary times
when symptoms indicated a possible recurrence; my daughter's
divorce; a crush fracture caused by disuse osteoporosis; and
estrangement from one of my children. At such troubled times,
my despondency is overwhelming. I tearfully and angrily cry out
to Christ Jesus to save me from despair.

When life's difficulties seem to assault me, I desperately need
God. In the words of Paul in Romans 8, I discover comfort and
consolation. I reflect and deliberate on the message that nothing
will be able to separate us from the love of God in Christ Jesus,
reading these words of hope over and over. Yes, the words ring
true. They sustain me and enable me to leave behind hopelessness
and pain. In their power they move me toward wholeness and life
abundant in Christ Jesus.

*Great Healer of body and mind, in times of distress, you are
the One who listens to my cries of anguish and understands my
torment. You walk with me in my pain and carry me when I
cannot walk. You minister to me with your healing presence and
empower me to journey from despair to life. Amen.*

Gay Holthaus McCormick

ʻWhom Shall I ʻFear?

The LORD is my light and my salvation; whom shall I
fear? The LORD is the stronghold of my life; of whom
shall I be afraid?   *Psalm 27:1*

Will the fear win? Those are the words a counselor once told me to tape to my mirror or refrigerator. I was dealing with some heavy life issues and feeling paralyzed by my fear of what might happen. You probably know that feeling—the *what ifs?* What if I try this course of action? What if it's the wrong choice? What if something goes dreadfully wrong? What if I get hurt? What if, what if, what if . . .?

Those questions of imaginary consequences had taken over my life. Of course, some of them might have actually happened. Realistically, we know that bad things do happen. But when we let fear of possible outcomes take control, paralysis results. I could not make any decision, good or bad.

Part of my resistance to facing my fear was the feeling that I didn't like the counselor. Maybe he was a jerk. Who can say? But his challenge stayed with me. I couldn't just brush off the message. Fear ruled my life—and that bothered me because I knew that God did not intend for me to live that way. God does not intend for any of God's children to live in fear.

Maybe it's my fighting nature, but I had to keep poking at that knot of fear until it began to unravel. Fortunately, I found a counselor who did not trigger my negativism. We worked together for a long time, probing and testing until I began to understand and work through that debilitating emotion. It was not easy work.

If you've ever spent any length of time in a serious counseling process, you know that you encounter bumps along the road. I remember reaching the place where I knew my old ways of living and relating were not healthy. But I still hadn't replaced those old habits with new ways of being. It took guts to break free of the old ways and move on to the next stage without knowing what came next.

I thank God that friends and family encouraged me to do this work. Perfect love casts out fear, it is true, but even God couldn't penetrate my defenses until I understood them myself. Together, we dismantled those barriers.

Thank you, God of emotional and mental wholeness, that you provide the help we need for the hard places of our lives. Amen.
Carol Franklin Sutton

February 18

Martha's Healing

Martha, Martha, you are worried and distracted by many things; there is need of only one thing.
Luke 10:41-42

The familiar story of Jesus' conversation with Martha at her home immediately follows the story of the good Samaritan in which Jesus tries to help us see the responsibility which accompanies the life of love. Jesus wants us to understand that if we claim to be ruled by the values of God, then those values must be tangible and observable in the choices we make and in the lives we lead.

Martha's story reminds us of what many women need little reminding about, that the excessive doing of the tasks of love can sometimes replace the heart of love with anxiety, resentment, frustration, and fatigue. The problem was not with what Martha was doing. The problem was with what Martha was doing to Martha. It was unusual for a rabbi to visit two unmarried sisters in their home to begin with. Martha, as the elder, was responsible for making sure that the visit went well. The laws and customs of hospitality were deeply ingrained both in her culture and in her heart. She wanted everything to be perfect for this important visit. She wanted to do her duty. She wanted everyone to be comfortable and at ease. The Scripture describes Martha's tasks (the Greek word can also be translated "service" or "ministry") as excessive, like a heavy weight that is dragged around. How common an experience that is for many women! Our desire to make our love for family and friends concrete can so easily get out of hand that we too feel as if we are dragging our duty around behind us like a lead weight. We, like Martha, can sometimes feel that no one in our family is cooperating and that even Jesus does not care what is happening to us.

Some have seen Jesus' response to Martha's cry of frustration as a rebuke that elevates Mary and denigrates Martha, that somehow values the gifts of contemplation and reflection over the gifts of service and action. I would suggest, rather, that in the gentle repeating of her name, Jesus is calling Martha back to her true self, back to wholeness and a calm delight that living out of our gifts in reasonable measure can produce. Martha simply needed to be reminded that blind adherence to duty, that excessive activity, even excessive activity for the good, can push us beyond our limits and turn that which should nourish us into a burden. Only when serving and doing are rooted deeply in intimacy with Christ and the power which comes from that relationship can we care with health and live in wholeness.

Redeemer of the oppressed, gently remind us this day of who we are that we may reasonably offer our gifts in love out of love. Amen.

Eugenia Gamble

February 19

Stand Up, Little Girl

Why do you make a commotion and weep? The child is not dead but sleeping. Mark 5:39b

When they came to the house of the leader of the synagogue, [Jesus] saw a commotion, people weeping and wailing loudly. When he had entered, he said to them, "Why do you make a commotion and weep? The child is not dead but sleeping." And they laughed at him. Then he put them all outside, and took the child's father and mother and those who were with him, and went in where the child was. He took her by the hand and said to her, Talitha cum, which means, "Little girl, get up!" And immediately the girl got up and began to walk about (she was twelve years of age). Those who witnessed the miracle were overcome with amazement. Mark 5:38-42

There was also a prophet, Anna. . . . She was of a great age, having lived with her husband seven years after her marriage, then as a widow to the age of eighty-four. She never left the temple but worshiped there with fasting and prayer night and day. At that moment, [when his parents brought the infant Jesus to the temple,] she came, and began to praise God and to speak about the child to all who were looking for the redemption of Jerusalem. Luke 2:36-38

The Corinthian women prophets with whom Paul had to contend regained their voices, their internal authority, because they heard the liberating gospel of Jesus: We are free, before God. No one—no priest, no husband, no community stands between you and God. We have authority to discern God's guidance. As prophetic women, we can reclaim our voices, even if we have submerged them for years. The years of regaining internal authority, filled with much prayer and some sacrifice, can help us to see the Holy and to speak forthrightly, bringing redemption to those who are looking for it.

Yet in our culture twelve-year-old girls still die—lose their voices—when they accommodate the cultural messages that tell them to relinquish (or diminish) the authority of their minds and bodies that they have trusted so far. They will not be free unless someone, speaking as the Christ, with the authority of the Anointed One, comes to them and says, "Little girl, get up! Your body, your mind, your soul is yours. You have authority to discern God's guidance."

God of longevity, may we who are between twelve and eighty-four finds ways to tell little girls to get up; to look for redemption as we listen to elderly female prophets; and to claim our own authority—before God. Amen.

Carolyn Stahl Bohler

Rocks of Eternity

The Rock, his work is perfect. Deuteronomy 32:4a

I am a lover of stones. When most people are looking at breathtaking scenery in areas of natural wonder, I am scouring the ground for interesting pieces of granite, limestone, jasper, aggregates, or whatever catches my eye. A friend of mine in New York City does much the same. When we travel anywhere together, we can be found hunched down near stream beds, on tops of mountains, near glaciers, at the seaside, and sometimes in city parks, scratching at the earth for a particularly interesting specimen of nature's art. We usually dispense with scientific identification procedures and spend time noting color, shape, and consistency. Then we speculate about the history of our treasures, essentially creating a story from a few of the clues revealed by the stone; we indulge our imaginations about what a particular rock may have *seen* or *felt* millions of years ago, and how aging, erosion, layering, ice movement, or great heat and pressure have created such a unique formation for us to see and touch.

Stones. Rocks. Rough and craggy, filled with holes, or smooth and rounded, pinks and oranges, greens and grays—earth tones, sky tones, sea tones. Speaking silently to us from all eternity. Creating soil and sand as they erode. Sustaining tiny plants, sheltering animals. Bringing forth first tools and fire at will. Becoming foundations for houses and roads. Developing into a part of sport and sculpture. A basic piece of earth with a longevity we cannot comprehend. They bring perspective. They form and shape and are formed and shaped. They encompass time and space. They share color and texture.

What a wonderful ancient metaphor for our Creator—and for what was created.

Rock of all times and places, gently form us in our time into the shape you would have us be. Amen.

Lisa Withrow

Inner Peace

*Now you are the body of Christ. . . . And God has
appointed in the church first apostles, second prophets,
third teachers; then deeds of power, then gifts of
healing, forms of assistance, forms of leadership,
various kinds of tongues.   1 Corinthians 12:27-28*

*The fruit of the Spirit is love, joy, peace, patience,
kindness, generosity, faithfulness, gentleness, and
self-control.   Galatians 5:22-23a*

Doubled up in pain, struggling to be a productive part of
society, Ani screamed out to God, You call me to works of faith,
but this body slaps me down. I am in agony. In agony to know
how to be faithful when I cannot *do.* The tapes of childhood
interpretations of God played over and over again in her mind.
Her body's life with an intruder that the doctors called "ileitis"
was unpredictably crippled.

Devotion to God turned Ani to the Holy Word, as the wise
women of her Armenian family had always done. As she read,
voices deep within her memory made themselves heard. Those
voices called her to pull in more from her clan in order to
understand that those tapes were notions from a linear system that
divided and reduced creation. These voices, however, called her
to a circular, all-encompassing knowing born and coded in her
genetic consciousness. Suddenly, she came to Paul. Her anger
flared. "The ultimate imprisoner of women! Even here he lists a
hierarchy of roles. There is nothing for me here."

The ancients continued to urge her. Ani read ravenously until
the simple verses of Galatians brought home a soothing, bathing
saline for the soul. The fruits of the Spirit are *being gifts,* and the
roles Paul lays out in 1 Corinthians are *doing gifts.* They can be
mutually inclusive.

Intimacy within the Word points the Eastern heart to wholeness
more like the Chinese word for peace, *Ping* (harmony; syn-
chronicity of flow), that allows for the Scriptures to move between
one another as in a dance for meaning. Corinthians helps us see
and name differing gifts, putting healthy boundaries to things.

Galatians contributes the wisdom of the Spirit to empower the flow and bring authenticity to one another. Being gifts call the doer to integrity of effort. The doer must ask, From what center do these efforts come? Being gifts call to those who struggle with disabilities, visible and invisible, to a ministry of presence. What is an apostle without self-control? What would a prophet do without inner peace? What is a teacher without faithfulness? What are deeds of power without love?

Gracious God of all knowledge, who thought the creation into being, thank you for the gift that calls me to seek out the way as a place and/or activity within myself and to recognize that to be is to do. Amen.

Ginna Minasian Dalton

February 22

Jubilee

You shall count off seven weeks of years, seven times seven years, so that the period of seven weeks of years gives forty-nine years. Then . . . you shall hallow the fiftieth year and proclaim liberty throughout the land to all its inhabitants. Leviticus 25:8-10

In the daily dance toward human wholeness, many of us know the partnership of an *inner child* who reminds us of both the graces and the sorrows of our early years, the ones that went into making us what we are. But as the years add up to fifty, sixty, seventy—*or perhaps eighty if we are strong* (Psalm 90:10)—another partner claims us, reminding us of who we are yet to become. She is our inner elder, the aging woman who lives within us, the woman who embraces us as we seriously begin to number our days.

The steps in which she leads us will become familiar as we count off seven years of seven years and hallow the fiftieth year, a threshold each of us crosses in the middle of life as we turn our faces toward the setting sun. That fiftieth year, the year of the jubilee, is a symbol of all the years to follow, and of the fullness that awaits us as we embrace ourselves as crones and women of wisdom.

Our inner elder introduces us to new thresholds that beckon us onward: detachment, letting go, living in a body that doesn't move quite as swiftly or ably as it once did, the searing pain of losing life companions. She initiates us into a different pace, one that is slower and more sober, convincing us that it is all right to rest in the presence of Lady Wisdom, the Sophia of God who may be new to us. She sings the music of this time with stunning regularity, whenever we pause to listen, the music of "proclaim liberty throughout the land." She reminds us that we whose spirits dance in this land of aging possess many freedoms. We possess the prophetic freedom to confront injustice wherever we find it. And we also possess inner freedom: to be whole, to be ourselves, to be God's. Finally, we possess the freedom to grow old, knowing that when we have finally numbered all our days, it will be time to go home.

Holy Wisdom, partner of all our years, be with us as we number our days. Satisfy us each morning with your steadfast love, and be with us as we step through the afternoon and beyond, into the evening of our lives. Amen.

Maria Harris

February 23

Taste and See

Ho, everyone who thirsts, come to the waters; and you that have no money, come, buy and eat! Come, buy wine and milk without money and without price.

Isaiah 55:1

Years ago, when asked to meditate on Communion, I was frustrated when the only image that came to me was of *Tutu* (my mother role model) and I standing at the sink cutting up ingredients for a special meal. Our object was not speed or precision, but *communion*. The hours ticked away, unmeasured, as we created stacks of peeled, cored, chopped, grated, or artistically arranged food. The goal, of course, was the beautiful table—overflowing with our gifts of preparation to be shared with our family and friends. There was so much love put in each little whittle of the knives and brandishing of the special kitchen implements. But at least as important as the final result was the time that led up to that magnificent repast. We told our stories, shared ourselves, remembered meals from times past, both happy and sad. We even dared to think toward the uncertain future. Grandpa had several strokes, and Tutu had been diagnosed with cancer. My marriage was shaky (we found that my husband's strange behaviors stemmed from a brain tumor). We didn't know that it was our last *communion* meal with our little family intact, but we somehow knew that each moment we shared the counter and the tools and the meal was precious. Not to be taken lightly. The words, prayers, and revelations that we shared could never be taken away. Our work was play, and what we experienced was *communion*. These times could not be relived.

What about our own experience of Communion? It too is simple. The elements are similar and yet sometimes varied—pellets, loaves, grape juice, wine—taken alone or in community. Shared in a sanctuary or on a stump in the forest.

When we commune together, let us remember that time and place are sacred. The simple elements shared by those early sojourners were sacred. Our community, family, friends, church members, and visitors are also sacred.

The place in which we worship is sacred, be it large or small, in or out of repair, mortgaged or paid off. Each simple act we perform in this sacred place puts us in *communion* with God. We don't know with certainty what lies ahead. But we can be present to each other and to God in the holiness of the *sacred now*.

Grandpa died just two months later. Tutu died three days after my husband was diagnosed with the brain tumor. She died the day after his first surgery. They were in the same hospital, she on the seventh floor and he on the fourth. The memory of that communion meal became even more precious as I sought to get through those difficult times.

Source of health and strength, help me never to take a moment for granted. Help me to see the sacred in the simple acts of my life. Remind me, when I am confused with details and needs, to be present to others and to you. Amen.

Karyn Shadbolt

Challenged

I praise you because I am fearfully and wonderfully made; your works are wonderful, I know that full well.
Psalm 139:14 (NIV)

She was a mischievous little girl, often throwing tantrums and helping herself to food from her indulgent parents' plates—until the morning she tried to snitch from a stranger who proved to be equally strong willed. The *battle of the breakfast table* would be the first of many battles of wills between Annie Sullivan and her charge, Helen Keller. Yet that morning was also a turning point after which Helen and Annie gradually began to trust each other. Helen made amazing breakthroughs in the next few weeks and finally, when Annie pumped water into Helen's outstretched palm, she did more than spell the word back to Annie. Helen understood. Not only did she realize that the word W-A-T-E-R stood for the cool liquid running over her hand, but that everything had a name. Helen probably learned one hundred words that morning, and went on to graduate from Radcliffe College. Where Helen's parents saw only a hopeless case, Annie saw a whole person.

While working at Butler University, I became acquainted with a wheelchair-bound student. Although most of the other students I observed clearly treated her as one of the gang, she told me her most common frustrations were people who were overly sympathetic or pitying, and those who treated her as if she were mentally, not physically, challenged. It is difficult to think of a physically challenged person as a whole person, particularly if that person has lost an arm or a leg, and many people react accordingly. Their first reaction is, "I wonder what's wrong with her," not "Look at how many challenges she has overcome." The next time you encounter a physically challenged person, remember that like you, he or she is *fearfully and wonderfully made.*

Creator God, you have carefully and lovingly fashioned us in your image. Give us the ability to see every person as a whole and complete masterpiece. Amen.

Jo Ellen Murphy

Love of God

*Lord, you have been our dwelling place in all
generations. Before the mountains were brought forth, or
ever you had formed the earth and the world, from
everlasting to everlasting you are God. Psalm 90:1-2*

When I was a child, I enjoyed picking June strawberries in my grandfather's garden. Later in the summer, I was eager to help Uncle Norman harvest green beans at his place in the country.

When I was twelve or thirteen, I wanted a garden of my own. Dad agreed that I could dig up a small plot in the backyard, if I would keep it weeded myself. I followed his advice and started small. I bought one package of flower seeds and planted and watered them. All spring and early summer, I faithfully went out to pull the weeds.

It was probably late June or early July when Uncle Norman came to visit. When I proudly showed him my little plot, he grinned. I had meticulously pulled up almost everything—except the button weeds. I had mistaken them for the flowers I had planted. Only one flower survived my vigorous weeding!

There is a kind of faith that focuses on the weeds, the *thou shalt nots*. Its adherents go well beyond the simple ten guidelines for living together in community found in the Ten Commandments. They pull the flowers from life, giving others the impression that God does not want people to have fun or to enjoy life. Their judgmental attitude makes it difficult for others to receive the grace and love of God.

When we focus on the negatives, rather than on God's love and grace, the gardens of our souls will lack the color, beauty, and fragrance God offers. We will be poor witnesses for the abundant life that is God's will for us and for others.

God of grace and love, help us to pull the weeds of negativism and judgmentalism from our lives, and to nurture joy, love, peace, justice, and grace. Remind us that if we want to help others receive grace, that we should pull the weeds—not the flowers of joy—from the garden of life. Amen.

Wilda K. W. (Wendy) Morris

Valuing Diversity

*All of them were filled with the Holy Spirit and began
to speak in other languages, as the Spirit gave them
ability. . . . In our own languages we hear them
speaking about God's deeds of power. Acts 2:4, 11a*

Look again at the story of the tower of Babel found in Genesis
11:1-9, and read it in juxtaposition with the story of Pentecost in
Acts 2:1-11. These two familiar stories, one from the Old Testament and one from the New, offer us insight as to how to respond
to an increasingly multicultural world. The stories serve as metaphors for three different approaches that are evident in our society.

When people think of wholeness in society, they often wish for
the imagined unity of the mythical age before the tower of Babel.
They imagine the possibility of such oneness when the United
States is described as the *melting pot*. This metaphor assumes
national, ethnic, and racial differences should all melt away, and
we should all become one, meaning that we should all act and
think alike.

While recognizing that this sort of unity in conformity is not
desirable, some see it as the only alternative to the other metaphor
that comes from the Babel story: the confusion of many tongues.
This many-tongued confusion is evident today in those who
emphasize difference to the exclusion of common bonds, an
approach sometimes called particularistic multiculturalism.

The New Testament story of Pentecost offers us a more useful
metaphor. Through the gift of the Holy Spirit, all were able to
understand each other, and each retained his or her separate
identity. This is pluralistic multiculturalism, not particularistic
multiculturalism. This is what is sometimes called not the melting
pot, but rather the *tossed salad* in which each ingredient retains
its unique texture and flavor yet enhances the whole.

*God of all peoples, help me to allow the gifts of the Holy Spirit
to enable me to learn to understand and appreciate others in all
their diversity so that I shall hear all persons speaking in their
own ways about God's deeds of power. Amen.*

Elizabeth V. McDowell

Surrendering to God

*God is our refuge and strength, a very present help in
trouble. Therefore, we will not fear, though the earth
should change, though the mountains shake in the
heart of the sea; though its waters roar and foam,
though the mountains tremble with its tumult. There is
a river whose streams make glad the city of God, the
holy habitation of the Most High.   Psalm 46:1-4*

A friend had been in an accident that caused a serious brain
concussion. Before the accident, she was an active woman—employed full-time professionally, a contributing citizen to the community, a caring mate and an involved mother of two teenage
children. For months after the accident, she struggled with her
impotence, including not remembering details, muddled thinking,
and an inability to focus. On the six-month anniversary of her
accident, she dropped by my house to talk.

After months of physical and psychological therapy, she was
still deeply depressed. "I'm a mess," she started out, "all I seem
to do is cry. I'm unable to return to work, I can't relate to my
children, and I'm not sure how much longer John will tolerate my
depression. I want so desperately to let go of the accident and
move on in my life. I think I need to surrender to what God is
trying to teach me in all of this. But I can't seem to figure out the
difference between surrendering and simply giving up."

We talked at length about her anger over the accident, her fear
that she would never recover, and her eagerness to let go. I
suggested she close her eyes and imagine a beautiful, deep flowing river. I asked her to envision that river as a symbol of her life
as God wanted her to lead it, and further suggested that for her to
get on with her life she needed to jump into the river. Choosing
to sit on the bank and watch the river flow by would be giving up.

In the river, sometimes you would need to swim your strongest
stroke, but always going with the current—the direction that God
wants you to go. After a while you decide you need to rest,
meditate, just be where you are. So you flip over on your back
and float comfortably with the current enjoying the fluffy clouds
and the overhanging branches of the trees. You let the birds

entertain you with their songs. You might get scared and decide to go back or to try to reach the other side, but you would be swimming against the current that could wear you out or perhaps ultimately defeat you. Learn to surrender to the current; work with it and experience where God is taking you.

Great Spirit, give me the courage to jump into the river, to have the strength to swim with all my might when needed, and to be aware of the times when I need to float and just be still. Amen.

Nancy Johns

February 28

A Woman's Way

"Go and learn what this means, 'I desire mercy, not sacrifice.'"　　　　　　　　　　　*Matthew 9:13a*

Lynda had come to me, her pastor, to talk about the recent breakup of the significant relationship in her life, to pour out her grief, and to talk about the wisps of a healing process on which she was only just embarking. We had talked, heart to heart, for more than an hour when we came to the subject of how she should handle the difficulty of communicating with her former partner, who was more than reluctant to speak frankly about what had happened between them. Lynda was seeking a way to acknowledge the truth that could potentially free each of them for healing and moving on.

"You know, Lynda," I heard myself saying, "perhaps the only thing you can do is take the bull by the hands, and . . . " I was first startled, then intrigued, by the accidental revision of the phrase I had uttered. I burst out laughing as I asked her, "Did you hear what I just said?" And a smile began to cross her face, too, as we examined the literalism of the phrase I had blurted out in contrast with what I thought I had meant. It was as if we had inadvertently imagined a new strategy: to meet your obstacle or opponent, not at the traditional line of offense, but with the reach of compassion.

Take the bull by the hands.

It's a vision that recalls the strangely comforting depiction of the biblical Martha in some little-known altar pieces of medieval

Europe. While popular art depicts Saint George slaying the fearsome dragon, here the heroine doesn't conquer or kill, but tames—leads the beast, bound only with her own skirts, through the village square.

To follow this new model for healing—this feminine model—is to take the bull by the hands, not the horns; to recognize the *humanity* in even the most *bullish* inner beast—not to conquer it by force but to encounter it with intentionality. Then we are already on the path to healing the inward places where we sternly judge ourselves.

Compassionate God, as you look deep into my eyes and love me, grant me in turn the courage to gaze fully into the depths of what I most fear; so that fear might become my teacher, and no longer distort my true self. Amen.

Gail Anderson Ricciuti

February 29

God Is Present

Pray in the Spirit at all times in every prayer and supplication. To that end keep alert and always preserve in supplication for all the saints. Pray also for me. Ephesians 6:18-19a

In 1981, my mother had a burst brain aneurysm, lingered for seven days in a coma, and died. I was in Massachusetts serving my first parish as a student pastor and flew home to be with my dad and sister.

Also in 1981, my dad had a ministroke. I left seminary and flew home with *fear* as the passenger in the seat beside me.

In 1991, a blood clot broke loose in my dad's leg and traveled to his lung. I was on retreat and drove to the hospital via the turnpike with my heart beating wildly and tears running down my face.

In 1993, my sister developed diabetic foot ulcers on both feet. She was hospitalized for months. I can remember how scared I was when I sat by her bedside and looked at her two bandaged feet.

In 1994, my dad had very bad pneumonia. It took days for them to find the proper medicine to treat him. I was terrified every time his fever rose. It peaked at 104 degrees, and he became delirious.

This year my stepdaughter, aged twenty-four, went to the hospital for routine surgery to remove an ovarian cyst. Only it turned out to be two huge tumors, and she had a complete hysterectomy. I was heartsick for her.

I am a committed Christian and the spiritual leader of a four-hundred-member congregation. But when my family members are seriously ill, my mouth dries out, my throat closes up, and I cannot pray. Mostly, in the health crises I have described above, I sigh and murmur incoherently. When sickness afflicts those who are very close to me, I depend on others. I count on intercessory prayer and its power for my loved ones and for me. And I recall what a favorite theology professor said to me fifteen years ago, "When you get off the plane, you will walk on a cloud of prayers which will uphold and sustain you."

Merciful God, thank you for those who pray for us and uphold us when we are unable to frame words. Amen.

Janet K. Hess

March

Water in the Wilderness

I give water in the wilderness, rivers in the desert.
Isaiah 43:20b

"You shall cross the barren desert but you shall not die of thirst. You shall wander far in safety tho' you do not know the way. You shall speak your words in foreign lands and all will understand. You shall see the face of God and live."[1]

I sent these song lyrics to a friend today, knowing these words had given me new life and hope in the midst of my wilderness of moving, an emptying nest, and a family illness.

"Water in the wilderness" took on profound meaning for me at that time. I knew I was in a wilderness. Nothing else can describe it. I had no choice but to go through it to reach the other side of wholeness, health, and a new life. But I learned I did not have to go through it alone.

I found "water in the wilderness," sometimes in unexpected places: looking at a gardening catalog, seeing pictures of rose-colored daylilies; sitting in the sunshine with a pastor friend outside the hospital; sleeping under a quilt made by my great-grandmother; lunching in the sun with a friend and laughing; accepting an invitation from a new acquaintance to get together; making pottery with a friend; reading Isaiah; planting petunias; being hugged.

In crisis we may not feel the presence of God as we wish. But as we look back, that water we receive in the wilderness is a gift from God, blessings from God's good earth: other women and men, the sun, the earth itself. Wherever you may be in your life right now believe the promise: "You shall see the face of God and live."

Watchful and caring God, be with us as we cross the wilderness. Open our eyes to the life giving streams around us. Help us find the water in the rock, in those hidden places close by. Thank you for the water that restores our soul. Amen.

Julie Fewster

Blessing in Disguise

*My brothers and sisters, whenever you face trials of
any kind, consider it nothing but joy, because you know
that the testing of your faith produces endurance; and
let endurance have its full effect, so that you may be
mature and complete, lacking in nothing.*

James 1:2-4

I am the oldest of four children in my immediate family. My father had diabetes. Statistically, one in four children inherit this chronic disease, and when I was ten years old, I developed diabetes.

All three of my siblings feel a certain degree of guilt that I was the *unlucky* one to be afflicted by this curse. I must say there have been times in my life when I would have gladly passed this cup of sorrow to another.

However, God has convinced me that I have been blessed—not cursed—with a chronic disease. Owing to the uncertainty of the number of my days, I learned early in life to rely on Christ. As the years progress, I have become more interested in spiritual things than what this world has to offer me. I have grown to understand that worry only chokes me and robs me of my happiness today. I will live the number of days God has planned for me, not one day more or less than that, so I have entrusted my life to him. I will invest the time I have in serving my God.

*Source of all life, help me to know that aside from you, there is
no security. My hope is in you alone! Amen.*

Brenda Marinaro

Spirit of Discontent

Whatchu can't have
you just can't have
who ain't meant just ain't in you
who be gone just ain't there
what ain't yrs/must be somebody else's
You gotta bring what you be needin[2]

When we were growing up, the message from every side seemed to be, Keep the rules, be good, and everything will turn out all right. So we did.

Little girls work hard on the sugar and spice and everything nice parts, especially for pleasing Mommy and making Daddy proud. Then there are the teachers who must be appeased. And one day boyfriends who could turn into husbands appear. After that children may be there to remind us of what is cool.

Work in the world adds other elements. As a clergywoman, I saw clearly that a subdued approach would aid the stages of ordination.

But somewhere between ages thirty-eight and forty-eight a hint of discontent that was previously hidden starts nibbling with an annoying regularity. Holes appear where one had not noticed something wearing thin before. Walls crumble, weaken, and could come tumbling down.

When what is real starts appearing without warning, the time is right to figure out what I *be needin'*. No one else is going to. All those people I please, as much as I love them, have no idea what will satisfy my creative, solitary self.

Of course reality is disruptive, even maddening. When parts of my honest self show up—like her or not—it is important to be kind to her, invite her in for tea.

Then I enlist the Spirit to help me, the same Spirit of creation who brooded over the dark waters, full of chaos, and brought forth a new world. This Spirit in me always knows what I need.

God of amazing joy, in the arrogance of being right, in the middle of anxiety, and especially in confusion, your solution is satisfying. Please quiet my mind, teach me to listen, and always, teach me to pray. Amen.

Audrey Ward

Joy in the Morning

Jesus wept.   *John 11:35 (NIV)*

Living with the reality of death gives one a keen awareness of limitations on time and presence. We experienced this when our son, Joel Keith, was diagnosed with HIV/AIDS at the age of thirty-six in February 1995.

The final Christmas we shared with him and his siblings was in 1993, at his instigation. Knowing there was no way they could surprise us by just appearing on our Florida doorstep, he called two weeks before Christmas and told me that my Christmas gift was going to be what I had requested. "Well, Mom, you're going to get it. We're all coming to Florida." What was my first reaction? I cried.

Happy memories were tucked away. Moments of love and laughter were shared in our small home by the nine of us. Mealtimes were centered on favorite foods and traditions, and we almost had to assign bathroom time. On that first morning we ran out of hot water for showers. Joel had gone first and spent too much time showering, shaving, and singing—all with the hot water turned on. In a sense, we were in a time of closure with him; we just didn't know it.

Since his death I've been given reading materials by consoling friends. A favorite is a booklet describing people like me as secondary sufferers. We are those who must watch through the pain, suffering, and even death of a loved one. In reading, I was inspired by my Scripture selection. Comprised in these two words, the shortest verse in the Bible, is a simple and clear message to all who mourn. Jesus was among our ranks. He was a secondary sufferer. Tears were his expression of grief when learning of the death of Lazarus.

I cry a lot. Healing comes in my tears. When I feel the tension begin to build beyond my endurance, I cry. Joel would call them bittersweet tears: tears for what was, whether good or bad. Tears for what will never be again. Our family's circle is diminished.

I cry for this son of mine who has died, but I've been crying far longer. Joel knew rejection because of his life choices, but never from his family. He was loved, unconditionally. We wept at his death because we loved him just as Jesus wept for Lazarus, whom he also loved. Joel loved God, and God loved Joel.

God of all comfort, may our tears of pain and loss be transformed into tears of joy as we continue to believe in the promise of eternal life. Amen.

Mary Jo Ferreira

Abundant Life

I have come that they may have life, and that they may have it more abundantly.   John 10:10 (NKJV)

I sometimes wonder if there is *life before death* (to use a phrase from Dorothee Soelle). It can be difficult to sit with parishioners or with clients in my psychotherapy practice and believe that there is such a thing as abundant life. The stories of abuse, abandonment, incest, and cruelty suffered by so many women are enough to make one weep in the face of such pain.

We have had the tendency to pause at the surface of Jesus' words. A dogmatic response does not address the depth of human suffering. Simplistic and rigid answers to the complexities of the marginalized people of our world not only are irresponsible, but indeed sinful.

Is there life before death? *Yes!* There is life before death if we are able to look and understand the meaning of the abundant life about which Jesus talks. What is abundant life? As I read and understand the Scriptures, it is a sense of becoming liberated from the inner wilderness of our lives. It is to experience the attention, respect, and validation of another human being who does not judge, but assists us in restoring our self-esteem, our sense of self, our worthiness through a loving and accepting relationship.

Jesus' example was clear in his relationship with women. The dramatic, caring, and even defiant way he reached out to the women with whom he established relationships changed their views of themselves.

Life abundant, life before death, has to do with the kinds of relationships that enable all of us to be restored to our original state of creation. In the midst of oppressive systems, including religious ones, we must never lose sight of the liberating power of Jesus' relationship with women and God's empowerment of strong and assertive women who continue to be resilient in the face of modern forms of stoning.

God of eternal might, help us to see that in the here and now, life is full of new and restoring experiences through our mutual relationships and together with God. Amen.

Rebeca M. Radillo

March 6

Healthy Anger

As the Lord has forgiven you, so you must also forgive.
Colossians 3:13b

Although she was pleasant most of the time, she could cut you to shreds before you knew what was happening. "Why are you mad?" I asked her one day after she snarled at me. "I'm not angry!" she spit out, her teeth clenched and her eyes narrowed, flashing slits. I knew her pretty well, and she was plenty angry. I also knew her faith was the most important thing in the world to her. So passionate was her desire to be a good Christian that she tried with her whole heart to cover her bedrock anger with smiles and *forgiveness*. Much later I found out she had a very good reason to be angry. Badly wounded as a child, she was very depressed, suffered migraines, and had seriously considered suicide.

Like many women, my friend confused Christian forgiveness with stifling her anger. They are not the same at all. A natural and healthy response to hurt, feeling angry is really the first stage of forgiveness. Anger says, *It was not OK to hurt me!* It is honest and mightily empowering. It cannot be rushed or stifled. It must be expressed in all its depth, although not necessarily to the one who inflicted the hurt. However, holding onto anger indefinitely can become spiritually, emotionally, and physically toxic.

Forgiveness is one of the most difficult tasks of our spiritual life, but the Holy Spirit keeps nudging us toward it. We are called to keep working with our anger and pain until we are ready to let it go. It is a process that can take time—months or even years. The truth is that genuine forgiveness is nearly impossible if we have been deeply hurt. We can't do it by ourselves, but God is ready to help us. God invites us to pray for healing of our hurts. God wants us to pray for the desire to forgive, or for the desire to desire to forgive. God responds when we pray to see the person who hurt us as Jesus sees her or him. God is delighted as we ask for help in letting go of the poison of resentment. With God's truly amazing grace, the ability to forgive is given to us.

Holy God of love and kindness, help me to be honest about my healthy anger. Empower me to enter into the process of forgiveness with you. Amen.

Tilda Norberg

March 7

My Belief, My Behavior

There are two things to do about the Gospel—believe it and behave it.[3]

After working more than forty years in a national church agency, some of my beliefs and many of my behaviors have been shaped by those years and responsibilities. Even in my fifth year of retirement I hold many of those experiences and learnings.

Creeping years and just plain weariness made it easy to relinquish national staff responsibility. But it was not easy to make the transition to a more local, family-oriented life. It requires great personal effort to adjust to local family and community needs without losing touch with the realities of national and global life.

I believe that God uses rather frail instruments, in the guise of ordinary people and everyday situations, to build God's realm on earth. I believe that each of us has unique gifts and abilities and that we must work hard to understand what God would have us do with them. I believe we must depend on that Source to lead us. I believe that family is to be valued, nurtured, supported, and corrected.

I believe there are constants in life. Location, status, and arena of responsibility may vary. In order to *behave* the gospel, one must translate and transfer prior experiences into current tasks and responsibilities. One must affirm that learning never ends and that

God is present in every situation. Behavior that promotes growth requires both inward reflection and outward action.

God of ages past and future, I give thanks for your constant presence through the many stages of my life. Help me always to believe and behave your word. Amen.

Theressa Hoover

March 8

Young Faith

I praise you, for I am fearfully and wonderfully made. Wonderful are your works; that I know very well.
Psalm 139:14

My daughter Sarah's education in theology started very young, when she was barely more than a toddler. It was, you might say, *boo-boo theology.*

In those moments when I had done all a mother could do to doctor whatever frequent scrape or cut or sliver-prick she had suffered, I'd look at her teary, still pained face and want to find something more. And so we started talking about magic, about the magic that God was doing in her body that very moment.

She wasn't interested in the science of it. She couldn't take in the details—how the injury itself immediately set off the chemistry and physics of healing, of plasma and cell activity, of the body's instant defenses in crisis and then its shift to rebuilding.

But she could listen to how from the very same moment she had been hurt, the healing had started. I would tell her (in nonscientific terms) how the hurt itself had started her body getting well. God is so close, I would assure her in the darkness of her room at bedtime, that maybe even before you knew you were hurt, God had started working toward your wellness. You can help the process, I'd point out, but you can hinder it—if you don't leave that cut alone. But there is nothing you can do or have to do to make healing happen.

As I talked with her of ouchies and this loving, healing God, I realized I was articulating my own theology of a God as close as the inner working of our own cells.

Someday Sarah will learn about the white blood cells and the plasma, and everything else. My hope is she will be struck by how her growing understanding of science does not contradict but underscores her faith—a faith that started with boo-boo theology.

Thank you, thank you, God, for how you are incarnate in my own body, in its marvelous, amazing, infinitely complex workings, and for how I see you in the healing care you give me and for how I hear you in each beat of my heart. Amen.

Beth Resler Walters

March 9

Connection

The old, old lesson of the art of meditation. To woo combinations and inspirations into being by a depth and continuity of attention and meditation.[4]

Wholeness is not simply the absence of disease or the achievement of good feelings, but a more positive state, one that integrates the breadth and complexity of experience. Holistic living invites joy without denying suffering and tragedy, remaining within the struggles of real life in this world.

For women who seek to live out an individual expression of new roles and relationships, the promise of wholeness offers sustenance for the struggle, an antidote for the stress of living between the *never again* and the *not yet*. After taking a bold step toward personal freedom or a public position on an issue, how many have felt a disappointing anxiety displace the expected exhilaration? The struggle occurs within us, as well as around us, and we can be surprised by its power.

Holistic living seeks integration, *making the connections* through understanding, as well as through relationships. These connections provide a web of meaning and strength; they are vital to our well-being. We do not need reminding that these connections are rarely easy to establish or maintain. Difficult relationships and stubborn interior issues can remain unresolved despite all our efforts and prayers. But in our seeking, in making even the little connections, we are knitting a little hope. May our attentions, to God and to each other, in the silence of meditation or the noise of the day, make powerful connections and *woo inspirations* to sustain us all.

Gracious God, hear our prayers of longing, for strength and insight, for the hope that sustains, even in the face of the world's suffering. Inspire us with new words and new connections; free us from the burdens of the past. Amen.

Holly Vincent Bean

March 10

Free Indeed

So if the Son makes you free, you will be free indeed.
                                                  John 8:36

"You've been married as long as I've been living!" exclaimed a classmate in disbelief. "Yes," I said, "I have a son your age." Following that exchange, I was treated a little differently. I keep reminding myself that for her, everyone over thirty is probably considered to be old. At age thirty-eight, I felt led to make a career change. This meant quitting a successful position as a health-care worker in the field of geriatrics and becoming a college freshman for the first time in my life.

The decision was a difficult one. Three years before, I was diagnosed with breast cancer that required radical surgery, and I was scared the cancer might return. I was afraid of being in the academic environment, of competing with brain cells much younger than my own. I feared the future prospects of receiving a Ph.D. at age forty-seven, and perhaps facing age discrimination when seeking work in my new field. Regardless, I know that I am where God wants me to be. This knowledge frees me from my fears and provides a sense of wholeness that instills a peaceful spirit.

Things are going well. I am now in graduate school, older than all of my classmates and practically all of my professors. My classmate's remark may place me in one category, but the message in the Gospel of John helps me celebrate who I am as an individual.

*Creator of all things, I praise you. Your Word refreshes my spirit
and fills me with joyful anticipation. Amen.*

Sally Olsen

Finding the Heart's True Home

*Lord, you have been our dwelling place in all
generations. Before the mountains were brought forth,
or ever you had formed the earth and the world, from
everlasting to everlasting you are God.*

Psalm 90:1-2

One of my best friends grew up in the American embassy in
China. She was raised by a Russian nanny, Lilinka, because her
parents were often busy or drinking. She still struggles with
homelessness.

All of us grew up in imperfect families, and many of us, deep
down, are searching for some place or someone to satisfy our deep
need for home, for security, for safety, for a place where we
belong.

Like Abraham and Sarah, we are all sojourners who have not
found our permanent dwelling places. The psalmist reminds us
that it is God who is our home. In Psalm 68 the poet wrote that
"God makes a home for the lonely. . . . God is a parent to the
orphan." The good news is that God's heart is a place of hospitality. It is a place where we can sit comfortably in our old slippers
and talk honestly about who we are.

Talking honestly about who we are to One who listens as
tenderly as Christ listened is perhaps the healthiest thing we can
do for ourselves (mind, body, and soul). We want many things in
this life; we search here and there for happiness. Underneath all
that seeking is a deep longing to be known as we are and to be
accepted anyway. We spend a lot of time and energy each day trying
to make sure that we are not alone, that we are not cut off from
others. We want a home base, a place of safety. Unfortunately,
we become so caught up in the experience of being a stranger on

earth that we forget that we were created to find our security and home in the heart of God.

If we are to be healed and whole, we must each discover that we are not alone; that when we are stripped to our most base self, someone understands. We need to know that we are cared for beyond all the wickedness of our deeds or the turmoil in our minds. We need to discover that when our spirit is naked, like the prodigal son, we are not cut off.

God makes a home for the lonely and is a parent to the orphan!

What comforting words these are! The heart of God invites us to come home, just as we are. We need to remember that the goal of life on earth is not perfect physical health, but union with God. God's first and foremost aim is to bring us into perfect harmony with God's love. Our physical life in this world was not meant to be permanent. John wrote, "Do not be worried or upset. Believe in God, believe also in me. There are many rooms in my Father's house, and I am going to prepare a place for you" (John 14:1-2).

Redeemer of the oppressed, in our seeking after safety and security, point us in the direction of your loving heart, that we might find rest and comfort. Amen.

Dorothy Lairmore

March 12

Seek the Lord

No one will be able to stand against you all the days of your life. As I was with Moses, so I will be with you; I will never leave you nor forsake you.

Joshua 1:5 (NIV)

What a valuable promise for Joshua to claim! I hope you will read the rest of the instructions that the Lord gave to him.

I am a *nontraditional student* becoming a registered nurse at the age of thirty-five—a challenging endeavor. This has meant many adjustments for our family. I wonder how Joshua felt when left with the task of leading the Israelites into the Promised Land. He had worked with Moses but now the ball was in his court, so to speak. Sometimes the big picture is just about too much to take in all at one time. When we feel overwhelmed, it is time to step back and focus on the most important priority. We cannot be all things to all people nor should we attempt to. Please read the rest of the Lord's instructions in Joshua 1:6-9. You are not left on your own—remember God is with you in all your circumstances. Truly, God is so good! Seek him each and every day. That is a positive action for each of us to take, just as Joshua had to take action in following the Lord to lead the Israelites into the Promised Land.

God of all comfort, help me to honor you by being faithful to the calling you have for me. Teach me obedience each day. Give me strength and courage to advance your kingdom. Amen.

Melanie Cooper

March 13

Graces of God

The thief comes only to steal and kill and destroy. I came that they may have life, and have it abundantly.
John 10:10

Here I sit outdoors being refreshed by the gentle breeze on this hot and humid day in Iowa. In one direction I can see six to eight miles, thirty to forty miles the other way. I could have chosen to remain inside and lament the weather. I opted for a better way of spending my time. I am choosing a life-giving situation.

As the breeze envelopes my being, I am aware of God's presence. The graces of God given as gifts for growth are as abundant as the blowing wind. They come to refresh and uplift one's spirit.

The grace of God can be accepted or rejected. To accept is to choose life. God desires oneness within ourselves. Time set aside to gain knowledge of ourselves is crucial to our becoming one, to our becoming wholly alive, to our becoming the person God intends us to be.

As we choose life-giving opportunities, we spurt ahead into new growth. At times this may stretch us beyond what we could have imagined for ourselves. Windows open; eyes brighten; our feet begin to dance. Horizons displaying newness burst forth in kaleidoscopic colors and patterns. A plethora of possibilities spring up. Exciting challenges take form—challenges that increase our potential to live life to the fullest.

God is a God of surprises. Look for God's surprises. Rejoice in their coming. Celebrate the newness. Enjoy the pleasures of the gift. An attitude of gratitude to God for the surprises expresses our acceptance of the joys in life. All is a gift to us.

As part of my evening prayer, I offer my words of thanks to this great God of ours for the surprises and joys of the past day. This prayer helps me realize how *alive* the day has been for me. This is life-giving. This is connecting me with the source of all life—God who loves me so much.

God who is the source of all life, thank you for the graces and surprises you shower down upon me. Assist me in choosing life-giving situations. Your loving support encourages me to live life to the fullest as I journey with you and others. Amen.

Millie Leuenberger

March 14

Blessed Presence

Lord, you have been our dwelling place in all generations. Before the mountains were brought forth, or ever you had formed the earth and the world, from everlasting to everlasting you are God.
Psalm 90:1-2

My mother died of breast cancer. Although she had a mastectomy, radiation, and chemotherapy, the cancer spread throughout her body. I recall moving through those days as in a fog. I went through all the motions of making arrangements for her funeral and burial, but I was detached from my feelings about her death. I don't remember very much of what happened or how things were accomplished. I do remember sitting on the sofa and being angry that she had left me, once again. I do remember being angry with God that God had allowed this tragedy. And so I refused to pray; I did not want to say a word. I sat and stared.

A friend from my church came to see how I was doing. I reported that I was okay. When she asked about praying, I said that I did not want to pray. She advised me that she was going to pray for me anyway and proceeded to do so without my consent. She prayed and I listened. I cried and explained my overwhelming sense of loss and pain to her. She remained with me for a while, checking to see if there was anything else she could do for me. After a time, she left.

I lived alone, but as I was sitting on the sofa, I heard a great sound as if from a multitude that was marching or walking from the rear of the house toward the front room. People seemed to be laughing and talking. My spirit seemed to leave my body and lay prostrate on the floor. I saw a female dressed in a white billowy gown dance into the room. She was young and gaily dancing. She was my mother. I recognized her spiritually, not physically. By this time, I seemed to be sitting again. She danced and then she lay down near me. I wanted to join her and must have communicated this to her, for she responded, "No, it's not time yet." With that, she departed, as did the sounds of walking and talking from the others.

Dear and precious Lord, I am grateful that even when I would turn from you, you have been faithful and have remained with and within me. I thank you for providing all that I have needed, for drying my tears, and for removing my sorrows. For your love, which seems boundless, I praise you. For your mercy, which overlooks my unworthiness, I honor you. For your grace, I bless your Holy Name. Amen.

Melbalenia D. Evans

March 15

Shared Friendship

In those days Mary set out and went with haste to a Judean town in the hill country, where she entered the house of Zechariah and greeted Elizabeth. When Elizabeth heard Mary's greeting, the child leaped in her womb.   Luke 1:39-41a

What unlikely friends: a pregnant old woman from Judea who had been barren all of her life and an unwed pregnant teenager from Galilee. But friends they were! Upon being told by the angel that she was pregnant, Mary immediately set out to unite with her friend Elizabeth. This must have been a difficult and lonely trip for this young teenager who had just received the most incredible message, but she went *with haste*. No trip was too difficult when she needed her friend and her friend needed her. They had to be together to share their secrets and mysteries and to bring healing and wholeness to each other.

Even though the text says that Mary "entered the house of Zechariah and greeted Elizabeth," I always picture Elizabeth seeing Mary coming and rushing out to meet her. They run to each other to embrace, and in that embrace passes much understanding and support. This understanding goes way beyond what words could express.

This is the way with special friendships. There are times in our lives when we must be together to share joys, dilemmas, sadness, pain. No matter the miles, we must be together to hold, love, laugh, cry—to share. Have you had a friend like this? You are blessed if you have. If you haven't, continue to seek and be open. If you've had more than one friend of this kind, you have been doubly blessed.

Spend a few minutes reflecting on your personal friend or friends throughout your life. What have they meant to you and you to them? How have they brought healing and wholeness to you? How have you brought healing and wholeness to them?

Creator of friends and friendship, our hearts leap when we think of our friends who are willing to share our pain and our joys, our best moments and our worst. Our lives would be empty without a special friend to go to with haste. We ask that you will continue to nudge us to be more available in our friendships. Help us to build friendships with those our own age and those like ourselves, but also help us to build friendships across the genera-tions and with those different from ourselves. Mary and Elizabeth learned from each other as they shared their fears and their faith. Help us to learn from each other. Keep us ever open to old friends and to the possibility of new friends. In our friendships, help us to bring healing and wholeness. Amen.

D. Elaine Tiller

ʹPrecious Gifts

It is more blessed to give than to receive. Acts 20:35b

A couple of years ago while visiting a small village along the Luapula River in Zaire, I was presented with a very special gift: six eggs.

Eggs are a precious commodity in Zaire. In spite of widespread malnutrition, eggs aren't often eaten in the villages, being used instead for bartering in the marketplace. Even though the young mother who presented them to me could have justified keeping those eggs for her family and the baby strapped to her back, she chose instead to present them to me, a stranger, as a gift; not because she was required to give them, not out of a sense of obligation, not because she thought she would get something in return, not because the eggs were so insignificant that she wouldn't miss them, and not even because she thought I really needed them. She gave because the joy of giving was rooted deeply in her community, in her culture, and in her very being. She gave with pride and gratefulness for having the privilege of sharing.

May we too learn to give from the richness of our hearts. Only then can we experience the wholeness of community that brings a hope for the abundant life our Savior envisioned for all of his children. May we discover the deepest joy of giving as we follow our Savior's admonition to feed the hungry, clothe the naked, comfort the sick, and visit the prisoners. Whether the hungry be in Calcutta or in Chicago, Nairobi or Little Rock; whether the naked be street children or village mothers, unemployed men or the aged; whether the sick be rich or poor, royalty or homeless; whether those in prison be brown or beige, or black or white; may we reach out to share with thankfulness and joyful hearts.

Compassionate, loving, and merciful God, out of the refreshing, bubbling, ever-changing stream of blessings in our lives, we come now joyful that we have been blessed with riches to share. Like a village mother who has tenderly borne the weight of the infant strapped to her back through the long hours of the working day, who now loosens the wrappings to hand the child to another to care for, we too now loosen the bindings from our possessions

*and acknowledge that what we have nurtured is not ours to keep
tightly bound to our beings, but ours to release to be embraced
by the community. May we share our riches, both material and
spiritual, with your children in need. May we do so joyfully
because we feel it a privilege to have something to give. Amen.*

Sharon Kirkpatrick

March 17

Change

*So we do not lose heart. Even though our outer nature
is wasting away, our inner nature is being renewed day
by day.*   *2 Corinthians 4:16*

Like many other college graduates, I thought our generation
would change the world in the sixties and seventies. I read certain
authors and thought their philosophies would change us all. Of
course, the world did change during those decades, shaped by
wars and economics and technology. But people didn't change the
way I'd hoped. Violence, crime, greed, pettiness, cheating—I
won't even try to list all the vices—are still rife. I may even
contribute to them in my own ways.

Injustice, as I perceive it, has always bothered me. Probably I
was given to ranting about it until, finally, someone in a discussion
group said to me, "Why do you always feel someone else has to
change?" What a loaded question! Like Pogo, the problem is *me.*
The answers begin and end with *me.* (I'm not leaving God out of
this equation. My relationship with God is part of me and shapes
what I do.)

Just prior to this awakening, I had been going through a
difficult stage of adjustment with my mother. As a widow she
moved close to us for support, and suddenly I was fourteen again.
Unasked-for advice and constant demands were a part of my life,
as well as a family and a full-time executive job. Guilt was the
hook, and I found it very difficult to deal with. A wise minister
pointed out that Mother was not going to change. I needed to
accept my adult life, to be interested in me, to love me. I was going
to have to make the adjustment: to accept my mother as she was
and change my thinking.

I'm still working on both aspects. I'm still prone to say, "Why don't they just . . . ?" rather than "What can I do?" At age ninety-one, my mother lives in an adult home, and I still find myself feeling guilty. But I am also being responsible. I cannot wait for others to act or to tell me what to do; I cannot expect others to change who and what they are. I must cope. I must act. I must make changes in my world. I must serve my God and live my life to be the best I can be, every day, every hour. God may work through me; God works also through others, and so I must respect those I meet and read about and disagree with and resent. The enemy may be *me,* but my hope for peace on earth also begins with *me.*

God of peace, work through me, change me, make me a peacemaker. Amen.

Cathie Burdick

March 18

Hallelujah! Amen!

But the angel said to the women, "Do not be afraid; I know that you are looking for Jesus who was crucified. He is not here; for he has been raised, as he said."

Matthew 28:5-6a

The blank pieces of paper stared back at me. These vacant pages had been whispering and shouting at me for days! "Fill in the spaces, cover the lines, write words of celebration and joy," they whispered! "Get on with it, make it the best ever, uncover the resurrected Jesus for all to worship and acclaim," they shouted!

I was a broken and grief-filled pastor faced with writing the Easter sermon. Our son had died on January 19, 1995. He was just thirty-one years old. My every waking and sleeping moment continued to be consumed with sorrow and suffering. How could I celebrate resurrection when death was all around me? How could I celebrate miracle life when tears and rage were my constant companion? How could I celebrate the astounding gift when life had lost all meaning and purpose? How could I possibly accomplish the task when my eyes were dim, my body bent, and my heart shattered? Our son is dead. What is resurrection? I don't know! I don't care!

If I could only know if my son was all right, I cried, then maybe the grieving shell would begin to crack just a bit. This was not a theological search or a doctrinal issue or a scriptural problem; this was a mother yearning to know. I always needed to know he was tucked in safely at night; that he was safe when playing and learning; that he came home safely from school, dates, ball games; that he was safe in college housing and classes; that he was safe in his employment, home travels, fun, and friendships. I needed to know—I had to know—Is he safe; is he all right; is he *home*?

It is late Saturday afternoon, the day before Easter Sunday. The page is slowly filling with empty thoughts and ideas. I feel wrung dry, vacant, and bare. "I can't do this," I screamed. "Someone has to rescue me. Someone! Please someone!" But the telephone was silent; no one knocked on the door. It was just me, only me and a few lackluster words.

The alarm was set for very early on Sunday morning. I had to have more paragraphs. As I set my feet on the floor, I was immediately enveloped in the sweetest, gentlest spirit I have ever experienced. Then the confirmation flooded my heart and soul: Kent is safe, he is with Love, and his hand is held by Jesus. *Someone* had come! I ran to my desk, wrote as fast as was possible, and laced the empty words with joy, celebration, hope, and peace. Jesus was safe! Our son was safe! The people said, "It was the most joyful, spirit-filled Easter sermon we have ever heard you give."

In the midst of the most wrenching sorrow, the Spirit graced my heart and stood me up to bear testimony to the miracle of life eternal! In the reality of total emptiness, the Spirit gifted me with the amazing assurance of life eternal!

Merciful God, the gift of your resurrected Son, assures me of your amazing and ever-present love. Even in the midst of life's most wrenching grief, your Spirit breaks through to speak to my soul words of hope. Accept the thanksgiving of my heart and listen for my whispered hallelujah. Amen.

Karen F. Freberg

Relax, God Is in Charge

But this one thing I do: forgetting what lies behind and straining forward to what lies ahead, I press on toward the goal for the prize. Philippians 3:13b-14a

"Relax, God is in charge" is the quote on a little card taped to the dashboard of my car. It reminds me of how very little about my life and work is actually under my control.

I used to equate the idea of living one day at a time and of trusting God for results with irresponsibility. Fretting seemed to make me more significant; I acted as if worry were my Christian duty.

What I forgot was that a Christian has only one duty: to commit her life completely to God. And if I don't live that way, no matter how much good stuff I plan and how much I actually accomplish, I wind up feeling unfulfilled and exhausted.

These days, I try not to treat God like some divine headwaiter to whom I give my orders. Now my prayers involve a lot of listening. My life is a whole lot less structured and a whole lot more interesting! When bad things happen, I ask God, How much of this is my fault? What can I learn from this? And (most important) what do you want me to do now? God always answers, although seldom as I would have expected, but the answer is always just right.

I take myself a lot less seriously nowadays. Sometimes I feel an incredible lightness of spirit. And my sleep is sweet.

Hope of all the ends of the earth, please help me remember which one of us is Boss. Amen.

Norma R. Jones

Betrayal

Nothing is at last sacred except the integrity of your own mind.[5]

To be betrayed by someone in whom you have put your trust is one of the most devastating experiences in life. To have your integrity questioned can ravage your soul. There is a visceral reaction to betrayal that is as debilitating as any disease. In fact, it can lead to disease. It can disquiet your mind. It can distress your soul. It can cause you to question your own ability to choose friends wisely. It can undermine your own self-confidence. It can disrupt your sleep and your digestive system. It can cause the darkness of depression to cloud your days. But it does not have to destroy you.

Jesus was betrayed by his beloved disciple, Judas, yet he said, "Friend, do what you are here to do" (Matthew 26:50). He accepted the fact that he could not control the betrayer's behavior. He also recognized that he would suffer the consequences of the betrayal. While we are not usually betrayed to the point of death, our sense of self may suffer as if it had died. If we will not let the power of the betrayer lay claim on us, that one will have no hold over us; our health, body, mind, and spirit will be sustained. Troublesome as betrayal can be, it does not need to sap the resources of our faith or whittle away at the strength of other relationships. While it may be difficult for us to call the betrayer *friend* any longer, we can maintain our sense of self by not getting in a power struggle with the betrayer. We do not need to fall to that level by being vindictive.

Through prayer and meditation, through the support of other friends, through a close examination of our own behavior, we can ask God to forgive the betrayer even as we forgive the person. We can confess any behavior that we sense has led to the betrayal and ask God to forgive us. We can seek to make amends with the person involved. If that is not possible, we can *let the experience go* and *turn it over to God*, asking God to give us the wisdom to learn more about ourselves from this encounter and to give us the strength to put the experience behind.

Remembering that each of us is a child of God and that nothing can separate us from God's love helps us to keep our perspective. Maintaining friendships with others who affirm us restores our sense of well-being. Healing our spirit after a betrayal is not immediate; it evolves over time.

God of grace, help me to forgive those who have betrayed me and strengthen my sense of self so that I will have no need to betray others. Amen.

Jean Anne Swope

The Better Part

Mary has chosen the better part.   Luke 10:42b

As preparations were being made for the United Nations Fourth World Conference on Women, an interesting impasse was reached on the question, What is woman? The question strikes at the core of current discussions of the role of women in today's society. While women have made progress in the United States, we are increasingly aware that abuse of women still exists here and that in many parts of the world the wife is still considered her husband's property. Also, the role of women in the church leadership is still restricted in many denominations and faiths throughout the world.

In the story told in Luke 10:38-41, we can see Jesus visiting in Martha's home. Martha's sister, Mary, is listening to Jesus' teaching when Martha comes into the room. She expresses her anger at Mary for not helping with household chores. Jesus intervenes saying, "Martha, Martha, you are worried and distracted by many things; there is need of only one thing. Mary has chosen the better part, which will not be taken away from her."

What is the better part? What is Martha missing by her attention to the household duties that seem overwhelming to her? Jesus is making a plea for balance in Martha's life. Be less anxious; set priorities to leave room for learning and growing spiritually.

Whatever our career, our household responsibilities, our social activities, we must strive to find the best part we can fulfill. We juggle our many tasks and responsibilities, striving always to achieve wholeness—physically, mentally, socially, and also spiritually.

Lord, help us to know ourselves. Strengthen us as we strive to find and occupy our special place in your world. Amen.

                                        Mable Doris Gooden

My Open Door

I believe that imagination is stronger than knowledge.
That myth is more potent than history.
I believe that dreams are more powerful than facts.
That hope always triumphs over experience.
That laughter is the only cure for grief.
And I believe that love is stronger than death.[6]

There is a group of us who meet once a week for sisterhood and prayer. I frequently lead the meditations. The women say that the following meditation has been particularly renewing and healing for them. It can be done alone or in any size group. You can do it while you slowly read through this article. You can read through the article first, close your eyes, and slowly go through the process yourself. Or you can have someone else read it to you.

I take a moment to get myself into a comfortable position. If I am sitting, I put my feet flat on the floor and uncross my arms and hands. I just focus on my breathing for a few breaths. I allow my mind to slow itself down as I breathe and begin to focus on my heart, becoming aware of its rhythm as I breathe. The heart is our culture's symbol for love.

I imagine there is a door in the front of my heart. I am the only one who can open the door. It opens from the inside out. When I am willing, I push open the door and let my love escape into the world. I breathe in love. I breathe out love. I breathe in again. I breathe out again. As the door of my heart opens, I notice all my concerns are right behind my love. I let my concerns out of my heart and into the world. There may be many concerns or few, big concerns or little ones. I let them out of my heart.

As my concerns leave my heart, I notice a door at the back of my heart. This door too can only be opened by me. As I pull open the door, *Divine Love* enters. I can feel the freshness of *it*. I can feel the energy in *it*. I allow *Divine Love* to be pumped throughout my body. I allow *it* to leave by the front door of my heart and enter the world. Now I am a conduit for *Divine Love* in the world. As I move through my week, I will remember this time. I am willing to be surprised time and time again by my experience of health and wholeness.

Boundless Infinity, Creative Spirit, I remind myself I am yours.
I live, breathe, move with your creation. Amen.

Kathie Murtey

March 23

Sacred Spaces, Healing Places

And that Christ may dwell in your hearts through faith.
Ephesians 3:17

On some busy days life seems to be a jumble of hard-rock pieces! There's the constant jangle of the phone and endless tasks to be done. Harsh voices reflect the hurt of rejection, personalities clash like cymbals, and troubled ones make pointed remarks. There is also the pull of the poor at our door and my own deep inner longing to see the hungry satisfied physically, spiritually, and emotionally.

Trying times challenge us to find places of peace and wholeness. These times push us to find sacred spaces to relax our bodies, rest our senses, and softly soothe the rough, painful edges of life.

I have found these healing places on high mountains and in quiet chapels, near running creeks, beneath sheltering trees. They are present in the sweet scent of a flower or in the hope that a rainbow promises. I find peace immersed in ocean waves or in an enveloping armchair, planting my tiny urban garden, or resting by a flickering fire. I treasure the times I am healed by a cherished memory or the voice of a friend. For me, all of these are holy ground.

Stronger souls than I have known wholeness in refreshing tears or in the fingering of well-worn prayer beads. Some have found healing amidst conflict or violence—even in dark prison cells. They, like I, have discovered the secret of sacred spaces. There are those times and places when, through the patient eyes of living faith, we are able to penetrate the darkness and recognize the overwhelming reality of God's presence within and about us. They are the moments of loving awareness of the invisible fullness in whom we who seek find our most sacred space—our peaceful dwelling place.

*Invisible but ever-present God, I give you thanks and praise
for the sacred dwelling space your unfailing love provides. Amen.*
Rose MacDermott

Role Reversal

*Do not cast me off in the time of old age; do not
forsake me when my strength is spent.   Psalm 71:9*

She sat on the couch, tears brimming, saying, "I need to talk to
you. I don't seem to be able to remember anymore." With a heart
as heavy as rock, with a choking lump in the throat, through tears
that could end a drought, I knew it was time to reassure my mother
that she, who had given me birth and had cared for me through
the vicissitudes of life, would not be abandoned in her declining
years. She had diminished four dress sizes in six months and
hardly looked like the soft lady in whose bosom I remembered
being comforted. She was, for me, the paragon of what a mother
should be: a loving, fiercely independent professional who nurtured her children to be self-reliant but was concerned for others
as well; a gracious conversationalist who could know a stranger's
life story in fifteen minutes through her genuine, gentle questioning; a generous woman who could always find a way to help
another in a financial pinch; a self-disciplined woman who held
high standards and taught us that with freedom comes responsibility; a wit with a story to humor us through almost anything. No
one is ever prepared to lose a parent, especially the mother who
bore you. Now it was my turn to provide succor for my mother.

It must have been difficult for her to have me take over her
investments, manage her cash flow, and secure power of attorney
over medical decisions and all other affairs of her life. But I
believe it was more difficult for her to have to admit that she was
no longer able to do all that she needed to have done. She needed
to be assured by me and by others in the family that her *doing* was
not nearly as important to us as her *being*. She needed to hear from
us that even though she was failing in health, with her body and
mind weakening, she was and is important to us; that the time it

takes to be present with her, to cry with her, to laugh, to hug and kiss, to talk, and to attend to her needs is a labor of love.

It is natural for her to fear abandonment because she no longer functions at her peak. It is also natural for me to get frustrated when our communication is disabled by memory loss. Still, our sense of wholeness is bound in our relationship with each other.

God of our circling years, be with those we love in their twilight years and strengthen us to be loving and caring vessels of your grace. Amen.

Jean Anne Swope

March 25

Wounded for Me

Jesus came and stood among them and said, "Peace be with you." Then he said to Thomas, "Put your finger here and see my hands. Reach out your hand and put it in my side. Do not doubt but believe." Thomas answered him, "My Lord and my God!"

John 20:26b-28

Why are those wounds still there? Why should the risen Christ still carry the signs of his suffering? Why does his glorified body carry such terrible reminders of his humanness? Why have the wounds not been healed? Why haven't they disappeared?

Every day for nearly two thousand years, Jesus must look at his wounded hands. How can he forget us? How can he ever escape from this world that taught him what it is to suffer? He is forever connected to us, to our pain, to our wounded, wounding selves. Look at your own wounds and you find the tie that binds you to others. No longer alone, you find yourself one with others. Loneliness and isolation dissolve and community begins.

Who can get through human life without being wounded? Not Jesus. Not us. Each of us bears wounds; each of us inflicts wounds. Parent to child, lover to lover, friend to friend, nation to nation, enemy to enemy. We live with the pain of our wounding.

We can ignore the wounds and strive to rise above them, numb ourselves to their pain, seek release in busyness, in addiction and denial. That is one way, but the wounds persist and bleed again when we least expect them.

It takes a long time, and patience, and repentance, and forgiveness, and still the wounds are there. They do not disappear but return to ache when the climate of our souls turns cold or clouded.

The wounds we carry are part of our identity. "Any known scars?" they ask when someone is missing. The scars are part of how we identify ourselves. The experience that caused them may never be talked about, but it does, nevertheless, become the scar that distinguishes our lives.

The wounds remain, but are healed. The healing begins with acceptance. Instead of running from the wounds as those disciples ran from the cross, like Thomas we reach out and touch them. We touch our own wounds, acknowledge them, know them to be part of us. We hold them out for Christ to touch and then they are transformed. No longer do we need to run.

So it is, O Lord, that you come to me and hold out your wounded hands. Touch me, you say. I know what it is to be wounded. Let me touch you and find a new way to relate to others. Let me touch you and find a new way to reach out to your world. Let me touch you and be healed. Amen.

Neta Lindsay Pringle

March 26

Be There

Could you not keep awake one hour? Keep awake and pray that you may not come into the time of trial; the spirit indeed is willing, but the flesh is weak.
Mark 14:37b-38

In Gethsemane Jesus was struggling very hard with what he knew was coming. He knew God's will was for him to be crucified in order to save us, but he did not want to die. Jesus, frightened and scared, was going to Gethsemane to pray and to work through the internal wars he was having. He asked Peter, James, and John to go with him, to be with him in his distress and trouble. He did not ask their advice; he did not ask them to do anything or say anything—he only asked them to *be there* as he struggled in prayer with his wants and desires and God's will for him.

Jesus needed friends to *be there* with him—not to do anything, but to be with him. The three disciples failed him. The three disciples fell asleep. Was the struggle, the suffering that Jesus was going through, too much for them? I suspect that this may be true. Jesus' pain was too much, so the disciples fell asleep in order to escape. How often are we asked to be there for someone who is suffering and needs a listening ear, a loving touch, a companion in one's hurt and pain. But instead of being there we fall asleep, give advice, or try to solve the person's problem. So often we are asked to hear the pain, to allow the pain, and to allow the other to find her own way.

We all go through our Gethsemanes, our times of great pain and hurt. We all need friends who will stand by us and be with us as we face these times and try to hear God's will for us.

God, bearer of our burdens, help us to bear one another's burdens by being there for each other in the times of great pain, suffering, loneliness, and decision. Help us to know how to listen and be available to each other. Help us to stay awake for each other and for the world. And God, let us know your presence in our Gethsemane times. Help us to feel your presence and love in our dark moments. Help us to remain open to your will being done in and through us as it was in and through Jesus. Amen.

D. Elaine Tiller

March 27

Giving It All You've Got

He sat down opposite the treasury, and watched the crowd putting money into the treasury. Many rich people put in large sums. A poor widow came and put in two small copper coins, which are worth a penny. Then he called his disciples and said to them, "Truly I tell you, this poor widow has put in more than all those contributing to the treasury. For all of them have contributed out of their abundance; but she out of her

poverty has put in everything she had, all she had to
live on."   Mark 12:41-42

In Jesus' day, widows didn't have it too good. There was no Social Security, no food pantries, no government subsidies, and no jobs. They had to rely on the kindness of extended family and friends, or on the handouts of strangers, and hope to marry again. Food was hard to come by; money, even harder. We don't know the circumstances of this widow in the story. We don't know how long ago her husband died, how old she was, or what her health was like. She had faith because she kept coming to worship in spite of the difficult circumstances dealt to her. She had courage because she gave all she had. She had dignity because it takes dignity to be a giver when you haven't got much going for you.

The widow gave more because she gave all she had. She gave more, because her story lives on to challenge each one of us to consider our giving. It's not up to us to make the giving enough to meet the need. It's not up to us to judge the hearts of those who give. We are called simply to examine ourselves and then give— out of our abundance, out of our need. Whatever our circumstances, giving returns blessings to the giver.

We never know who is watching. We never know what seeds our giving may plant. Let us cultivate the art of giving, and let us rest in the knowledge that God is the one who gives the increase.

Creator and Sustainer of life and all good things, accept this moment, the gift of my life. Accept the offering of my hands. Inspire in me a heart that seeks to reach out to others, both in times of abundance and in times of need. Amen.

Patricia A. Fraser

March 28

Seeing the Savior

And all my bones are out of joint; my heart is like wax.
Psalm 22:14b (KJV)

Shattered. Dying. Lost in inner space with no way out. The gap that separates God, self, and others is growing wider, not smaller. When depression and despair strike and death begins to look preferable to life, can we hold on to a faith that feels as though it has dried up, withered away, and left us abandoned? The author of Psalm 22 begins his plea with the words, "My God, my God, why hast thou forsaken me?" He keenly feels his separation from God. He then describes being surrounded by his enemies; no neighbors, just enemies. Separation from others. He has withered within.

What can one do, finding him- or herself in the space described by the author of Psalm 22? In the muted agony of self-loathing, in the barren wasteland of intellectualism, in the often fruitless pursuit of human help and human answers, can a light be seen in the darkness? What does the author of Psalm 22 do? Having depicted anyone's worst nightmare, the psalmist paradoxically comes up with a seemingly foolish and absurd answer to his predicament. He lavishly praises God. This same God who had forsaken him was absent when he most needed him, leaving his soul to sear in the heat of its own despair. *It is then that the psalmist, having knelt at the altar of his own emptiness, turns and kneels instead at the altar of God's fullness.* Powerless to effect his own salvation, he turns to the God who possesses the wholeness he seeks and who invites us to share in that wholeness. The journey in the psalm is one from the depths of negation to the heights of affirmation; from the uncertainty of life lived under one's own power to a life focused and centered on the One who is always at peace and is powerful enough to dispel the fears of this life that too often overwhelm us.

Can praising God restore one to health, to balance, to wholeness? Or is this merely the magic of positive thinking? Are we to replace our incomplete, negative self-image with a holistic, positive God-image and await our transformation? The author of Psalm 22 would answer yes. The psalmist's desire to praise God is his recognition that this God whom he appeals to is real. Too often we are unable to feel the presence of God in our everyday lives. We relegate God to the impotent position of an idea, a doctrine, a theology—instead of the living, breathing, *with me right now walking through my day God.* Not the distant *Our Father* but the *Here and Now Mother* who, like earthly mothers, is interested in every aspect of her child's day. But are we able to live moment by moment and sustain a perpetual sense of God's presence? Can we walk through this world with the strength to believe that we are always surrounded by God's Spirit?

Heavenly Creator, teach me to kneel before you this day and every day, to acknowledge your presence in my life, and to make your presence known in the world. Amen.

Lynn Forsberg

Prayer Warriors

Another angel . . . was given a great quantity of incense to offer with the prayers of all the saints on the golden altar that is before the throne. And the smoke of the incense, with the prayers of the saints, rose before God. Revelation 8:3-4a

Over a period of several years the pain from my neurological syndrome, reflex sympathetic dystrophy, was brutally intense. My energy was utterly spent coping with the pain. I yearned to be able to pray, yet could not. No energy remained for anything, not even prayer. My connection to the source of comfort and strength in my life, God, seemed to be blocked, which frightened me. And I felt guilty about my disconnection.

Serendipitously I received a gift from God—the revelation that I no longer needed to struggle. Others would pray for me and be my surrogates in prayer, my praying saints. In surrendering my ineffective efforts to these saints, I experienced a miraculous release from my feelings of fear and guilt.

Who were these praying saints who ministered to me? They were the congregation and Wednesday morning Bible study group of my local church, Sisters of Mercy, friends distant and near, and the faith networks of many. The prayers of my praying saints rose before God as a conduit through which heavenly life and healing flowed into my drained spirit. Through their intervention my heart was opened to receive God's healing presence. I now know what it is to experience the power, the joy, and the wonder of this divine gift.

God, I praise you for the power of the prayers of the saints which like the smoke of incense from golden bowls still rises into

your presence. Thank you for those who voluntarily take on the griefs and sorrows of others. As they have ministered to me, strengthen me to be able to do the same. Amen.

Gay Holthaus McCormick

March 30

Let's Not Pretend

Why are you cast down, O my soul, and why are you disquieted within me? Hope in God; for I shall again praise him, my help and my God.   *Psalm 43:5*

Why does it hurt so much to say, "I'm lonely?" As long as it is not said, it hides in back corners of the drawer, keeping the tangled busyness in front.

How can it be in lives so full of other people, whose wishes we let fill our days? We're taught to please, to hear the needs of others, and to meet their needs, while leaving our own unmet.

Psalmists and prophets often found the words to cry their pain, to open up their loneliness to God, and to call for help when there was no help within.

Why is it that our hearts are lonely, God? Is it until they truly rest in you? Just to touch each others' lives? To be part of the caring you began?

Creator God, help us to hear each other's inner cries, to listen for the words our sisters hardly dare to say. Show us where we need to reach out and help each other. Amen.

Carolyn Hall Felger

March 31

New Birth

By his great mercy he has given us a new birth into a living hope through the resurrection of Jesus from the dead.   *1 Peter 1:3*

Today is Easter Sunday. I have just talked on the phone with my ninety-two-year-old mother, who is many miles away. In just a few months she has slid precipitously down the slippery slope of memory loss.

I call my mother to learn from the staff how she is doing and, when she is able, to talk to her for a few minutes. She usually ends up giving the receiver to another, saying she can't hear or understand me. Projecting my own needs, I guess I call mother to bring some variety to her day. Within seconds of our speaking together, she has already mistaken present and past. "Did I go to church today?" she asks. I tell her, "Yes, the nurse to whom I just spoke told me you did," not telling her that she had to be taken out because of her loud, repeated proclamations, *This isn't a Catholic Church!* Two sentences later, she asks again, "Did I go to church today?" I realize, and accept, that I call her primarily for my own needs.

I've always been puzzled about time and eternal life. How can we humans have eternal life in our bodies without the passage of time? We measure the events of our lives—change, growth, decline—by time; how can we be without it? Is Mother's state of mind a forerunner of life without time? Perhaps I ought to be learning more from her about how relevant, or irrelevant, time really is. At the Easter vigil celebration last evening, the celebrant said that we don't need Easter when things are going well, but we want the assurance of something more when times are tough. For you, Mother, and for me, I hope in the resurrection of the body, in life everlasting, and for answers to my puzzlement about time.

Creator God, I thank you for the gift of my body at every moment of its earthly life, its death, and its resurrection. Let me care for it with love. Amen.

Mary Rehmann

April

ꟻresh Spirit

Purge me with hyssop, and I shall be clean; wash me,
and I shall be whiter than snow.   Psalm 51:7

My husband has often encouraged me to go *skinny-dipping* during our summer trips to an isolated lake in Wisconsin. Before experiencing the feeling of swimming *unencumbered*, it was very easy to decline the invitation. However, I found that once I tried it (in desperation due to lack of a good shower), I found it hard to resist!

In thinking back on that experience, the water rushing past and through and around all of my body, I remember feeling fresher and freer than I had ever felt before. It became obvious to me why water is such a powerful image in the Jewish and Christian traditions for healing, purification, and rebirth. Being raised Roman Catholic, I am aware that water has played an important part of my ritual life—I miss it as an Episcopalian. Every time Roman Catholics walk into a church, they dip their finger into water and anoint themselves. It is just a sprinkle, but it is a reminder of water—its power, the symbol of the Spirit.

Water—healing, refreshing water—oh, for the opportunity to immerse oneself and feel the Spirit washing over and through and around us as we seek to gain strength for the journey. Take a moment and mentally remove those things that encumber you, both physical and emotional. Now, dive into the fresh, cool, clean lake—and swim—letting the water flow over every part of you. Let the Spirit of God surround you with healing grace and power.

Oh healing river, send down your waters,
Send down your waters upon this land.
O healing river, send down your waters.
And wash the blood from off the sand. Amen.
        —Traditional Baptist Hymn

Jane Kamp

April 2

Sighs Too Deep for Words

Likewise the Spirit helps us in our weakness; for we do not know how to pray as we ought, but that very Spirit intercedes with sighs too deep for words.

Romans 8:26

As I stepped off the path and onto the gravel, I felt my foot slide out from under me. One foot curled back as I fell. *Snap!* I heard the bone break as I sat down on my leg.

"What's wrong?" my husband, Bill, yelled from down below.

"I think I just broke my leg," I yelled back.

"I heard it snap, Dad," Michael, my twelve-year-old, said, his face going pale in the sunshine.

"I'll go up to the top of the hill to get some help," Bill said.

Help? What help? We were visiting the ruins of Phaetos on the island of Crete. When we arrived at the top of the hill above the ruins, we had seen two elderly men selling souvenirs. Two old Greek men, bugging tourists to buy cheap souvenirs? Where's the help? We're two hours over the mountains from Heraklion, the only city on the island. A feeling of utter helplessness invaded me. I tried to pray. As the pain intensified, I couldn't concentrate. I felt panic rising up from deep inside. What if I couldn't pray? As if from outside myself I heard "Our Father who art in heaven," and realized the words were coming from my own mouth. Over and over again I recited that prayer, mindlessly repeating the familiar words.

My husband returned from his search for help. "You're not going to believe this," he said. "A German tour group just arrived in a bus, and on it is an Austrian orthopedic surgeon who speaks English!"

After helping my husband carry me up the hill to the car, the doctor found gauze in the bus's first-aid kit. The two old men, whom I had deemed worthless, ran off to the woods and returned with cut sections of bamboo for splints. I was arranged as comfortably as possible in the back seat of our rented car and rushed over the mountains to the only hospital on the island.

Two nights later, back at our hotel with a cast on my leg, my husband held my hand, saying, "Wow, an Austrian orthopedic surgeon who spoke English! Now that's help."

God of answered prayer, in my deepest need, when I am too ill, too tired, too miserable to pray, hear the prayer of my heart and answer. Amen.

Carol Spargo Pierskalla

April 3

Let God Transform You

Do not be conformed to this world, but be transformed by the renewing of your minds, so that you may discern what is the will of God—what is good and acceptable and perfect.   *Romans 12:2*

In the summer of 1943, junior high school was over. I was anxiously looking forward to the next big adventure—high school. In the month of July seven adolescents from our congregation attended a church camp held on the campus of a small college. That really felt like being grown up.

Our camp director, a handsome young minister, made the Bible come alive for me, especially the twelfth chapter of Romans. Paul's ideas made sense: we did not have to conform to the ways of the world; God loved us as we were. That sounded liberating to me, a thirteen-year-old dealing with a tall, gangly body.

Returning home from camp, I decided to make that chapter a guide for my living. Each night when the family thought I was asleep, I took out my little brown New Testament—the version printed for those serving in the armed forces. Because I wanted this to be a secret ritual, I even kept a flashlight beneath my pillow so that I could read my personal passage under the covers. Those words were so significant to me that soon I had committed the passage to memory.

Then came September. On the day before I was to enter high school, I entered the contagious disease unit of our county hospital with polio instead. Severe paralysis immobilized my entire body.

The ensuing months and years overflowed with the big world of rehabilitation—Sister Kenny hot packs, braces, special aluminum crutches, continually improving styles of wheelchairs, crusades for accessibility. As a teenager, I sometimes longed to sit with classmates up high in the stadium bleachers; I missed cruising around the neighborhood on my bike. But, upheld by supportive family and peers, I discovered new worlds that held satisfaction and meaning for me.

Although I can't wear tennis shoes or join in square dancing, my life has never been empty. I didn't have to conform to the world; bigger worlds claim my allegiance. As I grow in understanding radical Christianity, God continues transforming me inwardly. Insights brighter than all the flashlights on earth illumine my living.

Eternal Source of light and life, thank you for freeing us to live above and beyond conformity. Strengthen us to help transform this world in ways Jesus the Christ has shown us. Amen.

Dosia Carlson

April 4

Pressing On

Let us know, let us press on to know the LORD; his appearing is as sure as the dawn; he will come to us like the showers, like the spring rains that water the earth.   Hosea 6:3

Have you ever heard the expression, "If at first you don't succeed, try, try again"? It's not as easy as it sounds. Success in our world is an elusive dream. We are conditioned to compete in a global marketplace. Our best efforts can seem to be overshadowed by other more professionally packaged efforts elsewhere. Our world seeks immediate gratification, instant results. Long-range planning no longer exists because technology advances so quickly we can't keep up with it. Always one step behind the times, never quite measuring up, bombarded with the information explosion—it's enough to make anyone say, "Calgon, take me away!"

Who can make a difference in a world such as this? In a fast-paced, competitive world, it seems easier not to try than to fail. Yet who shall we become if we give up?

The measure of a person is not only in succeeding, but in attempting. Someone once said, "Expect great things from God, attempt great things for God." If I spend my life attempting small or meaningless achievements, my life won't amount to much. A homemaker became enthralled with a computer fantasy game and spent all her time trying to solve the game. Eventually she succeeded, but at what cost? She had neglected her children, the household chores, and her friends. In another city a woman who was unable to have children of her own began a summer tutorial program that helped keep children off the streets. They learned, played, and experienced God's love. When the woman became ill and could not complete the summer, others who saw the value of her work rallied resources in the community and continued where she left off. Which woman was the greater success?

Hosea called the people of Israel to return to the Lord. Hosea testified to God's abiding love and faithfulness to a wandering people. "Don't give up," cried Hosea. "Let us press on to know the Lord." It is worth taking the effort to know the Lord, Hosea asserts, because God is certain to come to us, as certainly as the sun will come up tomorrow morning. It is worth pressing on because when the Lord comes, there will be peace, like the spring rains watering the earth, and we shall be renewed.

God calls us to press on, to strive for that which is worthy. Most of all, God wants a relationship with us. As a faithful husband, God waits for us, longing to shower upon us rains of healing, nurturing love.

Ever-loving God, our guide and inspiration, when we are tempted to give up, spur us on. May we hear your voice calling to us, and may we press on—to know you, to receive your love, to embrace worthy goals and follow them through. Amen.

Patricia A. Fraser

April 5

Healing My Brain Tumor

Who will separate us from the love of Christ? Will hardship, or distress, or persecution, or famine, or nakedness, or peril, or sword?   Romans 8:35

I couldn't believe the doctor's words: "Joy, you have a brain tumor." My blood turned icy cold as I realized that I might die or become handicapped.

I asked the minister at my church if we could have a special service of healing for me. The following week at the service, the minister began, "Let us open our lives to God's healing presence." As I knelt at the altar, the members gathered round, laying their hands on me. I was surprised by the heaviness on my shoulders; it was almost like a burden. From inside my head came the words: "Be open to this need for healing." Suddenly I was aware of the earth beneath me, and I knew I was not alone. I was connected to every person whose hands were on me. We all needed healing in some way. We were carrying our woundedness, our brokenness, like heavy yokes around our necks. By prayerfully linking with each other, we shared the power of God's love with one another. Joining our human love and needs together, we connected with God's healing love. The laying on of hands was a reassuring pressure that we were not just isolated bits of thread, but rather part of a larger body with God. We were a beautiful, sometimes torn, tapestry.

Six days later, I went to the hospital. As I was taken into the operating room, I felt calm and peaceful. I told the doctors and nurses that I was turning everything over to God and to them. Six hours later I was wide awake in the intensive care unit, asking the nurses, "When will they do the surgery?" When I learned that it had been successfully completed, I kept saying, "I'm so happy. Thank you, God, for this miracle."

Only one week later, I returned to my church where the words of the Scriptures took me to green pastures and still waters. Yes, I was back in the church that had helped me walk through the valley of the shadow of death. Through my asking for help, God had turned a threat to my life into a promise of new hope and joy. I was at home in God's healing presence.

God who heals, thank you for the assurance that you will walk with us through the valley of the shadow of death. Help us to be open to the gift of your healing. Amen.

Joy Carol

God's Presence

Must I restore what I have not stolen?
Psalm 69:4 (Jewish Publication Society)

I remember the day this phrase leaped off the page at me, the day I read it in the Jewish Publication Society translation of the Bible. I did not understand the question, but I knew that for me the answer was *yes!* In answering the question, I opened myself to healing from childhood abuse in two ways. First, it brought me face to face with feeling abandoned by God during the abuse. *My God, my God, why did you forsake me?* And God answered me. I realized that when I was very small and terrible things were happening to my body, God was taking my soul away from my body and keeping it in a safe place so it could live and not be destroyed.

Second, I became aware of my belief that I could only heal if others admitted their fault and affirmed the reality of what had been done to me. Like the psalmist I cried, "In the day of my trouble I seek the Lord . . . my soul refuses to be comforted" (77:2). I realized I was crying out to God while refusing to open myself to God's healing. I was giving over to others the power to heal, which belongs only to God, and in so doing was allowing the life in me to be buried. I repented of my lack of faith, and God began working in me.

From this experience I know that our healing is not dependent on having the ones who hurt us take responsibility for what they did and for its effect on us. If this were true, I could never be whole. Those who hurt me are dead. I did not steal my body away from my soul; in fact, God was separating my soul from my *stolen* body, in order to keep my soul safe. But now, when by grace and spiritual work I am learning how to bring my body and soul together, I am restoring what I did not steal.

There comes a time when it does not matter who did what and when—or what was stolen. The question is, What restores life now? Yes, we must restore what we have not stolen—for the life of all.

Beloved Redeemer, who gives us life and breath each day, help us to remember you when we feel our life has been taken away

and we are alone. Help us to open ourselves to your healing touch
so that the seeds of life in us break open, ready to grow. Amen.

Jan Hoffman

April 7

Wounded Christian

Being a Christian means being held by Christ, chosen
by Christ, lifted up by Christ as the Good Samaritan
lifted up the wounded traveler in his arms.[1]

Being wounded is an experience that anyone who lives long
enough cannot avoid. It is the extent and depth of that wounding
that determines how long and how extensive the journey of
healing will be. Accepting that pain as a part of life is easy enough,
but it is living with personal pain that is so terribly difficult. The
process of healing is as different and diverse as people are.
Everyone must eventually look inward for wholeness. It is only
in the spiritual realm that our wounding can be taken beyond the
point of surviving into the place where we are conquerors.

It has been several years since the horrifying discovery that my
three young children were being physically and sexually abused
by members of our church while attending church activities.
Absorbing that reality was devastating. The ensuing days and
months of the unfolding trauma seemed more than we could
handle. Our children's innocence had been robbed, our covenant
with the church had been broken, and as parents, our confidence
in knowing our children and in being able to protect them had
been shattered.

Yet, in all of the pain, it was there that I felt God's powerful
hold on my life, and I was lifted by Christ as the Good Samaritan
had lifted up the wounded traveler. I began to see how Christ had
lifted the souls of my children, preserving and protecting their
spirits even in the midst of their abuse. I know that God's grace
is sufficient! God's presence does not grant instant relief or escape
from reality or deliverance from struggle, but if we are God's and
God is ours, then we may be healed from fear—fear of the present

and fear of what may come. Life becomes much bigger than flesh alone, and eternity becomes our hope.

Great Healer, deliver me from bitterness and anger. Help me rest in your love. Restore my hope, and lift me out of fear and into your arms. Amen.

Deborah Ulrich

No Right to Ask for Healing

The crowd sternly ordered them to be quiet; but they shouted even more loudly, "Lord have mercy on us, Son of David!" Matthew 20:31

The story of healing in Matthew 20 involves two blind persons calling out to Jesus in spite of the crowd's attempt to squelch their disruptive behavior. How interesting that it is the people following Jesus who suggest that the persons on the side of the road have no right to ask for healing! And what courage it must take to persist in pursuing wholeness when the crowd loudly insists that those on the margins should not be so selfish as to request healing for themselves.

Illness, by its very nature, disrupts the flow. It calls into question our life patterns, and yet it can free us to make changes. Illness is like a voice inside us that tells us what our lives are lacking, what is too much, or what is not life-giving.

Healing may come from being *selfish* enough to believe we deserve to be strong and well. It may come from reaching out for what we need, even in the face of those who tell us to be quiet. Such boldness can bring healing to our lives even when physical illness continues, because believing that we are created to be whole persons is in itself an expression of healing.

Loving Creator, healer of wounds and limitations and fears, set free in me your passion for wholeness so that I may invite healing into my life. Amen.

Cindy Farmer

God First

Choose life so that you and your descendants may live.
Deuteronomy 30:19b

We are bombarded with messages that tell us how to live: how to look, what to buy, how to think, and how to feel. These messages from our popular and religious culture teach us to compare our lives with images and with other people. When we do, we feel dissatisfied with our lives. We don't live up to *it*. Underneath the busyness of helping others live, we feel despair. We begin to believe we don't know how to live.

Before we can choose life, we first have to find it. God has promised to help us find the way. In the ancient covenant with the Hebrew people God said, "Choose life so you may live." God went on to say that choosing life involved loving, obeying, and holding fast to God. God again made a covenant in Jesus, who said, "I have come so that you might have abundant life."

How can those promises become real to us? Where is the life we are to seek and then choose? What, for us, is truly fulfilling and life-giving? As women who have been trained to give our lives away, how do we learn to inhabit our own lives, living them fully for ourselves, not just for others?

We can begin to seek our life by an act of meditation on our breath as it moves in and out of our bodies. When we intentionally breathe, we find ourselves. As we watch our breath move in, we feel calm. As it moves out, we feel release. Gradually, as we continue this centering process, a space is created in which Life can find us. As we breathe, we can become quiet enough to listen and to be present to life itself. The Spirit of God comes to us through human breath—when we take time to catch it.

Spirit of God, wake me up to my life. May I choose to live it rather than compare myself to others. Breathe on me, breath of God. Fill me with life anew. Amen.

Margaret Kornfeld

All Things New

See, I am making all things new.   Revelation 21:5b

Spring emerges with flowers, green grass, budding trees, fresh smells, and birds. We are reminded that new life is all around us.

One of the invitations to spirituality is to a new life of freedom and deeper love. As we examine the new life of springtime, how can we also be more aware of this invitation in our own life? Do we open our hearts and minds to God's transforming power, or are we walking around with our eyes and hearts closed to new life within our own souls and the souls of others?

Do we really believe in God's transforming power when we experience it, or do we respond to this promise with doubt, fear, or unbelief?

Just as it is a reality for the trees and flowers, transformation is also a reality for all of us. The challenge with spiritual transformation requires our hearts and minds to be opened before we can see the evidence and experience the wonder.

The invitation is before us, to be open and careful, to not get so caught up in the busy pace of life that we fail to see God's transformation and growth in ourselves and others. This spring, be aware of the resurrection that is taking place within yourself and others. God's transformation is taking place, and new life is all around us and within us and others. Be aware, "See, I am making all things new."

Gracious and loving God, help me to become more aware of the new life unfolding within me and others through your unconditional love and transforming grace. Amen.

Sara J. Davis

ʿNeveʳ Alone

And I will ask the Father, and he will give you another
Advocate, to be with you forever.   John 14:16

We don't like to lose what we believe is ours. Yet loss transforms our life journey. When we learn to walk, we lose the innocence. When we become ill, we lose our illusion of personal control and power. When we lose a love, we face our aloneness.

Loss is inevitable. Yet we want to avoid it; we pray that loss will not be part of our lives. For a while, we hold on to the belief that everything will be as it always has been. But eventually, this delusion fades away and leaves the blunt reality that life will not be as we want it to be.

We feel life has been unfair to us. We feel robbed of the destiny we thought was ours, and we feel powerless to make it different. Anger and resentment flow through us. We question the purpose of God and of human life. We challenge God and experience the vacuum of silence.

Yet this darkness cannot quench the imperceptible hunger that forces us to look again. In each loss there is a truth about limited capacity and about the boundaries of creation. Though we pray that God will change the loss that reveals our limits, God in grace will change our vision of who we are and who God is.

So how do our eyes come to see this new vision? When our souls are open to the truth, we will begin to see that God lives within us and around us, waiting for our worship, praise, and intimate conversation. Then we can respond to the tug of the Spirit and see God's eternal love and care for us.

We behold God, the great I AM. God will be God in all of life. God is faithful, and God's faithful promise of love is seen through our own history and the history of humankind. As we now can see this vision, we begin to know wholeness that is not dependent on our physical reality, but on the reality of God. We have found shalom.

Ever present Love, guide the eyes of our soul to see you so our
vision will change and we will behold you as God of all. Amen.
                                                    ʿOonnis ʿReese

Martha's Dilemma

*But the Lord answered her, "Martha, Martha, you are
worried and distracted by many things; there is need of
only one thing. Mary has chosen the better part, which
will not be taken away from her."*   Luke 10:41

How many times do we as women find ourselves in Martha's
position? Jesus and several of his disciples were guests in the
home of two sisters, Martha and Mary. Mary chose to sit at Jesus'
feet and visit with him. Martha, on the other hand, chose to be the
good hostess, seeing to everyone's comfort, yet taking no time to
enjoy her guests.

It seems in this passage that Martha became resentful of Mary
and so asked Jesus, "Lord, do you not care that my sister has left
me to do all the work by myself?" Jesus' response, reflected in
Luke 10:41, was probably not what Martha expected. Don't we,
as modern-day women, still fall into Martha's trap too many
times? We are so busy taking care of other people's needs that we
neglect our own. And then we wonder why we feel empty or
overwhelmed or sad, or, like Martha, feel left out and resentful.

Jesus' message for Martha and for us is that if we are to be able
to give our best, we must first fortify ourselves spiritually, as Mary
did by sitting with Jesus and learning from him and enjoying his
friendship. Jesus supported Mary's actions—"the better part,
which will not be taken away."

Devotional time is a *better part* for healthy living. Within our
devotions we can tell our God of our hopes and fears, our joys
and struggles; we can laugh and cry and sing praises and be totally
vulnerable to the one who knows us best. It is within this intimate
friendship that we are replenished and given focus.

Sweet Spirit, be the center and focus for all that I do. Amen.
                                                          Francine Stark

ʿTaking Care of the ʿWorld

*Come to me, all you that are weary and are carrying
heavy burdens, and I will give you rest. Take my yoke
upon you, and learn from me; for I am gentle and
humble in heart, and you will find rest for your souls.
For my yoke is easy, and my burden is light.*

Matthew 11:28-30

It was late that evening when the phone rang. It was my oldest
daughter calling at the end of her first week away at college:
"Mom, I am so homesick—I am so tired!" in a shaky, teary voice.
She went on to explain that she has been busy from early morning
to late at night discovering *campus life.* She talked of encouraging
her roommate, a rather shy young woman who had been very
homesick. "A couple evenings we even invited people in to see
our room and visit. That was great!" Then her excited tone
changed to a more quiet sincerity, as she said, "I really love it here,
but I've been trying so hard to be outgoing and friendly, meeting
people. I just wanted to stay in my room by myself this evening!"

Was I hearing right? My high-energy, life-loving, young
daughter was learning to recognize her need for rest and retreat?
I quickly affirmed her decision to take the evening for some quiet
time for herself. "You must be exhausted! It has been an incredible
week for you. You have a lot to process. You need some quiet time
for reflection." I also reminded her, "You don't have to take care
of the world! Right now, you need to take care of yourself—you
need to recharge."

Before we hung up the phone that night, she shared many more
stories, other concerns, and insights. She mentioned that this
coming Sunday, she along with two friends were going to church
together. As on other occasions, we talked about how it is important to care for ourselves, recognizing that we are wonderfully
created as beings with physical, mental, emotional, and spiritual
needs. As we ended our mother-daughter chat, I told her that I was
proud of her for many reasons, but now especially for two. I was
proud of her for being friendly and graciously hospitable, but I
was proud and happy for her most of all for realizing her need for
rest and wisely claiming that time for herself. Having spent only

one week at college, she seems to have learned some powerful lessons for life.

As women, we tend to become workaholics, as we strive to be *supermom* or do-it-all caregivers/nurturers/achievers. Only by learning to respect and value ourselves, as well as our need for balance, can we live as healthy and whole beings as God intended.

Gracious God, be with many young people, especially young women, as they leave the security of the home of their youth to discover where and how you would have them use their gifts. Help them to respect and value their specialness. Help them to stay in touch with themselves and with you, O God, our unmoving foundation and wellspring for life! Amen.

Sheryl Cross

April 14

Caring for Ourselves

But now more than ever the word about Jesus spread abroad; many crowds would gather to hear him and to be cured of their diseases. But he would withdraw to the deserted places and pray. Luke 5:15-16

Caring for ourselves is very difficult for most women. We are trained to do for others. Very early we learn to listen for children and to do homework, housework, or paid work. We learn that the external demands are much more important than the internal one.

Jean Baker Miller talks about this focus of women as their *webs of concern.* In her work *Toward a New Psychology of Women* she explains that a woman's self-esteem is based on her connections to others. Personal needs are always viewed in the context of the needs of those significant others. When we combine Miller's insight with all the encouragement from the church to be humble and giving to be faithful, too many women end up ignoring their own needs. They define giving to others as faithfulness. Self-care becomes selfishness.

This passage about Jesus, is very important. Luke says that many people came to hear Jesus and to be healed. Yet in the very next sentence of the same paragraph he describes Jesus' going to deserted places. These places are where Jesus might be alone to pray. Jesus would balance his care for others with time alone to care for himself. Luke, the physician, urges us to be like the Great Physician and take time out for self-care through prayer.

God of love and nurture, we women want to be faithful in your sight. Help us not to get caught up in our web of concerns so that we cannot see our need for time alone with you. We need the strength and guidance you give us. We need to know the depth of our souls. We need to feel refilled, so that in our care for others we have much to give. Help us distinguish between self-care and selfishness. Help us to follow the example of Jesus so we can face whatever comes our way. Amen.

Peggy L.T. Garrison

April 15

Tears of Happiness

Even in laughter the heart is sad, and the end of joy is grief.　　　　　　　　　　　*Proverbs 14:13*

We are incredibly complex people. This complexity manifests itself in the fact that two distinctly opposite feelings can exist simultaneously. Joy and sorrow are two such feelings that can exist side by side as if they were somehow partners. Often in our moments of greatest joy, we are also very mindful of our sorrow.

I was reminded of this truth on my wedding day. The experience of marrying the one I love and having loved ones all around my husband and me, witnessing our marriage vows, filled me with overwhelming joy. And yet hand in hand with that joy came feelings of sorrow because the two most important women in my life—my mother and my grandmother—were missing. My mother had died when I was only five years old and my paternal grandmother, who became my primary caregiver, died five years prior to my wedding. How I longed for them to be with me on this day. I know that my father and loved ones of my mother and grandmother were also feeling these two emotions. Right before the ceremony my mother's sister came into the room where I was to have my picture taken with her. As soon as we saw each other, tears streamed down our faces. I know those tears were tears of joy and sadness. This joyous occasion made us very mindful of my mother's absence. We did not have to say a word. Our tears said it all.

In remembrance of my mother and my grandmother, two roses were displayed in the sanctuary as my tribute to them. Joy and sorrow went hand in hand that day.

God of laughter, God of tears, we are very mindful of your goodness and love. We thank you for the gift of our emotions. Help us to sense your love and care as we experience both joy and sorrow in our lives. Amen.

Tammy L. Martens

April 16

Movement toward Reconciliation and Wholeness

For surely I know the plans I have for you, says the LORD, plans for your welfare and not for harm, to give you a future with hope.   *Jeremiah 29:11*

Physical deterioration, disease, evil, sin are inevitable parts of life. Each of us struggles with these realities. Yet faith proclaims that God desires wholeness for all of creation and is working toward that end. As Jeremiah writes, "For surely I know the plans I have for you, says the LORD, plans for your welfare and not for harm, to give you a future with hope." Faith is the confident sense of trust that we never have to endure the dark side of life alone. God is present with us, whatever the circumstances of our lives. God's Spirit enables us to accept that life doesn't have to be perfect to be good. It allows us to accept the imperfections of life and to weave these fibers—disease, broken relationships, cruelty—into a larger tapestry that also includes love and forgiveness and hope. Healing comes as we integrate the whole of these life experiences of mind and body and spirit into a new creation. Bishop Krister Stendahl of Harvard Divinity School has said that

God's agenda is the mending of creation. We can trust that God is active in creation, and is present to us as we seek healing and salvation.

In his book *The New Being*, Paul Tillich writes,

> Where these is real healing, there is this new creation, a New Being. Real healing is not where only a part of the body or mind is reunited with the whole, but rather where the whole in itself, our whole being, our whole personality, is united with itself. The New Creation is healing creation because it creates reunion with oneself.

This new creation promised in Christ is our hope as we seek healing for what is fractured and mending for what is ruptured in our bodies, the relationships we have with each other, and in our covenant with God. This new creation challenges us to live the abundant life even in the midst of brokenness, witnessing to God's love as *wounded healers*.

Compassionate, healing God, we are grateful that you call us to be colaborers with you in this movement toward reconciliation and wholeness. Make us new creations, integrating our pain and disease into the whole of life. We seek to follow Jesus' example as we allow God's love to work through us. Amen.

Joey Noble

April 17

Stand Up Straight

When he laid his hands on her, immediately she stood up straight and began praising God.   Luke 13:13

Her voice echoes over some forty-five years, but it remains clear, "Stand up straight!" Maybe you too had a mother who was concerned that you not slouch even if you were the tallest girl in your class. There's the echo of a mother's voice when Jesus says to the bent-over woman of Luke's Gospel, "Stand up straight." And his voice continues to echo over the centuries to women of all ages, "Stand up straight!" In the last century and in this country we have made great strides in enabling women to stand straight. We have tackled many of the big issues and won some. But there is still much in our world that cripples women and eventually weighs them down, causing them to walk stooped over. Invisible burdens carried on their backs that make it difficult if not impossible to stand up straight, to claim their rightful place in society.

Most of the women I know are bent over in their inner being, not by the big issues of the feminist movement, but by the little issues of every day:

Bent over by trying to meet the needs of all the people in her life

Bent over by the inability to live out the gifts God has placed within her

Bent over by society's judgment of her mothering or of her childlessness

Bent over by the demands of her husband's career

Bent over by dominating parents or an abusive spouse

Bent over by the expectation that of course she will marry

Bent over by grief or by loneliness

Bent over by people more concerned with her hairstyle than the persuasiveness of her argument

The story of the bent-over woman is our story. And I believe it becomes imperative for each of us to hear the gentle voice of Jesus say, *Woman, you are set free from your infirmity.* Jesus Christ came to set us free from the curse of Eden. He came to give us our own resurrection. He came to call each of us to stand up straight.

The healing touch comes in many ways. The struggle for equal rights and equal dignity is not a feminist political agenda. It is the voice of Jesus saying, *You are set free.* The companionship of other women isn't just a nice thing for the church to foster. It is the touch of Christ's body that allows us to stand straight by standing together. A constant probing to understand the uniqueness of being female in the world isn't an optional course for either men or women. It is the basis for understanding a creation in which God finds great delight.

God of unchangeable power, continue to touch each of us and gently remind us to stand up straight. Amen.

Lynn Vahle

Nature of God

My soul longs, indeed it faints for the courts of the
LORD; my heart and my flesh sing for joy to the living
God.   Psalm 84:2

Just when we think all our ideas about God and faith have come together in a neat little package and we can say, "This I believe," something shakes us up. Our very small church has a small and devoted adult discussion group. Since I became a member, it has studied a three-part series on mental, physical, and spiritual needs related to biblical passages and a series on ethics. A year ago we saw a video featuring a passage from Sallie McFague and decided to explore her book, *Models of God*. That book both strengthened my faith and shook up some concepts of God, causing me to rethink all the childhood teachings and the adult awakenings about the nature of God.

Deep inside me is a stirring that says God is much more than I ever dreamed, a cosmic being that is also a part of everyone on earth. Eternal life may not be what I expected. Some understandings of God are so much a part of my life that I cannot give them up because that would destroy what I have seen and now see as my purpose on earth. I have to come to terms with that and know that I cannot accept every insight that is propounded; my faith is mine to deal with and mine to live with. There's that word again—responsible. I'm responsible for what I believe.

One thing I have reaffirmed from these studies. I am responsible for the earth, for preserving it, for using its resources wisely. I am responsible, with God as my partner, and you and you and you. Only by letting God work through us, by being God's messengers and workers and lovers, can we hope to make earth a survivor. It's an important purpose, enough to give meaning to all our lives. Isn't that what so many of us are seeking today?

God of all wisdom and knowledge, who am I that your work on
earth should depend on me? I thank you for the beauty of the earth,
for its bounty, for all my blessings. I want to serve your purposes
on earth; help me to know what to do and when to do it. Move my
feet in the paths of your designs. Amen.

Cathie Burdick

ʻWings

God hugs you. You are encircled by the arms of the
mystery of God. [2]

When I close my eyes and envision the arms of the mystery of
God I see . . . angel wings. Wings of light. Wings that enfold me
when I feel most in need of protection. Wings that carry me when
I feel most in need of courage. Wings that fold softly around
me—like polar fleece on a cold winter's night—when I feel most
in need of comfort.

So much of the time I forget to see or sense the presence of
these healing arms. When I do open my inner eyes, it is like
turning on a light in a dark room: my mood lifts, my feelings are
transformed, and I can look at the difficult realities of my life with
hope rather than despair. In these moments of awareness of the
sacred presence, I know that I am not alone.

What a relief! This is no distant Spirit who lives far above me
in a vast heaven. This is a Spirit who comes close to me, who loves
me enough to take me in the arms of love and touch me. Just as
Jesus dared to call God the intimate *Father* (Abba), today I dare
to call God the embracing *Mother* as well. I slowly open my heart
to feel the comfort of her rocking, everlasting arms.

Most familiar God, today I thank you for your hugs. You always
surprise me. Most often, I do not expect the sudden sensation of
your presence. You just appear in my thoughts, and it is only then
that I remember to ask for your wise guidance. Even when I am
intentional about invoking your presence, when you actually settle
around my mind and heart like a comfortable old quilt, I am
amazed by your graceful appearance. Your timing is always a
mystery, and a gift. Today, in my gratitude, I promise to open my
eyes more often to see—to feel—the beauty of your soft, encircling
love. Amen.

Susan Savell

Broken Pieces

The vessel he was making of clay was spoiled in the potter's hand, and he reworked it into another vessel, as seemed good to him. Jeremiah 18:4

I see the potter working the clay. There are many small pieces that need to be joined together. The hands reach out to touch each of them and mold them one with another. They are all irregular, unable to be used as they are. We are like those pieces. God brings us to others and their strengths and weaknesses; we all become the whole.

But what is our purpose? As the potter shapes, there are many changes. Each shape could have served a purpose, but the potter is not finished. There are times in our lives when we think we are finished. We have met our needs, surpassed our goals, tackled our obstacles; then our world is upturned. We become like those broken pieces. But we don't lie there long. Those loving hands grasp each little piece, useless when absent from the Master, and begin to reform us beyond our own vision.

What about the finished clay piece? It must still be fired and painted or sealed, even though it appears ready. It will have to hold water, be washed, perhaps be broken again. And so, the firing. When have we felt *fired* or *sealed* as we were being prepared, without being aware of it? Heat encompassed us. We wanted out. But without the firing, the vessel wouldn't be able to hold what we want it to hold—the contents would seep through.

Loving hands apply the sealant with such a soft brush. Touching each inch. Nothing left out. We will not be sent to our use without being toughened and cared for in preparation. God's love is all those things: gathering our fragments, molding them for a purpose, the toughening of the materials. Then the loving strokes of the brush that say, You are ready to be used.

Refuge of those who put their trust in you, take my brokenness and create a vessel ready for use. I need your courage and care right now. Amen.

Karyn Shadbolt

Celebrate the Journey

*While they were talking and discussing, Jesus himself
came near and went with them, but their eyes were
kept from recognizing him.*   Luke 24:15-16

   This Scripture passage is taken from the story of followers of
Jesus on the road to Emmaus. They are not two of the inner circle
of disciples, but just ordinary followers of Jesus, like you and like
me. It was perhaps the saddest day of their lives. Maybe even
worse than the Friday before. Not only had Jesus been crucified
on a cross between two thieves, not only was Jesus dead, not only
had they lost the most important person in their lives, but to add
insult to injury, even his body had been stolen away. They could
not even go and mourn at the burial site because he was not there.
They loved Jesus. He had given meaning to their lives. And now
he was gone. There was no longer any reason to stay in Jerusalem,
and so they were, with heavy hearts, returning home to Emmaus.
   On the way they met a stranger who wanted to know what they
were talking about as they walked along. They wondered how this
stranger could be the only one in Jerusalem who did not know
what had happened to their friend, to their Master, to their hope
of salvation, Jesus. And so they told him the story of what had
happened those last three days in Jerusalem. And the stranger,
much to their surprise, beginning with Moses and all of the
prophets, told them how even this terrible tragedy was part of the
total plan. In the midst of their pain and loss, he gave them hope
and a sense of purpose. So much so that they invited him to come
into their house and stay for dinner so that they might hear even
more of this good news. And it was during the meal, during the
breaking of the bread, that their eyes were fully opened. They
recognized him as their Lord and Savior. Their night was turned
to day. They hurried back to Jerusalem to tell the other disciples
what they had seen and heard. "He is risen. He is risen, indeed!"
   We often find ourselves like those two disciples on the road
to Emmaus. Life at times can be very dark indeed. We lose a
job, we get very sick, we lose a loved one, or we become afraid
of some change in our lives, and the panic and pain are overwhelming. We place hope in something or someone, but that

hope dies. Tomorrow seems bleak and desolate. Like the men on the road to Emmaus, we do not have the total picture. We can only see a short distance down the road.

But each of us has a companion on our life's journey. One who knows the way. One who has been there already and understands the reasons and the purpose of the journey. I encourage you to share your pain and confusion with Jesus of Nazareth. Like the two on the road to Emmaus, tell him everything you know. Share your pain and your loss. Whatever your pain, he can understand. He will open your eyes and help you to find joy and hope once again. They asked each other, "Were not our hearts burning within us while he talked with us on the road and opened the Scripture to us?"

Lord Jesus, help us to remember that we are not alone on our journey, that you are with us always.

Mary L. Mild

Help in the Time of Need

So Joshua did as Moses told him, and fought with Amalek, while Moses, Aaron, and Hur went up to the top of the hill. Whenever Moses held up his hand, Israel prevailed; and whenever he lowered his hand, Amalek prevailed. But Moses' hands grew weary; so they took a stone and put it under him, and he sat on it. Aaron and Hur held up his hands, one on one side, and the other on the other side; so his hands were steady until the sun set. And Joshua defeated Amalek and his people with the sword.   *Exodus 17:10-13*

When I wake up each morning, I hit the ground running. There are children to be fed, dishes to be done, lunches to be packed, plans to be coordinated. Sometimes I work a whole day in two short hours. Then I go forth to a different kind of work, with its own demands and pressures. I'm often tired—stretched too thin and trying to do too much. I wonder, What wholeness can be found in such a life?

This picture of Moses at the top of the hill, trying to sustain the forces of God all on his own, is one I recognize. Moses is exhausted. He can't get through the challenges of the day by himself. Others need to help him. They put a stone underneath him, allowing him to rest. They hold up his trembling arms in theirs, and probably his anxious heart as well. Their companionship and their willingness to share Moses' burden save the day.

On many days I make the same mistake that Moses did. I attempt the impossible, trying to do it all myself. This is a destructive path. Salvation in this story—healing and wholeness, rest and the gift of a peaceful tomorrow—is won only when the challenge is shared. There is a lesson here for me, one I seem to have to learn repeatedly. To try to meet all my challenges on my own is destructive. God has not made me for such heroism. God has made me instead for partnership. In learning to share my burden and to welcome the strong arms of others, I am renewed. Healing begins.

God of helping hands, may I have the grace today to take your offer of nurture as seriously as I take your challenges. Give me, I pray, courage to accept my limitations and gratitude for the gifts and strengths of others. Amen.

Deborah Kapp

April 23

Mirror of Love

There are two ways of spreading the light: to be the candle or the mirror that reflects it.[3]

At eighteen, Pauline came to the city from the rural South bearing in her heart all the dreams of her impoverished family. An unfamiliar aunt took her in and promised education and a pathway out of poverty. They went to church on Sundays. *But they were so different.* The aunt expected her to act in ways she didn't understand—city ways, she guessed. One day they had it out, and Pauline left. After two weeks of staying with friends, she dropped out of school, lost her job, and was alone on the streets.

Pauline used to buy coffee for a group of homeless people by the supermarket near her bus stop. Now she went to them for help, and they took her in. She slept in their large cardboard box behind the store. In the darkness, she wept and prayed.

One night, a voice jolted her awake: *Pauline! Pauline! Come out! Come out!* She hadn't told anyone on the street her real name, and she was scared. Slowly she crawled out of the cardboard box. And there were the minister and a deacon from her aunt's church. "Thank God we've found you," he said. "We are your church family, Pauline, and we've come to take you home."

After a night at the pastor's house, Pauline was brought to stay at the women's residence where I work. Her church took up a collection for her expenses and helped her and her aunt reunite. Pauline is the only homeless woman I've ever met who was not raped or sexually assaulted on the streets. She lived through the darkness of the tomb and came out into the light of the Resurrection. And perhaps that pastor was the mirror that showed her that the Light was within her all along.

Thank you, God, for mirrors and candles. Wrap me, too, in the light of the Resurrection. And help me be a mirror today for someone else who is still in darkness. Amen.

Kae Lewis

April 24

Doing Justice

> "'You shall love the Lord your God with all your heart, and with all your soul, and with all your mind.' This is the greatest and first commandment. And a second is like it: 'You shall love your neighbor as yourself.' On these two commandments hang all the law and the prophets." Matthew 22:37-40

God made us for communion with God and with our neighbors. To love God is to be obedient to God and to be completely dedicated to God's presence and plan in our world. These *horizontal* and *vertical* relationships put us in a position to experience wholeness—shalom.

The prophet Amos calls us to avoid the hypocrisy of attending our religious services and ignoring the injustice that reigns around us and about which we do nothing. However, when we seek to be obedient to God and work against injustices in our society, we often experience situations that create much stress, fear, fatigue, and even anger. These are not the elements that make for wholeness.

Jesus has given us a model for doing justice—to feed the hungry, to give drink to the thirsty, to welcome strangers, to clothe the naked, and to visit those in prison. To work for these conditions can bring us into conflict with powers and principalities and bring condemnation upon ourselves. How then can we be faithful to God and experience shalom?

As we live in obedience to God, we have the promise that God will help us and be by our side as we carry out our tasks. When Jeremiah protested that he was too young to speak for God, God promised to give him the words to speak and to be by his side as he spoke them.

After commissioning his disciples to go out and preach to the nations, Jesus told them, "And remember, I am with you always, to the end of the age" (Matthew 28:20).

We are not alone as we try to live out our lives in obedience to God for God is with us, helping and sustaining us through the challenges and trials that we face. All we need do is offer our love to God and trust and know that God will keep his promises.

O God who is concerned even about a sparrow that falls to the earth, keep us in your care as we seek to be peacemakers and justice seekers in a world seemingly bent on self-destruction. Amen.

Dorothea Murray

April 25

Finding God

God has told you, O mortal, what is good; and what does the LORD require of you but to do justice, and to love kindness, and to walk humbly with your God?
Micah 6:8

Early this morning God and I took a walk. We were greeted by the doleful coos of mourning doves, by the chirp-chat of birds waking, and by the glorious rising of the sun. A morning breeze played gently around us. Each step welcomed the promise of this new day, and we relished every moment.

"This is where I am," God said. "My presence is everywhere. In order to sense it you must pay attention, consciously look for it in people and places, in every moment. Come, let me show you."

We walked along neat, well-kept houses where most people were still asleep. We noted the retirement center and nursing home, peopled with those in their final transitions of life. We listened to the hum of operations in a nearby factory. Other walkers and joggers greeted us cheerfully. Four For Sale signs dotted our circuit—more people in transition. Our walk took us through a college campus where people come to learn and to teach. We smiled at young boys and girls delivering the morning newspapers. Off to the right lives a woman newly widowed, already awake and grieving quietly.

"This is where I am," God said again. "My presence is everywhere. I am in and with all these persons. Every one!"

If you are in and with all these persons, then surely you are in and with me too.

Absolutely! There was a long pause. Then God laughed and said, "Now, let's get on with the rest of our day—the loving mercy and doing justice parts."

Nurturing Spirit, thank you for the you in me. Amen.
Jean Triplett

April 26

All God's Children

For the grace of God has appeared, bringing salvation to all.   *Titus 2:11*

Louise knew her decision to move Nana to the retirement home had been the right one from her own point of view—or least one of the best possible outcomes. Nana seemed happier there. She was surrounded by lots of people and activities. For someone with no memory, who lives only in the present, activity is a necessity. She and John picked up Nana on Friday nights for dinner with the family and on Sunday morning to take her to church. Louise took her for car rides to see the blazing color of fall and the azaleas in the spring.

At the age of ninety-one, Nana's heart gave out. She had been living in the retirement home for three years. Louise planned a memorial service for her there. Residents, staff, and volunteers came. Louise and her husband played piano/clarinet duets, their son played his banjo, and one of the volunteers played "I Want to Dance with the Dolly with the Hole in Her Stocking" on his guitar.

"It was her favorite because I always teased her about the holes in her stockings," he said.

Residents shared their feelings of loss. "Nana was so generous. If she had a cookie, she broke it in half to give me a piece, then she broke that in half to give someone else a piece—until she had nothing left."

"She brought me dandelions in the morning."

"Who will give me my hugs every day?"

As Louise listened to their stories, she realized how all these people had loved and appreciated Nana, that her presence had been a gift to them. Any lingering doubts about her decision to move Nana here were gone. The Spirit of God had led her to a solution that had been right for her—and for Nana. What a miracle!

Thank you, God, for leading us to the truth about ourselves and thus opening us to your truth—that we are all your children and you love us all the same, wanting the best for each one of us. Amen.
Carol Spargo Pierskalla

April 27

Finding Positive Goals

I will sing to the LORD as long as I live; I will sing praise to my God while I have being. Psalm 104:33

A teacher is a teacher is a teacher. One of the things we are taught to do is to think of nearly every interaction with students as a behavioral objective. So it comes as no surprise that I should approach my search for health as a series of behavioral objectives. When we think of health as an active quest, we can direct the course of our healing and wholeness. Every instant our bodies respond to stimuli. So the teacher in me looks for all the positive goals I can find. The surprise for me lay in where I found them—in the book of Psalms.

I have always been aroused by the power and the majesty of the Psalms, by their thunder and fire. They picture a God who gnashes teeth, delivers the faithful from danger, and wreaks vengeance on foes. I have been humbled by the Psalms' confirmation of God's covenant with people of faith. I have been moved by the art of the Psalms, by the singing and dancing, the sounding trumpets and clashing cymbals. I have known them to activate my senses, to call me to worship, to remind me of God's wondrous deeds.

But in my illness, I found a new use for the Psalms. In their ancient phrases and sensual descriptions, I found language to express the ups and downs of my daily struggle to get well. Their rich words gave voice to my journey; they formed behavioral objectives for me to attain.

I found comfort for pain: "To you, O LORD, I lift up my soul. . . . Relieve the troubles of my heart, and bring me out of my distress" (Psalm 25:1, 17).

I found strength for my battle with the evil of cancer: "The LORD is my strength and my shield, in him my heart trusts; so I am helped and my heart exults" (Psalm 28:7).

I found endurance to withstand difficult medical treatments: "Truly the eye of the LORD is on those who fear God, on those who hope in God's steadfast love, to deliver their soul from death, and to keep them alive in famine" (Psalm 33:18-19).

I found hope for days when despair was just around the corner: "The LORD heals the brokenhearted and binds up their wounds" (Psalm 147:3).

I found reminders of God's enduring promises: "I sought the LORD, who answered me, and delivered me from all my fears" (Psalm 34:4).

God of comfort and endurance and hope, I will indeed sing praises to you as long as I live. Amen.

Marguerite Mackay

Salty Christians

You are the salt of the earth. . . . You are the light of the world.   *Matthew 5:13a, 14a*

The winter of 1996 will be long remembered. Those on the East Coast will recall January's blizzard and tell about thirty or more inches of snow, being housebound until the plows released them, and long lines in the grocery store between storms. Those in the Midwest will remind each other of the long spell of subzero days and record wind-chill factors. Those in the military will think of the service personnel in the snow and cold in Bosnia or the adverse conditions in other conflict areas. In such a time as the winter of 1996, Jesus' words following the Beatitudes hold special meaning.

During January and February 1996, salt and light were especially valuable. Salt was important not because of its preserving power (as in Jesus' time), but because it melted ice and made our sidewalks and roadways safer.

Light and the power that generates it were also treasured. In the winter when the electricity goes out, we quickly learn how dependent on it we are. How fast our homes cool to an uncomfortable temperature, how much we want to read or do handwork when we cannot see, how hungry we feel when we cannot cook on our electric stoves! Without light, the streets are darker, traffic gets snarled, and civilization is threatened.

Jesus' timeless and timely words ring in our ears: *You are the salt, the light of the universe. Without you the way is treacherous and dark. With you there is safety and the path is lit brightly.*

In what ways are you *salty*? How do you make the path safe for others? How do they make it secure for you? In what ways are you the light? How do you make the road bright for others? How do they make it visible for you?

Light of the world, so shine in my heart and in my mind that I will be able to be your light for others. Help me to be a salty Christian in my words and deeds, this day and always. Amen.

Janet K. Hess

'Emotional 'Wholeness

Or do you not know that your body is a temple of the
Holy Spirit within you, which you have from God, and
that you are not your own? For you were bought with a
price; therefore glorify God in your body.
                                    1 Corinthians 6:19-20

We were in a familiar restaurant having lunch together, my nurse friend and I. I marveled at the energy she exuded. "I envy you your sense of self and assertiveness," I told her. A year and a half earlier she had gone through an unexpected and abrupt divorce, which her husband had requested. It devastated her. She was unable to function in her usual objective, professional manner. She found that the methods and techniques for coping that she had used for years no longer worked. She sought professional counseling and through this process received healing for her emotional and spiritual self, as well as new skills of assertiveness, improved communication techniques, and a better understanding of herself.

This experience occurred a number of years ago, when society was not as sensitive to emotional issues. Seeking counseling wasn't considered bad, but was thought to be a sign of a weakness. After five years in the mental-health field, I am saddened to see so many people still locked into the belief that getting help for emotional issues is a weakness. Many people, believing strongly in the virtues of independence and self-sufficiency, look down on or act superior to a person receiving such help. This attaches a sense of shame to the individuals who are trying to receive treatment for their distress. To the contrary, I have found that the clients I work with have a great deal of courage and fortitude in facing what is happening to them and in finding the coping skills that will help them reach their greatest potential. The beauty is that often they receive an abundance in return, far beyond their initial request for help.

Jesus promises us abundance, which was demonstrated when he asked for help from the disciples in feeding the crowds of five thousand and of four thousand. He took the meager amount of bread and fish the disciples gave him, provided for the crowd's needs, and supplied an overabundance of food. God will supply, not only our initial need, but also more than we ask for.

Receiving help for our *physical* well-being is socially acceptable. We consult an internist or surgeon, allow her to evaluate us, listen to her recommendations for care, ask questions to clarify exactly what is going on physically, and accept a plan of care. We know that if we want to be healed, it is best to follow the directions. Through the process we may adopt some new and healthier habits, find renewed strength to continue, deepen our spiritual bond with God, or begin to reevaluate our goals and priorities.

If only we could recognize that help for our emotional and spiritual well-being is just as acceptable. Taking care of ourselves—body, mind, and spirit—is not a luxury, but a way to show God our thanks for how God has made us. God gave us our body as a temple for the Holy Spirit. In order for that spirit to thrive, in order for us to reach the full potential the Spirit desires for us, we must care for the temple. The first step is to relinquish our whole body to God and accept help as needed, so that we can tend and nurture it. It's okay to be vulnerable—it's part of what makes us human.

God of everlasting health, thank you for your many servants in the healing professions. Give them wisdom and discernment as they minister to us. Make me sensitive to the needs of my body, mind, and spirit. Help me to care for them, that I may reach the potential you offer me. Amen.

Cynthia G. Haynes

April 30

The Presence of Faith

How can anyone be born after having grown old? Can one enter a second time into the mother's womb and be born? John 3:4

Nicodemus's encounter with Jesus takes place at night, reflective of the darkness and secrecy of the womb. How appropriate for the struggle that is to follow.

We can assume that Nicodemus, as a Pharisee and *a leader of the Jews,* understood the life of faith to be one of study and action, a matter of outward doing that involved the mind, the reason, and ordered activity. Certainly he saw Jesus' role in terms of Jesus' performance of *signs.* Pleasing God and manifesting the presence of faith consisted in matters that are largely under our control, that is, what we do.

But just as Jesus confronted the rich young ruler with a call to a kind of action the young man could not face, so here Jesus confronts Nicodemus, and us, with an image for the life of faith that radically differed from Nicodemus's view.

Jesus pictures us as children still in God's womb. Our lives as God's people—God's babies—are not primarily something we do, but something that happens to us. They are not our activities in relation only to a distant God, but an intimate process in which we are connected and fed as with an umbilical cord to the God who is laboring for our freedom. They are the process of our birth, a process fraught with risk and pain both for us and for our mother.

When we see this metaphor only as a description of what happens in our baptisms, we lose its value as an image for all of our Christian lives. We are being birthed by God—in pain and struggle. We experience the contractions of the birth process. Some of them fail to move us toward being the people we are becoming; that is true in any birthing. But in the midst of the pain and the gasping, the throttling uncertainty, it is God who is suffering even more than we, in order to bring us finally forth as her new creation, her own.

Mother God, in you we live and move and have our being. Sustain us in the painful places of our lives. Feed us with your own body and blood. Comfort us when we are afraid. And bring us forth into the light of your face and the joy of your presence, as you rejoice also in us. Amen.

Katherine Griffis

May

Living Water

Jesus answered her, "If you knew the gift of God, and who it is that is saying to you, 'Give me a drink,' you would have asked him, and he would have given you living water."　　　　　　　　　　　　*John 4:10*

The story of the Samaritan woman has always touched me. I have read the story many times and have portrayed the woman in drama. With her I have felt loneliness and rejection. This is a wonderful story of God's forgiveness. My focus has always been on the Samaritan woman: her condition, her confrontation, her confession, her commission, and her commitment!

Just recently, in studying this passage again, the words of Jesus spoke to me in a new way. What did Jesus mean when he offered "living water"? My thought suddenly became centered on Jesus and the offer and what it means to me in my life.

Living water! Water is essential to all of life. Without it nothing lives. As I thought about water in all its forms, many images came to my mind: Sitting on the bank of the backyard creek in deep depression, the gentle ripples cascading over the rocks calming my troubled heart. Watching the rains come to the parched garden and seeing the withering plants being revived and sustained. Standing at the base of the Iguassi Falls and listening to the roar of the cascading water and feeling the power in the force of the water. Looking up as the water in the form of mist rose from the falls and formed a rainbow and remembering all of God's promises. Walking in the newly fallen snow, which the sun caused to sparkle like diamonds, filling me with the beauty of living water.

The Samaritan woman is still essential to the story, but it is more than her story; it is my story as well. *Jesus offers me living water*. Water that is essential to my life in service and wholeness. This living water that will calm me, revive and sustain me, empower me, remind me of God's promises, and fill me with beauty.

Thank you, Lord, for giving us living water. During times of depression and dryness you are there to renew us and restore us to a life that is filled with your Spirit. Amen.

Evon Laubenstein

Support

Bear one another's burdens, and in this way you will
fulfill the law of Christ. Galatians 6:2

During my many years specializing in older-adult ministries, I was a strong advocate of support groups. Again and again I witnessed the strength gained when a small group of people under wise leadership shared their struggles as caregivers. Many of them were adult children seeking guidance in making decisions with or for aging parents. Hearing how others in similar situations were learning to cope gave hope and enlightenment, especially to those new to caregiving roles.

When our agency organized a conference for people interested in facilitating support groups, we were amazed at the response. We had anticipated that perhaps twenty-five or thirty would register. To our surprise we had to cut off registrations at 150 persons. Such a variety of needs were being addressed through groups of people with similar situations: bosom buddies (post-mastectomies), mothers of twins, Alzheimer's disease, chronic fatigue syndrome. On and on went the list of issues represented by participants.

Although I could professionally espouse the virtues of well-facilitated self-help groups, I did not fully understand the impact of such gatherings until I went to one for my own needs. My experience started with a lump in my leg. In young adult years I had surgery for a mass in my left thigh. Thanks be to God—this was only a benign tumor.

However, seventeen years later another lump developed near the site of the first one. "Aha," I thought, "another benign tumor." Not so. This time surgeons confronted me with the unwelcome report of a liposarcoma in my thigh requiring intensive radiation. Thus began a new pilgrimage in my midlife years.

Family and friends offered phenomenal support. Yet I longed to share my feelings with others who were also confronting cancer. Without much effort, I located about ten people going through radiation or chemotherapy. They too wanted to probe their reactions and explore ways in which faith could provide hope for each day. Our support sessions, held in private homes, always included periods of prayer. How earnestly we prayed for each other! Some did not experience cures, but all of us sensed a healing beyond medical treatments. We rejoiced in God's presence binding us together, enfolding and upholding us, individually and as a group.

To you, great Healer of hearts, minds, and bodies, we bring our gratitude for the ways your Spirit can bind us together. As you support us, so may we find ways as Good News people to support one another. Amen.

Dosia Carlson

May 3

Partners

A Partner is someone you work with on a big thing that neither of you can do alone. . . . On the days you think I am not doing enough, and on the days I think you are not doing enough, even on those days we are still partners and we must not stop trying to finish the work. Is the world finished yet? and God answered, I don't know. Go ask my partners.[1]

When have you finished a project or task on your own? Thank God, we are partners! Each week I make a list, and then as projects are completed, I cross off the done deal. What happens is that the list gets old, more than a week goes by, and more things are added than are completed. Has that happened to you?

It is rare that everything on my to-do list is finished. Interruptions, crises, higher priority items from my boss (or from myself), family calls—all help to rearrange my day. But when I come to reflect on the day's happenings during the last few moments late at night, I recall that what the day brought was exactly what was needed. It may not have met my expectations, but I know that God was present in the midst of all the happenings.

God of all compassion, help us to rest and to awaken refreshed for the new possibilities that are sure to come. Be our partner in this world of possibilities. Amen.

Kathleen Clark

Letting Go of the Past

This one thing I do: forgetting what lies behind and straining forward to what lies ahead, I press on toward the goal for the prize of the heavenly call of God in Christ Jesus.　　　　　　*Philippians 3:13b-14*

We all carry our pasts with us. Much attention has been given to the influence of families of origin, birth order, and early childhood experiences on how we develop into adulthood. Personality development theory has focused on the question of "nature or nurture" in determining human identity and ethics. Current wisdom agrees that much of who we are is intricately linked with our past experiences.

What about the parts of our past that have been negative or harmful? Sometimes we seem to be trapped by our past experiences and are unable to find our way beyond them. Anna is a young woman who was raped at knifepoint by her boyfriend. She is afraid to develop new relationships with men because she doesn't trust her own judgment. Maria's husband was killed in a car accident by a drunk driver, leaving her alone with the responsibility of caring for her three-year-old child and unborn baby. Anger and bitterness have been her constant companions as she works cleaning houses, trying to keep the bills paid, while someone else gets to be with her children. Janet developed Crohn's disease as a young teenager and missed dating, hanging out, and going to the prom because of digestive problems, stomach pains, and surgeries. She lives a life of isolation and shame, despairing of ever having a relationship with a man. Most of us have some past experiences that hinder our ability to live fully and productively today.

The journey toward healing is not an easy one. The first step is recognizing what is holding you back and naming it. The second step, often a long and arduous one, is letting go. Paul speaks of "forgetting what lies behind and straining forward to what lies ahead." Paul had a lot to forget. He had persecuted Christians in the name of Roman law. The suffering and even death he had brought to others might have haunted him. The self-delusion that came to clarity when he met Jesus on the road to Damascus struck him deaf, dumb, and mute for three days. Yet once he came to know who Jesus was, and once he heard God's call in his life, he let go of his past, his former goals, even his identity as a keeper of Jewish law. He chose to give himself up to something greater, allowing God to transform him into something new.

We must let go of what lies behind. We are called to let go of our hurts, as well as our sins. In order to let go, we have to look into the closets of our pain and sort through them. Once we see what is holding us back, we need to let go of it. We can offer it to God, who is powerful enough to bear it for us. Letting go frees us to move ahead, to grasp something new, to allow God to heal and transform our pain into something beautiful. This doesn't always mean that our circumstances change, but that our hearts become soft and open to love and grace. Remember, God cannot place forgiveness and mercy into hands that are already full.

God of the past and the future, gently pry open our hearts that are clutching pain from our past. Grant us courage to see what holds us back, to name it, and to let it go, even as we let ourselves go into your loving arms. Amen.

Patricia A. Fraser

May 5

Choose Joy

May the God of hope fill you with all joy and peace in believing, so that you may abound in hope by the power of the Holy Spirit. Romans 15:13

Avoiding lopsided living has been a challenge in my life ever since the day I was born! I can recall my parents telling me how serious I was as a child, frequently observing and analyzing the events before me.

The social gospel of Jesus Christ made a marked impression on my life, as did John Wesley's commitment to *social holiness*. Many current events bothered me then and still do. The teeter-totter of life seemed tipped in the direction of sorrow and despair when I contemplated the enormous poverty in the world, oppression of women and children, the destruction of the ecosystem, and particularly during the 1960s, 1970s, and 1980s, the possibility of nuclear annihilation. Life seemed dim and hopeless. God seemed far away. How easy it was to become swept into the negativism, forgetting the joy in life and forgetting that God is present in both our sorrow and our joy. During midlife (call it a crisis!), I found myself searching for some kind of balance because I knew that life held much more than sorrow, and I wanted it!

Henri Nouwen writes in his book *Here and Now* that sorrow and joy can live together but that "joy does not simply happen to us. We have to choose joy and keep choosing it every day." The act of *choosing* joy is, perhaps, the greatest challenge before us. It requires a deliberate, conscious decision and, at times, requires enormous energy. For us social activists, choosing joy ain't always easy!

To choose joy means taking a step toward wholeness, for I believe that God has given us capacity for both. "It is in the choice that our true freedom lies, and that freedom is, in the final analysis, the freedom to love," writes Nouwen.

So, life is better. There are now times when I take deep breaths and smile at the same time. The joyousness of living is present even through times of sorrow. God is our strength. God does love us beyond measure. And God calls us to love and care for one another and also to rejoice! The world is filled with beauty waiting to be claimed. Choose joy!

Although the world can seem heavy and desolate, O God of truth, we find comfort in knowing that you are with us, giving us strength and will to celebrate all of life—its sorrow and its joy. Help us to find a balance in our lives that will bring us a sense of wholeness, hope, and peace. Amen.

Linda Bales

The Wonder of Myself

*For it was you who formed my inward parts; you knit
me together in my mother's womb. I praise you, for I
am fearfully and wonderfully made. Wonderful are
your works; that I know very well. My frame was not
hidden from you, when I was being made in secret,
intricately woven in the depths of the earth.*

Psalm 139:13-15

I am continually thankful for the wonder of myself, that whole
person who is mind, body, spirit—a unique work of God's creative
process. I discover that the whole is more than the sum of my parts
and that my whole being is wrapped in mystery.

I am recovering from a mindset that sees the world as fractured
and atomized. This viewpoint constructs each individual person
as separate from every other person and from the created world.
With this viewpoint, even individual persons can be seen in parts,
as when the womb is separated from the woman, or when the spirit
has nothing to do with the body. I am recovering from a mindset
that tells me that I can abuse my body with stress and overwork
without reaping consequences in my mental and spiritual outlook.

I feel keenly the loss of community, for I know that my
wholeness depends on my relationships with other persons and
with creation.

I laugh at women and men who believe they are self-made and
that they have received no help from others in their achievements,
for I know the mystery and wonder of a God-given wholeness that
enables me to see the ways in which we are connected and
dependent on each other. I am no longer afraid to be vulnerable
to others, for I can celebrate the wonder of myself.

Because God knows me, even in my inmost parts, and loves
me as I am, I know that I am lovable. I can give and receive
love.

*Creator of heaven and earth, who knows me and loves me
as I am, I am grateful each new day for the wonder of my life
and for the life around me. You have surrounded me with
persons to love and with new discoveries to make. I am*

awestruck at the wonder of all of your works. I am finally silent before your great mystery. Amen.

Carolyn Henninger Oehler

May 7

Time with God

In the morning, while it was still very dark, he got up and went out to a deserted place, and there prayed.
Mark 1:35

I have a morning ritual of riding my bike. It's born out of the craziness that comes with living downtown. I go out to a quiet place where the sky meets the cool water of the Pacific Ocean. As I huff and puff my way up to my "secret place" on this particular morning, a heavy layer of fog hangs over the city, its gentle mist embracing me with its arms. There is no one in sight, just me and God.

I stop to catch my breath. Gone are the noisy sounds of garbage trucks, honking horns, and busy people scuttling off to work. All that remains are the sweet sounds of birds chirping, fog horns blowing off in the distance, and the *drip, drop* of dew falling from the trees.

As I gaze out into the misty nothingness, I pause to speak with God, sharing my soul and the troubles that weigh on my heart. I consciously try to feel the all-encompassing love that surrounds me. I thank God for the precious tranquility of the morning, for this momentary escape alone with my Creator.

I mount my bicycle to begin the journey home. As I ride down the hill, I feel lighter inside, a little more alive. Perhaps it's because I've left my burdens and fears with God. Perhaps it's because I know I don't have to face this day alone.

On those mornings I declare myself *too busy* or *too tired* for my morning ride, the days tend to get a little more crazy, a little less serene. I often think of Jesus and the lessons taught by the way he lived. Jesus, who, no matter how busy, went off alone and took time for himself to pray.

When I get caught up in my list-making, commitment-filled,

overbooked schedule, I need to remember that everything else falls into place when I take time to be with God.

Creator God, no matter how hectic life can get, may I always make time for you. Amen.

Kristen Corselius

Loving Myself

Remember, no one can make you feel inferior without your consent.[2]

It is not always easy to remember that we can be in charge of our feelings. Strongly negative words and behaviors can be devastating at times.

An extremely important step in interactions with others is to keep clear in our minds that critical or negative words are always worth evaluating. Each of us has the right to decide whether such words and behaviors honestly fit and need to be considered, or not.

No matter who speaks the words, we are in charge of our reactions to them. Being respectful and caring of ourselves is a loving action, both for us and as an example for others.

As you go about the business of this day, please carry this message with you: I can care for myself in loving ways. I can reflect thoughtfully about interactions with others; I do not have to swallow unfair negative statements.

Almighty Giver of good, please help me to love myself enough to take care of myself. Amen.

Julia D. Brodie

Quiet Trust

*In quietness and in trust [confidence] shall be your
strength. . . . For the LORD is a God of justice; blessed
are all those who wait for him. Isaiah 30:15b, 18b*

A favorite coffee mug reads, "For healthy growing . . . we need
some quiet time." Preparation to lead a spiritual-growth study on
The Interior Life in the early 1980s marked a high point along my
personal journey toward wholeness. The devotional and contemplative writings of many, past and present, reflected their involvement in the hard work of prayer and meditation—of *waiting for
the Lord, the God of love and justice*—on behalf of the whole
world. *This* was the place of preparation for effective engagement
in that to which the God of love and justice called—and calls—in
efforts to counter hatred, bigotry, self-centeredness, and all the
isms that crowd our days.

Several thoughts from those writings and reflections still stand
out and continue to instruct. In one of her visions, the fourteenth
century mystic Julian of Norwich was reminded by God, "It is I,
the Might and the Goodness of the Father-hood; the Wisdom of
the Motherhood; the Light and the Grace that is all blessed Love
. . . the Trinity . . . the Unity." Dame Julian also wrote that *prayer
oneth the soul to God.*

Evelyn Underhill warns against the danger of a *lopsided Christianity,* concentrated only on service and obligations, without the
balance of waiting for God: "We mostly spend our lives conjugat-
ing three verbs: to Want, to Have, and to Do. . . , so that we find
ourselves in perpetual unrest,..and forgetting the fundamental
verb, to Be . . . [in the presence of the One who is!]." Wise counsel
for many of us as women who somehow never learn when to say
no or to keep our *active* and passive selves working together
instead of competing!

Lessons often need to be relearned. In the past eighteen months,
the death by suicide of a brilliant, promising sixteen-year-old
family member; the attacks on and misinterpretations of the event
in which some twenty-two hundred women (and a few men) from
around the world came together to celebrate and experience God's
continuing revelation and presence among us, as Wisdom and as

accepting Love; the increased sense of growing political insularity and repression—these and more led me first to increased busyness, to *reacting* instead of acting effectively. Finally, however, they led to my finding again the strength and renewed wholeness that come from the quietness and confidence of waiting on the one who is all love, all justice, all wisdom, and all wholeness.

Loving God, grant that each day we may be renewed, strengthened, and made whole in your presence, for acts of love and caring and justice in those places where you have put us. Loving Mother, caring Father, perfect Wisdom, and comforting Presence. Amen.

Elaine Gasser

May 10

To Feel

But look, I am going to seduce her and lead her into the desert and speak to her heart.   Hosea 2:16 (NJB)

Seduce me:
Breathe on my flesh.
I want to feel, to yearn, to call.
And reach for what is not visible, for what I do not possess,
    what I cannot domesticate.
Shy and fearful, I fill my mind with obstacles and busyness.
I think:
I am wonderfully made; and neglect the Author of my life, the
    Word I Am, the Book.
I feel safe with my little god, my little thoughts.
My little fears.
Lead me: By myself, I am lost.
you are the Way. Teach me.
the desert:
A place to be avoided.

Women of my age seek company. Safety in numbers. But you call me into the wilderness. A landscape of utter solitude and dependence on manna and quail. A place where no thing grows by human hand.

*Speak to my heart, Lord. Tell me who I am. You deconstruct me,
and I am slain. Thank you for the hard places. Thank you for the
dark places. Amen.*

Diane Bonner Zarowin

A New Beginning

*As for me, I am establishing my covenant with you and
your descendants after you.*   Genesis 9:9

Noah and his family were happy when the time came for them
to leave the ark, I imagine. Who wouldn't be after several months
on a boat with a zoo?! I used to imagine that they just stepped off
the boat, looked around, saw the beautiful green life growing,
smiled at the shining rainbow, picked up their suitcases, and went
off to build a new home and life. You know, everyone lived
happily ever after.

But now, after seeing the residue of hurricanes and floods, I am
aware that houses and bodies and street signs and pet bowls don't
just dissolve like salt in a glass of water. One has to clean up before
one can rebuild. One has to grieve before one can accept the reality
and magnitude of any loss. One has to make peace with and lay
to rest what is no longer. One has to decide to move forward, and,
I have found, one has to rely on faith in order to do so.

Often when I *begin anew,* I want to step into a new day, as if
walking off a boat and into an environment cleansed and new. But
life isn't that easy. Rebuilding what, in some cases, took weeks,
even years, to create doesn't miraculously happen overnight, as I
sleep. It's a choice, and it requires effort. Sometimes I hold on to
something I do not really want because at the very least it is
something. Rarely does this work out for my best. Nor does it
convey a living testimony of my faith in Christ.

Sometimes, when I'm really daring or strong in my faith, I risk
the feeling of losing everything in an effort to discover what is
really most important. When I do this, I feel I am discovering
God's will for my life. In this way, when I begin again, I step into
a new day, agreeing to sift through the rubble and to allow myself

to be sad and confused about the loss. I risk losing control; I give up attempting to control that which I do not want to face—the unknown. Instead, I rely on God, who knows my footsteps even before I step off the boat into the mud and a new beginning. When I do this, I choose to begin the work of planting new seeds and patiently waiting for growth. I endeavor to trust in God's covenant with me and to believe that God does indeed help me to rebuild my life. His convenantal promise has never failed me.

Watchful and caring God, please help me to begin anew by giving you control of my waking and sleeping hours. There is much that I need to let wash away, much that I need to sift through. With each decision, Lord, I request your guidance and your strength. Help me to give away that which separates me from you—my will. Teach me, I pray, your will be done. Amen.

Debra Sutton

May 12

Life's Struggles

Do not, therefore, abandon that confidence of yours; it brings a great reward. For you need endurance, so that when you have done the will of God, you may receive what was promised. For yet in a very little while, the one who is coming will come and will not delay; but my righteous one will live by faith. My soul takes no pleasure in anyone who shrinks back.

Hebrews 10:35-38

Life is difficult. It has been said before, in many ways, but this statement always evokes a knowing nod or a wry smile of acknowledgment. Is it because we are mostly prepared for what life brings only in later years after having lived through it? We all attest to difficulties living in a complex and stressful world. Is it that we were never prepared for happiness and joy? Expectations lead us to anticipate the opposite. How unprepared I have been in the face of simple fun and joy. I have been paralyzed by receiving the rich blessing heaped upon me by my Lord. It seems we are not prepared for the good or the bad that happens in life.

Life is unfair. Parents of dying children know about unfairness.

Considering today's news headlines there is no way to describe world happenings as equitable or righteous. It wasn't fair for Jesus to be tortured by being hung up in the air with spikes through his body. His Father knew it wasn't fair.

This Scripture assures me that life is difficult and unfair, but it exhorts: Hold on! Persevere! Be God's people in action! Your confidence in Christ and your daily struggle really make a difference in both your own life and everyone else's. And know that your confidence in God will be richly rewarded. The King is returning.

Watchful and caring God, thank you for your words of confidence. Because of you I can face the issues of life. With confidence I can live a life of faith in you and be your servant. Amen.

Pam Gurley

May 13

The Power of Prayer

If you believe, you will receive whatever you ask for in prayer.   *Matthew 21:22 (NIV)*

One of those days Jesus went out to a mountainside to pray, and spent the night praying to God.
Luke 6:12 (NIV)

I recently moved into a new home. Exhausted from all there was to do that week, I happened upon my journal book. That's one of the joys of moving (and believe me, there are not many!); you find treasures and keepsakes that you have not noticed in a while. Sitting down on my bed, I began to flip through the pages. The first thing I noticed was there had not been an entry in over two months. "How neglectful," I thought. I flipped back a little farther to see how it was with my soul just a few months before. As I began to read my petitions to God, I was reminded of the distress that I experienced much earlier in the year. The prayers that I had lifted to God were written with a calm assurance and absolute surrender, that I was comforted by my faith—my faith in the God who claims me.

Sometimes our life journey leads us to a place of total surrender, a place where our only alternative, our only hope, can be in Jesus Christ, our Savior and Redeemer. At moments like these we are called to prayer and meditation so that our spirit may be one with God. In these times we can feel the power of prayer, manifested as the Holy Spirit steps into our life and begins to sort out the tangled web of confusion that has bound us up hopelessly. As the Spirit steps into our dilemma, a space begins to separate us from all of the rhetoric and chaos that stand in the way of our wholeness. How affirming it was for me to find that in the seven months that had passed, every prayer I had uttered had been answered by God, and each concern had been resolved.

Now my goal is twofold. First, I will strive to send all my prayers to God with the utmost assurance that they will be answered. To utter them, even when I am not in distress, with the same calm surrender that allows God to do the most complete work in me. Second, I will strive to reclaim the daily time set aside to record my thoughts, dreams, hopes, and prayers for my todays and my tomorrows. There is such power in prayer and such grace in God's response to it. Jesus had all of the power that this universe could offer, and yet the only tool he used was prayer. It was all that he needed to walk amongst us and bring us eternal life. What a blessing it is to know that same power is available to you and to me.

Gracious and everlasting God, we give thanks for the joys of this day. Continue to guide and direct us that we may walk daily in your will and in your way. Help us to entrust to you more and more the prayers of our heart so that we may ignite the full power given to us by Jesus Christ. Amen.

Denise R. Mason

Godly Parenting

*Is there anyone among you who, if your child asks
for bread, will give a stone? Or if the child asks for a
fish, will give a snake? If you then, who are evil,
know how to give good gifts to your children, how
much more will your Father in heaven give good
things to those who ask him!* Matthew 7:9-11

Would any of you who are parents give your child a stone when she asks for bread? Or would you give him a snake when he asks for a fish? In this passage, God is compared to a loving parent, giving her child the very necessities of life. Bread and fish—food for a healthy journey.

The family is in a spiritual-health crisis today. There is plenty of rhetoric about children being the future, but how much sacrifice are we making? What do our actions, our lives tell our children about the family and the world? Are they learning about sacrificial love, patience, tolerance, compassion, and understanding? In a world filled with violence and hate, are we teaching repentance and forgiveness?

This summer I worked as a legal assistant in the Child Advocacy Unit of the Legal Aid Bureau in Baltimore, Maryland. All of our clients were children whose parents gave them stones and snakes in the form of drugs, alcohol, and violence. Some modern-day stones and snakes are easy to see, but others are more subtle. Harsh words, abusive discipline, lack of time, even an abundance of things can be snakes we give our children. Discerning between the snakes and the fish is always a challenge.

Many parents are working hard *to provide* for their children. Provide what? How are we providing for their spiritual health? Are we giving our children *things* or tools to enable them to be compassionate human beings? *Toys R Us is not the answer.* Parents who share and demonstrate God's love offer their children the beginning of a healthy life. Prayer and Bible stories at home, as well as participation in an active faith community, are bread and fish for a healthy start. Our children are our future. Hopefully, we are providing for them as our loving God provides for us.

God of forgiveness and understanding, you provide for us like a loving parent. Help us to provide for our children with a healthy beginning to life within your family. Amen.

Meg Oliver

May 15

Trust God's Process

God is our refuge and strength, a very present help in trouble. Therefore we will not fear, though the earth should change. Psalm 46:1-2

One of the things that continues to influence me from my undergraduate thesis, "Theology's Contribution to the Liberation of Women," is a new understanding of God. God: not as a noun, but as a verb—the verb "to be" or "to become." The idea of God as the power of being feels *right* to me, and it has been one of the images I've embraced when thinking of and struggling with where God is in my life.

My mother has often said to me, "trust the process," which means, trust that situations and events occur for a reason; life will work out as it should. As I've experienced the need and the necessity to do this, I've begun to hear *trust the process* as *trust God's process.*

Until a few years ago I was obsessed with and addicted to food. I was a compulsive overeater, complete with frequent binges, distorted body image, and little that wasn't somehow colored by the thought of food and weight. There came a point, however, when I decided to take a look at some powerful but unacknowledged underlying issues that began bubbling into consciousness as possible origins of this obsession. One issue I could no longer ignore was the impact of being sexually abused as a child by my grandfather. With the decision to confront this, doors came flying open, and I began to recognize God's process in my life. I was presented with situations and people that helped to clarify where I had been and what I had been through, and this strengthened who I was becoming. As I began to admit how events in my life had impacted me, that impact decreased.

In an amazingly short time, I felt free of this obsession with food, and I now find that journey affecting my life in some wonderfully positive ways. One spring, after being confined to bed for six months with a pregnancy, and then adjusting to new parenthood and recovering physically, I finally felt ready to work professionally again. As a psychotherapist in private practice, I had worked mostly with women on issues of self-esteem, anger, conflict management, and personal boundaries. Deciding to return to work, I received an unsolicited job offer to consult in a weight-management program as a group therapist and educator.

I now find myself at the point where my personal journey and my professional journey meet. Having dealt with my personal history, I am now better able to hear the pain and fear of my clients and better able to see God in their struggles *to become*. I can now honestly trust that there is a way through it all. I've also become aware that where I am now and what I am doing professionally could only have happened through my trusting in *the process*, in God-the-power-of-becoming.

God of all righteousness, help me to continually trust in the power of your process in and through my life. Amen.

Yolanda Turner

May 16

Surpassing All Understanding

And the peace of God, which surpasses all understanding, will guard your hearts and your minds in Christ Jesus. **Philippians 4:7**

It was October of 1981. I was sitting beside my father's bed in the living room of my mother's house. Snow was gently falling outside, enhancing the atmosphere of warmth and safety inside. My father began groaning as he struggled to bring air into his diseased lungs. I was reading from the Psalms, and the sound of my voice seemed to bring him some comfort. Unable to bear hearing his pain, my mother left the room, going into her bedroom and closing the door.

Kneeling on the floor beside her bed, she began imploring God to relieve her husband's suffering. She was justifiably distraught and upset. Her *precious Jim* was dying, and all she could do was stand by and watch.

Into her mind came the phrase, You cannot give peace if you don't have peace. Understanding that this was a direction for her, she prayed for peace in her own heart so that she could pass that peace on to her husband. After regaining her composure, she returned to the living room.

As she entered the room, she stopped in amazement. I was singing to my father.

Peace is flowing like a river,
Flowing out from you and me,
Flowing out into the desert,
Setting all the captives free.

When my mother told me later of her experience, we marveled at the way God works to help us in times such as these if we are open to receiving that help. The warmth and safety of God's love is no illusion; they are the reality of our faith.

Loving God who knows our every pain and loss, in our helplessness and despair, fill us with your peace. Amen.

Carol Spargo Pierskalla

May 17

The Therapeutic Touch

Now king David was old and stricken in years; and they covered him with clothes, but he gat no heat. . . .
Let there be sought for my lord the king a young virgin.
. . . the damsel was very fair, and cherished the king, and ministered to him: but the king knew her not.
1 Kings 1:1-4 (KJV)

One would presume that the great King David could have beautiful blankets of sheepskin and bear, of wool and mohair, the best the kingdom could offer. But clothes and blankets did not warm him, the story goes. It was Abishag lying next to him that brought heat and comfort. Every once in a while, the language of the King James version hits the right note, as here where it is said that Abishag cherished the king, an embrace of affection and respect, but the king "knew her not," the reticent expression the KJV used to let us know that they didn't have sex.

We so often associate touch with sex, relegating other tactile encounters to a brief handshake, a polite hug, a quick kiss on the cheek. Our physical restraint has been shaped by cultural decorum and phobias, by family openness or taboos, by our own changing comfort level of engagement with others. But here is one of the body's basic senses being denied. If eyesight is failing, we get glasses; we have our hearing checked; we please our palates on a daily basis; we cater to our sense of smell with soaps and flowers and air fresheners. The danger of touch that is inappropriate or unwanted has tipped the scale against its necessary and useful place in our lives.

Close to the heart of faith healing lies the complex, mysterious interaction between the healer and the seeker. What the mind perceives and what the flesh receives often act in concert to trigger the body's ability to mend itself. The affinity is so strong that, according to Dr. Dolores Keieger, the transformative energy can be achieved when hands hover close to the area of pain, even without making direct contact. So why neglect this powerful sense? In Mark 5, the woman who had suffered twelve years from a relentless hemorrhage ("suffering much under many physicians and spending all she had," v.26) believed she didn't need to see Jesus or hear him. She thought that if she could just touch his garment, healing would come through this powerful connection.

Most of us are not in the position of trading our best woolen blanket for a human counterpart, but we can take a clue from our near-human companions, the great apes. Their ritual grooming practices aren't just for whiling away the hours. The closeness and care relieve stress, calm the struggle for dominance, and strengthen immune responses. While your coworker may be alarmed if you try to pick bugs off her back, you can find healthful ways to incorporate healing touch into your life. Get or give a massage. Have your hair shampooed. Rock a baby or hold a friend's hand. Allow yourself the expression of all your senses.

God of love, teach me the wonders of touch, to be at home in my body and to be welcoming to others. Amen.

Abigail Hastings

Affirming the Lessons

I waited patiently for the LORD; he inclined to me and heard my cry. He drew me up . . . and set my feet on a rock. . . . He put a new song in my mouth, a song of praise to our God.   Psalm 40:1-3

In December 1973, my husband, Myron, and I listened as the emergency room doctor observed that my body was in the grip of some kind of systemic infection. The doctor showed only minimal concern.

Over the next two weeks my condition worsened. I became weaker. My memory faded, my sense of balance disappeared, my vision blurred, my central nervous system malfunctioned, my speech faltered. It was the worst of times for a thirty-four-year-old wife, mother, and professor. Later I learned that I had experienced a close brush with death.

After thirteen months the diagnosis came: *Chronic Epstein Barr virus localized in the central nervous system.* Prognosis: Chronic and long-term.

Why did it happen? Why me? I probably will never answer those questions adequately, yet I can deeply affirm the lessons I've learned. Here are some of them.

1. God's presence often comes through other people. Many people were channels of God's grace and love. I'll list only a few examples: the theologian who brought me large-print books, the small boy who steadied me as I walked, the families who brought meals.

2. Attitude is critical. I was resistant and angry. I resented the virus which could be active the rest of my life. "I can't cope with this," I declared. My friend responded, "Jan, you have great coping gifts. It's not that you can't; it's that you won't." I have!

3. Health is a choice for discipline. Dealing with chronic EB virus is a matter of long-term life management. Daily choices involve appropriate exercise, adequate rest, meditation, relational support, and sensible diet. Some days the choices seem to flow naturally; other days I have to prod myself, *Do it!*

God of grace and presence, thank you for your abiding love,

*steady and trustworthy even when illness strikes. Open our minds
and hearts to life's lessons. Amen.*

Jan Chartier

May 19

Lord, Help Me

*The LORD God helps me; therefore I have not been
disgraced; therefore I have set my face like flint, and I
know that I shall not be put to shame.   Isaiah 50:7*

There are days when I look in the mirror and criticize the person
I see staring back at me. I've been noticing a few dimples and
creases in unflattering places, and I lament my unfulfilled dreams
and bruised relationships. I get caught up in the should have's and
ought to have's that I didn't do. I used to find myself lamenting,
"Lord, help me!" That phrase had become a reaction to what I
saw, rather than a real prayer. Fortunately, when I caught myself
saying that one day, I decided that I should make that a real request
of my Creator. But help me to do what? To push back from the
table and put my plate in the sink rather than to get the second
helping? To complete those thirty sit-ups every day? To find the
right foundation garment? To go back to school? To make that
phone call or write that letter to reestablish a relationship?

As I prayed and meditated on this request to God, I heard the
small, still voice of the Holy Spirit say "I love you; can't you?"
As I considered this rumbling inside my spirit, it occurred to me
that I must first accept myself as I am, dimples and creases and
all, and I must acknowledge my gifts and talents, as well as the
relationships that are strong and healthy. Therein lies my strength
and my help from God. This is not about vanity; it's about loving
this person that God created. It's about doing the best that I can
for myself, so that I have the capacity to give the best that I have
to my God and to all of the others whom God has created.

*Holy Creator, thank you for my life, for my gifts and talents,
and for the loving relationships I have. Help me to be what you
intend. Amen.*

Francine Stark

ʻExpectations

And what does the LORD require of you? Micah 6:8b

Daughter, your faith has made you well; go in peace.
Luke 8:48

Robed and ready to process for the morning worship service, the guest minister was approached by an elder who, handing her a book, said breathlessly, *Oh, you haven't a hymnal.* Smiling, the minister took the hymnal, opened it, and entered the sanctuary. Although the partially sighted minister could not see one word of print, she had learned that people were more comfortable if she held an open hymnal. They expected it of their minister.

How many things we do because people expect it. Most of us have learned from observation and experience how to function effectively. When because of choice or necessity we deviate from the commonly accepted pattern, we are often considered to be disabled or not functioning properly. I have been in some traditionally male-dominated situations in which benevolent male colleagues, seeking to be helpful, have said to me, "No, no, this is the way it is done." Their way was the way. Nevertheless, there continue to be thoughtful women and men who, recognizing that God has created us with many differences, have challenged society not to place a value on these differences but to understand and celebrate them.

"Don't concentrate on what you do not have. Concentrate on what you do have." This sage advice, offered by a famous retinal surgeon who could not walk or stand without the aid of crutches, helped me to better understand what God expects of me. When our faith controls our actions, we are free from the expectations of others to find that God has provided a way for us, a way that makes us whole.

Many of us have learned that living a new way, a different way, requires confidence and courage. To constantly try to live up to the expectations of others is exhausting, even soul-destroying. To seek to be all that God has created us to be is exhilarating and life-giving.

I give you thanks, O God, for the different ways in which you make me able. Help me learn to center on my abilities and to live by your expectations. When people would define my actions by their expectations, give me strength and patience. Heal the wounds of misunderstandings and judgments. Fill me with the power of that faith that would make me whole. Amen.

Nancy T. Heimer

Children of God

Let the little children come to me, and do not stop them; for it is to such as these that the kingdom of God belongs. Truly I tell you, whoever does not receive the kingdom of God as a little child will never enter it.　　　　*Luke 18:16b-17*

Whenever Christmas or birthdays approach, my secular self thinks of all the gifts I need to buy and wrap. At the same time, my church self is reminded of God's gift to us—the precious baby Jesus.

Now that I have grandchildren who are active toddlers, I have a daily reminder from God that children are gifts! These children awaken in me my own sense of self when I see them hurting, struggling, testing.

The children look at me and at their world with fresh, wide-open eyes, uncynical attitudes, open hearts. I see them react spontaneously to the daily events in their young lives; what they feel is who they are.

Close observation of children can help us. Just look at how complicated we have made our lives! A child's simple honesty can serve us well. Oh, to look at the world, once again, with such wonder and amazement, enthusiasm and excitement! So many gifts await us when we do that.

Children instinctively trust those who take care of them. We can learn to trust once again and to believe that there is a power greater than ourselves that has us and everything in our lives under control. Everything is okay.

God, with your help, our children can shine like the sun. You hold them today in the palm of your hand. You can do the same for me, if I will just let you. Amen.

Carole Jeanne Kane

May 22

Never Alone

For freedom Christ has set us free. Stand firm, therefore, and do not submit again to a yoke of slavery.
Galatians 5:1

"That's just a crutch," say the scorning voices. "Surely you can do better than that! Don't lean on anyone. Don't lean on anything. Surely there is something wrong with you that you would need that!"

Yes, there is something wrong with me. My ankle is broken. My whole leg is in a cast, and without a crutch I cannot walk. Sure, it's something to lean on. Thank goodness it's something to lean on! Thank you, God, that there is something to lean on. Without this strong stick, I would go nowhere. I would be stuck in this chair all day long. I don't move too easily with the crutches, but at least I do move. I can get around. I can manage.

So it is with my soul. There is something broken inside of me—inside all of us, if we would only admit it. Sometimes I am strong —stronger than people know. Other times I limp. I lose my balance. I am in great danger of falling.

If I am to get through life, I need a strong, sure crutch on which to lean. I need something that will not break or bend. I need something strong enough to bear the weight of my brokenness. I need something that will hold me until I am strong enough to walk alone. Something—someone—on whom I can depend.

The trouble is, it's so easy to choose the wrong crutch. Some could become part of my life forever. They want to keep me crippled. They would block my freedom. They would limit my independence. Some crutches become addiction. They would only cripple me more. They would destroy my independence.

They would never let me stand on my own two feet. There is always the danger of getting used to being supported.

When the cast comes off my leg, what will it feel like to move without all that weight that drags on me? Will I be strong enough to walk on my own? For a while I will use the crutch, just for balance. Just to be sure.

The day will come when I will put it down and walk free and strong on my own. That doesn't mean I want to be alone. I still want those who will walk with me. I do want them to know the difference between being a crutch and being a friend.

So it is, O Lord, that I choose you to lean upon. I choose you knowing that when I am weak, you will hold me. You will keep me in balance. When I would lean too hard, you will say, "Do not be afraid. I will walk beside you and catch you if you fall, but you have the strength to walk straight and tall—and when you do that, I will still be here." Amen.

Neta Lindsay Pringle

May 23

Renewed Strength

But those who wait for the LORD shall renew their strength, they shall mount up with wings like eagles, they shall run and not be weary, they shall walk and not faint. Isaiah 40:31

I went out for my run, as usual. It wasn't easy because my husband had just left for yet another year of separation. The military life is not an easy one, but it seemed like we'd had more than our share of separation, and I feared that our fragile relationship would not survive another year apart. As I rounded the first corner, my strength and resolve seemed to melt away, and the tears began to flow down my face. How would I make it? It all seemed too impossible and too overwhelming. Just then I began to hear the bird singing. It seemed to follow me along the streets of town, around every corner, through the woods. His song rang out to me, and I found myself remembering words and a melody. At first it was just in my head, then I began to sing:

"Why should I feel discouraged, Why should the shadows come, /Why should my heart be lonely And long for heaven and home, /When Jesus is my portion? My constant friend is He: /His eye is on the sparrow, And I know He watches me./ I sing because I'm happy, I sing because I'm free, /For His eye is on the sparrow, And I know He watches me.[3]

With each word, the burden seemed to lift, and I realized that I didn't have to get through the year by myself. I knew that I had a helper who would run with me each step of the way, no matter what happened. I knew that there was no place that I could go or be that was away from God's love and mercy. And that makes all the difference!

Thank you, loving God, for walking with me and guiding my decisions today.

Nan Jenkins

May 24

Count It Joy

My brothers and sisters, whenever you face trials of any kind, consider it nothing but joy.   James 1:2

I was anxious as I walked into the grocery store. I had been diagnosed recently with metastatic breast cancer in my lung, a stage 4 cancer for which there is no cure. I was anxious because I was sure I would see someone I knew who would stop to chat and ask how I was. My voice would shake, and I would have to mention that I had cancer. I hoped I would not cry.

Months later I walked into that same grocery store with a smile on my face. I still had the cancer and there was still no cure in sight, but I no longer felt like the victim. I was thrilled to be alive! Did these people know how lucky they were to be grocery shopping? What a joy to meet a friend! And if they said, "How are you?" I responded with a hearty "great!"

Moving from intimidation to confidence, from terror to resoluteness became a spiritual journey for me. I discovered along the way that I truly wanted to live. I discovered along the way that I was a very valuable person who needed to take time for myself.

I discovered along the way that I could say *no* to volunteer positions I might resent. I discovered along the way that I could ask for someone to deliver meals, clean my house, and care for my children. I discovered along the way a loving and devoted husband, a husband whose positive traits greatly outweigh any personality quirks I once wanted to change. I discovered along the way that I could take charge of my decisions about my treatment, I could exercise, I could make fresh fruit and vegetable juices, I could eat only healthy foods, and I could meditate.

Can cancer bring joy? Yes—if joy is knowing what is truly important in life: forgiveness, acceptance of others, caring, sharing, friends, family, and the value of each day. Yes, if you realize that the love of God can never be taken away.

Gracious God of unending love and support, thank you for coming into our lives and for turning fear into hope, peace, and joy. Amen.

Jean DeGraff Tischler

May 25

I Believe in Miracles

And remember, I am with you always. Matthew 28:20b

"There's no reason for her to be alive," the surgeon told my husband. "There must be a lot of prayers somewhere." And there were. From the moment Wendell told my mother I had been thrown from the car and run over, she prayed. Within minutes a chain of prayer stretched from a group of college classmates in a Sacramento park across country to New York. The power was indescribable.

I believe in miracles. My husband lifted the car, and I scooted out from under it—both physically *impossible*. We were three hundred miles from home, and total strangers from church cared for our two small children (thankfully unharmed) until friends could come for them. The surgeon who was called had just returned from Sweden and used a new technique, tong traction, to mend my crushed pelvis. (Our other possible doctor, we learned, always put patients in a body cast, and I would likely never have walked again.) My mother came, fed me, stood for hours massaging my toes, keeping the blood circulating in my feet. (The bed was on eighteen-inch blocks, and I was in eighty-five pounds of traction.) Mother gave me life then, too, as she had when she birthed me. Call it adrenalin, caring, luck, coincidence, whatever you choose. To me they are miracles, true gifts from God.

During those interminable four months, unable to turn or move, healing came to me from so many sources: husband, mother, doctors, nurses, aides, cleaning people, family, friends, letters, cards, soft music, other patients, ministers, priests, remembered Scripture, and always the continued prayers from coast to coast. Each night sleep came as I repeated two phrases over and over: "Lois, I am with you always!" . . ."Though I walk through the valley of the shadow of death, You are with me." And God was there.

Loving, healing Creator, thank you that your love and power are always deep within us, healing us in whatever way healing is needed, and making us whole. Amen.

Lois Pew

May 26

Crying Out

A voice says, "Cry out!" And I said, "What shall I cry?"
Isaiah 40:6a

Cry out! Cry out in thanksgiving. Cry out in pain. Cry out for justice. Cry out for liberation. What shall I cry? My cries differ. When they come from the time and place of wilderness, they are calls for clarity, discernment, meaning. When they come from the time and place of abundance, they are shouts of laughter, joy, celebration. Then there is the routine. What shall I cry in my daily work, in my daily relationships? Routine does not excite me. Routine feels safe, but also deadens my spirit. Crying out doesn't enter my mind very often during times of routine.

How is it that God moves in daily living? Routinized schedules, meetings, appointments, even a routine of hectic busyness can block the creative, playful, compassionate nature of God's Spirit. I find that when I look for meaning in every element of the day, the routine cannot block the presence of God. *What shall I cry?* becomes *What shall I see?* and *What shall I hear?* today. By wondering what is in store in the department of meaningful surprise, I find that I watch my day quite closely to find God moving. Simple as that concept sounds, no matter how many times people have said those words, it amazes me how real the experience of God becomes on a daily basis when I look, listen, and *expect* a life-giving surprise.

What shall I cry, O God? That you transform daily living through expectation of meaningful surprise. Enable me to watch for it. Amen.

Lisa Withrow

May 27

Job Security

God is our refuge and strength, a very present help in trouble.　　　　　　　　　　*Psalm 46:1*

In 1989 on a crisp November day, I went to work as I had done for the last twenty years at the same company. It was a Friday, and I was looking forward to a busy weekend.

Layoffs were occurring. In previous weeks I had experienced sorrow as I watched longtime friends and peers be released. They were people with families to support, and they were among the most valued employees. I was in that category as well, but I thought that I had no reason to worry about my job. My responsibilities and job description, along with years of service, protected me. Or so I thought.

Just after the Thanksgiving holiday, the boss called and asked me to come to his office. I was not prepared for the news that I was losing my job of twenty years. I was in total shock and felt that my life was being torn apart in those moments—the news was so severe. I was also told to take all of my personal belongings home with me. I would not be allowed to come back at a later time. I hadn't driven to work because of bad weather, and I explained that I didn't have a way to take everything. My boss said he could take me home, and he also offered to call a taxi. I chose the boss—somehow that seemed right.

When I finally got home, I just sat in a chair for a long time without moving. I didn't answer the door and I let the phone ring. I was in a daze and I did not talk to or see anyone. It was morning before I fell asleep. When I awoke, I felt as if there had been a death in my family.

My job security was replaced by uncertainty and stress. Little did I know that I was beginning a six-month search for another job. As time passed, my hope diminished. I felt that I would never get my life back together. My severance pay was almost gone when a friend called me and said there was an opening at our world church headquarters. I learned that the salary would be less than one-half of my former earnings. I accepted the job but advised them that I would continue to look for employment that offered greater financial security.

It is now six years later, and I am still working for the church. I feel that it has been by God's grace that I have been able to manage. I have had to make adjustments, and that hasn't always been easy. Sometimes I worry about bills and unexpected expenses, but somehow I have enough. I enjoy my work and I have friends that I love and care about. I am thankful for the relationships that have nurtured and affirmed me.

Thank you, God, for sustaining us by your grace, and for your presence with us in good times and bad. Amen.

Connie Le Elgan

May 28

Godly Rituals

This is my body, which is given for you. Do this in remembrance of me.   Luke 22:19

When Jesus said to his disciples, "Do this in remembrance of me," it was during his last meal with his closest followers sitting beside him. He gave them a tangible way to remember him in the ritual of breaking bread and drinking wine, the same ritual we celebrate regularly when we observe Communion.

Certain rituals can be healing if we use them to benefit us in times of brokenness or times when we feel depressed, lonely, or afraid. The act of doing something that evokes a pleasant memory or even a sad memory can help us put things in perspective and move toward wholeness and balance.

I recall experiencing emotional highs and lows during my adolescence, as is typical of young people. When I was feeling low, I would sit at my piano and play songs that reflected my mood. Soon my sister would be sitting beside me on the piano bench, and we would begin singing duets. Before long, I was no longer in the dumps. This unconscious ritual was healing for me each time it was repeated.

When events in our lives cause us to feel less than *together,* rituals in our daily routine can be a comfort of sorts, if we let these small acts remind us that there is still some semblance of continuity in our lives. Just taking in the daily newspaper, listening to the weather forecast, reading the Sunday paper in bed with our morning coffee—these insignificant activities help us realize that we still have these things to appreciate. These small everyday rituals lend structure and meaning to our daily lives.

If we go through the motions without thought, like going to church every Sunday or partaking of Communion without remembering why we are there, life can be empty and meaningless. If we make the effort to consider each thing we do, we may even learn to give up some activities because they are meaningless, or worse, harmful. If we live each day listening for others' sadness or brokenness, we might find a way to sit beside that one and offer an ear or a shoulder to lean on. We can live intentionally renewing ourselves—physically, emotionally, and spiritually.

Living and Giving God, help us to remember the value in our daily rituals. Help us remember that the ritual of breaking the bread and drinking the wine was given to us to renew us from brokenness to wholeness. Thank you for the richness of daily routines, for weekly chores, for monthly and yearly rituals that add blessings to the full circle of our lives. Amen.

Elizabeth Okayama

Serving Jesus

*He touched her hand, and the fever left her, and she
got up and began to serve him.*   Matthew 8:15

I had been sick for two weeks, first with hepatitis and then with
strep throat. My doctor, knowing I was single and having to cope
alone, announced he was putting me in the hospital. I could choose
any of the city's three hospitals, he said. I had no doubts: I had to
go to the smallest of the three, Mercy Hospital, founded by the
Sisters of Mercy.

I had to go to Mercy Hospital, I feverishly believed, because
there one of the nuns—a short, quiet, older sister, I imagined—
would come and lay her cool palm on my forehead. And I would
be healed or at least feel a lot better.

I checked into Mercy. The nuns, it turned out, were away on
their annual retreat. I got well anyway.

But my vision of that little Sister of Mercy and the healing
power of her gentle, cool hand remains strong, and I still believe
in it. Any mother or father who has set a fevered child to sleep
with a soothing hand, anyone who has turned to massage therapy
to counter the effects of stress, any nurse or doctor who has
stroked the hand of a person on the way in or out of surgery,
anyone who has been placed in the center of a circle of friends
praying for healing—anyone with that experience also believes
in the power of touch.

Research years ago in a foundling home pointed out that
infants who were not touched and held failed to thrive and in some
cases died, even when there was no obvious illness or other cause
of death. It would be illogical to assume that babies grow to
become adults who no longer need caring touch for their physical
health.

There is something holy about touch, about bridging the chasm
of the inherent loneliness of being human. Perhaps it creates the
same connection that's referred to in the phrase "whenever two
or three are gathered," as my friend Zach Thomas says in his book,
Healing Touch. But it is a language our hands can once again learn
to speak.

I remember, my Creator, the power you have placed in my

hands—power to soothe, to comfort, to assure, to support, to bless, and yes, to heal. May I use it to bring glory and honor to you. Amen.

May 30

The Baker Woman

He told them another parable: "The kingdom of heaven is like yeast that a woman took and mixed in with three measures of flour until all of it was leavened."

Matthew 13:33

Jesus, who brought us the image of God as *Abba,* a loving, nurturing parent, brought other images as well. God as a baker woman is one suggested by this parable.

Remembering my grandmother in her farmhouse kitchen, putting heaps of flour into her oversized mixing bowl to make bread and rolls, is not difficult. She did not need a measuring cup. She knew the ingredients by heart and the amounts by feel. At the correct time and in the appropriate way, she would add the yeast. She would knead the dough skillfully, then set it aside to rise. Eventually the dough would be divided into loaf pans and dinner sized rolls for a final rising before baking. In time her blacktop stove would be sending wafts of heavenly aroma into the air. The taste was scrumptious.

With this memory, it's not difficult to visualize God working busily as a baker woman within God's domain. In this parable, there are three measures of flour. That's fifty pounds of flour—a lot of bread! Kneading and preparing God's domain is a large task. Yet to this task, Baker Woman God brings tender, loving care, adding just the right ingredients, including the all-important yeast. It's not just any yeast, either. In Matthew 16:6 Jesus advises the disciples against *the yeast of the Pharisees and Sadducees* to convey to us that his message is the proper leaven.

Jesus provides the leavening that helps us to experience God.

In knowing God, we can see that God goes beyond male. Yes, God goes beyond female too. After all, God is God.

When God is God in our lives, good things can happen. God's leaven can work quietly within each of us for positive change. God's reign can bring peace, justice, and love to us and to our world.

God as a Baker Woman. What a compelling image!

God, let your dominion work powerfully within us as yeast works within bread. Form our lives in ways you would have us be. Whether Baker Woman, Abba, or however we understand you, help us to know you in the fullness of your love. Amen.

Julia D. Shreve

May 31

Trusting God

In the beginning God created the heavens and the earth. Now the earth was formless and empty.
Genesis 1:1-2 (NIV)

We have been taught to think of formlessness or chaos as bad, something that needs to be ordered. We have been taught that our best work is work that keeps us in control. In attempting to structure chaos, however, we miss a truth. (Not to mention, as any woman knows, that it's an impossible goal.) Often we see ourselves as failures in direct proportion to the amount of confusion in our lives.

Take another look: chaos, or undisciplined randomness, is the creative soup for something new—new thinking, new ways, new relationships. We think of chaos as bad because it is uncomfortable, even painful. As the old ways break apart, the discomfort and inconvenience are much the same as the pain of labor. God, it seems, would have us understand that we cannot always be in control and do not need to be. To trust in the chaos is to risk an unplanned outcome by allowing God to have control. "Trust me," say the Scriptures over and over again, and yet we persist in trying to control, to make ourselves secure. Paul in Romans reminds us that nothing can separate us from the love of God. Why not let go and trust God to take you where spiritual soaring is possible—to a life that is filled with the joy of expressed potential instead of self-doubt and protection.

Help us trust, Lord. Help us trust enough to search for and believe that all things work for good. Help us to fly with the angels. Amen.

Anne H. Brady

June

Woman of God

And just then there appeared a woman with a spirit
that had crippled her for eighteen years. She was bent
over and was quite unable to stand up straight.
                                            Luke 13:11

I had been standing on the sidewalk outside of the royal palace of Bangkok, when out of the corner of my eye I saw her. Her hair was thinning and gray. It was twisted into a knot at the back of her neck. She wore a simple, black cotton dress, and her feet were covered with slippers so thin that the heat of the pavement must have seared the soles of her feet. It was almost one hundred degrees with matching humidity. Yet there she was, bent over so that her upper body was parallel to the pavement. Tied onto her back was a huge load of cut wood. She balanced the load with her hands, holding the ropes around the wood and her body.

This woman living in the twentieth century was to me a powerful image of the bent-over woman in the Luke story. How alike they were! One was the victim of an evil spirit that kept her in bondage and prevented her from being an active member of her community. The woman in Bangkok was marginalized from the community by the grinding poverty of the lower class.

Jesus healed the bent-over woman in the temple, even though he knew that the powerful leaders of his faith would rebuke him. Jesus knew that one of the reasons for his ministry was to heal and to make whole persons who were oppressed by the injustices of life—physical, emotional, spiritual—or by the actions of unjust systems.

Jesus knew that God had created people to live in community with each other and with God. God's people were to share their gifts and resources with each other in order to benefit all within the community. To live this way brings wholeness and reconciliation. It is God's plan lived out.

Gracious God, help us to hear again and again the message of Jesus to heal the sick and hurting persons in this world. Give us the courage and strength to be like Jesus and make the task our own. Amen.

                                            Sally Graham Ernst

ᴍy Delight Is in Her

And you shall be called by a new name
that the mouth of the LORD will give.
You shall be a crown of beauty in the hand of the LORD
. . . You shall no more be termed Forsaken,
and your land shall no more be termed Desolate;
but you shall be called My Delight Is in Her.
Isaiah 62:2b-4a

Divorce is devastating. Whether signifying the end of a marital relationship or the separation of any two people who are ending a deep relationship, there is no easy way to part.

When I hear people say, "We don't believe in divorce," referring to their family or religious affiliation, I say, "Who does?" We believed in our companionship, or we would not have been together long enough for coming apart to matter very much. It doesn't seem to make a lot of difference who makes the final decision; both feel the wound.

There is relief at the end of constant argument, of course. There is peace in a household no longer torn apart. And the tension of not knowing, suddenly settled, gives the signal that it's time to move on, however immobilized one might feel.

But even when the arrangements are as amicable as possible, there's the emptiness just the other side of homecoming. Family patterns for holidays are fractured, and some friends seem to become part of the property settlement.

Brokenness begins to mend with attention to the basics: nourishment, exercise, and sleep; pleasure in the company of constant friends; the blue of the sky and the wind in the trees. To sit down, light a candle, and taste the flavors in good, simple food is solace. It helps to feel the textures of the clothes I am wearing, too, and choose the ones that are comforting to me. I am still connected—here, now.

Time moves on as I maintain the discipline of returning messages, keeping appointments, and answering letters. Through it all, I must remember to pause, be still, and listen for a new name. The sound may be a quiet one; it requires my full attention.

Thank you, Lord, for your crown of beauty; thank you for lessons in living this beauty from the inside. Amen.

Audrey Ward

June 3

Set Free

You will know the truth, and the truth will make you free. John 8:32

It was a warm, sunny afternoon. The birds were singing and there was a slight breeze. I had just gotten comfortable in my patio chair with my Bible and my journal. I needed some quiet time. Out of the corner of my eye I saw something moving by the bedroom window. I got up and moved closer for a better look. There, caught in a large spider's web, was a beautiful monarch butterfly. It was flapping its wings trying to get free.

I picked up a twig and tried to free it. The butterfly fell to the ground on the grass at my feet. As I bent down to look closer, I could see one of its wings was damaged. The edges were ragged and torn from the constant struggling to free itself. As hard as it tried, it could not fly. That's when I noticed a piece of the web still attached to its wing. In its weakened condition, it took little to hold it down. I gently picked it up and removed the remaining web. It flew from my hand to a nearby bush, then lifted by a gentle breeze flew away, free from the web, free to fly wherever it chose.

As I sat back down I thought, "What a beautiful lesson, Lord." The butterfly, symbol of new life, set free. There are things in my life that bind me, paralyze me, and no matter how I struggle I cannot free myself. Only truth can set me free—the truth of God's love and grace—the truth that I am loved unconditionally.

We need to ask God to free us from the things that bind us and keep us from growing and becoming whole. To be free of the past and its fears like the web imprisoning the butterfly.

Thank you, Creator God, for butterflies, for the beautiful symbol of new life. Free us with the truth of your love. Amen.

Donna Authelet

Images of God

So God created humankind in his image.
Genesis 1:27

Every person is created in the image of God. Each moment of life you and I are called to participate in creation by our thoughts and actions. Think of the images that you ascribe to God—creator, lover, forgiver, healer. Are there more images of God? Name your list of God's images. Now identify these images of God in your own life. See the opportunity for you to be creator, and agent of love, forgiver, healer in your thoughts and actions.

Bible stories and life stories demonstrate that each day is an opportunity to live in the image of God. Which of these images is most important to you? How are you participating in God's creative process? The importance of the image, as well as how the image is lived out, changes according to the gifts that we are using and the situation in which we find ourselves.

It is part of the creative process to be open to the present moment and to participate using the gift of God's images that are relevant. Awareness of the present moment brings quiet to my mind and peace to my heart. Confusion and anxiety tend to abate. That is God's grace acting in my being.

Thanks, God of hope and joy, for our part in the creative process. Amen.

Patricia A. Smith

Turning Points

Then the devil left him, and suddenly angels came and waited on him. *Matthew 4:11*

As life goes on, we collect losses until we come to resemble a barnacle-encrusted old sea turtle. Distress and disappointment, disease and death become familiar companions.

Distress over life's limitations is only normal. There is always so much more one has to say, so much more to do. It is disappointing if we are not needed as before. Yet, can identity and self-esteem become tied too tightly to one's role in the family, career, or social circle?

We are humbled—and angered—by the nibbles and bites that disease can take out of our bodies, bodies we do not always recognize as our own. Death was once the occupation of the old. But because of AIDS, horrific regional conflicts in many countries, and the trend toward random violence, it has become a preoccupation of the young.

But no season of loss lasts forever. There is a turning point. Light does return, weakly at first, but surely. There is staying power in the ability to love, to reach out through the loss to new energy. We learn we can trust the spiritual forces of turning, renewal, and resurrection. Indeed, we may be closer to holiness at these turning points than at any other time.

The story of Jesus' forty days in the wilderness is instructive. Jesus faced every human experience, but refused to test the divine powers that popular wisdom attributed to the Messiah. He chose instead a path that is open to each of us—faith in the promises of God. He reached deeply into his memory of the Scriptures and his experience of God's love. In the wilderness and again on the cross, Jesus reached through physical pain, betrayal, and despair to that level of unbroken light that is God. That light shines through his brokenness—and our own—with its promise of eternal life.

God of hope and joy, help us to trust the light and its promise of new beginnings. Amen.

Peggy Billings

June 6

Open My Ears

Hear my prayer O God; give ear to the words of my mouth.   *Psalm 54:2*

An old friend from whom I had not heard for years unexpectedly called to urge my attendance at a class reunion. Time and distance provided her few opportunities to travel to the area, and she hoped I would be there since I lived nearby. Prior to her plea for my attendance, I had been ambivalent about the event.

On the morning of the reunion, we had a chance for the usual update about our lives. Later in the day, as we walked by ourselves to the evening picnic, the conversation changed. She began by acknowledging my church involvements. And then with some hesitancy, she stated that she had not included *church* in her life for years. Not wanting that to be a barrier between us, I somehow found the right words that encouraged her in further conversation. She talked first of her grief over the difficult death of a classmate who had been among our close friends. Our dialogue continued in a search for meaning in our friend's life and death. Engaged in listening to each other, we found ourselves sitting apart from the activities of the reunion picnic. Our conversation moved to stories of turning points and meaning in our own lives. The integrity of her questions and insights precluded glib responses on my part and drew us into a common hearing of each other.

Suddenly, a new voice intruded. Another class member had singled me out, wanting to know about my work in the church. A member of the same denomination, she listed people she knew and meetings she attended. I acknowledged those I knew, adding a few names to the denominational list myself. But I allowed this exchange to go on too long, and too late I recalled that this jargon meant nothing to my friend. It was she who had raised the greater questions of meaning and wholeness. In those minutes, she was effectively excluded by institutional talk. The other class member departed, but the opportunity for mutual searching with my friend had vanished.

God of this day, your grace calls us to create community. Open us to hearing the unexpected voices of truth outside our established routines and structures. Strengthen us to give voice to those excluded in our common search for wholeness. Amen.

Julie Tulloch

The Woman Who Touched Jesus' Cloak

He said to her, "Daughter, your faith has made you well; go in peace, and be healed of your disease."
Mark 5:34

The story of the woman with *severe bleeding* is recounted in three Gospels. It is a story within a story, a brief happening as Jesus was en route to the home of Jairus, whose young daughter had died. This unnamed woman was seeking health and wholeness; she found it in Jesus the healer.

The woman had been ill twelve years. She had been treated by many doctors and had spent all her resources, but no one was able to cure her. Imagine her physical and emotional exhaustion!

Additionally, she was ceremonially unclean; she was contaminated. According to Jewish law, anyone who touched her or touched anything she touched was also unclean. She was an outcast: lonely, ostracized, spiritually depleted.

Even in this desperate situation, she had not given up. On this day she was seeking help from Jesus, whom she had heard about. As she was jostled by the crowd, she was saying to herself, "If I can just touch his clothes, I will get well" (Mark 5:28).

She did touch Jesus' cloak; her bleeding stopped at once. Jesus turned and asked, "Who touched me?" The disciples didn't take him seriously: "The people are all around you, crowding in on you." When Jesus persisted, the woman came forward and told her story. He responded directly to her, "My daughter, your faith has made you well."

Today women are physically, emotionally, and spiritually drained for many reasons. Health and wholeness may come through persistence and searching, as it did for this unnamed woman. It may also come as women who are lost in the crowd are offered love, affirmation, and support by caring friends.

God of all compassion, fill my cup; I lift it up. Come and quench this thirsting of my soul. Fill my cup, fill it up, and make me whole. Amen.

Barbara E. Campbell

Acts of Healing

To another [is given] gifts of healing by the one Spirit.
1 Corinthians 12:4-11

As the twentieth century approached, my grandmother, then a young mother abandoned with two children, enrolled in nurse's training in a trade center of the Pennsylvania lumbering industry in the Allegheny Mountains. After brief months of hospital training, she was assigned to accompany a recovering surgery patient for a month or more of health care that could include laundry, food preparation, and child care. To be a nurse was to be a nurturing friend for the whole person. I remember her stories of patients too sick to transport over log roads to the hospital, so the surgeon and the now-more-seasoned nurse would move into the kitchen where the water boiled in a copper wash boiler on a woodburning stove. The long table became the surgical table for the physician and the nurse. Often in such situations, the nurse stayed for two months caring for patient, family, and household. Healing was personal, extending into all phases of life; the long encounters brought lifetime friendships.

Nearly a hundred years later I am surrounded by dramatic contrasts in health providers: dozens of highly trained men and women, assisted by every diagnostic tool, touching dozens of persons each day. The encounter can be very short; names will not be held in deep appreciation fifty years later. One thing is often the same: the person-to-person support in seeking health and wholeness. I learned early that healing is not only professional—*gifts of healing* often are with the one in the hospital bed.

My grandmother and I shared a common task. She was primary caregiver to the seven-year-old child, my sister, left paralyzed by raging fever in the days before antibiotic drugs became available. Forty years later I was left as the caregiver for my sister, but from her limited body she exercised the gifts of healing, her Spirit gift. Her wheelchair in the sideyard was a listening post for toddlers in their first explorations; high school boys on their way home from football; old men lonely and repetitive; and anyone who needed a listener, a word of encouragement, or a glimpse of life from the potential of faith.

Heal the hurt within us.
Heal the wounds inflicted upon us.
Heal the memories that haunt us.
Heal the feelings that drag us down.
Place within us the potential
to facilitate our own wellness.
Be wholly in us
who hunger for wholeness every day of our lives. Amen.[1]

Joyce Anderegg

June 9

Wholeness Is
Believing in Yourself

"Sir, even the dogs under the table eat the children's crumbs." . . . *So she went home, found the child lying on the bed, and the demon gone.*   Mark 7:28, 30

For many years I was both disturbed and intrigued by this passage. I could neither understand nor accept Jesus' refusal of the woman's request, and I felt challenged by the woman's confidence and courage. In order to challenge Jesus the way she did, she must have been totally sure that she was right!

I saw in the Syro-Phoenician woman what I wanted in myself. While I was ready and willing to speak up for the justice due to others, I was far behind when it was on my own behalf. Modesty and humility, precious things for a woman to pursue according to my Hispanic cultural background and my Christian faith, held me to clear and defined limits. While it was acceptable and even expected of me as a good Christian woman to help others, it was selfish to help myself. It took many life experiences, tears, and much prayer for me to finally learn and accept that the opposite is true. You cannot do for others what you cannot do for yourself. Wholeness cannot be obtained by denial. No matter how much one is able to love others, there is no "shalom" until one is able to affirm oneself and to claim one's space. It was this fierce determination to affirm herself and to claim what she thought was just for her that led the Syro-Phoenician woman to confront Jesus. And on doing that, through her wholeness, she became an instrument of wholeness to Jesus. She enabled Jesus to enlarge the perspective of his own mission!

Thank you, God of all creation, for you gave me life and made me your daughter. So many times I have allowed others to make me feel less. You gave me gifts, aspirations, and dreams. So many times I have consciously walked away from them under the pretext of a humbleness that hid my fears and self-doubts. You were insistent with me; you pushed harder until I was able to be whole again. Muchas Gracias, Señor!

Yolanda Pupo-Ortiz

June 10

One Day at a Time

The readiness is all!

She is at the stepping-off place in life. Mid-twenties, graduate of a fine college, with a career that took off even before graduation, and recently committed in marriage to a very special man. And in the midst of it all, the diagnosis: multiple sclerosis, nerve sheaths being stripped of their protective fatty layer, the gradual decline in nerve function with many possible effects.

How do I comfort her? What do I do? What can I say?

One day at a time. Maybe yours will be the more benign form—gradual loss of some refinement of control with many years of productive living. I've known friends whose cases were like that.

Read and learn as much as you can; we've made such strides against diseases. (Does a compulsive search for knowledge give us the illusion that we are in control?)

Wait and see before starting the treatment of choice—daily injections that must continue *forever* and which, according to the doctors, mean that pregnancy is prohibited. Reconsider your plans for having your own children.

God gives us being, a breath at a time, one creative opportunity at a time. You were ready for this challenge, and your husband, your families, and friends are ready too. Every breath you have taken, each one of ours, has brought us to this stage in our journeys. We will discover courage in common with each cell that breaks down.

All-wise and knowing God, we ask to accept what we do not know and to be confident that we will know what we need when the time comes. Let us be grateful for today, not fearful of the future, nor clinging to or regretting the past. Thank you for giving us friends and family to walk with and to walk with us. Amen.

Mary Rehmann

June 11

Creative Gifts

Why should we all use our creative power . . . ?
Because there is nothing that makes people so
generous, joyful, lively, bold and compassionate, so
indifferent to fighting and the accumulation of objects
and money.[2]

A couple of years ago, a friend invited me over to watercolor with her. I had never done it before. I liked it so much that I bought paints and brushes of my own right away. Now I spend hours putting blobs of color on paper and telling myself how beautiful they are. As one book I read says, "Not even Picasso could make blobs exactly like yours."

I never thought of myself as an artist because I couldn't draw. Now I'm learning that art is more about seeing than holding a paintbrush and that almost anyone can learn to draw. In *Drawing on the Right Side of the Brain: A Course in Enhancing Creativity and Artistic Confidence,* Betty Edwards explains that all children begin as artists. Most of us give up on art in elementary school when we are unable to make the transition from unself-conscious Crayola drawings to more realistic ones. The children who figure out how to draw get encouragement. The rest of us learn to say, "I'm not an artist." (Just like many of us say, "I can't sing.")

Now I am learning to draw and paint. Most of the time I feel like I am about five years old. I try to have fun and avoid feeling embarrassed. It is more important to me to enjoy the process of making art than to like the product.

The delight that comes from painting has invaded my whole life. I'm beginning to remember what it felt like to be a child and to play. I have more fun now. I worry less and feel better. Making art is an important part of my spiritual practice and my well-being.

God of all creation, teach us to recognize you in the beauty of your creation and to delight in our own creativity. Help us to enjoy your world and to treat it gently. Amen.

Jeanette Stokes

June 12

Broken Vessel

When he laid his hands on her, immediately she stood up straight and began praising God.   Luke 13:13

Jesus broke a number of traditions and taboos one sabbath day when he reached out to a woman with a spirit that had crippled her for eighteen years. She was quite bent over and was unable to stand up straight.

There she is—bent over,
'Can't look us in the eye.
She's probably a sinner . . .
It's sad to see her cry . . .
But why should we be bothered?
We turn, and look away,
Until a voice within cries out:
She's kin, we hear Christ say.
Her brokenness is our concern,
Her burdens ours to bear.
There must be ways to empathize
And let her know we care.
For we are often broken, too,
And need a listening ear.
We're part of one community
In Christ, who knows our fear.
Love takes the risks of touching,

Of reaching to convey
Whatever gifts we have to share
With others on life's way.
Then, when we feel bent over
And long, ourselves, to see
New Life emerging from despair,
We'll hear, *Stand tall! You're free!*

Source of deliverance and help, in whose love we are made whole, grant me strength and courage to live with confidence and compassion today, offering hope to others. Amen.

Lavon Bayler

June 13

Choose Life

I have set before you life and death, blessings and curses. Choose life so that you and your descendants may live, loving the LORD your God.

Deuteronomy 30:19-20

I am a chaplain. Most of the people I know have a chronic illness or physical challenge. Over and over again I am faced with the question of what health and *abundance of life* really mean for these people I love. Is it possible that healing is not the same as *curing*, that wholeness is not the same as physical perfection? Yes, it is not only possible; it is the truth about human life.

No matter what circumstance we are in, the same fundamental choice is open to all of us. On this day, in this present moment, will we choose to engage in activities and behaviors that will lead to life? Or will we allow ourselves to destroy the potential of each day through attitudes and pursuits that make our lives a living death?

My friend Elsa was almost completely paralyzed by Lou Gehrig's disease when I met her. She learned to hold a stick in her mouth and tap computer keys to spell out her thoughts, letter by letter. Elsa had more love and a richer inner life than most physically mobile people. She chose to engage life as fully as it was possible for her, given the tragedy that had occurred in her physical body.

Another friend Ada was frustrated by the limitations created by her broken hip and failing eyesight. She chose to focus her intense rage upon the daughter who visited her regularly, until the relationship reached the breaking point. By alienating her closest relative, Ada lost this source of support and moved further in the direction of choosing death even in the midst of life. She is a miserable person now.

Seeking wholeness and healing is primarily a spiritual task because illness is not always merely physical. We must be guided by daily prayer, silence before God, worship, spiritual friends, and the experiences of people who have walked through *the valley of the shadow*. God gives us the same choice each day, but it takes careful awareness to discern what truly brings us life.

Steadfast and loving One, help us to experience your great love for us. Open us to the knowledge of what is most life giving, and help us to embrace it. Increase our appreciation for your rich blessings, which are present no matter what hardships we face. Amen.

Julie Ruth Harley

June 14

God's Beloved Daughter

And when Jesus had been baptized, just as he came up from the water, suddenly the heavens were opened to him and he saw the Spirit of God descending like a dove and alighting on him. And a voice from heaven said, "This is my Son, the Beloved, with whom I am well pleased." Matthew 3:16-17

You are God's beloved daughter in whom God is well pleased. So often we have difficulty remembering this fact. We worry that we are not good enough, do not give enough, don't have time enough. We tend to take the worries of the world upon our shoulders. Let us remember that we belong to God and so does the world. Our task for today is simply to receive God's loving and healing embrace. We must know in our minds, hearts, and bodies that we are beloved and precious, made in God's image.

Jesus Christ received the voice of God blessing him in baptism as he began his ministry. Take a few moments in silence to breathe the love of God into your lungs. Fill yourself with the breath of life. Notice God's presence radiating from within and around you. You are God's beloved daughter. On this day, may you go forth to serve Christ, to spread God's love, and to celebrate with the joy of the Holy Spirit.

Beloved God of grace and glory, be present with me on this day. May I be fully aware of your deep love for me. Grace me with your healing presence. Place in my path opportunities to serve you today. Amen.

Cynthia A. Maybeck

June 15

Receiving from Others

I don't talk about miracles, I don't talk about being born again, or about God's chosen people or the blessings of a particular church. I am pleased to have known the people I have found inside the religious community. I feel fortunate to have known my need for them and also to have felt the continued resistance in comprehending the Holy Who.[3]

Several years ago, I found myself in a forest of Puerto Rico with eleven of my brothers and sisters of the United Church of Christ. Our denomination was working with the indigenous citizens, helping to empower them as they sought to maintain ownership of land bordering the magnificent beaches. We were the guests of a native family who were celebrating the fact that electricity was being brought to their shacks just that day. The matriarch of the clan helped support the family by selling along the tourist-laden street native foods that she had prepared. This day, however, we were her guests, and as we were entertained by her family and ate her sumptuous food, I was overcome by such a feeling of awe. She was giving us a gift—an offering of food. How often in my life do I think I am the person with the gifts? How can I freely accept an unconditional gift from the *other* when she could barely feed her own family? A sense of God's presence overcame me during this meal. All I had read about sharing bread came to life. Here we were, twelve *church* people, seated on crude benches, being served Communion by a black goddess who embodied Christ for us. Her toothless grin radiated such love, such peace, such thankfulness. I was transformed!

Fortunately for me, I have learned that not only can I feed others, but I can become vulnerable enough to be fed. I can be fed each day by the *other* if I allow myself to be open to God's presence. To break bread with the *other* is a gift, especially when the food is a gift freely given, and received.

Gracious and loving God, help me to always be open to receive the gifts of life from others. Speak to me when I become too independent—make me realize that by receiving the gift from the other, we can together be freed to love more deeply, dance more wildly, and celebrate life more fully. Amen.

Ann Leslie Hanson

June 16

Forgiveness and Justice

What does the LORD require of you but to do justice and to love kindness?   Micah 6:8b

And forgive us our debts as we also have forgiven our debtors.   Matthew 6:12

The selections from the Tao couldn't hold my attention that particular morning. I sat in a small church sanctuary, its walls and ceiling draped with T-shirts from the Kentucky Clothesline Project—visual and personal reminders of women and children who have been victims of abuse. The horror of one particular baby-sized shirt kept grabbing me away from all other thoughts. The caption: "Feeding and diaper changing time wasn't always what it appeared to be." An all-too-graphic line drawing accompanied the words.

From the open Tao a flowing Chinese character whispered,

Forgiveness, forgiveness, while the harsh scrawl on the baby shirt pleaded, *Justice, only justice.*

Justice and forgiveness come together along a very fine line to create the wholeness—shalom—of God's reign. According to the prophets, empires fell because of the mistreatment of women and children. God's justice was determined by the quality of human justice toward the widows and the orphans. Yet God was willing to face the injustice of humanity so that we could have the grace to forgive one another as we want to be forgiven.

Living in God's reign requires that our justice be tempered with forgiveness. And our forgiveness can only be complete with justice at its side. God offered unconditional forgiveness only when the price was paid. The fine line in the wholeness of God's reign should be mirrored in each of us who live that reign.

God of forgiveness and justice, give us the intent and the grace to be just and forgiving, as you have been with us. Amen.

Mona Bagasao

June 17

Who Me?

You did not choose me but I chose you. And I
appointed you to go and bear fruit, fruit that will last.

John 15:16a

Jesus was trying to convince the disciples of their calling to a special job. Today Jesus still chooses us to bear fruit where we are planted. Jesus chose me! What an awesome thought. I have been singled out to do a special task at a specific time in my life.

The disciples perhaps said, "Who me? Surely not me." The same thing happened to many that God called and chose for a specific task. Remember the story of so long ago when some donkeys wandered away from the farm and got lost. The donkeys belonged to Kish, who sent his son to look for them. Saul's search brought him face to face with Samuel, who recognized him as God's choice for king of the Hebrew people.

Like Saul, many of us can't believe that we have special talents that would mark us for servanthood. Saul's initial reaction was,

"Pardon me, you must have the wrong person." God used lost donkeys to get Saul's attention and to bring him to the place where he was willing to serve.

God says to us today, "I chose you and appointed you, and if I have chosen you, I will give you the tools to do the job." Moses was given a rod to bring water from the rock; David, a stone to kill Goliath; the small boy, a lunch to feed the thousands; Martha, her home to offer hospitality; and Mary, her devotion to worship the Lord."

What has God given to you and me? When we are chosen, we are also equipped. It is not always easy to accept that God can use me and my talents. God has given me a ministry of encouragement, listening, and laughter. Laughter isn't a gift I would have asked for, but God has seen fit to give it to me, and it is my responsibility to use it.

Proverbs 15:13 tells us, "A happy heart makes the face cheerful," and Proverbs 17:22 says, "A cheerful heart is good medicine." Laughter can be used to make a point, to get your audience with you, or to ease a tense or stressful situation. And it just makes you feel good.

On several occasions Jesus said, "Be of good cheer, I have overcome the world." So remember, you can be happy because Jesus said, "Be of good cheer."

When God calls, answer, "Yes, Lord, what do you want me to do?" Believe that you will be given the necessary tools to accomplish the task.

God of today, yesterday, and forever, thank you that you indeed have called me. May I always be ready to say, Yes me! Amen.

Evon Laubenstein

June 18

God's Presence

We have gifts that differ according to the grace given to us.   *Romans 12:6*

I do not look disabled: no hot pink wheelchair as an identifier. I do not use a shiny, chrome-plated pair of crutches. You will not know me by the soft, graceful fluttering of hands in conversation.

There is no gentle-eyed and unwavering guide dog by my side to distinguish me as a person with a disability.

Since visited by a mysterious virus in March of 1989 I have dark circles under my eyes, momentary lapses in my conversation due to short-term memory loss, and the unexpected pain of my soft muscle tissue tearing, tearing. There is also the quiet and persistent body and mind-numbing lack of energy that gives chronic fatigue immune dysfunction syndrome its name. I am but one among millions with a hidden disability. No known cause. No known cure.

Early on in the illness, I waged a daily battle with despair along with the sometimes hourly management of pain and concurrent gnashing of teeth and shaking my fist at God. Loss. First my old, active circle of friends. Running. Backpacking. My size-ten body and ten-hour work days. Then my career, woven seamlessly with my self-esteem.

Finally, life in the slow lane—the cleansing, ritualistic burning of my daily planner in the fireplace and the absurd *gift* of my briefcases to the local homeless shelter. *Ahhhh.* Signing off from the drudgery of daily carpool and church committees led by points of order.

What was left in the long white hours of quiet? The unexpected gift of time—watching a pair of doves making love on my window sill. Time to brew a pristine pot of tea by leaf and to have lunch with friends without looking at my watch. Connection, uninterrupted with my children and husband, no longer penciled in around appointments and meetings. Reading for the pure joy of reading and creating with bits of string and cloth— the tools of women since antiquity. Learning the limits of my body and knowing the sacred meaning of the word no. At last, finding a way to dance with God unencumbered by duty or the need to be perfect.

Holy Mother, thank you for providing a comfortable place to rest my fevered brow and aching body. Thank you for the precious gift of time and for helping me to understand that I am precious even when I am not engaged in anything other than simply being. Amen.

Sharon Kutz-Mellem

Loving Ministry

To every thing there is a season, and a time to every purpose under the heaven:A time to be born, and a time to die.   *Ecclesiastes 3:1-2 (KJV)*

To have been able to serve at the beginning and ending of the spectrum of this existence we call life has been a privilege for twenty-two years of my nursing career. After being a housewife and mother for sixteen years, I returned to my profession as an RN and reentered the working force as an OB-GYN nurse. Much had changed in the intervening years. Many things that were previously recycled by sterilization now were disposable. But childbirth was just as much of a miracle as it had been when I witnessed it during my training days. The fact that I was present to assist a new life coming into this world always caused tears to fall. Needless to say, at times that emotion was a bit inconvenient, as I was *scrubbed* and considered *sterile* at the time, and drying one's tears was not possible.

After serving in this capacity for almost ten years, I worked in other departments until 1980, at which time the hospital initiated the inpatient hospice service. This consisted of seven specially trained nurses, a chaplain, and a medical director. I applied for this area of nursing care and in August of 1980 began caring for those who were dying. It is a different kind of nursing, inasmuch as our goal was to make each patient's remaining time on earth as comfortable and enjoyable as possible. There was no hard and fast rule in regard to the care. The patient dictated his or her needs and wants; the family was also involved. I, as a staff person, felt my life enriched by caring for and being able to know and love each one of them personally. My feeling was that I received from them so much more than what I contributed to them. I recall the poet, the rancher, the devoted mother of five, the photographer, the Catholic nun, the young man of eighteen, and on and on. I remember vividly having to awaken sleeping relatives to tell them of their loved one's passing. Their reactions were usually calm and grateful that their loved one had been able to be in the hospice setting.

As they were nearing the end of their existence, the majority of them felt that belief in Christ held much hope for them, for he would never abandon them. In the time left them, they would experience a joy even when circumstances were not joyful. They were able to have a patience that was sustained by the Holy Spirit and the faithful prayers of many.

O Lord of all compassion, let us always have hope, be joyful, patient, and faithful in prayer. Amen.

Gloria E. Applegate

June 20

God's Overwhelming Presence

The light shines in the darkness, and the darkness did not overcome it.   John 1:5

As a young missionary in Brazil, I lived in a small four-room house that was owned by Mrs. Little, an unschooled but enterprising grandmother. Her son and his family of twelve lived in a cement shoebox house on the same small lot. The entire family earned money by making and selling dresses at the weekly street fair. I helped when I could, but was usually off training adult literacy teachers or restoring an abandoned library so that it could be used again.

One summer the thermometer climbed to 117 degrees in the shade. Water was scarce, and what was available was contaminated from the open sewage ditches. I felt desperately ill. My fever kept climbing until suddenly, in the early morning hours, I knew that death was near. I knew also that God was overwhelmingly present with me in that room.

I prayed for the strength to get help before delirium overtook me. I called out, and Mrs. Little woke up only to become immobilized with fear that I would die. She stumbled back to her room sobbing, unable to help me. Suddenly a six-year-old grandchild appeared in my doorway. He had crept into the house in the night in hopes of finding a cool spot to sleep. He was able to run across town and bring back a missionary colleague and her sister, who was a visiting nurse. They found ice to lower my fever and cared for me until I was able to make the two-hour trip to a doctor several days later.

In those dark moments near death, it never occurred to me to die. I knew that God's strength surrounded me and carried me through. Later on I learned that I had been suffering from typhoid fever as well as amoebic dysentery. I had survived against great odds. What was a mystery to the doctors was very clear to me. There was another Healer there whose light shone in the darkness and could not be put out.

Great healer God, help me to trust in your presence and your power, even in my moments of disbelief. Help me to find within myself that light, your light, that illuminates choices, that empowers me to expand my dreams, and that heals me where I am wounded. Amen.

Kae Lewis

June 21

Waiting

For the creation waits with eager longing for the revealing of the children of God.   Romans 8:1

My reflections about what kind of revelation creation longs for in our ecological age takes me back to my hospital visit with a six-year-old cancer patient last year. "I'm going home today," Lea beamed, "and I'm going to play outside in Mama's flowerpots." Lea's mother explained that a month earlier her child had arranged some outside plants into the shape of a face. Then, placing her stick "thermometer" into the geranium mouth, she declared the earth had a fever and wet down an old rug to cool the brow of her newly discovered friend. "The earth needs a nap," she said.

I'm afraid Lea is right. The earth is sick and tired. In a consumer-oriented society that values unlimited growth, the earth and many of her creatures never get a day off. Using goods and services and people as objects, we not only deplete nature's resources, we also devour our own spiritual reserves. This body we have ravaged is our own.

Sisters, all of creation waits with eager longing for us to replace egotistical notions of health—shortsighted notions of how *we* can heal *our* individual bodies—with the ecological call to protect the energy and health of all that is and will be. Creation waits with eager longing for us to realize that our feverish search for health will cease only when the brow we cool is larger than our own foreheads. Creation waits with eager longing for the children of God to reclaim with joy a deep kinship and connection with all of life, valuing creatures and other biotic forms not only for what they can give but because they are loved by God. Come, sisters, all of life longs for this health. It is *ours.*

God of all creation, we confess we have wearied your body with overuse. Stir in us a desire to love and care for all that you love. Amen.

Penny Ziemer

June 22

God's Power

And what is the immeasurable greatness of his power in us who believe, according to the working of his great power.　　　　　　　　*Ephesians 1:19*

The neonatal intensive care unit where I work is a very high-tech environment—certainly far more than I envisioned when I entered nursing and on some days more than I would like it to be. But we do have access to some remarkable equipment—all of it powered by electricity. Once a month there is a generator check to ensure, in case of a power failure, that the emergency generators will kick in. Even though this has been routine for years, there is still a slight apprehension as the hour approaches. Shortly before 3 P.M., the check is announced, and the nurses station themselves at the bedsides of infants on respirators. The switchover is accomplished in a matter of seconds, but the nurse must be prepared to take over for the respirator and give the vital breaths by hand if the connection to the power source is broken for any length of time. We have the ability to do this, but as time passes the rhythm becomes more erratic, and overall the breaths are less effective than the electrically powered respirator. The vital sign monitors are so amazing that the push of a button will show what the baby's heart rate was at 9:21 A.M. last Tuesday. But when power is interrupted, this most sophisticated monitor becomes disoriented and inaccurate. There are a multitude of infusion pumps in the unit (as many as eight on a critically ill infant) delivering life-sustaining nutrients, fluid, and medications. If disconnected from the power source, these pumps will automatically switch to battery and will operate quite well under their own power for a time. Eventually they will signal *low battery* and finally stop operating entirely.

It occurs to me that throughout our lives, we are seeking to reconnect to our power source. Most of us are periodically reminded that without our connection to Christ, our source of power, the rhythm of our lives becomes erratic, our life-sustaining faith weakens, and we become exhausted trying to function under our power. Finally, we even lose our orientation.

Spirit of life, we give thanks that you are always available to us with your sustaining and directing power if we maintain the connection. Amen.

Lois LaFon

June 23

Sound Mind

God did not give us a spirit of cowardice, but rather a spirit of power and of love and of self-discipline.
2 Timothy 1:7

"One to five years." The oncologist's words slashed us as he gave my best friend, Phyllis, his prognosis following her mastectomies. As we sat in silence in the car before starting home, Phyl said, "I can't leave the children that soon. I won't leave them. They won't be ready. God hasn't given me a spirit of fear, but of power and love and a sound mind. I'll do whatever I need to do. I'll live!" And she did, for fourteen creative, productive, love-filled, suffering, giving years. She left to her children, her friends, her church a legacy that never will be forgotten.

Because Phyl's system had always reacted strongly to any drug, chemotherapy was violent and debilitating. Yet four different times she endured it. Radiation gave more time, and experimental hyperthermia, painful as it was, held the vicious cells at bay longer. Her children gave unstinting support, writing her poems and letters, giving her ways to visualize the good cells overcoming the bad in her bloodstream, phoning, praying, letting her know always how much they loved her. Her church and her friends upheld her in every way possible. She gave back with full measure, running over.

Phyl taught classes on pain and healing, on personal and spiritual growth. Her visits to a beloved Christian counselor were shared with us. She served as chair of the church board and taught high school youth in Sunday school. On the day she learned that the cancer had spread throughout her system, she still gave witness to her faith at the evening's worship service. Six months later, when her time came to leave us, she said goodbye to each child. Friends streamed to her bedside, expressing their love and saying farewell. She was the same beautiful self in death that she had been in life as she moved into her next experience—totally healed and completely whole.

Thank you, Healing Spirit, that you have given us a spirit of power and love and that you give us the strength to live that power and love each day. Amen.

Lois Pew

June 24

A New Direction

If I . . . settle at the farthest limits of the sea, even there your hand shall lead me, and your right hand shall hold me fast.   *Psalm 139:9b-10*

Pennsylvania is a beautiful state. I've heard about Oil City, Pennsylvania, for years. It was a logical place for an executive in the business of crude oil transportation (that's my husband, Rick) to visit when he met with other executives occasionally. But when Rick told me of an impending move to Oil City, I was devastated!

I had always lived in Parkersburg, West Virginia! This man wanted to uproot our family and move us 240 miles (four hours) from everyone and everything I loved! He wanted to disturb my secure nest of family, friends, neighbors, church, and a job I loved!

Anger welled up inside me. Anxiety overtook my being. I was upset with Rick, Pennzoil, and everyone. But wait a minute! If I believe that nothing can come to me unless it passes my heavenly Father's approval first (and I do), who moved me to Pennsylvania? And if he moved me to Pennsylvania, the kicking, screaming, and rebellion I felt must be worked through, as tough as it was and still is, to some degree. Some healthy grieving was necessary, but I saw that God would help me as I took baby steps toward wellness, wholeness, and a search for his direction and leading into ministry opportunities even in Pennsylvania.

Regardless of your life situation, you too have opportunities to minister! Yes, even you in your situation! Open your heart and mind to the creative ways that God can involve you in ministry for his kingdom!

God of all creation, help us look to you for guidance, security, and opportunities to serve. Help us map out baby steps to build our confidence as we go. Amen.

Brenda Marinaro

June 25

Love the Lord

You shall love the LORD your God with all your heart, and with all your soul, and with all your might.
Deuteronomy 6:5

*David danced before the LORD with all his might. . . .
Michal daughter of Saul looked out the window, and saw King David leaping and dancing before the LORD, and she despised him in her heart.*
2 Samuel 6:14-16

For most of my life, my spirit was in conflict with my body. I had learned to despise and punish my body, to view my appetites as the enemy to be subdued and my physique as something shameful to house my soul. The change took place when I learned to dance.

Dancing, my spirit soared free! Dancing, my body became my joy, my release, my worship. I found that my appetites were a natural signal of need to be welcomed as a friend. No longer ashamed of my body, I began to think of it as a beautiful temple of God's Spirit and to treat it as precious. The words of the Shema returned to my thoughts, and I wondered what it meant to love the Lord with all my might. I used to imagine a pinched face, muscles taut, straining to love. I was much like Michal, despising joy.

Our body, mind, and soul are meant to be as one, as our God is one. If we despise any part, we become disconnected, brittle, and anxious. When we treat ourselves as precious, anointing and caring for ourselves as a temple of God's holiness, we become as one.

Love the Lord with all your might. Dance with joy and abandon! Taste each morsel of food and sip slowly each glass of wine and be grateful! Bathe in the waters and anoint your body with oils. Relish each loving touch as a moment of holiness. Know that your body is a precious gift and treat it as such. The Lord your God is one God, and you yourself are made to be as one—whole and holy.

Mighty One, make me as one, body, heart, and soul, dancing with joyous abandon in gratefulness for life. Amen.

Peg Shelton Williamson

June 26

Seasons of Life

For everything there is a season, and a time for every matter under heaven: a time to be born, and a time to die.　　　　　*Ecclesiastes 3:1-2*

As a nurse, I am accustomed to initiating discussions about a living will/advance directive with patients to determine the type of care that they prefer if they become incapacitated. Does the patient have a living will? Does it include *Do Not Resuscitate* instructions? The conscious decision of an individual to consider the advantages and disadvantages of life-support systems and to provide written instructions to family and professional caregivers is very important when a health-care crisis situation arises.

Mother was an eighty-four-year-old widow who was always busy: going out to breakfast, lunch, or dinner, shopping, taking a trip with friends, attending a church activity. It was sometimes hard to find her home unless I made an appointment. Her latest hobby was learning to knit. She loved to care for her home and yard. The telephone call from my cousin informing me that Mother was not feeling well, followed by her emergency admission to a hospital with a short-term terminal illness, was unexpected.

Fortunately, mother had communicated her wishes to me and her physician. Her conscious act to live in my home, in familiar surroundings with family, until life ended, without the assistance of life-support measures, provided the opportunity to share some of the most precious moments of a lifetime.

Great Healer of body and soul, remind us that to everything there is a season, even a time to die. Give us the courage to consider and record our wishes, whatever these may be, since they are an important aspect of health and wholeness for those we love. Amen.

Marilyn O. Harris

June 27

Old-Fashioned Sin or Bad Habits?

I appeal to you therefore, brothers and sisters, by the mercies of God, to present your bodies as a living sacrifice, holy and acceptable to God, which is your spiritual worship.   *Romans 12:1*

Current national newspaper headlines suggest that Americans are indeed sacrificing their bodies, but not in the "holy and acceptable" ways of Paul. How ironic that habits the church once denounced as *sinful* have become primary health *issues, concerns, problems,* or *crises* of the whole society. Consider these: increased cigarette smoking among youth; high birthrate among young, unwed teenagers; deaths caused by drunken drivers; lotteries; and addicted gamblers.

When was the last time you heard a rousing sermon about sin in general or a particular individual action? *Sin*—the transgression or deliberate disregard of divine law—has fallen on hard times. Rules went out of vogue in favor of "do your own thing."

My church youth group in the mid-forties had rules of *Christian conduct,* some positive *to do*'s and several *sins* to be avoided: smoking, drinking, card playing, going to the movies, and *necking* in the backseat. Even a popular song reminded us, "It's a Sin to Tell a Lie."

We memorized Scriptures, including the Ten Commandments, Romans 12, and other sayings of Paul to reinforce ideas of holy living. Our leaders stressed breaking old habits, but we often saw the rules as ways to take away all the fun. We were reminded, "Be not conformed to this world, but be transformed by the renewing of your mind"(Romans 12:2).

Transformation is indeed necessary. These matters demand attention from the church, as well as government, school boards, and nonprofit coalitions. Churches have not abandoned their ideals and doctrines; but their voices are muted.

These issues by whatever name are impediments to physical and spiritual wholeness. In a society that rejects rules and champions individual rights and local control, a way must be found to establish a common good. Who will set the standards? How is responsible decision making to be taught for the health and safety of individuals and the society as a whole?

Great Comforter, grant us wisdom, grant us courage, for the living of these days. Amen.

Barbara E. Campbell

Skunk Medicine

*Be pleased, O LORD, to deliver me; O LORD, make
haste to help me. Let all those be put to shame and
confusion who seek to snatch away my life; let those be
turned back and brought to dishonor who desire my
hurt. Let those be appalled because of their shame who
say to me, "Aha, Aha!"*   Psalm 40:13-15

A friend held out a deck of animal cards used by certain Native American groups as sources of guidance and wisdom. "Pick one," she said. "Let your aura surround the deck and pick a card."

I picked a skunk. "It figures," I thought. It had been a rough year. "Now listen to this," my friend said. "Here's what you can learn from the skunk."

Skunk medicine is about power, gentle power. The skunk commands respect by its very presence. It is not provocative or aggressive. It will not kill you, but it will make a lasting impression on you if crossed. So the skunk waddles around with a sense of sureness; it is both nonthreatening and self-confident.

The guiding principle in skunk medicine is to use that self-respect to attract and inform others. People are naturally drawn to those who live out of a centered, fearless self. To find that sense of calm and to project it to others is a gift we can give each other, as we all seek to live the abundant life God offers to us and desires for us.

The other side of skunk medicine is the practice of recognizing and confronting those who would deplete your strength. Psalms is replete with references to "smiting the enemy," a vengeful view of the world that gets turned on its head in Jesus' teachings. But there is a certain wickedness at work when we confront those who kill our spirits. To ask God for help in living with these *enemies* is not to say you want them struck down (oh, not literally anyway); it is to admit that they diminish you, often at great emotional cost. You do not have to pass judgment on them or despise them. Just be alert to the ways that they divert us from realizing the richness of God's Spirit in our lives. To let this negative energy take over is to give them more power than is right.

To complicate the dynamic, it is rarely the stranger who exacts such a toll from us; often it is a boss or family member or close friend who shamelessly taunts, "Aha, Aha!" But to put on the armor of God—this is, to celebrate who we are as we are—is to give ourselves a new kind of protection, one that does not allow our spirits to be quashed and our souls to be robbed. At least not without putting up a big stink.

Guardian of my life, give me strength to resist those who would snatch away my spirit. Teach me the self-respect that is rooted in your view of me, that of loving-kindness and joy in who I am. Amen.

Abigail Hastings

June 29

Dance, Dance My Heart

Dance, dance my heart—For our God is listening; our God is listening to your melody.

I first learned this phrase from an anthem that our seminary choir sang. It reverberated as a deep chord in my life, for I participated in a seminary liturgical dance group where I was learning to dance.

Let me explain. I approached dance with great fear. I have problems telling left from right. My gracefulness often matches that of an elephant. Who else falls up stairs? Being a *big* kid— taller than other kids my age and some of my teachers—I was chosen to be one of the *boys* at square dances, so I learned the wrong part. Dance was not a language that I or my body knew.

Seminary was a freeing time when I broke the rule that only men were students. I learned all about worship as I had always wanted. It was the early 1970s, and I was coming to know myself as a woman, not a *girl*. My faith moved from being experiential to being an integration of knowledge and experience. I was growing stronger.

In the middle of this experience was the dance group. Often I would have to drag my weary body over to the group, only to come home invigorated. I saw us put religious meaning into visual form—worship came alive. These words about dance acquired special meaning.

The most important meaning came when my grandmother died. I knew that I was grieving. I could feel the tears inside, but they would not come out. The funeral was not the place. My cousins and I were *trying to be brave*. Being alone did not work either. I finally went to dance class. After doing our usual stretches and beginning exercises, we were given time for us to put together our own dance.

I remember my choosing to dance death. I began with the active and moved to the inactive. I wanted my body to experience what my soul felt had happened to my grandmother. So I danced until I ended up on the floor in a ball with finally only my hand moving. And then that stopped. As it stopped, the tears came. The grief was released. My dance class became a blanket that embraced me and let me cry.

That experience taught me the depth of meaning in my dance phrase. "Dance, dance my heart"—dance whatever you feel. "For God is listening; God is listening to your melody." God will not only hear, but will receive whatever we experience in our heart. This is true whether what we feel is celebrative or full of grief.

For me, "Dance, dance my heart" is a call to liberation and an assurance of God's presence. Both help me feel whole, regardless of what happens.

God who knows me more intimately than I know myself, receive my dance of life. Help me to know that whether grace-filled or stumbling the dance itself is faithfulness. Help me to dance from my life into my death with eyes fixed on you. Amen.

Peggy L.T. Garrison

June 30

The Barrier of Assumptions

Do not judge, and you will not be judged; do not condemn, and you will not be condemned. Forgive, and you will be forgiven. Luke 6:37

Not long after I began pastoring three small churches on the coast of Maine, I was warned about Hollis Davis. Word had it that he did not approve of women ministers, and he would not hesitate to make an issue of it in public if I were to meet him at a community gathering. As he was not a parishioner in one of my churches, I decided to avoid him. I did not need to seek out a confrontation about this issue; I had plenty to do as the pastor of people who affirmed their female minister. Occasionally I would see him across a room at a town meeting, but I never came face to face with my alleged critic.

A year passed. One morning I ran into the village store for the newspaper. As I looked over the shelf of canned baked beans, my eyes locked into those of Hollis Davis, who was shopping in the next aisle. I had almost forgotten about him, but there he was, ready, no doubt, for a fight. I smiled at him and nodded hello. I was in no mood for a debate on women's ordination in front of the candy counter, so I quickly eased myself out of the store. Safe.

Later, the phone rang. It was Hollis Davis. Could he come see me? I resigned myself to the inevitable encounter with my closed-minded adversary. The following morning as Hollis sat down in my office, I prepared for his attack. Hollis leaned forward, put his face in his hands, and began to cry. He had just run for a local public office and had received three votes. He was feeling rejected, a failure and a laughingstock. He had come to me, he said, because I had smiled at him in the store the day before. I flushed with shame. He said he had no one else to turn to; he needed a pastor. We talked. We prayed. I felt so humbled by his trust and so ashamed of the assumptions I had been carrying about him for so long—assumptions that had fabricated a huge barrier between us.

Hollis and I became friends. He and his wife brought me a gift of fresh bread, which we broke together. They eventually became active in a nearby Pentecostal church, where their pastor was a woman. Several years later, I stood at Hollis's graveside, saying goodbye to the friend who unknowingly taught me a profound lesson about the destructiveness of assumptions and the gift of God's healing grace in disproving them.

Healing God, thank you for breaking down the barriers that our assumptions create. In you, reconciliation is never impossible! Amen.

Priscilla Dreyman

July

Jesus' Life-Giving Water

Everyone who drinks of this water will be thirsty
again, but those who drink of the water that I will give
them will never be thirsty. The water that I will give
will become in them a spring of water gushing up to
eternal life.   John 4:13-14

Jesus tells this to the Samaritan woman, who knows well the triple oppression of race, sex, and class.

For many years I happily pursued a career while also envying friends who were having babies. Finally I had two small, exquisite children, but I found life at home sometimes lacking. Then I discovered Anne Morrow Lindbergh's *Gift from the Sea*,[1] in which she describes mothers as pitchers perpetually spilling themselves out in dribs and drabs, draining their *creative springs* but not replenishing them.

I definitely knew my wellspring was going down the drain rather than watering a well-remunerated career, as my husband was continuing to enjoy. What I did not know was how to prime my pump.

Lindbergh found that solitude refilled her pitcher. I began to seek time alone—first by leaving the children in the church nursery so I would have one hour a week to worship quietly, then by dedicating their nap times to something that was of compelling interest to me.

As the children grew, my husband (and strongest ally) understood my need to take courses, to go on retreat, even to write a book. I began to sip Jesus' *life-giving water* and to identify and celebrate God's wondrous presence in my life. I was being prepared for a new career and for ministry as God's special agent in my home, workplace, community, and church. I discovered that what I do really matters to God. Although solitude is rare, today my pitcher *runneth over.*

Heavenly Mother and Father of us all, challenge us to discover the source of the spring that provides life-giving water so that we may drink deeply and never again thirst. Grant that we may rejoice in your day-to-day involvement in our lives and enjoy the peace that our friend and companion, Jesus Christ, has promised. Amen.

Sally Mitchell Bucklee

July 2

Praise God!

The heavens are telling the glory of God; and the firmament proclaims his handiwork. Day to day pours forth speech, and night to night declares knowledge. There is no speech, nor are there words; their voice is not heard; yet their music goes out through all the earth, and their words to the end of the world.

Psalm 19:1-4a

There is no agreement on the exact meaning of the Hebrew word translated "music." It may be translated as *line,* as in line of music, or as *call.*

From earliest childhood, little girls seem to understand language better than little boys. All through school, girls seem to have a readiness for language skills. Yet girls learn that society prefers that they keep quiet. They learn that teachers respond more favorably to what boys say in class; they learn that the announcers of this world are mostly men; they learn that people hear what men say at board meetings, in churches, at trials, and at social gatherings, but not what women say.

But we read in Psalm 19 that not all speech is with saying, not all telling is by talking, not all knowledge is linear. After all, the very heavens tell of God's glory in soundless invocation; the days and nights greet each other in wordless benediction; creation fits together in rhythm and contour.

Many women of my generation (born before/during/after WWII) have not said their words. We have paid for that silence with the emotional and physical symptoms of stress and resentment. And the world has paid, too, by not hearing what we might have said about caring for our common space, about taking responsibility for the very young and the very old, about the fragility of individual life and planet life. Our words might have gone out to the end of the world, but we have kept them inside, where they have sometimes wounded us.

Perhaps by watching and listening—the interplay of light and dark, the sacredness of seasonal changes, the essential habit and necessity of giving praise—we can finally get it right, learning patience from the passage of days, learning diligence from the eternal utterances of space, learning strength from our interior harmony with creation.

Holy Voice, teach us to speak health; teach us to praise you with our tending, our sharing, and our silence. Help us to know that the words of our mouths and the meditations of our hearts are acceptable to you. Amen.

Cathy Carpenter

July 3

Abide in Me

I am the vine, you are the branches. Those who abide in me and I in them bear much fruit, because apart from me you can do nothing.   John 15:5

Someone has wisely said:

Within this earthly temple there is a crowd.
There is one of us who is humble and one of us who is proud.
There is one of us who loves his neighbor as himself
Another cares for naught but fame and self.
There is one of us who is brokenhearted for his sins
Another unrepentant sits and grins.
Of such infernal trouble I'd be free
If only once I could determine which is me.

Dr. Lesslie Newbiggin helped me to see that the priority claim upon all professing Christians is *to abide in Jesus Christ*.

Jesus went on to say in verses ten and eleven: If you keep my commandments you will abide in my love, just as I have kept my Father's commandments and abide in his love. I have said these things to you so that my joy may be in you and that your joy may be complete.

As we abide in Jesus Christ, something of the fragrance of his Spirit is made known in all we think and say and do. When unexpected illnesses occur and problems and disappointments pour overwhelmingly upon us, we remember that we, the branches, are pruned that we might bear more fruit.

Almighty and ever living God, whom to know is eternal light, whom to love is perfect peace, whom to serve is fullness of joy, we praise and thank you for the gift of yourself in the person of Jesus Christ. Enable us to so abide in him that we become increasingly like him in thought, word, and deed. Use us all to the praise of your glory and the extension of your community of love. Amen.

Allene M. Ford

July 4

Formed by God

The LORD God had not caused it to rain upon the earth, and there was no one ['adam, "human being"] to till the ground ['adamah]; but a stream would rise from the earth, and water the whole face of the ground ['adamah]—then the LORD God formed a man ['adam, "human being"] out of the ground ['adamah], the dust.

Genesis 2:5b-7a

Genesis 2 describes a graphically female earth (a stream would rise), which is still virgin: not yet rained upon or tilled.

Out of the ground of this female earth God creates the first human being, the trees (verse 9), and the animals (verse 19).

Instead of subjugating or invading the earth, God establishes a partnership of rain and tillage with that human being—earth's own child, scrabbling for nourishment at her breast. How appropriate in a world where agricultural labor is often woman's work.

The story says that we are *grounded,* at home, in our bodies, which constitute us even before God's breath enters us; and through which we share in a common substance with all other living things and with the earth herself, so that we are at home also on the earth.

It tells us that our bodies are good, valuable, beautiful—formed by God's fingers playing in the dust. And that we participate—men and women both—in the femaleness of the earth, which is part of their goodness.

And it tells us that we are connected, both to the earth from which we come, and to God, who has lovingly made us and with whom we bring forth new creation—for food, but also for delight.

God of all creation, open our eyes to the beauty of our bodies this day. Teach us our connectedness to the earth and to you. Let our streams, too, give water to the earth. Amen.

Katherine Griffis

July 5

The Lady Is My Shepherd

The LORD is my shepherd, I shall not want.
Psalm 23:1

This has been a very hot summer. And bright. As I enter the damp coolness of the hospice, I surrender to the artificial light.

By now most residents know that I am a chaplain. As I walk the corridors and enter the rooms, I seek eye contact. Who wants to talk? Who wants to pray? Who wants company? A hand to hold?

Gently, I move toward those with AIDS.

Death doesn't look any different here—sunken eyes, hollow cheeks. Bodies become skeletal, and they gasp to delay the last breath. It is not easy to die.

And yet I walk.

Where are you, Lady?

I feel your light and your presence, and I hope for miracles. Not for the body, surely, for that cure would be short-lived indeed.

But a miracle, nonetheless.

Bodies, minds, and souls, turning to you in obedience and surrender. I think we each have the same task: to take time seriously; to learn how to live into faith, love, and friendship; to lay down the cares of the day; to die for each other.

But there is so much noise in the world; so much static.

Make of me a clean heart, Lady. Help me to release my agendas and my prejudices, my fears—help me to learn how to pray beyond that which comforts me, beyond that which keeps me safe. The Lady is my shepherd. Amen.

Diane Bonner Zarowin

July 6

Praise the Lord!

Breathe on me, breath of God.

Breath is the gift of life. We come into life with the first breath filling our lungs and providing the oxygen for our bodily functions. Then the body begins the rhythm of inhaling and exhaling, taking in the oxygen and releasing the carbon dioxide. With each breath you and I are provided the nutrient for life and the release of a potential poison. The breath provides each person with a mediative moment for healing and restoration to wholeness by following the rhythm of breathing.

When you and I find ourselves in need, seeking the awareness of God, the breath that is taken in and released can be a means to center our life in the creative moment of birth and rebirth to bring acceptance, insight, and renewal:

Breathe in . . . receiving, breathe out . . . letting go

Breathe in . . . receiving, breathe out . . . letting go.

Focusing on the rhythm of breathing allows us to be reminded of God's gift of life and God's gift of reconciliation in the present moment.

Gracious Giver of knowledge, help us to let everything that breathes praise the Lord. Amen.

Patricia A. Smith

ʻWomen Seeking ʻWholeness

*One of the scribes . . . asked him, "Which
commandment is the first of all?" Jesus answered,
"The first is, . . . 'you shall love the Lord your God
with all your heart, and with all your soul, and with all
your mind, and with all your strength.' The second is
this, 'You shall love your neighbor as yourself.' There
is no other commandment greater than these."*
                                    Mark 12:28, 30-31

In a society that is frail, fractured, and frazzled, we have
become women desperately seeking wholeness. The amount of
money we spend on health clubs, therapy, and spiritual retreats
demonstrates how we long for balance in body, mind, and spirit.
That balance is critical to our survival and to our health.

I am a pastor, a single parent of two teenagers, and a committed
worker in many arenas. Keeping the balance of body, mind, and
spirit is a high priority. I know that if I do not exercise and eat
right, my mind and spirit suffer. If I do not study, keep my mind
challenged, and make healthy choices, my body and spirit suffer.
If I do not take the time to nourish my spirit through prayer,
worship, meditation, and working with my spiritual director, my
mind and body suffer.

The power to be balanced, whole, healthy women is not something we will find outside ourselves. It starts within, with hearing
and responding to the gentle, yet strong, rhythm of the love in
whose image we are created, which gives us life. When we look
in a mirror, that love empowers us to say "I love you" to ourselves
with a love that accepts, affirms, and heals. That love, the love of
God, is the centering focus of our wholeness.

Jesus provided the wholeness model long ago when he said we
are to love God with all our heart, soul, mind, and strength. This
was and is the way to optimum living. In so doing, loving
ourselves and our *neighbors* will come to mirror the whole and
balanced relationship we have with God. What a gift we as women
can offer! As we walk through life this day, may we step forward
in the wholeness that empowers us!

*God of compassion, may the connectedness of body, mind, and
spirit be made whole by the power of your love. Amen.*

Liz Lopez Spence

July 8

Inner Strength

*A woman said, "Speak to us of Joy and Sorrow" . . .
"Your joy is your sorrow unmasked. And the selfsame
well from which your laughter rises was often times
filled with your tears. . . . When you are joyous, look
deep into your heart and you shall find it is only that
which has given you sorrow that is giving you joy.
When you are sorrowful look again in your heart, and
you shall see that in truth you are weeping for that
which has been your delight."[2]*

A woman must recognize and be in touch with her inner
self—sensitivity, courage, love, and hope as a source of strength
and renewal. From this source she can replenish her sisters who
are without that inner peace and steadfast drive and enable them
to reach out to the poetry often trapped within them. From the
pain of oppression and humiliation felt by so many battered and
bruised women can come the renewed spirit of self-affirmation,
self-reliance, and self-love. It is upon the wings of our shared
laughter and tears that we discover our commonality as a bond of
strength and support. It is that invisible connection between the
homemaker and the business woman, the physician and her
abused patient, the actor and her audience, to which she speaks
of joy and pain.

*God, you who are perfect love, let us form a latticework of
women's souls ever connecting across the globe. Let us weave a
blanket of peace and safety, sewn by women's hands and hearts,
over the world. Amen.*

Jackie Underwood

ᴅo ᴺot ᴡorry

*And can any of you by worrying add a single hour to
your span of life?*   *Luke 12:25*

I constantly need to remind myself that this question is rhetorical. Jesus assumed an answer of no. I tend to live my life as if I
believe the answer is yes. I come by the tendency honestly. My
mother is a world-class worrier; I like to say I learned from the
best.

It has been clear to me for a long time that energy spent
worrying about things over which I have no control is energy not
available for the more important tasks of life. Recently I have
realized that even worrying about those things over which I do
exercise some control (as opposed to acting on them and then
letting go of them) is also dysfunctional. But doing something
about either one—there's the rub!

Midlife has brought the realization that life is short, that so
much that seemed important, particularly in my work, is marginal
at best. What I have come to value above all else are quality
relationships, creative expression, and a sense of balance between
being and doing. Worrying tends to create a barrier between
myself and each of those treasures. For example, I have recently
rediscovered the role of art in my life. The hours I spend painting
are filled with a sense of joy and peace. However, as I began
showing my work to friends and basking in their approval, I
found myself worrying about the product rather than savoring
the process. When a colleague suggested that I sell some
paintings as a benefit for a project we both love, I was flattered.
But that night I awoke in a frenzy of anxiety, worried that I didn't
have enough paintings, that they weren't good enough, that no one
would buy them. I realized that I was in imminent danger of
having the one thing in my life that is pure joy and free of stress
polluted by worry. I was on the edge of turning my play into
work.

Jesus reminds us that worrying is not only dangerous for our
physical and emotional health. It can be spiritually depleting as
well: If God so clothes the grass of the field, how much more will
God clothe you! Do not keep worrying. The line between doing

our part in God's creative plan and inflating the importance of our role to the point where we cease to trust God's grace may be a thin one, but it is an important one.

Gracious God, remind me every day that the choice is mine between worry that depletes and trust that refreshes. Nudge me toward trust and wholeness. Amen.

Peggy Halsey

July 10

Stubborn or Persistent

Yet because this widow keeps bothering me, I will grant her justice, so that she may not wear me out by continually coming. Luke 18:5

Earlier in my working career I was a federal government midmanagement employee. On one occasion I was engaged in a heavy discussion with my manager. He wanted me to follow a strategy that I thought was inappropriate, not because of moral or legal issues, but because I thought his approach would not be effective. In the heat of the discussion he said, "Barbara, you are being so stubborn." From somewhere within me came some references to being born under the sign of Taurus the bull and then the response, "I am not stubborn, but I am persistent." The response broke the tension, and we were able to proceed with a more productive conversation.

In that moment of tension, I did not remember the persistent widow. In the text from Luke (18:1-8), Jesus tells the disciples the story of a widow who constantly appealed to a judge for justice in a situation where she perceived she had been wronged. Although the judge tried to ignore the widow, her persistence in pressing her case caused the judge to relent and to respond to her appeal. Jesus tells the story to illustrate the need for unceasing faith and prayer. "God . . . will quickly grant justice to them." The judge saw her as stubborn; Jesus recognized her persistence.

I think of that widow often. She is a role model for me. In these days when I feel weary, I remember how she persisted, and my strength is renewed. When a problem seems entangled and impenetrable, the persistent widow reminds me that the goal is reached only when you press on, unceasingly.

To wear down injustice requires constantly calling attention to its existence. There must be ongoing efforts to thwart the barriers constantly thrown in the way by those who have not yet seen the light. The strength and wisdom to persist comes from remembering always to cry out to God day and night. God will grant justice in God's time. The persistent widow assures me of that.

Gracious God, please do not let me become too willing to wait or so comfortable that pushing on is forgotten. Enable me to have the clarity of vision to see the possibility of the reign of your justice on earth. Open my heart to understand your will, and grant me the strength to do it. Amen.

Barbara Ricks Thompson

Gaining Understanding

We know that all things work together for good for those who love God, who are called according to his purpose.   *Romans 8:28*

The dark creeping tendrils of despair, anxiety, and hopelessness wrap around my whole being. Depression saps energy, vision, and hope for each of us touched by its tendrils. It may come crashing down suddenly, or it may seep into our lives so slowly that we hardly see it becoming a part of life.

Depression or other disability (either mental or physical) exists in many of lives. There is a real tendency to treat all the difficult parts of our lives as invaders. We then turn our work of coping into a fight against this thing that we try to reject and cleanse from our being. However, I truly believe that all disability is a part of our being, a part of who we are. God calls us to accept all of our being and to move forward into life, using all the gifts we are given.

This is not to say that God asks us to glory in our disability as a great gift. Each disability is a part of the physical world. Every part of our life is affected by the presence of depression. When it touches our lives, we must recognize that it exists and accept it as part of reality. The sapping of one's hope for the future drags upon the affirmation of our faith—that God works for good in all things. Yet we must each know that our struggle gives us understanding and experience that are never gleaned by mere reading and study.

God's people walked in despair for forty years in the wilderness. Indeed, that is what formed an odd group of individuals into a community. The struggles we experience help us create new understanding and grant us the freedom, the possibility, and the promise of creating bonds with others who are in need in new and different ways.

Loving God, I pray that you will wrap your loving arms around me so I may accept who I am and where I am. Grant that I may know your presence in my life and share my gifts with others. Amen.

Gay Gilliland-Mallo

The Pearl of Great Value

Again, the realm of heaven is like a merchant in search of fine pearls; on finding one pearl of great value, he went and sold all that he had and bought it.
Matthew 13:45-46

It seems to me that the vision of wholeness is the pearl of great value and the realm of God on earth evolves when we do all in our power to acquire our pearl.

The vision of ourselves as healed, balanced, accepted, centered, optimal, light, and joyful comes as but a rare glimpse. Yet the sheen of the pearl is unmistakable and endlessly attractive. The soul knows its origin of wellness, wholeness, shalom, and unity. Granted a glimpse in that moment of being, we see our potential clearly. In that moment we love ourselves deeply. We are the pearl of great value. The moment lives on in our minds as a beacon. And so, the quest begins. We commit ourselves to becoming whole persons.

When we start out, we can never quite anticipate the cost of that pearl. The cost of wholeness demands literally tens of thousands of dollars. For some, it entails the healing of the physical body and great health-care expenditures. For some, it is the long-term outlay of spiritual and psychological energies to loosen whatever binds us. For some, it is breaking loose of destructive relationships. For some, it means relocating to find our own sacred ground. For others, it requires the consistent practice of journaling, shaking loose the stress, and paying attention to what we take in and the inner ecology. And for all, making whole will take endless patience with God's time.

Around us, women are making these moves. Women climb out of potholes and ditches because they have glimpsed the great value in themselves. Their fortitude, in turn, has encouraged others to stretch, grow, and become strong. As each woman becomes strong, her community becomes strong.

The realm of God is ushered in one pearl of great value at a time.

Watchful and caring God, let me love myself as a pearl of great value. Amen.

Amelia Chua

July 13

Limitations

And this is my prayer, that your love may overflow more and more with knowledge and full insight to help you to determine what is best, so that in the day of Christ you may be pure and blameless.

Philippians 1:9-10

I want to do it all.

I can't, and I know it.

I can't because it's impossible. *All* is a task too big for any one person. If I try, I'll end up . . . pick one: feeling guilty, feeling incompetent, feeling like a failure.

Also, I can't because trying may well make me sick. I had CFIDS (Chronic Fatigue Immune Deficiency Syndrome) for three years, and my doctor has told me in no uncertain terms that the illness can kick in again if I don't take care of myself.

That's the kicker: taking care of myself. It requires so little. Eating three meals a day. Resting when I'm tired rather than collapsing when I'm exhausted. Pausing. Choosing where to plant my energy rather than sowing it haphazardly. Doing some art every week. Balancing my need for regeneration against the needs of others for my presence and attention. Paying attention to my own body's requirements.

It's easier for me to conceive of saving the world (not single-handedly; I have three friends who will help) than it is to imagine eating breakfast every day of my life for the next forty or fifty years. Apparently I think that ten minutes a day is the critical factor in accomplishing—what? Not all my hopes and dreams. Just what I want to do.

I can't do it all, whether we're talking about what I want to do or all the self-care I need to take; I can't do it all. So maybe it's time to determine what is best and then try living into those choices.

God of ages past and future, remind me that it's not more time I need. It's more love overflowing with knowledge and more insight. Amen.

Mary Cartledge-Hayes

July 14

Stages of Life

Then suddenly a woman who had been suffering from hemorrhages for twelve years came up behind him and touched the fringe of his cloak, for she said to herself, "If I only touch his cloak, I will be made well." Jesus turned, and seeing her he said, "Take heart, daughter; your faith has made you well." Matthew 9:20-22

The woman had been bleeding for many years, a condition that many women experience as they age. A deep yearning for healing drew her to break all social codes and religious laws and, taking a great risk, to touch the fringe of his garment.

From birth to death, the process of aging is a body and soul event for many women with many associated risks, changes, losses, and grief. In midlife, in particular, we can feel very much alone. In the context of a society that places great value on youth and physical beauty, a society filled with many devaluing messages for aging women, we can begin to feel invisible.

Out of necessity, we must plumb the depths of our faith and interior lives seeking our God-given beauty, wisdom, and power. We must touch the garments of one another, drawing strength and healing so that we might encounter a transformation of the spirit as well as the body, as we experience *the change of life.*

Transforming God, in all stages of my living, give me the necessary courage to take risks and touch the garments of others so that I might experience the healing support I need to make this journey called life with all its changes. Amen.

Karla McGray

July 15

Momentary Affliction

And my God will fully supply every need of yours according to his riches in glory in Christ Jesus.
Philippians 4:19

More than thirty years ago, I was aboard a freighter, sailing with my husband and one-year-old son to *the uttermost parts of the earth* to South Korea where we were to live for three years as missionaries. This verse with its glorious promise was ringing in my ears as we sailed under the Golden Gate Bridge in San Francisco into a world unknown. Would God's promise really prove to be true, or was this only a nice sentiment in an ancient book? Now, thirty years later I can say yes, with authority, having experienced the reality of God's presence in that promise that brings health and wholeness.

God gives us strength and comfort through life's inevitable crises as they come to us. It was a great learning for me when I came to the realization that, indeed, suffering is going to come to each of us in one form or another. Following on the heels of this truth was God's promise that God does supply every need so that we can learn to rejoice and give thanks no matter what circumstances we find ourselves in, "For this slight momentary affliction is preparing us for an eternal glory beyond all comparison."

(2 Corinthians 4:17). Indeed, our God of all mercies and comfort does comfort us in all our affliction, that we may comfort others with that same comfort and in the process become whole.

God of all comfort, may we be strengthened with all power according to your glorious might for all endurance and patience with joy, giving thanks to God who has qualified us to share in the inheritance of the saints in the light. Amen.

Norma S. Mengel

July 16

Encouragement

Therefore encourage one another and build up each other, as indeed you are doing. 1 Thessalonians 5:11

Children starve for lack of education just as they starve for lack of food. As my car stopped at the home on the edge of the cotton field, little heads popped up in the window beside me. "Colors! Colors!" they shouted.

I laughed and got out of the car with my sack of blocks, some old crayons, and a brown paper bag to *color*. My job was to help this mother use the materials at hand to work with her children. The goal was to teach her how to help her little ones get ready for school.

The home had no toys. The linoleum, a pattern I remembered from my childhood, was almost worn away. The lights were dimmed in an attempt to keep the home cooler in the blazing Arkansas heat.

This was my third visit to the home. Although the mother had chosen to take part in the Parents as Teachers Program, she had not participated in our lessons so far. She seemed more comfortable sitting quietly and watching me with the children.

When the children finished coloring, I produced some blocks. The children dove for their share like cowboys in the old movies as the *grub* was placed on the table. When they settled down, they had no idea what to do with the blocks. I was beginning to work with the child next to me when I noticed the mother leaning forward in the chair. As I watched, she picked up the blocks and began to fashion a creation for each of her children. I watched as she assumed her role as her children's teacher.

God of steadfastness and encouragement, help us to never take for granted the skills our parents taught us. Help us to share these skills with others. Amen.

Jackie Bryant

July 17

11/6/19 # The Amazing Grace of God

The LORD is my rock, my fortress, and my deliverer, my God, my rock in whom I take refuge, my shield, and the horn of my salvation, my stronghold.   Psalm 18:2

Have you ever reached a point of powerlessness in your life, when you felt all alone in a seemingly hopeless situation? Being moral and imperfect, we often find ourselves caught up in the vicissitudes of life, without anywhere to go or anyone to turn to. How devastating this can be in a world where humanity knows no compassion or forgiveness, and when God appears to leave you defenseless and alone in a merciless world.

There is an answer. It is called God's amazing grace—an outpouring of love that comes when you least expect it as well as an assurance that everything is all right because God has you in his ever loving care. In the words of songwriter John Newton, "Through many dangers, toils, and snares, I have already come; 'tis grace hath brought me safe thus far, and grace will lead me home." Very often we lean on our family and friends instead of putting our faith and trust in God, who will never forsake us or leave us.

The amazing thing about God's grace is that it is sufficient to meet all of our needs. Because of this, it passes all human understanding. How could God be so kind, so wonderful, and so marvelous to a humanity that often seeks its own destruction? Why does God often give us another opportunity at life? What is it that God demonstrates to us by this mercy that seems to always fill up our cup and never let it dry out?

The message is that we must love each other as God has loved us. When we are recipients of God's grace, we show gratefulness by extending that same grace to others. That is the test of Christianity. Can we forgive someone else as we have been forgiven? God's grace allows us to understand the magnitude of God's work in our lives and gives us a desire to leave what has placed us in bondage and to get closer to our deliverer. When all else goes awry, we can find peace in knowing that God's grace is sufficient for us!

Our Creator and our Teacher, help us to love each other as God has loved us. Amen.

Berlinda A. Love

July 18

Forgive Others 2-5-20

Jesus said to him, "Not seven times, but, I tell you, seventy-seven times."   Matthew 18:22

According to the traditions of the rabbis, the Jews of Jesus' day were expected to forgive others only three times. After the third offense, you would not be asked to pardon the offender. Three pardons were enough. Thus when Peter offered to forgive his enemies seven times, by the standards of the day he was being generous. Jesus, thank goodness, is even more generous. Does this mean that we should keep account of offenses and how many times we have forgiven someone, up to the seventy-seventh time? No. The number seven was special in Judaic culture, representing completion and perfection. Jesus' *seventy-seven* is not a mathematical equation, but a symbol of unlimited forgiveness. He tells us to forgive completely *every single* time—that forgiving our brother or sister completely should be an echo of the Lord's complete and perfect forgiveness of us. With complete forgiveness there is no keeping score, no keeping track, no keeping account.

In refusing to forgive our sister or brother, we erect walls around ourselves, walls designed to keep offenders out. In our hard-heartedness, we attempt to install a ceiling over our heads to keep God from softening our attitude toward those who have offended us. Do we realize that the walls we build to keep our brothers and sisters out also serve to keep us *in*? Unwillingness to forgive doesn't just punish the offenders, it punishes *us*, keeping us in a prison of our own design.

I'm reminded of a ~~congressman~~ Senator who was a POW in the Vietnam War. He spearheaded the efforts of our government to reestablish diplomatic relations with Vietnam, much to the anger and misunderstanding of some of his fellow Americans. Over and over they protested, "How can you? After what they did to you?" It was difficult to understand that he had forgiven the Vietnamese, truly forgiven, and that the reconciliation he was now experiencing freed him finally and totally. If he had not forgiven, he would have remained a prisoner.

Not being Jesus, all of us find complete forgiveness to be very difficult. ~~If I were to show you my personal offense ledger, it might demonstrate that though I say I've forgiven you, there is little I've forgotten.~~ With the Lord's help, though, ~~I~~ we can tear down the walls that separate ~~me~~ us from ~~my~~ our brothers and sisters. ~~I~~ we can let Jesus in through ~~my~~ our ceiling. ~~I will forget, and~~ ~~I~~ we can completely forgive—even seventy-seven times.

Redeemer and Deliverer, help me to forgive myself and others as many times as you forgive me. Amen.

Leah E. McCarter

July 19

Adding Cubits to Your Life

He said to his disciples, "Therefore I tell you, do not worry about your life, what you will eat, or about your body, what you will wear. For life is more than food, and the body more than clothing. Consider the ravens: they neither sow nor reap, they have neither storehouse nor barn, and yet God feeds them. Of how much more value are you than the birds! And can any of you by worrying add a single hour to your span of life? If then you are not able to do so small a thing as that, why do you worry about the rest?" Luke 12:22-26

In days gone by, there were tense feelings about whether the crops would fail or babies would survive. Now, in spite of all the conveniences of modern life, we nevertheless find ways to compound anxiety, to bring it into a booming business that requires stress management. Adrenaline, once so necessary in stimulating us to fight or to flee, now seems in a race to set rocks in neck muscles, twists in the lower back, and knots in the stomach.

We may need to evolve to a higher form of life to be truly free of the concerns of food, shelter, and daily life as the Scripture suggests; just considering the birds of the air or the lilies of the field can have a beneficial effect. When I've considered the city pigeons about all I can, I vicariously experience nature, notably through such poets as Mary Oliver. I read her walks in the woods and feel my own breathing slowing and becoming more restful. I discovered that Lamaze breathing was less relevant to childbirth than daily life where little cleansing breaths carry me along. To feel the peace that passes understanding, to nurture a life that is centered and calm, actually teaches your body how to cope when adversity hits. There is evidence that tranquility gets stored, saved for the next time a crisis arises, and that the body then uses this hidden reserve to blunt the severity of future anxiety attacks. You could say that tending emotional health is like money in the bank for one's physical resources.

If you really are set on adding that cubit to your life, however, a recent study showed that people who have two or more sources of emotional support tend to live longer. Just having someone to talk to, feeling there is a safety net, and being distracted from obsessing about the problem all prove helpful in times of crisis, says James House (*New York Times,* December 15, 1992). He also observes what those in ministry already know: "[Even] if there is nothing to be done, people, like other animals, are comforted by the mere presence of someone who is close to them."

God of joy and gladness, be present in my life in ways that help me breathe deep the beauty of this world. Comfort me with the peace that passes understanding, that what life I am given may be grounded and sure in your infinite love and mercy. Amen.

Abigail Hastings

An Overwhelming Feeling of Calm

*And hope does not disappoint us, because God's love
has been poured into our hearts through the Holy
Spirit that has been given to us.*   Romans 5:5

It happened the year I felt the props being knocked out from under me and my life falling apart. My best friend moved out of town. A month later the minister for whom I had worked for over twenty years died suddenly. Later that week I learned my youngest brother was facing probable brain surgery.

The morning of the scheduled tests and surgery, as I was driving to my work, I was filled with an overwhelming feeling of calm, of great joy, and a sure knowledge that everything would be all right.

I still feel that there was healing. There was no surgery, but tests led to a diagnosis of a rare brain disease for which, then and now, there is no known cure. My brother learned how to live with the disease. His patience, courage, and outgoing, loving spirit endeared him to all—family, friends, and nurses who cared for him.

The last fifteen months of his life he lived with me. Because of that morning nine years earlier, I carried with me the assurance of hope that I could do what was necessary and that if it was too much for me, help would come.

Heavenly Guide and Protector, deep thanks for the many times I have been sure of your presence in critical times. Help me to keep more constantly in prayer that I may share with others this assurance and answer your call. Amen.

Alice Cotabish

Envision a New Creation

*For I am about to create new heavens and a new
earth.*   *Isaiah 65:17a*

Apparently written in hope of restoration from the Exile, this
passage envisions God's new creation as a time of joy, health,
peace, and prosperity for all. Jerusalem will be a place of delight;
people will live to old age; the wolf will lie down with the lamb;
and all will have sufficient shelter and food, the fruits of their own
labor. "They shall not build and another inhabit; they shall not
plant and another eat" (Isaiah 65:22).

I find it necessary to return again and again to such visions in
the Bible. It reminds me of what I am living for—a new creation,
a new social order. Sometimes in our struggle against injustice, I
forget that protest is not the goal; transformation is the goal, the
end. It also reminds me that feminists and other justice activists
must find ways to hold together concerns of healing, social justice,
and ecological justice, with a new creation, a new order in which
all living beings participate.

One important way to hold on to a vision of a new creation as
we work on different activist agendas is to put ourselves in
conversation with and make ourselves accountable to those in
other struggles, particularly with those in this society who have
even less access to social power and privilege.

Just the other day, I received notice of a major conference on
religion and the environment with almost no attention given to
issues of racism, classism, sexism, and other forms of social oppression. Insofar as my understanding of that conference brochure was
accurate, it is a conference that denies in practice the biblical
vision of a new creation.

What is your vision of a new creation? How similar to or
different from Isaiah's is it? How do women and men of all colors,
how do lambs and wolves, fare in your vision? How is healing
related to social and ecological justice in your vision? How do
you hold yourself accountable to others working on different
agendas; how do you hold others accountable? What, if anything,
should you do to bring your own activism into the larger context
of a biblical vision of new creation?

God who stands with those who plant but do not eat, we open our hearts and minds to your vision of a new creation in which all people, wolves, and lambs will eat their fill and enjoy one another's presence. Amen.

Elly Haney

July 22

The Power of Touch

Children were brought to Jesus for him to place his hands on them. Matthew 20:13 (NIV)

Several months ago my cousin's child was born prematurely, weighing only two and one-half pounds. Since then, the child's parents have gone to visit the neonatal intensive care unit a half-dozen times daily to hold him, literally loving the baby into life through tender touching. We are all affirmed by each other's touch—from infant-parent bonding on through a mother's gentle stroking and a father's playful bouncing or in the friendly arm-in-arm stroll of childhood chums. In maturity it is the heartening handshake and pat on the back that encourage us. Life's hurts and hardships are often healed by a dear one's caress or a sweet lover's kiss.

When our own special touch is expressed through arts and crafts, composing or gardening, we not only experience who we really are inside, but we also reflect to others our participation in the touch of a bountiful Creator. These creative, beautiful, sometimes playful, often fruitful endeavors are the visible expression of our inward selves. They touch others in ways we can only imagine.

I will always remember a dying friend asking me with his sad eyes to bless his forehead with a much appreciated *Spirit* pin I had given him. The blessing of the church with the holy oils of initiation, strengthening, forgiveness, healing, and anointing are outward touches that symbolize inner acceptance, growth, comfort, and commitment. In the heart of our prayer, God touches our soul so intimately that we can never again doubt the divine presence at our center.

We all have our own stories to tell of these graced, sacramental touches. We give and we receive through touch. We know that touch can bring us closer to each other and to God. It is worth our time to examine our use of this gift of God and to remember that the touch of Jesus never did remove the proverbial mountain, but it did take away the stone in front of a tomb.

Creator God, whose touch brought forth the cosmos and my own small but loving self, teach me to appreciate and use this precious gift in ways that will bring all I touch closer to you. Amen.

Rose MacDermott

July 23

Enlightened Vision

My teacher, let me see again.   Mark 10:51b

"I've been living in my head too much," I thought as we rode along the interstate. "I've been so worried about my writing projects that I've missed seeing the summer wildflowers or savoring the cool wet pines. I feel like the blind man on the side of the road. I need Jesus to restore my sight, too."

At that moment, my husband, who was driving shouted, "Look!" and pointed to the rear window of the car.

Jolted from my meditation, I turned and gasped at the view framed by the back car window. San Francisco Mountain, twelve thousand feet high, thrust its sawtooth top into a gigantic vertical shaft of light: an enormous rainbow! The highest peak seemed to have punctured a cloud bursting with light which now poured in streams of yellow, orange, red, green, and purple down the mountain slopes. I was stunned!

The blind man was even more stunned; he saw Jesus. Jesus wants to stun us with the same sight: himself. That's why God breathes rainbows across skies and caresses mountaintops with dazzling light. To get our attention. To exercise our eye muscles. To focus us on the eternal. To pull us toward God's face. To see God, close up.

God of everlasting wisdom and vision, save us from too much thinking and not enough looking. Open our eyes. Jolt us with rainbows over our shoulders. Stun us again and again. Show us yourself. Amen.

Amanda Palmer

ʼReflection on Life

He called a child, whom he put among them, and said,
"Truly I tell you, unless you change and become like
children, you will never enter the kingdom of heaven.
Whoever becomes humble like this child is the greatest
in the kingdom of heaven. Whoever welcomes one such
child in my name welcomes me." Matthew 18:2-5

When I answered the phone, to my great joy and surprise, it
was my ten-year-old grandson Daniel calling long distance.

"I have to write an essay about someone in my family, but I
can't use my mom or dad, so can I use you?" I had never been
used in this way before, but I was touched by his ingenuous
request—and flattered. I assumed that a maternal grandmother
hadn't been specifically assigned, and that he did have a choice
between me and his other grandmother. Besides, it's not every day
you get to talk about yourself—especially to someone who shares
your love of chocolate and hangs on your every word.

Dan explained that his mother had already supplied some of
the family *stuff* about who was born where and to whom, but he
had more questions that only I could answer. (Actually, he said he
had to fill a whole page, and even if he wrote BIG, what *stuff* he
had wouldn't be enough.) "Okay, Grandma?"

"Fire away," I replied enthusiastically.

For the next two or three minutes, the telephone wires between
California and Iowa surged with names, ages, dates, places—all the
cold statistics that seemed somehow warmer when I was living
them. But there was so much more to tell, like my excitement at
hearing child prodigy Ruth Slenczynski play the piano in a concert
hall in St. Louis. But then Dan apologetically interrupted, "Sorry,
Grandma. That's all I need. Thanks. I love you. Bye." His page was
filled!

"I love you, too, Daniel," I hastily added just before the phone
clicked on the other end. I sat there, cradling the phone in my
hand, feeling a little like a pile of discarded Christmas wrappings
after all the presents have been opened—colorful, but used! We'd
come full circle!

Later, his mother sent me the essay. As it turned out, the last line was *stuff* his mother had supplied. With all due respect (I'm sure) Dan had closed with: "Grandma loves the beach and lying in the sand and drinking her five o'clock vodka tonic." His teacher liked it. "Very nice job, Daniel," was written in the corner with one of those happy-face stickers.

I hope I get as favorable a review when I've filled my page.

Heavenly Savior, in you mercy, help us to use you in everything we do, and open our hearts to ways we can use one another to glorify your kingdom. Amen.

Nina H. Pohl

July 25

Obeying Jesus

Very truly, I tell you, when you were younger, you used to fasten your own belt and to go wherever you wished. But when you grow old, you will stretch out your hands, and someone else will fasten a belt around you and take you where you do not wish to go.

John 21:18

My Lord, God, I have no idea where I am going. I do not see the road ahead of me. I cannot know for certain where it will end. Nor do I really know myself, and the fact that I think that I am following your will does not mean that I am actually doing so. But I believe that the desire to please you does in fact please you. And I hope I have that desire in all that I am doing. I hope that I will never do anything apart from that desire. And I know that if I do this, you will lead me by the right road though I may know nothing about it. Therefore, I will trust you always though I may seem to be most and in the shadow of death. I will not fear, for you are ever with me, and you will never leave me to face my perils alone.[3]

Thirteen years ago I was a member of the diaconate board in my church, and my pastor suggested that I take the training and become a hospice volunteer. Hospice is a centrally administered program of palliative and supportive services that provide physical, psychological, social, and spiritual care for dying persons and their families. Services are provided by a medically supervised interdisciplinary team of professionals and volunteers. Hospice affirms life. It exists to provide support and care for persons in the last phases of incurable disease so that they might live as fully and as comfortably as possible.

Hospice has enabled me to be a more caring person who listens not only with my ears but also with my heart. God is always at work in our lives, conforming us to the image of Christ, to help us become what he created us to be in relationship to himself for the sake of others. As we love God and become clothed with Christ, God enables us to be mutual agents of his abounding grace.

Help us, God of our salvation, to love you and to imitate Christ in taking the gospel to our confused, hurting world. Amen.

Betty Susi

July 26

God's Plan

You have kept count of my tossings; put my tears in your bottle. Are they not in your record?

Psalms 56:8

Picking myself up off the sidewalk (but not before I looked to see if anyone saw me make a three-point landing, glasses flying one way and me the other), the tears started to fall. "No, Lord, this can't be happening, not now anyway! It's not fair!" But it had happened. I knew my wrist was fractured. Somehow, I managed to get through the heavy double doors at my church and collapsed on the stairway leading to the fellowship hall. It wasn't long before a friend came along and retrieved my husband from the festivities of Christmas decorating. To the emergency room we went where we found out the bad news: both arms and my knee were fractured! I had to be admitted. But it was the Tuesday before Thanksgiving, and seventeen people were invited to our home for dinner. Even worse, my first children's book had just been published and the autograph party was Saturday! Between the pain of the fractures and the disappointment of not being at my book signing, the Lord had lots of tears to collect and put into his bottle that night and for many nights to follow! "What possible good can come of this?" I wondered.

The answer didn't come overnight, but come it did. Because of my unusual plight the local TV station came to do an interview. The word got around and *Benjy's New Home* began to sell, but that wasn't the best of it. Teachers heard about me and asked me to come and speak to their classes of all ages. Because of that one fall, God used me to tell my story and in the process tell his story of hope and love through Jesus. Yes, all things did work together for good!

Thank you so much, dear Jesus, that you can and will use the most difficult circumstances in our lives for your glory and good if we only let you! Thank you that you care about our tears so very much that you actually collect them! Amen.

Bonnie Scherer

July 27

New Ministry

I planted, Apollos watered; but God gave the growth.
1 Corinthians 3:6

I am seeing a seed sprout for ministry in the city. The youth want to serve supper at Peter's Retreat, a residence for men and women with AIDS. A mother and teenage daughter have volunteered for supper preparation at Center for Hope. Another mother wants to bring her nine-year-old with her to serve a meal.

It's the children, youth, and families that are giving us energy for this project. It is new energy, a new seed, sitting in the soil, eager to be watered and nurtured.

It didn't just happen. We spent the winter praying, planning, researching. Last year the teenagers and their advisers spent a week serving lunch in a soup kitchen. They came back changed; the children at the center had touched them. They told us the story one morning in worship about children who came to the Kids' Cafe at night for supper. About kids eager for a glass of milk. We saw the tears of our teenagers. And now we see once again their quiet and firm commitment to make a difference.

What is the seed growing in you? What is the seed sprouting

in your congregation? Take a magnifying glass. Look closely. Be aware of that seed. Water it. Nurture it. And give God thanks for the growth.

Life-giving God, we thank you for new life springing up within us and around us. Open our eyes to see it. Open our hearts to nurture it. In the spirit of the resurrection and new life in Christ we pray. Amen.

Julie Fewster

July 28

God's Gift of Healing

To another faith by the same Spirit, to another gifts of healing by the one Spirit.   1 Corinthians 12:9

Standing on a sidewalk in a quiet town on a beautiful day, I was unexpectedly hit by a speeding out-of-control car, thrown into a plate glass window, and knocked unconscious with a fractured skull and serious injuries to my head, neck, and back. When I finally tried to open my eyes, I realized a stranger was kneeling beside me in the shattered glass on the sidewalk and was talking to me. "You're going to be okay, but I want you to lie very still and to stay awake for me. Can you promise to do that?" Although I had one overwhelming desire to close my eyes and go to sleep to escape the terrible pain in my body, I knew it was important to make every effort to do whatever this kind woman told me.

She waited for an ambulance with me and rode to the emergency room of the hospital. This loving stranger stayed by my side telling me I would be okay and encouraging me to stay awake a little longer. Through her strength and caring, never leaving my side, this guardian angel spun a healing and protective cocoon around me blocking out much of the trauma and fear that an accident victim experiences. Doctors have since told me that she likely kept me from slipping into a dangerous and deep coma, and she may have saved my life. So I am alive today to tell this story.

I am very grateful for this courageous woman. She could have chosen—as most people would have—not to get involved with a stranger who had been hit by a car and was lying in the street bleeding and unconscious. But she chose to kneel in the shattered glass spread around me like a carpet on the sidewalk and to reach out with healing love to help that stranger survive.

Lord of glory and of life, thank you for the many wonderful gifts you give to us each day. Help us to know how to use these gifts so we can best serve you and our brothers and sisters throughout the world. Amen.

Joy Carol

July 29

The Healing

Very truly, I tell you, the one who believes in me will also do the works that I do and, in fact, will do greater works than these. John 14:12a

In the movie *The Cure,* an awkward teenage boy, Eric, be-friends his eleven-year-old neighbor, Dexter, a kid rejected by everybody else because he has AIDS. Their friendship turns into a sometimes outrageous adventure, including an attempt to float more than a thousand miles down the Mississippi River in search of a Louisiana doctor reputed to have found an AIDS cure in the swamps near the river's end.

At first Eric is as wary as the others of this boy with AIDS, but he becomes Dex's passionate advocate, determined to discover a way to stop this illness. They hope for a cure when they brew teas made of every leaf they can find, all carefully documented in their notebook-paper research journal. They decide that since healthy food hasn't helped, the opposite may be the answer, and both gorge themselves bilious on candy bars. All of it, however, fails. In the midst of one of their devilish pranks on hospital personnel, Dex dies.

As Dex's strong, single-parent mother drives Eric home from the hospital, she starts wailing her grief and pulls the car to the curb. Eric throws his arms around her and, in his own tears, cries, "I just wanted to cure him. But I didn't." The mother's face suddenly shines. "Oh, but you did, Eric. You did! For the months you were his friend, you made it go away!"

Few of us fully believe Christ's prediction that we too will do miraculous works like his, such as healing. But just as Eric did, every one of us has, at the very least, that healing power for others—the power to make illness, depression, injury, and even the nearness of death go away, even if for just a few minutes. By living fully, our jokes, our stories, our adventures, and our very presence grab hold of life for others—and for ourselves.

My God, help me feel and live out the fullness of life in all situations, so that I can offer and use that power to counter the pain of illness and the fear of death, whether it's for myself or for others. Amen.

Beth Resler Walters

July 30

Memories

I consider that the sufferings of this present time are not worth comparing with the glory about to be revealed to us. . . . We know that all things work together for good to those who love God, who are called according to his purpose.   Romans 8:18, 28

My grandmother is eighty-five years old. We are very close because I lived with her after my parents divorced when I was a sophomore in high school, the same age my own daughter is now. My grandma was widowed in her early sixties, but she had a job as a cook at our small local hospital. She would rise very early and go to work and be home just before I would get to the house after school. She did not have much money and still does not, but I never seemed to notice because she made sure I had those things I needed. Grandma has always been there for me, and now, even though it is a real struggle, I am trying my best to be there for her. She married a wonderful Christian man the same year I got married. Now, almost twenty years later, he is in a nursing home, and she spends part of each day with him.

This past fall she began calling me to ask what day it is. I knew that was not a good sign. Her short-term memory is very poor now, not even a year later. She doesn't know that she doesn't know and thinks she can do the things she always has; only she doesn't and she can't. My heart bleeds for the situation and the thought of losing her. It is as much a concern for me as it is for her. I do know though that our Lord watches and cares for her and that I get to be a part of this process. Realizing that God has good things in store for her, I can more easily endure this process. God knows us both better than we do ourselves, and I am confident of this promise in Romans 8:28.

Thank you, Lord, for your mercy and love not only in the good times but especially in the hard times. Amen.

Melanie Cooper

July 31

Building Trust

For surely I know the plans I have for you, says the LORD, plans for your welfare and not for harm, to give you a future with hope.   *Jeremiah 29:11*

Every time I find myself in situations that are uncomfortable or unfavorable toward me, I remember this Scripture. But still I find myself time and time again doubting *something*—my gifts, my talents, my skills, my understanding. Because of all the times that God, like a mother, has been there to see me through, I find it difficult to admit that it is actually God that I doubt. *Is it okay to doubt God? That is my issue.*

If my goal is spiritual wholeness, then doubting may be part of the process. Especially when I admit to myself that I am not in charge of anything, God is. My life has been bought with a price, and I should glorify God in my body, which includes my mind.

Trusting God did not come easy for me. Although I was *brought up* in the church, God was like Santa Claus. Communication was expected only when you wanted or needed something. It was only in adulthood that I learned about a personal relationship with God. God is really interested in my future. Therefore the Almighty wants to be involved and included in my present and in my past.

God promised never to leave me or forsake me. Even my loving parents can't make this promise. The more I tried God and studied the Word, the easier it became for me to trust and obey.

Do I still sometimes have doubts? *Yes!* But now I know that it isn't God that I doubt, but my ability to follow the leading of the Spirit.

God, my spiritual parent, even when I have doubts, thank you for being eternally faithful and present. Like a parent, point the way that I might follow your Spirit. Amen.

Mary B. Lovett

August

Jesus Touched Me

One man was there who had been ill for thirty-eight years. When Jesus saw him lying there and knew that he had been there a long time, he said to him, "Do you want to be made well?"　　　　　*John 5:5-6*

The man was lying by the Bethesda pool, waiting to be the first to enter the pool after the stirring of the water by an angel of the Lord. It was believed that whoever stepped in first, after the stirring of the water, would be made well. The man complained to Jesus that no one would carry him into the pool, that others would enter before he could lower himself in to be healed. With that, Jesus told the disabled man to "stand up, take your mat and walk" (John 5:8). Without knowing who Jesus was, he obeyed him. The man was not healed because he had a long-standing faith in Jesus. The man had never met Jesus before that day. The man did not go into the pool. Jesus bypassed the miraculous healing powers of the stirred waters and instead used his words to heal.

When I'm traveling for business, at the end of a long day of meetings, I sometimes indulge myself with the pleasure of sitting in the hotel whirlpool or hot tub. In the therapeutic hot pool of stirring waters, my weariness seems to disappear. After soaking in the tub, I feel renewed and energized.

What is it about water that is stirred up that heals? Was the pool at Bethesda really stirred by an angel? We've all heard of healing ourselves with the power of positive thinking. Jesus healed those who had faith as well as those who didn't know who he was, like the man at the pool. There are some who claim to be healed by faith healers.

If you were sick in mind, body, or spirit and were asked, "Do you want to be made well?" wouldn't you respond with a resounding yes? Where do we find the source of power for healing—in stirred waters, in our minds, in the words of Jesus? Should we go to Hot Springs, Arkansas, where perhaps angels stir the waters, or can we seek the power to heal within ourselves through meditation and prayer? Can it be by embracing Jesus' words and doing what Jesus tells us to do? Not only to "take your mat and walk," but to live out the words of his commandment, "You shall love your neighbor as yourself" (Matthew 22:39).

Great Physician, watch over us who sometimes lack faith in ourselves, who stay stuck on our own mats of self-pity. Make us open to hearing Christ's words. Move us off our mats and out where you need us to be. Amen.

Elizabeth Okayama

August 2

Joy through the Pain

You will have pain, but your pain will turn into joy.
John 16:20b

Wholeness is not always a matter of healing. Sometimes it means finding a higher quality of life that embraces physical and emotional conditions, which will get worse or improve only slowly. Friendship and laughter can be key ingredients in being whole.

I met Jane and Margaret at Mary Elizabeth Inn, a women's residence. Jane is an artist recovering from a brain aneurysm that left her in a coma. Against great odds, she has overcome more than all her doctors and therapists said was possible. She says it is because she surrendered her life to God in those awful unconscious moments when her life hung in the balance ten or so years ago. Jane's aneurysm occurred after a hiking accident in Alaska when her foot slipped and she plunged down a cliff.

Margaret was already her best friend. When Jane's husband divorced her and her children turned away because of the personality changes brought on by the aneurysm, Margaret remained Jane's friend.

Years later they independently arrived in San Francisco. By this time, Margaret suffered from a deteriorating lung condition, carried an oxygen tank, and rode in her motorized wheelchair wherever she went. Margaret held Jane's power of attorney in financial matters, and they took great delight in going to the social services department and waiting for an unsuspecting worker to assume that Margaret instead of Jane was the client. Margaret died quite suddenly, but her courage and positive outlook continue to inspire Jane and others who are on healing journeys.

Thank you, eternal Source of peace, for the choices that shape my life. Help me to improve the quality of my life through laughter and prayer, by letting friends know I care, and by nurturing relationships that are inspiring and healing. Amen.

Kae Lewis

August 3

Shining Gold

There was a ladder set up on the earth, the top of it reaching to heaven; and the angels of God were ascending and descending on it.   Genesis 28:12b

It was a dingy, out-of-the way airport in the middle of the night, and I sat there feeling dowdy, accompanied by two young children and a husband, waiting for a plane that wouldn't come till morning. As I wandered through the terminal, suddenly down the stairs from another gate came an amazing sight: a bevy of brilliantly dressed young women. Their floor-length dresses had diamond-encrusted gores on their trains, and their faces glittered with diamond dust. Exotic feathered hats perched on their heads. They tripped down the steps and into the terminal chattering vivaciously (and rather empty-headedly, I thought). Later they returned to the plane, enjoying their excursion but self-contained.

Off to the side stood their chaperon, an older woman, her face full of wrinkles and wisdom. Somehow I mustered the courage to approach her—and later I rushed back to my husband: "She spoke to me; she likes me; she's going to talk to me again."

Soon after, I woke up, and for days delight would wash over me at the memory of those young women—empty and silly, but absolutely gorgeous! And I would feel again the old woman's welcome.

Then one day, I recognized what I had seen: the ladder and the angels. And God who had talked with me in that place.

Wise Woman God, come to us in our wildernesses. Grant us

those visions of delight that nourish us. Show us the beauty and the worth we cannot see in ourselves. Show us your face. Amen.
Katherine Griffis

August 4

I Will Heal

I will restore health to you, and your wounds I will heal, says the LORD.   Jeremiah 30:17a

What did you call them when you were a child? Those hurts, those *owies*, those *boo-boos* that were a part of tripping over tree stumps, falling on gravel, slipping on ice. They were part of childhood, as was their healing.

What was necessary to heal those *boo-boos*? With loud sobs and wet tears I would look for my mother, letting her know how badly I needed her, admitting my pain. My child self knew that I needed my mommy's hug and magic kiss with the words, "There now, that will make it all better."

My mother, however, was convinced of the need for cleaning with lots of soap, hot water, and Merthiolate, that stinging, bright orange badge of honor that elicited as many tears as the original *owie*. A Band-Aid to keep things covered was a further badge of honor. With time, most of the scars went away, although some especially deep ones remain to this day.

As an adult I still get them: wounds, pains, ouches. Living and aging and caring open me up to all sorts of hurts, physical and emotional.

I have discovered God's healing in my life as adult wounds heal. I still cry, letting God and others know that I need their attention. I still need a hug. Sometimes I need the harsh reality of an antiseptic—some way to combat poison and infection. When wounds sit unheeded, untended, they cannot begin to heal.

Most of all it takes the healing magic of time. Time is the great healer, cliché though that may be. The deepest, most jagged, most painful wound in my life has healed after eight years. Yes, it has left a scar. Sometimes, touched in a certain way, there is still a tender feeling, pain that remains.

Knowing that caring friends, reflective counseling, and time can cure the pains to come helps me feel healthy today. It is health based on confidence in a God who cares about our restored health and healed wounds. And it is in that confidence that I can accompany others through their need for healing.

Kiss it and make it better, O God of healing. As we bring our hurts and the world's wounds to you, hold us tenderly in the palms of your loving hands. We ask, assured that you want us all to be whole. Amen.

Carol Q. Cosby

The Lord's Day

This is the day that the LORD has made; let us rejoice and be glad in it.　　　　　　*Psalms 118:24*

Hear these words from the psalmist. Say the verse aloud. What do you hear? What do you feel? A day does not go by that I do not find myself saying aloud or hearing the words of this Scripture in my mind. The verse has become an important part of my life, providing comfort and reassurance in my daily activities.

I discovered the verse as a call to worship during the Sunday morning liturgy. The words have been said many times without much meaning. Then one day I heard the words speaking to me. It was during a time of crisis, and I was struggling. The words of the psalmist called me to see God in the midst of the crisis. I was not alone. The day presented new opportunities. I celebrated the creative choices of that day. Embracing that day and the days that followed gave me the strength to face the daily challenges of life knowing God's presence and gift of daily creation.

Today, I say the verse and am reminded of the partnership of life available to each of us. I see the network of life unfold before me and hear the invitation to participate in the infinite nature of creation.

Giver of every good and perfect gift, thanks for the eyes to read the psalmist's words, the voice to speak the words, the ears to hear words, and the opportunity to experience healing and to celebrate each day. Amen.

Patricia A. Smith

August 6

The Only Constant Is Change

For everything there is a season, and a time for every matter under heaven: . . . a time to weep, and a time to laugh. Ecclesiastes 3:1, 4a

Changes, big changes, have been the most significant factor in my life in the past two years. I have lost my father, changed careers, and have seen many of my friends and neighbors move from my neighborhood. And now, our only son is leaving home for college five hundred miles away. All are expected occurrences in the life of a fifty-year-old female in our times, but they feel monumental when they are happening to me personally.

With all of this change comes a sense of loss and feelings of anxiety. I have tried to experience the grief that comes with closure and departures, even when it has meant facing deep pain. Yet at the same time I have recognized that the pain makes a positive statement about the good that went before. The good in friends, the good in rich vocational calling for twenty-five years, the richness of the family relationships.

During this process of change I have also found a sense of excitement in the new aspects of life: a wonderful new career, new colleagues at work, new grassroots communities to meet, new friends who appear on a regular basis.

Anchors have been crucial to me as I have sometimes felt like "a motherless child" in wandering through the maze of shaping a new life. Because I no longer have to commute two hours a day to work, I now have time for daily morning meditation. I am now into my third year of reading Anne Wilson Schaef's *Meditations for Women Who Do Too Much*, along with theologians and daily Bible readings. I walk to work, so I benefit from the new hour of exercise and breathing fresh air every day. I also continue my regular experience of community gardening. Getting my hands into the soil at least three times a week is crucial to literally grounding myself in reality, which is essential to my total health.

This has been a priority for me for the past fifteen years. A garden provides many of the ingredients for maximum physical, mental, and spiritual survival. I never leave the garden without feeling better than when I entered it. It gives me a sense of my creatureliness as I work with plants and experience the animals as companions. Whether I work alone or with other adults and children who share the wonder, I know that the garden is there for me as one of the gifts of being fully human.

Yes, change is one of the few "constants" in life. I have learned that change is manageable if one faces it with assurance that the basic values and some fundamental disciplines remain as anchors.

God of change and infinite stability, guide and comfort us as we face big changes in our lives. Grant us the wisdom to know when and how to make changes when necessary. Amen.

Ellen Kirby

August 7

Hope in Christ

Only faith can guarantee the blessings that we hope for, or prove the existence of the realities that at present remain unseen.
Hebrews 11:1 (The Jerusalem Bible)

The holiday season is one of our happiest times. We give thanks for our blessings and await the arrival, anew, of the Christ Child. For children, days move slowly as they await their season of gifts.

I discovered two masses in my breast just before that joyous season. I looked in the mirror, and there it was—a dimple. I had read that a dimple on the breast is a warning sign for cancer. I knew I could dissolve into tears or meet the enemy head-on. I chose the latter.

I kept my secret until after the new year so that joy would abound for my children and grandchildren. Following a mammogram and a positive biopsy, a series of tests produced evidence of metastatic cancer. It was everywhere, including the liver—or so some radiologists said. I was given seven months to live.

I knew that if I called on God, my cry would not fall on deaf ears. My parents introduced my sisters and me to Jesus Christ when I was a child. And God's presence has been clear to me from the days I lay in the shade in my mother's garden and carefully examined the blades of grass and the tiny creatures crawling on them—no two alike. Overhead, clouds each had a different shape. No one but God could have created such beauty and variety. As the years passed, I learned to call on God at every turn in my life. Now, in this crisis, I called on God, certain that I would be heard.

Prior to surgery, I lay in bed one night and the strangest thing happened. A warmth seemed to engulf my whole body—from my toes to my head. I *knew* it was the hand of God.

I had a modified mastectomy the day after Easter and endured six aggressive treatments of chemotherapy. Tests performed afterward revealed no evidence of cancer anywhere. Two years have passed. I am cancer free. I thank God for Jesus by whose stripes I was healed.

Thank you, God, for healing. Thank you for the privilege of busily serving my Master because I "ain't got time to die." Amen.

Juanita Locker Ivie

August 8

Take Nothing for the Journey?

He ordered them to take nothing for their journey.
Mark 6:8

How peculiar: take nothing for the journey. It's politically correct, maybe—simplifying one's lifestyle and all that. But my work requires me to travel constantly. Even if I could imagine getting along without clothes and makeup, surely no one expects me to leave behind the tools of my trade: books, papers, packets, videos. It's obvious Jesus was talking to men—they're not the ones who have to worry about being sure there's enough food, and whether there's going to be a laundromat en route. Imagine a young mother, loaded down with bottles and diapers and toys and teething rings and strollers and all the other necessary paraphernalia of infancy, being told to "take nothing for the journey!"

Of course I know it is meant as symbol and metaphor; that it is about becoming unencumbered, about being focused on what's really important. But still . . .

Recently, I heard that line in a new way, a way Jesus may not have intended, but that's the beauty of words of wisdom—they take on new meanings in new times. I heard "take nothing for the journey" in the same sense that one might say, "I wouldn't take anything for that experience." This journey is so valuable, so rich, so full of possibilities, that I will take nothing for it. I won't sell it or trade it or even invest it for later. This amazing journey has been freely given to me; the only possible response is to live it to the fullest. And perhaps it is not only the big journey, my life, that can be viewed this way. Could I possibly see all the smaller journeys—to Atlanta to do a workshop, to San Francisco to consult with a community project, to Oklahoma City for a board meeting—as gifts too precious to squander, rather than obligations to fulfill?

God of all my journeys, help me to travel light. But even more, help me to remember to savor the trip, and to go with thankfulness. I will take nothing for the journey! Amen.

Peggy Halsey

August 9

More like Jesus

When did we see you hungry, a stranger, naked, lonely, homeless?　　　　　　　based on Matthew 25:37-39

"There is a woman at the door," said a volunteer at our cold weather shelter. "She looks scared." As I walked toward the door, I could see her standing on the porch—wet, scared, and forlorn. I welcomed her, invited her into our shelter, and began the process of making her as comfortable as possible under the circumstances. She refused the food, accepted a cup of tea, and I found her a place to sit.

There were about thirteen people there that night. All but Maria (that's what she said her name was) were single, homeless men.

I could tell she was not *homeless* and was very uncomfortable in our little bungalow shelter. But she had no place else to go. As the volunteers and I proceeded to settle everyone down for the night, I was able to spend some time with Maria and hear her story.

She had come to the city from another part of the state. She had been staying with her aunt, but she could not stay there any longer because of rental restrictions. She was three months pregnant. The father of this baby was demanding that she have an abortion. She said that she would not do that. She could not go back *home* because she already had a five-year-old that she could not take care of. What could she do now?

We made her as comfortable as possible. She finally accepted the offer of a sandwich and another cup of tea. We found her a blanket for the night and arranged floor space with myself and another female volunteer.

When morning came, I gave her my business card and asked her to call me at the office where I knew that I had resources available that would be helpful to her. She accepted the card, but said she wanted to go to where her aunt lived. After she had some breakfast, a volunteer walked her to the bus stop to make sure she got on the right bus.

Sometimes in the *shelter business* you wonder if one night, even if it's in out of the rain, is really worth the effort. Do the brief moments we have with some of these hurting, desperate people really make a difference?

There she was, standing in the dark night at our open door—cold, wet, tired, scared, and pregnant. Sound familiar? It should. I believe that we made a difference that night in Maria's life. We invited her in and offered her what we had. No conditions, no judgments. Our lights were on and we were there!

"I tell you, whenever you did it for one of the least important of my children, you did it for me!" (See Matthew 25:45.)

O God, help us to be there with the door open and the lights on. Help us to be loving, caring, compassionate, nonjudgmental to all who need to come in out of their darkness. Amen.

Shirley Ferrill

Trusting in God

*I hereby command you: Be strong and courageous; do
not be frightened or dismayed, for the LORD your God
is with you wherever you go.*   Joshua 1:9

When I first memorized those words, I didn't think I would be
holed up alone in a doctor's office waiting, with my heart in my
mouth, for a computer to spit out the course of treatment that I
would be following for the next year to try to eradicate a colon
cancer that had already spread throughout my lymph system
leaving me with a 15 percent chance to live. All the surgery that
could be done had been done, and now it was up to a computer
that was located hundreds of miles away to make a random
selection. Whatever happened to personalized medicine?

At that very second, I realized that even though the computer
was in charge of me for the moment, that computer was ultimately
run by a power much higher than it. I closed my eyes and prayed,
"Lord, let my random selection be a number three." Number one
was no treatment, and number two was oral chemotherapy only.
Because I am a registered nurse, I knew my best shot at life was
number three, both oral and intravenous chemotherapy.

When the doctor returned to give me the results of the random
selection he said, "I don't understand this. I programmed you
yesterday and you were a number one—no treatment. The clinic
just called to tell me the computer had made an error. You are
suppose to be a number three. The computer has never made a
mistake before; this is really strange. I just don't understand this!"
I said, "This is neither strange nor is it a mistake. It's called prayer
power, pure and simple!" This incident was my own personal
miracle. God was with me, giving me strength and courage and
taking away the terror in my heart. He was still in charge, modern
equipment or not. He runs the universe and he does not disappoint!

*Rock of our lives, you have commanded us not to be afraid.
Thank you for being so close to us. Feeling your presence, we do
not need to fear what this world can do to us. Amen.*

                                        Bonnie Scherer

Women Disciples

*But all his acquaintances, including the women who
had followed him from Galilee, stood at a distance,
watching these things.* Luke 23:49

The women disciples of Jesus must have been an amazing
group. They were in the crowds that gathered on Galilean hillsides
to listen and learn at the feet of Jesus. They found time—amid
days filled with gardening, gathering, grinding, washing, cleaning, cooking, baking, spinning, weaving, sewing, bearing, and
caring for children—to nurture their spirits.

Some of them even dared to leave the safety and security of
home to follow Jesus to Jerusalem. The Gospel writers neglected
to record their names. Probably their multiple duties as food
gatherers and preparers continued amid all the uncertainties of
first-century travel. Did they carry pots and pans and dishes on
their backs as they walked those long miles? It must have been
quite a camping trip!

We, whose lives are complicated by so many things, can hardly
imagine how days must have unfolded for these women. (Those
who are homeless today, more than their middle-class sisters,
might understand.) I like to think that, in spite of all their difficult
responsibilities, they had one priority above all others: learning
from Jesus and seeking to live by what they heard and observed.
(That's what *disciple* means.)

Frightening events in Jerusalem brought a vicious denial of the
way of wholeness and health that Jesus' love had demonstrated.
When their leader was nailed to a cross, Luke tells us, the disciples
"stood at a distance and watched." But a few of the women drew
near. They were the last friends at the cross and the first friends
at the empty tomb. Their witness to the Resurrection made them
the first evangelists among the disciples. We have an amazing
heritage from these spiritual ancestors!

*Amazing God of ages past, present, and future, keep us from
being distracted by all our things from the opportunity to follow
Jesus into fullness of life. Amen.*

Lavon Bayler

Living in Victory

I praise you, for I am fearfully and wonderfully made.
Psalm 139:14

As a young woman, I was afflicted with a frequently fatal disease. My despair after diagnosis was dominated by grief and death. What seemed most real to me, as I lay in my hospital bed, was death. I was most aware of my sick, unlovely body. I felt guilty for being so ill and being a burden on my husband. I railed at God: *Why? Why?*

After a terrible night of grief and tears, a good friend walked into my hospital room. He was a fellow Christian who, the day before, had learned of my illness. He prayed with me that morning, and a wonderful encounter occurred. *I let go of death*! I felt my life flow into the life of God! Everywhere was life. I felt as though I was floating above my diseased body, alive and well. The words came to me: "It is okay to be who you are." I knew that I was alive in the life of God, whether I lived or I died. The freedom of this hour became the long process of a miraculous healing.

Am I fearfully and wonderfully made? *Yes*! Because of the great love of Jesus I can declare joyfully with Paul: "I can do all things through him who strengthens" me (Philippians 4:13). Jesus told a leper he healed, "Your faith has made you well" (Luke 17:19). We are healed either in this life or in death: "Death will be swallowed up in victory"(1 Corinthians 15:54).

Is my body imperfect? Yes! Aftereffects of illness tell me that! With limitations, am I okay? Yes! Can I live and love the way I am? Yes! Can I serve the Lord the way I am? Yes, yes, yes! Each day of my life is a gift from God that I share with others.

God of steadfastness and encouragement, thank you for loving me. Thank you for life! Amen.

Rebecca J. Dobson

Sunflower

*Very truly, I tell you, you will weep and mourn, but the
world will rejoice; you will have pain, but your pain
will turn into joy.* John 16:20

Sunflowers and their cousins are abloom everywhere this time
of year. They grow near the treeline in high mountain meadows
and in the hot and humid fields a few feet above sea level. Each
one seeks the sunlight as it moves across the summer sky.

Sunflowers are in vogue again. Not only are they the focal point
of expensive paintings, they also cover shirts, napkins, and bright
dresses. They hang in artificial array in craft shops and in homes
where they bring some cheer to chaotic lives.

Sunflowers are bright yellow and cheery around the outside
and dark in the middle. I understand. I too have been encouraged
to put on a happy face and keep the dark stuff private. It has taken
a long while to comprehend that the dark too has great value. We
are both yin and yang. Our sunny petals fall away, but seeds of
new life come from the dark interior. Creativity and new possibility are waiting to take root when we accept the pregnant
possibilities in the seeds as potential given to us.

The sunflower, Good Friday dark and Easter bright, is so
grace-full!

*Grace-filled Creator, help me to accept who I am, to acknow-
ledge my gifts, to learn from my mistakes. May I learn to cherish
the valleys as much as the mountaintop experiences. Amen.*

Belva Trask Duncan

Sisters

*But, by far, the best gift I ever got [from my sister] was
an original framed needlepoint. . . . In just a few words
it summed up the eternal essence of our relationship. It
simply said, "A sister is a forever friend."*[1]

My brother-in-law was admitted to the hospital for a planned routine operation. It turned out to be anything but routine. One complication after another developed—a corrective second operation, an abscess, an open-wound method of healing the incision, a severe case of dehydration, and, what became most serious, a fever, indicating infection. He remained in the hospital for twenty-seven days becoming thinner, weaker, pale, and diminished. He endured unending medical tests, hourly probing and tubes everywhere. My sister stayed at his side through it all. She has never been inclined toward nursing, but with a little effort learned how to care for him and change the bandage. She talked with the doctors and nurses in a calm voice and asked intelligent questions.

As the days went by, there was growing concern for his recovery. We could hear the fear in my sister's voice. There was nothing we could do. The doctors seemed to be taking proper steps. The nurses took good care of him day and night. On our many family phone conversations, we said to each other, "Patience. We must have patience with the doctors, with his body to heal itself, with ourselves to wait for positive reports."

By day seventeen, I had traveled four hundred miles to be with my sister. Another sister took time off from work. The two of us sat with her in silence at the hospital, chatted with her at mealtimes, reviewed the day's progress with her late at night, listened to reports by the doctors and nurses, and talked cheerfully to our brother-in-law when he was awake. Once he asked me from his bed, "Why? Why is this happening to me?" I could only answer, "There is no answer to why."

Sometimes the three of us would be silly, telling family stories and laughing. It was good to laugh. Once we had a picnic lunch on the hospital lawn next to the high-rise garage. Each morning at their home we would gather on the king-size bed waiting until 7:00 A.M. when the first phone call was made for the updated report from the night nurses.

Many times my sister would say, "I didn't know how much I needed my sisters to be with me." We didn't ask many questions or tell her what to do. We just sat with her. We gave little advice on how to cope with her utter frustration with the doctors. There was no talk about our fear for her husband's life. Being sisters, we knew there was nothing else to do but be at her side.

Healing Spirit, you are always a surprise to me. When I look for the hope you bring in one place, I discover it in another. You have reminded me that comfort of the soul is a wonderful gift we have to offer to those who care for the sick. Thank you for the mysterious healing power of the ministry of presence. Amen.

Gini King

August 15

Hope in God

Why art you cast down, O my soul, and why are you disquieted within me? Hope in God; for I shall again praise him, my help and my God. Psalm 43:5

Society tends to view depression as an illness, a form of mental instability. I prefer to see it as a barometer of the condition of our souls, like optimism, exhaustion, spiritual discipline, or physical fitness.

Having experienced an extended depression after my first child was born, I now have some strongly held convictions about what depression is, what it isn't, how it should be viewed, and what it tells us about ourselves.

From my vantage point on the side of recovery, I learned that depression isn't a personality defect, a sign of weakness, or a result of a sinful life. It isn't something to be ashamed of or embarrassed by. It is, in my opinion, a product of imbalance—profound sadness that comes from your life being out of balance in any number of ways. In some cases, the imbalance comes from chemicals or hormones either lacking or overflowing. In others, it's from life circumstances that don't fit who we are or who we want to be. In cases like mine, it's an intricate weaving of many factors—chemistry, circumstances, and personal history not yet healed.

My own imbalance was corrected by a combination of medication, psychotherapy, and making changes in my life to reflect the values that were most important to me. For many of us, recovering from debilitating depression can be not only a liberating experience at a particular point in our lives but also a yardstick by which we can measure the rest of our journeys. Now I can experience joy, contentment, and wholeness in life in ways I never understood before. I can recognize bliss when I experience it because it so outshines the despair I once felt. I don't think I'll ever again wait so long to get the help I need to move beyond depression.

I believe that God stands with us through the despair and rejoices as we use whatever means are necessary to help us return to a higher plane.

Gracious Giver of knowledge, thank you that there are so many tools I can use to regain the balance I need to live life as you intend. May I have the wisdom to know when I need help and the courage to seek it. Amen.

Kristy Arnesen Pullen

August 16

Faith in Tight Places

You who live in the shelter of the Most High,
who abide in the shadow of the Almighty.
I will say to the LORD, my refuge and my fortress;
my God, in whom I trust.   Psalms 91:1

You have cancer. I was to hear those words three times in the space of three months. Each time the blow seemed to strike harder than the time before. The last time was breast cancer. I felt totally helpless and unable to cope at times, but when things became really difficult and it seemed as if there were nowhere to turn, God would intercede and give me the peace of the Holy Spirit.

This year the words were somewhat different, but they were even more devastating. *You have a brain tumor. You must have an MRI at once!* Fear, tears, brokenness, and an unmeasurable grief seemed likely to overwhelm me. Since I am claustrophobic, the thought of that tiny tube around my head was almost unbearable. On the morning of the test, I went into the test room, got prepared, and tried not to be afraid. As they were moving me into the tube, my heart cried out, "Jesus, come with me." Do you know what I discovered? Jesus fit into that tiny tube right beside me. He drove out the fear and brought blessed peace.

What will happen with the tumor? Only our God knows at this point, but one thing I do know is that Jesus Christ will go with me wherever it leads and that he will give me peace in the dark night of the soul. Ultimately, he will bring the sunlight once again.

Almighty God, who comes with me even in tight places, I do not know what the day will bring, nor any of my tomorrows. What I do know is that you will hold me close and stay with me through it all. Amen.

Frances Breton

August 17

God's Child

Blessed are the merciful, for they will receive mercy.
Matthew 5:7

Many people think of nursing homes, or long-term care facilities, as places where people go to die, not to live. This is far from the truth in the facility where I work. Residents are given the opportunity to live the quality of life that they choose and are encouraged to be as active as possible. I think of Gail who came as a six-month-old infant. She was born in a day and age when parents were encouraged to place infants with disabling conditions in institutions. Although physically disabled, she was bright and cheerful, and she made many friends. She had many *mothers* among the staff and thrived under their attention. She actually became more adjusted and well-rounded than many children with disabling conditions who grew up at home and were spoiled. She graduated from high school and business school, and at one time even went to live in the community with supportive services. However, she was lonely and missed her community—her family—so she came back. She was a lady who took charge of her life and in the end, I suppose, her death. She lived a full and active life for forty-five years and had made an impact on so many people that there were between three to four hundred people at her memorial service. People came from her community and from the greater community. She was born with a disabling condition and survived many operations, including the amputation of both legs while she was still very young. Having been abandoned by most of her biological family, she had lived in an institution all of her life, and she was remembered by hundreds. She was not a saint. She did not show compassion and love to all, and she had a temper. But she always forgave everyone.

God, you created us in your image and you surround us with familial love, as you did Moses. We are reminded that you are sufficient for all our needs. Our wholeness is not determined by the number of limbs we have as much as by how we live our lives. Thank you for the models that you provide for us. Amen.

Jacqueline Sullivan

August 18

Lord Help Me!

Then Jesus answered her, "Woman, great is your faith! Let it be done for you as you wish." And her daughter was healed instantly.   *Matthew 15:28*

Jesus had just finished preaching when he departed into the coasts of Tyre and Sidon. He was confronted by an unnamed Canaanite woman begging for mercy. The woman had a daughter who needed help, but the woman did not say, Help my daughter, she said, *"Lord, help me"* (Matthew 15:25).

The woman had come up against the realization that some situations are too big for humans to handle. The woman was so persistent, so determined, so tenacious that it was clear that she knew that she needed help. The woman understood the problem to be her problem, she did not say, "Lord, help my daughter," she said, "Lord, help me." Without question the woman's daughter needed help, but she was addressing a mother's inability to help her daughter. I can remember the times when I have cried out to the Lord for help with a problem that one of my children was experiencing. I asked the Lord to help me when there seemed to be nowhere to turn. I asked the Lord to help me when my children seemed to have stepped off the road and become distracted by some demonic enticement.

Faith got Jesus' attention. The disciples said, "Send her away." After all, she was not one of the chosen children of Israel. She was just a Canaanite woman, a woman of a different race. Jesus knew the disciples had discriminatory thoughts in their minds, so he told the woman that he came to the lost children of Israel, and it was not right to give the children's food to the dogs. The woman answered that *the dogs were allowed to eat crumbs that fell from the master's table.* When the woman said that, a new and wonderful thing happened. Jesus answered her, "Woman, great is your faith! Let it be done for you as you wish." And her daughter was healed instantly.

Jesus responded to sincere, genuine, authentic faith. Jesus responded by healing the daughter because of the faith of her mother. Formerly, people gained access to God because of their race, their faith, and because they were descendants of Abraham. Now, they gain access to God through faith in Jesus Christ, alone. There are no racial boundaries, no denominational boundaries, and no gender boundaries. It was the woman's faith that caught the attention of Jesus Christ, and it was the woman's faith that elicited the response she requested, namely, a daughter who was healed and a response from God. Faith that is real, faith that is authentic, is faith that God responds to with an answer. There is no problem that is too big for God. There is no disease that is too dastardly for God. There is no situation that is too sinister for God. Carol Antrom, writer of contemporary gospel music, has written of God's sovereignty and acknowledges that God "can do what no other power can do."

One day I cried out, "Lord, help me." I was sick and the doctors did not know how to cure me. God heard my cry, cured my illness, and made it possible for me to be a medicine-free, seizure-free epileptic. On another occasion, I cried to the Lord concerning my own daughter, and the Lord picked her up and turned her around and placed her feet on solid ground. Your own life may be filled with difficult problems. If you have faith and you turn to Jesus, you can be like the Canaanite woman who cried out, "Lord, help me," and after a while and by and by God will hear your cry and say to you, "Woman, great is your faith! Let it be done for you as you wish."

Most heavenly and all-wise God, I need your help with my family; my people have chosen to turn from you and turn to the world. I can't handle these situations by myself, but I know that with your help a change will come. Please hear my cry and answer my plea. Amen.

Dolores E. Lee McCabe

August 19

Friends

I do not call you servants any longer, . . . but I have called you friends.   *John 15:15a*

Debbie, Harriet, Laura, Lucille, Frances, Ralph, Steve, Rocky, Demaris, Jeanne, Susan, Ann, Gary, Sarah, Jerry, James, Mike, Brenda, Mary Ann, Chris, Sarah, Charla, Jill, Peggy, Kevin, Jean, Joyce, Lynne, Martha, Jeanne, Jeannie, Pat, Lena. That takes me up to about 1984. These are my friends, people who have shared my life. Some have been with me since I was less than a year old. Some came into my life and cared for me at particular moments and then moved out of my life. Some come and go. Take a moment to think about those people in your life who have been real friends.

In this remarkable conclusion to the fifteenth chapter of John's Gospel, Jesus presents us with an amazing truth. We have been chosen as Christ's friends, and, in Christ, we are to be friends to one another. Webster's dictionary defines a friend as "a person whom one knows well and is fond of." What distinguishes a friend from an acquaintance? How does the fondness grow and how is it maintained?

A friend is someone who is there for us, who exhibits love in a concrete way, even at personal cost. A friend is one who wishes us well, who sincerely wants her friend to be and become all that God dreams for her. A friend rejoices when things go well and prays and tries to help when things are going less well. A friend knows the difference between her friend and herself and resists the subtle competitions that can sour any relationship. A friend listens and shares from the heart. She is alert for the meaning behind words and, having heard, will not withhold the truth.

Friends tell us what they see. Friends take our hands and go wherever it is that our journey takes us. They may become frustrated. They may think we have taken a foolish path. They may tell us over and over what they see. But they will not take their hands from ours. They will forsake us neither when the chips are down nor when they are up.

That is the kind of intimacy, safety, joy, and play that God longs for us in our human relationships. That is also the kind of relationship that Christ offers us in the divine relationship, one who cares for us concretely, one who wishes us well, one who listens, one who tells the truth, one who will not abandon us in sorrow, stupidity, or joy.

Friend of the heart, make us worthy friends of yours and of those friends of yours with whom you bless our lives. Amen.

Eugenia Gamble

August 20

Healing from Within, Just Beautiful!

And wherever he went, into villages or cities or farms, they laid the sick in the marketplaces, and begged him that they might touch even the fringe of his cloak; and all who touched it were healed. Mark 6:56

To teenagers, looks are everything! But I don't look good.

Never mind that I could play the piano, that I was a majorette, that I was president of Student Council, and that I had beautiful hair (or as one kindly deacon told me every Sunday, even on a bad hair day!). I wasn't pretty with a bilateral cleft lip and palate.

Wonderful parents, loving sisters, encouraging people, made me feel good about myself, but the mirror did not. Solution: avoid mirrors, don't talk, become a recluse. Impossible. Alternate solution: learn to accept me, since others did. Possible.

Once at a Billy Graham crusade, one of the *helpers* laid hands on me and yelled at God, "Heal her, Lord." "Wait a minute," I said. "I am healed." The quick reply was, "No, God doesn't want you to look like this." "Oh yes she does," I countered and marched defiantly away.

Indeed, I am healed. My healing was brought about by excellent doctors, surgeons, dentists, prothodontists, speech therapists—all instruments of God, no doubt about it. I felt great.

When I was a young adult, an acquaintance invited me to a Spiritual Frontiers healing service. I went, wondering what I would do with my prosthesis if suddenly the palate closed and teeth formed. I hadn't even brought a box along for it.

Through the years, I've discovered a different kind of wholeness. There may be a visible cleft, but the invisible wholeness wins, hands down.

It's been a long time since I've been a teenager, a long time since I worried about my appearance, and a long time since I learned that the Great Physician brings wholeness of a far more lasting nature.

Creator God, we offer to you our brokenness whether it be physical, mental, or emotional. We give it to you for your healing touch. May we reflect your beautiful wholeness since we are imaged in you. Amen.

Grace T. Lawrence

August 21

Contentment

But the fruit of the Spirit is love, joy, peace, patience, kindness, goodness, faithfulness, gentleness, self-control.   Galatians 5:22-23a (NASB)

It's not often that I stop a salesperson in the middle of a sales pitch. And even more rare that I render anyone speechless. But I accomplished both these feats within recent months. I still find it amazing.

The telephone company salesperson called to try to convince me to add additional phone services. I declined, but he kept trying. Finally, he asked me why I didn't want anything more. I responded, "because I am content with what I have." After a brief silence he answered, "Well, I don't hear that often, but it's a good reason!"

The person I rendered speechless, if only for a moment, is a close friend. Over the years, we have talked about my many struggles: life with a physically and emotionally abusive husband, infertility, low self-esteem, divorce, career losses and changes, adjusting to being single again. She listened as I shared my frustration, anxiety, restlessness, discontentment, fear. We talked about my anger toward God and my questioning of what was happening to me, and why. Other times, I shared the praises of feeling God's touch, of truly knowing that the Lord has a plan for me, and of the delight of answered prayers.

Recently, she asked me how I was doing, if I was still considering quitting my job and moving out of state. (I had thought that would be a good solution to *getting away from it all*.) And I said, "No, I have decided I am content with where I am."

It has taken a lot of work to become content. It also seems to have just happened. But probably, really, it has happened because I decided that I wanted to be content. I determined that it was okay to be me, I allowed myself to ask for God's help, and I accepted the miraculous results. It was just like when I accepted Christ as my Lord and Savior. That was a conscious process too. I set aside the doubts and questions, conceded that I was worthy of God's love, admitted that I was a sinner. I asked for forgiveness, and I accepted God's grace, love, direction and manifestations in my life. Sure, both contentment and faith will continue to be day-to-day efforts, but the results are still exciting and amazing. And, occasionally, those results leave me speechless.

Lord, thank you for the peace of God, which surpasses all comprehension and guards my heart and mind in Christ Jesus. Amen.

Beverly Burns Erskine

My Beloved Child

You are my Son, the Beloved; with you I am well pleased.　　　　　　　　　　　　　　　　Luke 3:22

Luke describes Jesus' baptism as God's acknowledgment of Jesus' *Christ-ness*. In that acknowledgment one word stands out: beloved. God says, "You are the beloved." At that time, Jesus was approximately thirty years old, finally coming into his own as the one with a great and terrifying ministry bestowed upon him.

I believe that no ministry, however large or small, however quiet or evident, can be sustained without a sense of being a beloved child. Counselors tell us that the inner child is a crucial part of us—pay attention, they say. Social workers and health professionals tell us that almost every move we make in our relationships with children forms and shapes who they are. The *child* is everywhere—in us, around us, beside us.

Ah, but to feel beloved, that is the difficult part. Love has taken on romantic, sentimental meaning in popular media. Compassionate, caring love makes the news only during times of disaster when people pull together. The love of God becomes a buzzword in religious institutions. How does one feel beloved in the way God loves?

When alone, I light a candle for my prayer time. Sometimes I break bread by myself. Often I feel a sense of melancholy or loneliness during these times; however, I also find that these times of light and breaking of bread fill me, within the melancholy. For God speaks clearly there. Then I know the sense of being one of the many beloved that goes beyond love of friends and family. Then I know that when I break bread with others, there is something present stronger than my own feeling—that we are beloved together.

Loving One, teach us to know that we are deeply loved. Amen.
Lisa Withrow

August 23

Beauty Is Skin Deep

You gave me skin and flesh and knit together bones and
sinews.   *Job 10:11 (TLB)*

Have you ever stopped to think about your skin? Skin is that amazing, soft, protective covering for the body that has many characteristics. Skin mirrors our general state of health. Our face may flush from a fever, appear pale when we do not feel well, have a rosy glow from cold weather, or blush when we are embarrassed. Skin has other wonderful characteristics such as being waterproof, offering protection from bacteria, containing our bodily fluids, and having the ability to heal itself whether the wound results from a tiny pinprick, a paper cut, or a major surgical procedure.

Skin has another important function—the sense of touch. A superficial burn from a hot iron or stove causes us to withdraw quickly. The loving touch of a spouse, child, or friend adds pleasure to our day. The sense of touch provides the opportunity for each one to reach out to others during times of health, illness, and unexpected circumstances. We can also experience the sensation of touch for ourselves.

Thank you, loving Creator, for making me so wonderfully complex! It is amazing to think about. Your handiwork is marvelous—and how well I know it. Amen.

Marilyn O. Harris

August 24

God Is Present

The heart knows its own bitterness, and no stranger shares its joy.   *Proverbs 14:10*

One of the ironies in life is that we are not alone, yet we are alone. This is the human experience. There is a place in all of us that cannot be penetrated by anyone except God. I believe this is felt profoundly by someone who has experienced the death of a loved one.

My best friend and I were away together for a weekend in March of 1991, when my friend received the most dreadful phone call of her life. Her parents had been killed in a car crash. From that moment on, I watched and listened as Linda tried to deal with such a tragedy. To this day, I still do not know the depth of agony she has experienced. Only her heart knows that. As much as I want to penetrate that deepest part of her pain, I cannot. She carries that alone. Spiritually, however, there is one who does know as no other. The psalmist cries out, "O Lord, you have searched me and known me" (139: 1). Comfort for pain ultimately comes from God alone. He is the only one who can penetrate that innermost part of our being where all pain and suffering reside. In fact, he knows that part of us better than we know it ourselves. I think of that wonderful spiritual that goes, "Nobody knows the trouble I've seen, nobody knows but Jesus." This certainly is an accurate description of our human experience.

My friend still carries this tragedy with her, but she also carries with her the fact that God indeed knows her like no other.

Watchful and caring God, I am thankful that you know me like no other. Thank you for your grace and love that sustains me through all of life's difficulties. Amen.

Tammy L. Martens

Receiving Help

I praise you because I am fearfully and wonderfully made; your works are wonderful, I know that full well.
Psalm 139:14

When I was a child, I experienced a problem that I now thought was totally behind me. Only rarely did it come to mind. I came to realize that perhaps it was influencing my life, especially my family, more than I knew. Having grown up in a family that did not encourage sharing problems, it took a lot of incubating before I was ready to talk with a *counselor*. In the hope of freeing others to do likewise, I share my experience.

I turned to a friend who works with women and their lives and found help. She provided the name and phone number of a local counselor. It took two and one-half years, help from another adviser, and concerned discussions with my husband and two trusted friends before I was ready. I knew what needed to be done but was unable to do it effectively, to finish it and put it behind me. We want to believe that Christian reading, experience, forgiveness, and prayer—our dependence on Christ—should be enough to solve all our problems. But sometimes Christ's answers are found behind the door of a counselor.

I asked lots of questions on the first call for an appointment.

Reassured, I signed up. Her job was to ask questions. My job was to be open and responsive, ready to work when ideas and responses came to the surface.

I need to keep working in certain areas, and I know where she is if I need a catch-up session sometime in the future. I would encourage therapy and counseling if you have some persistent unhappiness in your life.

Gracious God, we thank you for the way you have made us, and for all who help us grow into the free people you want us to be. Amen.

Anabel Moseley

Chicken Little

God did not give us the spirit of cowardice, but rather a spirit of power and of love and of self-discipline.
2 Timothy 1:7

During my recovery from cancer surgery and then a year of chemotherapy, I spent a lot of time reading, praying and meditating. I had to deal with a lot of fear and anxiety—some normal, some caused by chemicals. One of the books I read that really blessed me was *When The Heart Waits* by Sue Monk Kidd. It's about transformation and spiritual growth. In one of her chapters she uses characters from childhood stories to illustrate ways in which we live out our lives. One of them was Chicken Little. Remember that story?

> Chicken Little was ambling along when an acorn fell on her head. Her fear exaggerated the acorn into a piece of the sky, and she scurried into a cave crying, "The sky is falling! The sky is falling!"

We are like Chicken Little when we feel like the sky is always about to fall. We withdraw in fear and avoid taking risks. Perhaps you have had experiences in your life that taught you that life can't be trusted. We let fear run our lives. *What if I make a fool of myself? What if I fail? What if, what if?*

God has given us a spirit of power and love and self-discipline. We can keep going and growing in spite of our fears. We can update those old recordings from our childhood that tell us that life is to be feared. We can also deal with the abnormal fears that we create ourselves.

God of unchangeable power, help me to release my fears and trust in your love and power. Amen.

Donna Authelet

Fruitfulness

By contrast, the fruit of the Spirit is love, joy, peace, patience, kindness, generosity, faithfulness, gentleness, and self-control.   *Galatians 5:22-23a*

As a child, I lived for a while near an orange grove in Florida, where I came to appreciate waiting for fruit-fullness. Fruit doesn't just happen. Fruit begins only as future possibility. On the way to fullness is the green, growing time; days of hot sun, longing for water, the necessary cold snap, those weeks of deep bitter juices. Only with tough time is fruit-fullness. So with the fruit of the spirit: love and joy, patience and kindness, being generous, being faithful, being gentle. Only over time and the graced life in-the-Spirit comes self-control. The fruit does not burst forth already grown with baptism, with being born, and being born again. But the seed—ah, the seed is given. "We will reap at harvest time, if we do not give up" (Galatians 6:9b).

Someone shared with me the "Toddler Property Laws."

> If I like it, it's mine. If it's in my hand, it's mine. If I can take it from you, it's mine. If I had it a little while ago, it's mine. If it looks just like mine, it's mine. If I saw it first, it's mine. If you are playing with something and you put it down, it automatically becomes mine. If it's broken, it's yours.

Somewhere between toddler and child of God, many of God's children grow into fullness. We usually know them when we see them. We call them *saints.* Sometimes we call them sister, or friend. We know within ourselves the growing times: the un-ripened moments of selfishness, the half-ripened struggles to bear with those who *push our buttons,* and sometimes the grace-filled joy—when we know patience, live into generosity, choose kind-ness. When we realize within ourselves that the lusciousness of grace, spilled out and overflowing, has prevailed.

Spirit of the living God, fall afresh on me. Spirit of the living God, fall afresh on me. Melt me. Mold me. Fill me. Use me. Spirit of the living God, fall afresh on me. Amen.

Dorothy Savage

August 28

When Decisions Get Tough

*Then Jesus said to the Jews who had believed in him,
"If you continue in my word, you are truly my
disciples; and you will know the truth, and the truth
will make you free."* John 8:31-32

Louise was struggling with taking care of Nana, her mother-in-law. Nana lived in her home, and she was with Louise all day, every day. Nana followed her everywhere, including shopping, since there was no one at home to watch her.

"She's so slow!" Louise complained to her husband, John. "And she follows me around all day saying, 'Don't get old, Louise. Don't ever get old.' As if I could stop it!"

As Nana advanced further and further into Alzheimer's dis-ease, Louise's life became more and more restricted. She hired someone to be with Nana while she searched for an appropriate care facility—appropriate for a confused old woman who loved nature and cats and people.

Finally, in desperation, Louise enrolled in a seminar for caregivers. "Examine your heart," the teacher said. "Why are you really doing this? What is it you hope to gain? The approval of others in your congregation? Your spouse's approval? It will help when you see your own motives."

One morning while writing in her journal, Louise realized her own need. *What I really want,* she wrote, *is for Nana to love me. I've always wanted her to love me.* Tears streamed down her cheeks. It was too late. The real Nana wasn't home anymore.

Within a week, Louise found a retirement facility on a wooded hill, with wildflowers on the grounds, a younger resident happy to earn a little money by making sure Nana was properly dressed and present at meals. And while she was looking at the room, a cat appeared in the window! The final sign! Louise enrolled Nana in the facility's craft classes three days a week. A month later, Nana went willingly to live there with her new friends.

God of us all, help us to be aware of our deeper needs so we can be free to make the necessary but sometimes difficult decisions in our lives. Amen.

Carol Spargo Pierskalla

August 29

God's Plan

For surely I know the plans I have for you, says the LORD, plans for your welfare and not for harm, to give you a future with hope. Jeremiah 29:11

As the manager of a Christian bookstore, I meet many different people on their journeys through this life. Some are bubbling over with joy, others are weighed down by the burdens of everyday living. Still other are *just looking.*

One day, I found myself sitting on a bench near a handicapped man in a wheelchair. He was unable to speak and laboriously wrote on a pad and handed it to me, "Warm day for shopping." We exchanged notes with similar small talk. A few days later, I saw him again. After a few notes, he wrote, "You pity me, don't you?"

Shocked at his directness, I nodded yes.

The next note was a long one. He wrote: "Please don't. I consider myself special, chosen by God to show the reverse side of the coin. For without people like me, how could you recognize God's perfect works?"

All at once I felt different about him—and myself. Now when I get down and discouraged about my limitations and my own multiple sclerosis disability, I know perhaps I, too, have been chosen for the reverse side of the coin.

You and I are the greatest miracle in the world! Again I was reminded that we are chosen by God to fulfill his special purpose.

Our God is all-loving—he wants the best for us.

Our God is all-knowing—he knows what's best for us.

Our God is all-powerful—he can and will do what's best for us.

What are you waiting for?

I have it all—wife, mother, grandmother, bookstore manager, inspirational speaker and singer, community volunteer, church worker, interdenominational Bible-study leader, world traveler. And I have multiple sclerosis. My goal is to inspire, entertain, and make people think. My disability has not become a stumbling block but a measuring rod by which I can evaluate the most effective use of my God-given abilities.

Great Healer of body and soul, thank you for teaching me that I am just the way you created me to be. Amen.

Marlys L. Kroon

August 30

Do Not Worry

Do not worry about anything, but in everything by prayer and supplication with thanksgiving let your requests be made known to God.   Philippians 4:6

My first thoughts on waking that morning centered on all the administrative details for which I was responsible. As coordinator for a major conference set to begin in a few hours, I anxiously reviewed my checklist: get out packets for registrants, contact custodian about extra chairs, add several more sets of brochures to resource table, put out signs identifying registration area. Other things to do tumbled about in my brain.

Fortunately, committee members for this conference had agreed to serve in numerous capacities, such as arranging for refreshments at break time. I had conducted this successful conference for several years, so why was I feeling stressed this morning?

While gulping down my orange juice and toast, I scribbled out fresh reminders of announcements to make at the opening session. I even glanced again at the list of people who were preregistered, old friends plus names new to me. They'd all be coming with high expectations, and I didn't want to disappoint them.

"God help us all," I murmured under my breath. "Don't let me forget anything or goof up on my responsibilities." Exhaling this prayer on the run, I hurried out of the house into the freshness of a cool February morning.

Before shoving my briefcase and several bags into the car, I glanced up at the western sky. There approaching the horizon was a descending moon—still bright. The crisp beauty against the steel blue sky made me exclaim, *Wow.*

Then I turned and faced the east. As if on cue, the sun was rising. Apricot, crimson, and peach shades of clouds stretched out with ever-changing hues. Although sunrises and sunsets in the Southwest desert often bewitch our eyes, this moon-sun spectacular caught me off guard.

Suddenly words and a tune formed in my heart. I began singing a jazzy little song: "I'm not in charge of the sun; I'm not in charge of the moon; I'm not in charge of the birds in the air . . ." More words and music bubbled up. The middle portion of my song went, "but I am responsible for." Inwardly I recited a clearly organized plan for the day. My creation concluded with the same melody but altered words: "So I give thanks for the sun, and I give thanks for the moon, and . . ." Inhaling deeply the wonder of that new day, I drove confidently to the church. On my lips and in my heart were God's latest gift to me.

We give thanks, God, that you, not we, are in charge of the universe. Amen.

Dosia Carlson

Say Yes

*For surely I know the plans I have for you, says the
LORD, plans for your welfare and not for harm, to give
you a future with hope.* Jeremiah 29:11

Health, healing, and wholeness—not asking for perfection but functioning as well as possible. Consider the following verbs for a future with hope, which have been gleaned from living through significant health crises.

1. *Say yes* to the will to live in the freedom of this temporary condition, and say yes to the will to die, to let go what has already gone.

2. *Diddle and putt and generally pause* when the pain howls.

3. *Redefine healthy* as celebrating life with enthusiasm again. *KILO*—root word of health, holy, healing, hallow, and wholeness—swells to its fullness—the Hebrew blessing of *shalom.*

4. *Rouse the spirit* of the curious soul child inside who refuses to stop finding another way.

5. *Eat of the marrow* that asserts a whole being's serenity wanting to be as healthy as it can be.

God of many deliverances, who has plans for us, sustain us in the balance of trying to find ways around barriers while granting what we cannot do despite strength of will. Remind us that while hindrances intrude and threaten to undo, they are a small part of who we are. Amen.

Dallas A. Brauninger

September

Resting in God

*My God, my God, why have you forsaken me? Why are
you so far from helping me, from the words of my
groaning? O my God, I cry by day, but you do not
answer; and by night, but find no rest. Yet you are holy,
. . . In you our ancestors trusted . . . and you delivered
them. To you they cried, and were saved; in you they
trusted, and were not put to shame.   Psalm 22:1-5*

How often I have uttered similar words. Why God? Why have
you abandoned me? Why do you not ease my pain, deliver me
from this? Where are you, God? The feelings of anger, frustration,
despair, hopelessness, and of being alone and abandoned lie heavy
in these words. We all go through moments in our lives when we
feel alone and abandoned. In the midst of it, we search for that
ground on which we can stand. For the psalmist, the ground was
in remembering how God had been faithful in the past. We also
find strength by remembering God's faithfulness in our lives and
in connecting with those who can remember with us or even
remember for us.

An image that helps me in these dark times comes from a very
quiet moment in my life, a time of preparation for the then-
unknown challenges that lay ahead of me. I was on retreat and
paused for a moment beside a river. Heavy rains had left the waters
raging well above the river's normal banks. The turbulent, muddy
water forced tree limbs and debris downstream. Suddenly, in the
midst of these treacherous waters, a deer struggled along, caught
in the current. I wanted to call for help. Something had to be done
to save the deer from this perilous situation. I felt caught. As my
fear and desperation grew, there was at the same time an inner
prompting that said, "Be still and wait."

I looked again and became aware that the deer was not fighting
or panicking. Rather, she calmly allowed the water to bear her
downstream. To my amazement, the current carried the deer to
the inner side of a curve below me. She gracefully stepped out of
the water onto dry ground and ran off into the woods.

Similarly, God bears me up as I go through the turbulent,
muddy waters of my life. I need only rest in God's arms. Resting

in God's arms does not take away the turbulence or the muddiness of the flood. Rather, it allows me inward stillness. God's strength and presence bear us through the turbulence to dry ground.

Giver of peace, be with us when life challenges us. Grant us an inner stillness where we can accept your loving embrace and find rest, strength, and courage in your arms. Amen.

Debbie Deane

September 2

There Is a Time for Everything

For everything there is a season, and a time for every matter under heaven.   Ecclesiastes 3:1

I am drawn again and again to this passage, in times of struggle and in times of joy. It's a reminder that life is always full of motion and activity. Movement stops only when death occurs—life is the story of ever-changing movement. Life has many aspects and many parts that always relate to each other. The time we spend at work affects the time we spend with our family. The time we spend in nurturing ourselves affects our relationships with others. *There is a time for everything.*

We must learn to move with the flow of our life. At times there are more work demands; at other times there are fewer. It is not that we must try to eliminate or control any aspect of our life. We simply need to know that change always comes. *There is a time for everything.*

Even in the midst of great struggle, there are times when promise is seen. In those times, when there is great joy, there is likely to be some sense of struggle. When we feel weak and helpless, we can develop the seed of great strength, and when we feel powerful, there is the seed of gentleness. *There is a time for everything.*

The gentleness required for being present with someone is a strength that offers our own vulnerability and our own experience with another person. Such gentleness offers a place for others to meet us. If one always holds the controlling power and tells others what to do, the seed of gentleness has little chance to be planted. *There needs to be a time for everything.*

As we strive to live faithful lives, change is always on the forefront of our living. Today's situation is different from yesterday's or from last year's. It is much like realizing that the rules for a two-year-old child are not like the rules for a teenager. God calls me to seek ways to act faithfully in the situation in which I am now living. Remember that the faithful answers for today may not be the faithful answers for tomorrow. *There is a time for everything even as change is always present.*

God of judgment and compassion, I pray that I may sense that you are traveling with me in the journey that is mine today. Grant me the grace to accept change in my life. Amen.

Gay Gilliland-Mallo

September 3

There Is Healing in Forgiving

Love your enemies, do good to those who hate you, bless those who curse you, pray for those who abuse you.   Luke 6:27-28

The year 1982 was very difficult for me and my family. Our son and daughter were involved in a student strike at the University of Puerto Rico. The situation became so severe that a SWAT team was called onto campus. Every morning we took our kids to the university, prayed with them, and sent them in with fear and trembling, wondering if we would see them alive again.

During a prayer meeting we were asked to pray for all the parties involved in the strike, including the police. Not only could I not pray for the police, I could not pray, period. I felt like a dry well. As I struggled to free myself from the hatred I was carrying, this prayer came to my heart and my lips: "God, help me to forgive as you forgive me." Healing came to my life. The shackles were shattered and the burden lifted. I was free again, free to praise and free to pray. What a wonderful sensation!

So many women have been bound in hatred for so long—hatred toward people who abuse and mistreat us; hatred toward institutions that want to keep us in submission. That is one impediment that *you* can vanquish. It happened to me and it can happen to you.

God of forgiveness and understanding, help me to overcome the obstacles that keep me from being healed in my soul and, therefore, from having abundant life. Amen.

Miriam Z. Gutiérrez

September 4

Part of One Another

For just as the body is one and has many members, and all the members of the body, though many, are one body, so it is with Christ.   *1 Corinthians 12:1*

People sometimes ask how I can work in settings like a hospital emergency room, a drug rehabilitation program, or housing and support services for the homeless. In some ways the answer is easy for me; how could I do otherwise?

The writer of 1 Corinthians suggests that we are all part of one another. I do not think this ends with our family or our church or even our neighborhood. Today, perhaps more than ever, we are all connected. When someone else hurts, it hurts us as well. When the rain forest is destroyed, it affects the environment for all of us. The amount that we pollute the earth affects others around the world.

If I do not speak out against violence, especially violence against women and children, then I am condoning it. If I don't try to help those who are homeless, I am accepting the fact that some people will not have a place to stay. If I don't try to make a difference, I am indicating that there is no hope.

We are many parts but one body! We may not be able to change everything in every place, but we can make a difference. And as all the parts work together, we all are healthier.

Gracious God, ruler of all people on the earth, help us to recognize that we are all one. Help us to see those who are in need as our sisters and brothers. May we be aware that as others hurt, we suffer as well. Help us see how we can make a difference. Amen.

Nelda Rhoades Clarke

To Heal by Sharing Joy

A cheerful look brings joy to the heart, and good news gives health to the bones.   Proverbs 15:30 (NIV)

Pleasant words are a honeycomb, sweet to the soul and healing to the bones.   Proverbs 16:24 (NIV)

So much of what we hear on the news and read in the paper is bad news. And we are quick to repeat it. Wouldn't it be wonderful if all we needed to do to achieve good health were to be cheerful and to spread good news?

Those who dwell on the negative side of life have difficulty seeing the bright side of situations. They tend to bring down the spirits of those around them. They often have physical ills, and they seldom feel good. Persons with sunny personalities, on the contrary, rejoice in small blessings; they bring joy to others and health to their own bones. They always have a smile ready.

At a recent conference of church secretaries, one of the presenters was Dr. Humor. He talked about the importance of laughter in our lives—laughter can transform us. Showing us humorous cartoons and telling us funny true stories, he kept us all laughing for the duration of his presentation. Isn't it true that after a good laugh, you have a sense of well-being, a kind of euphoria?

The prescription for a happy heart and healthy bones in Proverbs sounds easy—and it is free. If we heed the words in Proverbs, we can work at being joyful and speaking pleasantly.

It isn't hard to compliment a coworker or thank a family member for a kindness. As Christians, we can spread the good news and tell the stories we know so well about Jesus and his love. And as we heal ourselves, we may bring healing to others.

Loving and caring God, who knows when we are hurting in body and soul, teach us to heal ourselves by sharing joy and by spreading the good news of your son, who died that we might all be whole. Amen.

September 6

Conceived by the Holy Spirit

But just when [Joseph] had resolved to do this, an angel of the Lord appeared to him in a dream and said, "Joseph, son of David, do not be afraid to take Mary as your wife, for the child conceived in her is from the Holy Spirit."　　　　Matthew 1:20

For the sixth year in a row I attended Judson Memorial Church's annual production of *Christmas Wrappings,* Al Carmine's eclectic musical presentation of the entire biblical Christmas story, from the *begats* clear through to Herod's slaughter of the infants. I especially loved the choral numbers. Those sixty voices singing from the side and center aisles, resonating in the dome overhead, produced *surround sound* that vibrated in my bones and electrified my cells.

I had forgotten it by February, when the vision came. When I wasn't totally absorbed by the work I loved, I ruminated on the thought that I was not likely to become a biological mother in this lifetime. I was over thirty-five, single, and not unhappy with my life. I had never experienced any burning desire for motherhood, but it was certainly a profound and life-changing growth experience for most women. I would probably miss that experience. I needed to absorb what that meant to my life as a woman.

That February morning I heard the music before I opened my eyes. My room was absolutely filled with a swirling chorus singing the chant, "Holy Mary, Holy Mary, Holy Mary, Holy Mary." And then came a solo voice, "For that which is conceived in you is of the Holy Spirit." As long as I wanted to listen, they sang for me.

I gave heartfelt thanks for the confirmation and the message: that which is conceived in me *is* of the Holy Spirit—the ideas, the programs, the sermons, the songs. That is the fruitfulness that is mine to offer the world.

Divine Beloved, thank you for the privilege of cocreativity with your lively Spirit. Keep me open and receptive in my inmost parts. Thank you for blessing my fruitfulness, that it may benefit your beloved people in the fullest and best way. Amen.

Noel Koestline

September 7

All Women Are Healers

To heal ourselves is a reclamation of the power we all have as living beings to live in harmony with the life energy and to fulfill our potentials as creatures among many on the earth.[1]

It is time. It is time for women to reclaim their power to heal: to heal ourselves, to heal others, to heal the world. There is a spiritual dimension to healing that has been forgotten or suppressed too long. We know the power that can be gathered from the earth around us and channeled into our bodies for energy and healing.

It is time. It is time for us to take control of our own bodies and to direct our own healing. It is time to believe our own experiences. It is time to listen to our own truths and to act.

It is time. It is time to find energy and solace in meditation and in the companionship and strength of other women. It is time to share our healing energies toward the healing of the earth, for we are all of the earth and our healing is tied to the healing of the planet.

It is time. It is time to rejoice and to celebrate life. It is time to think of ourselves as whole and beautiful, as worthy and passionate, as loving and wise.

Guardian of our lives, help sisters to see that it is our right to live and to be whole. To know that healing will not come from outside, but from ourselves united. Amen.

Karolyn Holm Burkett

Is There No Balm?

Is there no balm in Gilead? Is there no physician there? Why then has the health of my poor people not been restored? Jeremiah 8:22

During a recent visit to Los Angeles I read an article in the *LA Times* describing the difficult choices facing the LA county commissioners to close either several major county hospitals or all the neighborhood-based health clinics. What a choice! We know that public hospitals, especially emergency rooms, are the only sources of medical care for the poor and the uninsured.

As *caregiver* women we are the ones who escort children, older parents, relatives, and friends to the doctor and hospital. As employed persons, we are overrepresented in the low-wage or part-time jobs that do not provide health benefits. Increasingly, professional women who are *downsized* or are hired as contract workers have seen their guaranteed health care disappear. What is happening to God's vision of an abundant life for all?

Is Jeremiah's lament our only response? *No!* The religious community worked hard for health-care reform. More than thirty thousand women were mobilized through Church Women United to study and act on behalf of universal health-care coverage. God intends us to be coactors on behalf of justice and righteousness for all God's peoples.

In the African American spiritual "There Is a Balm in Gilead," we sing: "Sometimes I feel discouraged, and think my work's in vain, But then the Holy Spirit revives my soul again."

Binder of wounds, let us be revived and be moved by the Holy Spirit to continue to work in our local communities to provide health care for all. Amen.

Patricia J. Rumer

September 9

Feast on the Moment

For everything there is a season. Ecclesiastes 3:1-22

There is a wonderful old retired pastor who declares that his goal in life is to find some humor in every day and to share it. He has learned to delight in fleeting moments of life, to feast on little bits of humor he finds each day.

As I examine my goals for each day, I wonder what I have learned in sixty-six years.

Some time ago I resolved to devote my time and talents to people, not *things*. I want to value persons, not possessions. I will leave the dishes unwashed and the beds unmade to spend time with family and friends. I want to feast on the moments that involve personal contacts and personal service.

I will not think of happiness in relationship to grand events. Rather, I will hold precious little islands of happiness in every day. I will not think of happiness in terms of what others do for me, but rather find happiness in giving.

Time is fleeting and life is at best brief. As a Christian, I look forward to a life forever with my Lord, but I want to live this earthly life as fully and as lovingly as I can. I want to recognize that many of life's most precious moments are easily missed. It will be my intent to go with the child who wants to show me some newly discovered wonder. I am determined to take time to listen to the disorganized words of the old, who desperately need attention. I pray for wisdom to respond to the cry for help and love in sad eyes.

God of all generations, in each bit of joy, in each moment of happiness, in each expression of love, allow me to recognize your gift, and I will give you the glory. Amen.

Kathleen A. Moore

Stirring with Resentment

*Do not repay evil for evil or abuse for abuse, but, on
the contrary, repay with a blessing. It is for this that
you were called—that you might inherit a blessing. For
those who desire life and desire to see good days, let
them keep their tongues from evil and their lips from
speaking deceit; let them turn away from evil and do
good; let them seek peace and pursue it.*

1 Peter 3:9-11

Granny Lindsay was known by everyone in the neighborhood.
She lived to be over one hundred years old. Her house was only
a few doors down from the church house where I served on the
staff. When I needed a good dose of perspective, I walked down
to see Granny. She had eyes that danced with life, even as her
body edged toward death. Stories tumbled out of her as she told
of picking cotton and going to bed with cracked and bleeding
hands and feet.

One day I asked Granny, "What was the hardest time in your
life?" I expected stories of poverty and prejudice from the racist
soil of her heritage. Instead she told me this story:

It was just a few years ago when my younger sister
Emma came to live with me. Emma was sick, and there
was no one left in the family but me to care for her. What
could I do? I took her in. Kin is kin. But it didn't take my
heart but two or three days to be filled in every crook and
crevice with resentment. She was the baby sister my
daddy loved best. Emma wasn't disciplined like the rest
of us. The hickory stick never crossed her legs. She was
spoiled through and through. The world revolved around
Emma, and the rest of us kids stood around her holding
resentment. Even as an adult, she was queen of complaint.
No one could do enough. When she came to live with me,
she expected me to be her maid. She would moan and
groan if I asked her to help. Well, I couldn't stand it. My
resentment grew so big that it smelled up the whole house
like a mess of collards cooking. So I got down to some
serious praying. Every morning I'd stir a pot of grits, her

favorite. As I stirred, I asked God to remove this mountain of resentment. I stirred and I prayed day after day. Plenty of grits went down, until finally God set me free. You know what finally did it, don't you? No, ma'am. Did you run out of grits? No, child. I started feeling deep down that I couldn't love her. But I loved the someone who knew how to love her. And that was the beginning. I even got where I could laugh at myself and Emma—us two old women hobblin' around tryin' to make do. Emma eased up a bit, though she still could complain, but it doesn't stand in my way anymore. I just go on. I even have some love in my heart—a dab and a dash is a start. God is might big, child, might big.

Beloved God, come to our aching hearts. Stir us with your disturbing and healing Spirit. Whisper forgiveness in our ear and splatter us from head to toe with grace to love again. Amen.

Nancy Hastings Sehested

September 11

Stirring Up Gifts

When I call to remembrance the genuine faith that is in you, which dwelt first in your grandmother Lois and your mother Eunice, and I am persuaded is in you also. Therefore I remind you to stir up the gift of God which is in you through the laying on of my hands. For God has not given us a spirit of fear, but of power and of love and of a sound mind.

2 Timothy 1:5-7 (NKJV)

This Scripture became important to me several years ago, especially when I focused on the reminder to "stir up the gift of God which is in me," reminding myself and others that God already dwells within. We need to remember to stir the ingredients of God's indwelling spirit and not let our relationship become stagnant.

When my grandmother died recently, this passage added depth to my relationship with God. Granny and I had been very close, and I feel blessed to have had her in my life for so long. The difficult part now is to keep claiming her spirit and her presence, even though she is physically absent.

This Scripture passage now challenges me to remember that part of my faith journey began because of the faith that dwelt within my grandmother. The spirit of God's unconditional love, gentleness, and humor certainly were regularly *stirred up* and shared within Granny and passed on for others to receive.

God invites us to remember those who have touched our lives with genuine faith and have been companions for us on the journey.

Grandmother God, help me to remember your gentleness, your kindness, and your open arms and lap that are always ready to receive me. May I remember that your indwelling presence is now being stirred up within me, to remind me that even death cannot separate the true spirit of life-giving relationships. Amen.

Sara J. Davis

September 12

Rock of Ages

The rain fell, the floods came, and the winds blew and beat on that house, but it did not fall, because it had been founded on rock.   Matthew 7:25

My great-grandmother Ma Rachel Bell passed away this past summer at the age of 108 1/2. When I was a child, Mama Rachel always *seemed to be older than old* to me, although at the time of my childhood she would have been in her seventies and eighties. After Mama Rachel turned one hundred years old in 1987, I figured that since she made it this long, she had no plans of ever leaving.

My father's sister admonished me once for using euphemisms such as *passed away* or *passed on* for death. She said when we used words like that we were avoiding the obvious. What is obvious to me, as I reflect on my great-grandmother's life, is the vast quantity of life she encountered in her 108 1/2 years. She was born the daughter of slaves. She had been a widow since the year

1914 when her husband was taken in the great influenza epidemic. Consequently, she raised six children alone. We always marveled at how she pulled together the pieces of her life. We knew her to be an exceptional quilter. We grieved openly when failing eyesight prevented her from carrying on this craft after her eighties. Much to my surprise, I learned on the occasion of her death that she was a country doctor of sorts; undegreed and unlicensed, but the administrator of home remedies for palsies, infirmities, and afflictions that arose among the people on the few blocks of a community where she lived for most of her life. Further, her empathetic spirit sensed when any of her *children* were feeling poorly. My eighty-six-year-old grandmother, Mama Rachel's daughter, tells stories of her mother's knowledge of her children's physical distresses, even when they had not told her or anyone else.

Despite the fact that four of her children preceded her in death, Mama Rachel had a strong policy of never grieving for those who had passed away. She preached that it would be faithless to grieve someone else's passing into a better place. So in the spirit of the theology preached by one who had seen so many pass before her, I grieve not her passing, but fancy somehow her position as she was welcomed into God's commonwealth by those she loved and those who loved her, including my father.

I heard of Mama Rachel's passing the day I was preparing to leave the country for a ten-day commission. I went to visit my great-grandmother's home shortly after my return. I desperately wanted an item that would remind me of Mama Rachel's fortitude, strength, and position in the family for nearly a century and a decade. My great-aunt gave me permission to take a rock of petrified sand and sediment that my great-grandmother had gathered quite some time earlier, which had laid posed on the porch in front of great-grandma's vacant rocker. That rock reminds me of how great-grandma was able to make it through the rains and the winds and not be felled. Her foundation was the rock we call Jesus; Ma Rachel Bell was a wise woman.

The rock I took from my great-grandma's home now resides in one of the more sacred areas in my home as a solid reminder of what God can do and does do through the ones we know and love.

Eternal God, whose omniscience extends so much further than our finite minds can comprehend, I thank you for the blessings and gifts your servants have left for those who for a season remain. May we be comforted by a sense of the eternal as we serve thee daily. Amen.

Cheryl F. Dudley

September 13

God's Agenda

You prepare a table before me in the presence of my enemies; you anoint my head with oil; my cup overflows.   Psalm 23:5

Heavy clouds filled the October sky. My husband, son, and I had left my in-laws' home in Chattanooga to drive back to Kansas City. I was irritated. It was three o'clock before we were driving on the interstate, and my plan had been to leave by noon. We had reservations at my favorite Kentucky State Park motel, and I wanted to arrive before dark. We were sixty miles from the park when the setting sun unexpectedly pierced through the clouds. Golden rays sprayed across treetops and through bare branches. Gradually the road opened out into flat land. The sky, once hazy with banks of gray and white clouds, now spread out in soft pink, aqua, and lavender. Brilliant reds and yellows streaked through the cumulus mass. We were surrounded by a canopy of color. *He prepares a table before us.*

God nurtures us in so many ways. If we had left earlier, we would have missed this beautiful sunset. Agendas help us focus, but they can also cut off opportunities for spontaneity and surprise. Has God ever placed a table before me that I have not recognized or claimed? I'm sure I've skipped some of God's meals when I've been too busy for meditation. I need many moments with God if I hope to see and accept what has been spread for me.

On a large piece of paper draw a four-legged table big enough to fill two-thirds of the space. Think about the many ways that God nurtures you, focusing specifically on the past week. Write words or draw symbols on the table to represent how you have been fed.

Not only has God prepared a table for me, God has done this in the presence of my enemies. Who are my enemies? My worst enemies can be those thoughts or voices within me that squelch my potential. Mental-health therapists and writers attribute this to our internal critic. "What makes you think you can do that? Gina can write a lot better than you." When these thoughts overwhelm us, we become immobilized by fear and indecision. We miss out on God's feast for us.

Clarissa Pinkola Estes, in *Women Who Run with the Wolves*, claims the enemy is our internal predator whose job is to block our attempts at new journey experiences. This predator uses our fears and weaknesses to bind us.

Think about your internal enemies. Write words or draw symbols around the table to represent them. Release them to God.

Thank you, God of light and sun, for the promise of your table. Help me, daily, to discern who my enemies are and to deal with their power over my thoughts and actions. Help me to assert my true self, made in your image, as I struggle on my journey today. As my cup overflows, may your healing oil nourish my soul. Amen.

Cynthia G. Haynes

September 14

Wanting to Be Healed

When Jesus saw him lying there and knew that he had been there a long time, he said to him, "Do you want to be made well?"   John 5:6

The birth of our first child was unexpectedly difficult. My doctor and I had planned for a natural delivery. However, after fifteen hours of labor, I abandoned the original plan and readily agreed to have saddleblock anesthesia. When it wore off after several hours, the baby wasn't any closer to being born than before. Finally the doctor realized that the baby was in a breech position and attempted to turn it. I was ready to give up, convinced that I was dying.

As I drifted out of consciousness, I remember seeing only my obstetrician and a nurse. At that point the most amazing experience of my life occurred. I entered a long tunnel, turning like a corkscrew. At the end was a brilliant light (which I learned many years later was typical of the accounts of people with similar experiences). When I came to the light, I felt totally loved, accepted, and peaceful. God was present in an awesomeness that is beyond my power to describe. I felt ashamed for ever having taken life for granted and the power of love lightly.

There then occurred a dialogue of consciousness beyond words in which I ultimately requested that I might return to the physical world to complete some things I had started. I wanted to be with my husband, who was a graduate student in seminary at the time. What was to be the fate of my unborn child? Given the choice, I knew I wasn't ready to leave the world yet.

Miraculously, my request was granted, and I felt myself beginning to rotate back through the tunnel—this time in the opposite direction. The hospital room was full of medical technicians. However, the first person I focused on was the brand-new, tiny being who was lying on my tummy. As I watched in awe, he took his first gasp of air and started to cry. He was fighting for life too!

I burst into tears of joy—gratitude for life and for another chance to be with my new family for a while longer.

Like the man by the pool of Bethesda, I clutter up my life with myriad excuses and reasons for not being at peace with myself— whole and cured. I recall the experience that showed me how ephemeral this life is, and my gratitude for every hour and every day is renewed.

God of the past, present, and future, thank you for life and for the freedom to participate in our own healing. Through your grace help us to stop wasting our time on this earth with excuses and complaints and with lack of appreciation for the life you have given us. Amen.

Carol McCollough

Yes, Jesus Loves Me

Though I walk in the midst of trouble, you preserve me against the width of my enemies; you stretch out your hand, and your right hand delivers me. Psalm 138:7

She stood by her, staring out the window. The room was dark; she had yet to raise the blinds.

I entered the room. "Good morning." No reply. "Good morning," I said louder. "How are you?" I walked toward her. She turned her head and body in slow motion. "Hi," her voice was soft. In the shadows her facial features were obscured. "Let me open these blinds for you. It's lovely outside."

The sunshine illuminated the entire room. She looked to be about forty-five years old. Her skin was evidence of a hard life. Dark circles surrounded her eyes, and when she smiled, deep lines shaped her mouth. Her name was Mary. This was her third hospitalization in six weeks.

"I am scared. Doctor says I may have AIDS. I know I've got pneumonia. Sometimes it's hard to breathe. I haven't done anything to get AIDS. I'm separated and I'm a good mom. I've been a decent person for over ten years. I can't have AIDS, can I? Reverend Betty, is God punishing me?"

I took her hand and asked her to tell me about the God who knows her name. She told me of the God of her childhood who was distant and frightening. The God of her adolescence was one who pronounced strict rules that she struggled to keep. The God of her adulthood appeared in and out of her life. When she was alone and desperately in need of comfort, she remembered the affirmation, "Yes, Jesus loves me." She began to cry. Again she whispered, "Yes, Jesus loves me."

God of many deliverances, I'm dependent on you. Help me to remember your ways. Speak to me now. You've always brought me through. Lord, I'm dependent on you. Amen.

Betty Wright-Riggins

Safe in God's Arms

Death has been swallowed up in victory. Where, O
death, is your victory? Where, O death, is your sting?
1 Corinthians 15:54-55

Forty years ago, early on a spring morning, I fell asleep at the wheel. My car crossed the road, broke through the guardrail and plunged diagonally down an embankment, coming to rest against a tree. I awoke at the guardrail, and my twenty-three years of life passed before me, just as legend has it. I had time for a quick regret that I would never marry before the car came to a stop and I sought a way to escape.

Later I realized that I had not been afraid of dying. Seven years after the accident, during a lingering illness with a high fever, I *dreamed* a long arborlike vision with Jesus beckoning at the other end. I had a new baby then, and pleaded that I wasn't ready to die. I awoke that time, too, and recovered to raise my family. Thinking about the episode brought back the same reality—at no time did I feel fear or panic. Instead, there was a kind of serenity.

Minor though these episodes were in the light of tragic accidents and terminal illnesses, they shaped my life by bringing me face to face with the possibility of death. How I will react to the end of my life is unknown, but all my life I have believed that I do not need to be afraid. God has promised something better, and my trust is in God.

These experiences did not make a daredevil out of me. I am not adventurous. I experienced great qualms about hot-air ballooning and white-water rafting, although both turned out to be great fun. I am not comfortable risking my life. My hope is that in whatever form death approaches, I will meet it with faith and with strength and with courage, knowing that I do not need to fear this adventure because God will be there.

My Guardian and Guide, I thank you for all the moments of my life that have shaped the person I am today. Use me for your work in the world and be with me when my life draws to a close. Take my hand and draw me into our next great adventure together. Amen.

Cathie Burdick

ʼBlessings

*The boundary lines have fallen for me in pleasant
places. . . . Therefore my heart is glad, and my soul
rejoices; my body also rests secure. Psalm 16:6a, 9*

"The boundary lines have fallen for me in pleasant places." Not
everyone can say that, and surely few can say it all the time. Yet,
it is true for more of us, for more of the time, than we usually
acknowledge. My work with women and children in crisis brings
me face to face with life's pain daily. Seeing the beauty and joy
of life takes intentional effort. Wholeness requires me to center
periodically on the blessings of my life, without fooling myself
that I deserve them or that I have earned them.

Recently I had to confront my own ungratefulness. A friend
and I had planned to meet at the beach for a restful weekend after
weeks of work and travel. The night before, the path of Hurricane
Opal looked ominous, so we decided that she should cancel her
trip, though I would try to get there, since I was to speak en route
at the dedication of a new ministry for imprisoned women and
their children. The hurricane changed course, my day went
smoothly, and I ended up alone at sunset, driving a rental car
toward the beach in gorgeous weather. I was bitterly disappointed
and was beginning to shed a few tears of self-pity, when I heard
my own voice (or was it the Spirit using my vocal cords?) say
aloud,

> Get a grip, Peggy. You have just spent the day with
> thirty-five women who have long prison sentences and
> will miss their sons' and daughters' childhoods. You
> learned that the director of the program, who smiled as
> each woman received her certificate of completion of a
> parenting course, got the news last night that her hus-
> band's cancer has spread. You spoke with a colleague,
> instrumental in developing the prison ministry, whose
> fifteen-year old daughter ran away from home last week-
> end and is now hospitalized. Now about your problem,
> the one you are crying over . . . You have to spend a
> beautiful weekend alone at the beach.

Needless to say, I grinned, dried my eyes, and arrived at the beach deeply grateful for God's grace in the form of rest and renewal.

God of all our days, the painful and the pleasant, give us perspective and humility. Amen.

Peggy Halsey

September 18

Solitude

Deep calls to deep. . . . at night the Holy One's song is with me, a prayer to the God of my life.

Psalm 42:7-8 (Adapted)

Solitude—the still and sacred space carved out within by hands chafed from the duties of the day, by hearts bruised in relationships, by minds wrought with anxious deliberation, by souls excluded, disowned, devalued, and torn. Solitude—herein resides the hallowed place where the Holy One heals graciously, listening attentively and responding honestly amid the shadows of the night, through the whispers of conversation and the cries of confrontation, disclosing the beauty and the struggle of encountering the realities of a woman's life.

Do we dare frequent this place even in the darkness of the night? Will we finally shed our frenzied, frenetic pace to journey to this realm of solitude? And why, as women, do we fail to seek the timeless reconciliation, the awesome truth, the reenergizing renewal afforded here?

For deep calls to deep as our longings thirst for the one who stirs us to stillness, who sings our name, calling us from the crowds and the chaos without, from our complicity and self-neglect, to be refreshed.

Surely the Holy One has called to the depths of your being; surely grace has ushered you into solitude, to temper and to transform the cadence and tempo or the lyrics of your life-song.

Yes, the risks of soul-full health, nurtured and energized in handcrafted stillness, may mirror the need for change, for redesigning day-to-day spirituality, for disturbing the fragile note of safe tranquility so tightly grasped in the clamor of the day, in interactions with those who are different, powerful, or threatening. Yet the voice of God within calls forth in poignant wonder to reword a woman's prayer of trust that we will be revitalized by night and by day.

With you, O Holy One, we speak in this still small place within us. In the intimacy of solitude, where we meet you and our selves more fully, may our health and our wholeness be nurtured by the new life-song you teach us to sing. Through our prayer this night, may deep call to deep within all women in profound and life-giving ways, by your grace. Amen.

Greta Wagner

September 19

Closing the Caregiving Door

Be pleased, O LORD, to deliver me; O LORD, make haste to help me. . . . I am poor and needy, but the LORD takes thought for me. You are my help and my deliverer; do not delay, O my God.   *Psalm 40:13, 17*

Our son was attacked by multiple viruses that left him *functionally paralyzed* from the neck down when he was eleven. It was a long journey back to health involving physical therapy for eighteen months. The shock came when this neuromuscular disorder recurred following each new infection. For twelve years our family lived on alert that within a few hours we could move into the caregiving mode for weeks or perhaps months. Repeatedly I became the *caregiving mom.*

The day came when the cause (a deeply embedded, fully developed, fifth wisdom tooth) was identified and removed. Recuperation took several months, but from the beginning we knew this journey was radically different from previous recoveries.

We rejoiced for our young adult son. A bright future replaced uncertainty and doubt. It was a new day of freedom in his life. It was easy and joyful for me to focus on the dramatic changes in his life. The changes in my own life were obviously real, too; but they seemed elusive and challenging to clarify. Much of my forties and early fifties had to keep caregiving for my son as a top priority. I could shelve the issue only temporarily. Finally, at age fifty-four, I was free to close the door on this situation.

Now I face growth questions. How shall I fill those caregiving spaces? What new patterns need to replace the old ones? Into what human endeavors shall I pour my energies? There were and continue to be few immediate and definitive answers. As time passes, I am filling the spaces with meaningful pursuits. I have been learning the art of patience as I wait for the Lord's direction. It is quite a challenge for an impatient soul like myself!

God of our lives, teach us the art of waiting upon your leading when new doors of freedom open for growth toward health and wholeness. Amen.

Jan Chartier

September 20

'But by God's Grace

But by the grace of God I am what I am.
1 Corinthians 15:10a

It has taken me sixty years to accept that the apostle Paul was right! For too long, I thought I was *less than* or *not good enough*. When I was in my first church Children's Day program at age five, I was to recite a long poem from memory. (I have always memorized quickly and easily.) I had not heard the other children's parts until practice on Saturday. As the others recited, I listened intently. Somehow, I felt that I was not as good as the rest.

On Sunday, when it was my turn, I had the whole congregation laughing. What I did was repeat verbatim the speech of the child who preceded me, a speech I had heard only twice!

Even as an adult, I have found myself trying to offer someone else's gift because I doubted my own. But I am the only person in all creation who can offer my own special gifts. I don't feel this way because I was liberated by feminism, or because I have four degrees, or because I am a respected professional. I have changed because my God affirms me—not in terms of *you're better than* or *you're worse than*—but because God says that who I am is right, who I am is enough.

I still work on believing that. Before every sermon I preach, before every new job I begin, before each new social situation, before (and during) all confrontations, I tell myself the best thing I know to say: "By the grace of God I am what I am."

God of all creation, thank you for my faith in you—and for your faith in me. Amen.

Norma R. Jones

September 21

Lessons of Life

Even though I walk through the darkest valley, I fear no evil; for you are with me.　　　　*Psalm 23:4*

My family gives a wonderful gift: a positive outlook on living, aging, and dying.

I remember Aunt Carrie, almost ninety-eight years old, lying on her deathbed. No machines. No tubes. Only an attendant to keep her comfortable. She opened her eyes, spoke my name, and closed them again. I stroked her forehead and remembered her in younger days.

"If you have your health and your family, you are rich." She would speak and laugh simultaneously as she wove her thread through material. A modest seamstress, she was one of the happiest people I knew. She refused medical intervention to prolong her life needlessly. Ninety-eight was long enough, she thought.

Her body filled with fluid. The doctors would say she died of congestive heart failure. No—she just knew when to let go and die gracefully of old age.

Poet May Sarton wrote, "Old age is not an illness, it is a timeless ascent. As power diminishes, we grow toward the light."[2]

My father refused a pacemaker at age ninety-two. He had fought (and won) enough battles with disease—cancer, broken pelvis, heart attack. Now, he said, he did not want to go back to the hospital. One day, as the doctors predicted, his heart skipped a beat and he fell over. He died as he lived, fully engaging life.

My widowed mother shovels her driveway after the Blizzard of '96: twenty-four inches of snow at age eighty-one. "I just stop and rest every fifteen minutes. I'm doing fine," she assures me on the phone.

I still receive lessons on living and aging.

Source of health and strength, help me to live fully the life you give and to trust you when the time comes to let go. Amen.

Adele K. Wilcox

September 22

Combating Hopelessness

For God did not give us a spirit of cowardice, but rather a spirit of power and of love and of self-discipline.   *2 Timothy 1:7*

Those days come when the sky is gray, when we feel tired through to our bones, when unresolved issues from the preceding night scream loudly in our minds and hearts, and when the tasks of the day seem more than we can handle—but handle them we must. It is on these particular mornings that I give myself ten more minutes in bed no matter what. I pull what little resources I feel I have to focus on the Holy Spirit in me that Christ promised would be with me always to guide, teach, and empower me. Rather than focus on my feelings of helplessness or weariness, I focus on that Spirit of God, giving its power full reign, not only on the spiritual part of me, but also over my body and mind. While I take deep slow breaths, I breathe in love and exhale sadness; I breathe in power and exhale helplessness. I breathe in the love of God and exhale hopelessness.

What I find is that nothing is hopeless and that we are not helpless when we give recognition to the empowering force of the Holy Spirit in us. By the end of the ten minutes, I find that the unresolved issues from the night before and the tasks of the day are still present, but my attitude about them has shifted. I realize that it is a new day with new possibilities and that even the gray sky cannot overshadow the gift of the glow within me given by the Holy Spirit.

Thank you, loving Creator, for the gift of your Spirit that dwells and works and moves inside of me, giving me love and power to face each day. Amen.

Francine Stark

September 23

Too Busy for Quiet Time

Many crowds would gather to hear him and to be cured of their diseases. But he would withdraw to deserted places and pray.   Luke 5:15b-16

"Too busy," I mutter to myself, "too busy for quiet time." Have you looked around and noticed only those who need you and only the many obligations that wait to be met? Jesus had the same experience. With all the hurt in his world, he could have had a permanent, twenty-four-hour-day, seven-day-a-week job as a teacher and healer. But he knew that he could not do his job alone. Unable to hold back the surge of those whose needs would never abate, Jesus took himself out of their field of vision so that he could renew his relationship with God and thereby find his own center.

How do we make our teacher's example real in our own hectic, noisy lives? "Be still and know that I am God," sings the psalmist (46:10). Let us regularly seek the stillness and the silence. This seeking will sometimes remove us physically from the outside turmoil for a brief or extended retreat. Even when this is impossible, however, we can learn to find the stillness within. Breathe deeply and slowly, concentrating on the inhalations that fill your throat, lungs, and belly with life-giving air. Concentrate just as intently as you exhale, moving every bit of air up and out of the body. As you breathe, allow no thoughts, whether lofty or mundane, to capture your attention. Notice the thoughts, as you do any external distractions, and then let them go, returning focus to the breath. Allow obsessiveness to fade, as plans for the future and attachments to the past give way to God's eternal here and now. See if you do not feel calmer after this meditative break, more ready for work—perhaps with a prayer of praise on your lips.

Spirit, breath, and movement of air are expressed by one word in Hebrew, as they are in Greek, Sanskrit, and several Asian languages. Where breath is savored and stillness is cultivated, there can our Creator fill and move us.

Keeper of the stars, instill humility when I am led by pride to imagine that my own busywork keeps the world spinning. Give me permission to stop the clock so that your Spirit can fill me. You are the air that I breathe, O God. Help me to know, as Jesus did, that it is in you that I live and move and have my being. Amen.

Marie Roberts

September 24

No Coincidence

Blessed be the God and Father of our Lord Jesus Christ, the Father of mercies and the God of all consolation, who consoles us in all our affliction, so that we may be able to console those who are in any affliction with the consolation with which we ourselves are consoled by God.

2 Corinthians 1:3-4

This side of heaven we will never fully understand the purpose and meaning of pain and suffering in our lives. God does not promise that our lives will be free of sickness, heartache, and pain, but God does promise to be with us in the midst of it and to comfort us in all our troubles (2 Corinthians 1:4).

Several years ago, I experienced the dread of many women—a diagnosis of breast cancer. God sent so many people to me to administer the comfort that he promises. The most reassuring thing that anyone could do or say to me was to tell me, "You are on my daily prayer list" or "My church circle is praying for you." Literally thousands of prayers, many from people I will never meet, were said on by behalf. I will always believe that those prayers resulted in the supernatural sense of peace that I maintained throughout radical breast surgery with reconstruction, six months of chemotherapy with total hair loss, and radiation treatment.

Since I was victorious in my fight with breast cancer, God uses me to offer encouragement to others experiencing the same ordeal. It's been said that *coincidences* have put me in contact with women facing the same diagnosis.

A couple of weeks ago, I found meaning in today's Scripture passage. Yes, God has called me and is showing me who I can comfort and the same wondrous comfort that I received.

God of many deliverances, I praise you as the Great Comforter and ask that you open my eyes today to see those who are in need of your comfort. Amen.

Carolyn Carpenter

September 25

Choose Life

I call heaven and earth to witness against you today that I have set before you life and death, blessings and curses. Choose life so that you and your descendants may live.   Deuteronomy 30:19

Choose life. These words confirm that we come up against wanting to choose death. Then, despite our reaching toward wholeness, the will to live and the will to die fight inside us. Even those of us who carry too much steadiness to yield to the will to stop grapple with it. Perhaps the very shadowy presence of the will to die excites the stubbornness of the will to live.

I have had many occasions to call it quits. The body was in too much pain, the challenges felt too handicapping, or the day's supply of energy was exhausted. Early on, I found the safe time to give up. At night, on the pillow, I can just stop. A morning person, I know I will wake with at least some energy for wanting to continue. In the night, an idea frees itself to enter the turmoil. Growing to trust that hope will burst into a solution, I let go of the terror of the will to die. It does not lessen the struggle but sets it within a fuller perspective.

This hope comes from God. Whether it is Spirit-always-aware

or God-planted within us as our given capacity for ingenuity, hope overshadows us, speaking of a Presence that stays with us inside the suffering.

Great Healer of body and soul, encourage us as practicers of life to enter all our feelings with the trust that we can choose life. Amen.

Dallas A. Brauninger

September 26

I'm Always Thinking of Going Back

When Lot's wife looked over her shoulder, she turned into a pillar of salt. Pillars hold things up, and salt keeps things clean, but it's a poor exchange for losing yourself.[3]

Freedom is expensive. It costs so much that we're tempted to make returns. Going back—to a home that hurt, to a job that stressed—seems all right after all.

The more I focus on back there, the less I am able to make here and now a welcoming place to live. Memories have a way of dropping off sharp edges that hurt too much to store inside. The fragments that are left feel more comfortable in reminiscence than their reality was when we lived it.

In this softer reverie, however, I may doubt past decisions I have made. Those doubts connect with today's loneliness or worry, and as a result, I begin to think that denying parts of my own life is all right in negotiating for companionship or security.

Or maybe it's the magic of compelling need. Someone else's need can draw with greater intensity than one's own, and it does have the power to enchant. But remember, there is neither peace nor justice in self-destruction.

Mother and Father of mercy and of love, when voices from the past call out to me, I thank you for teaching me how to focus on what counts right where I am, right now. Amen.

Audrey Ward

Forgiveness

Be merciful, just as your Father is merciful. Do not
judge, and you will not be judged; do not condemn,
and you will not be condemned. Forgive, and you will
be forgiven. Luke 6:36-37

We often use this Scripture to describe how we ought to treat others, forgetting that it applies to us too. It is not helpful to waste time applying hindsight to our choices and actions, except to learn. To waste time shaming ourselves for our inability to make ourselves perfect is unchristian. Hindsight is not fair. *All* of us do the best we can with the information we have, the energy, and the capacity. It's time to cut ourselves some slack here and apply this Scripture to ourselves.

Trust the Lord; forgiveness is offered *before we need it.* Before we screwed up, God forgave us. We have no right to hang on to judgment. We cannot see ourselves clearly.

God of my salvation, remind me that I am your beloved child, lift my weary heart into your hands, and breathe the breath of a renewed faith in forgiveness for myself. Amen.

Anne H. Brady

Praying

Devote yourselves to prayer, keeping alert in it with
thanksgiving. Colossians 4:2

I pray with my eyes seeing against my darkened lids a hungry child, a crying woman, a ravaged land, a warming fire, a rising sun, a soaring place.

I pray with my ears, lifted on strains of Bach and Beethoven, Handel and Mozart, hearing angels sing; moved by poets whose passionate words shape wings for my faith, giving expression to my inarticulate longings; pulled to intercession by voices from the margins, moans from the oppressed, silence from the voice-less.

I pray with my fingers, writing my pain, touching in love, tracing tears on the earth's cheeks, reading the Braille of humanity's despair and hope, clenching and unclenching in supplication and longing.

I pray with my heart.

Hear my prayer, life giver, mother, compassionate one, sister, spirit of hope, safe place, cosmic dancer, lover, mystery, home. Amen.

Carolyn Henninger Oehler

September 29

Hand in Hand

"'To love him with all the heart, and with all the understanding, and with all the strength,' and 'to love one's neighbor as oneself,'—this is much more important than all whole burnt offerings and sacrifices."   *Mark 12:33*

Balance and wholeness go *hand in hand* as we journey about
   this God-given land.
On some days we labor and take little rest.
On some we attach each task with great zest.
We work and we work until day is done.
No time to ponder if our race will be won.
Yet balance and wholeness should go *hand in hand* as we
   struggle and toil.
Please, God, give us a hand.
My body is tired. My feelings are numb.
My soul seeks God's presence. My mind has gone numb.
Where's balance? Where's wholeness, when energy's low?
O guide me, dear Savior, in the way I must go.
Take time for renewal. Spend time in the sun.
Share time with another in a spirit of fun.
Read tales of the love shared by servants of yore.
And glory in wonders of those gone before.
Those others have suffered and died in his name.
Our works may seem feeble compared to their fame.

Each day in our own way we all do our parts
To reach out to others with Christ-centered hearts.
Yes! Wholeness and balance are found *hand in glove*
If we enter each day with a heart filled with love.

Our bodies, minds, hearts, and souls hunger for your presence
within. Guide us as we seek to balance our lives. May we respond
as you would have us. Help us live with love for all. Amen.

Susan L. Scavo

September 30

Trust in the Lord

Blessed are those who trust in the LORD. . . . They shall
be like a tree planted by water, sending out its roots by
the stream. . . . In the year of drought it is not anxious,
and it does not cease to bear fruit.

Jeremiah 17:7-8

Trust in our time is a dubious concept. Globally and personally,
with violence or its potential all around us, how can we trust
persons or God? And if we trust, how can we know blessing? Is
it not more likely that we will be caught off guard and suffer for
it?

Jeremiah assumes a capacity to trust, but for some of us, trust
is not a given; fear is more our experience. We may have to learn
to trust by sending roots down through what seems to be parched
desert sand, hoping to find a stream or underground river bed that
will provide nutritive flow. We can find such nutritive sources,
even when much around us seems chaotic or unsupportive. Part
of trust in the Lord is celebration of what is given us. Some of us
are surrounded by good in the form of both persons and experiences. Others of us must look hard and long to find trustworthy
persons or elevated moments or positive events in our lives. But
all of us are capable of remembering some experience that has
brought us joy, even if long ago. To recover the memory and to
bring it into consciousness as a feeling experience that is ours in
the present is like putting roots into a stream of life. Once again,
for an instant or an hour, we celebrate joy. That joy is our

connection with God. It becomes a rootlet through which further nourishment and joy may flow. As the roots take hold and we know joy again, fear diminishes. We do not deny the reality of danger, but we stand as straighter trees, less vulnerable to violence, able to make life-affirming decisions that separate us from violence, and able to be intentionally nonviolent toward those whom we might otherwise make the victims of our frustration and our unhappiness.

Creator Spirit, who nurtures us though we are unaware, open our hearts to the joys we have known, that we may know joy and trust in the present and no longer vigorously disclaim the good that we may find in our lives. At the same time, keep us aware of the dangers we walk among or even produce, so that we may find healing ways to resolve them. Amen.

Janel Cariño

October

Parched Places

*Then your light shall rise in the darkness and your
gloom be like the noonday. The LORD will guide you
continually, and satisfy your needs in parched places,
and make your bones strong; and you shall be like a
watered garden, like a spring of water, whose waters
never fail.*   *Isaiah 58:10b-11*

It was a Saturday evening. I had just finished a favorite dinner
and was sprawled out on my bed. While surrounded by the lush
sounds of Bach organ music and the smell of a flickering, vanilla-
scented candle, I read and absorbed the comforting words found
in Isaiah.

It had been two years since I was widowed. My daughter had
moved out of our home, having recently completed college.
Living alone was proving to be singularly difficult, and weekends
left me feeling particularly isolated. My mobility then and now is
very limited due to a physical disability. I experienced loneliness
as a giant vise crushing my chest, an acute, excruciating, torturing,
very physical pain, a loneliness intensified by the isolating nature
of my disability.

Feeling utterly bereft, I cried out to God for nurturing and
affirmation, for healing of my parched places. For that day, there
was a transformation. Through words of Scripture, in a manner
that I do not understand, I found a channel, a connection to the
watered garden Isaiah writes about. I experienced the movement
of the Holy Spirit, bringing comfort through these and other words
of Scripture, and emerged renewed, nourished, and watered. They
are a mystery, these waters that never fail. When next I revisit this
terrible pain of loneliness, I trust that the spring of water, experienced before, will again renew my spirit.

*Loving and nurturing God, it is only to you that I can turn when
my spirit becomes a parched place. You renew and fill me so that
instead I become like a watered garden. Amen.*

Gay Holthaus McCormick

ˆWaiting with Anticipation

*He [Zacchaeus] was trying to see who Jesus was, but
on account of the crowd he could not, because he was
short in stature. So he ran ahead and climbed a
sycamore tree to see him, because he was going to pass
that way. When Jesus came to the place, he looked up
and said to him, "Zacchaeus, hurry and come down;
for I must stay at your house today." Luke 19:3-5*

Zacchaeus wanted to see who this Jesus was, but he was short
and the crowd so large that it obstructed his view. I can imagine
him standing on his toes, moving side to side as he tried to peek
through the gaps, only to have those on the route blocking his view
of Jesus. So he went on ahead, climbed a tree, and waited. Waited
in anticipation—knowing he would see Jesus with his own eyes.
And Jesus came and looked at him and told him to hurry up and
come down for today "I must stay at your house." Zacchaeus
prepared. He did what he could to see God. Then he waited. He
was available and waited with anticipation.

Sometimes we too are surrounded by crowds that seem to block
our access to God. Sometimes the crowds are composed of
people, sometimes pressures from work, demands at home, challenges to our physical health, or worry and preoccupation with
other concerns. There are times when we cannot move the *crowds*
and we can not see past them. Part of our journey is in learning
how to wait with anticipation even when the *crowds* loom over
us. Zacchaeus climbed a tree and waited. For me, daily quiet time
has become my tree where I learn to wait with anticipation. For
others, it may be weeding the garden, going for a walk, listening
to meditative music. It is that space where the crowd will not block
us, where we personally can be in God's presence. It is that space
where we can wait expectantly.

Waiting and being available to God is what we are able to do.
Then it is God who invites us down to be at God's side. It is God
who comes to dwell within us. We need to be available and wait
and then be open to allow God to come inside and with our whole
being respond to God's love through the ordinary moments and
happenings of our lives.

God of our joy and anticipation, sometimes life just gets crazy and unmanageable. So many things demand my attention and energy. So many people want to have a part of me. Allow me to stand in the midst of this chaos to wait expectantly for you that I might respond with my whole being to your grace. Amen.

Debbie Deane

October 3

I Can Do All Things

So God created humankind in his image, in the image of God he created them; male and female he created them.   *Genesis 1:27*

When my cousin was two, his mother took him with her when she went shopping. A kindly woman leaned over and asked, "And what is your name?"

"Eddie No," was his prompt reply. He had been told *no* so many times that he thought it was part of his name!

The "nos" are a large part of our socialization. As women most of us have been taught what we cannot do—sit with our knees apart, climb trees, do math, be independent, or be in charge. Women in different religious and cultural contexts have been given somewhat different sets of negatives, but almost all of us had these "nos" repeated so often and so subtly that they became part of our identity.

When Eddie became a little older, he learned that "no" was not a part of his name. Some of us find that the "nos" still stick to us. It is hard for us to break through and be what God has called us to be, to do what we really think we should do and what we really want to do. Sometimes it is others who set up the barriers; other times internalized sexism makes us conform.

It helps to remember that we are made in the image of a God who refuses to be boxed in. When Moses asked for the name of God, the reply was "I am who I am." Perhaps an even better translation is "I will be who I will be." We cannot control God with our definitions and categories; God will be God.

Will we hear when God calls us to break down the boxes that keep us from being what we are called to be?

Blessed Creator, free us from the negatives that tell us what we cannot be, so that we may reflect your image and do your will. Amen.

Wilda K. W. (Wendy) Morris

October 4

How Long, God, How Long?

A man was going down from Jerusalem to Jericho, and fell into the hands of robbers, who stripped him, beat him, and went away, leaving him half dead. Now by chance a priest was going down that road; and when he saw him, he passed by on the other side.
Luke 10:29-31

When we as women are not safe to be fully who we are—body, mind, and spirit—our being is wounded. We are like the man whom the robbers stripped, beat, and left half-dead. How many of us are survivors of childhood sexual abuse? How many of us have suffered physical and verbal abuse from a spouse or a family member? How many of us have had to hide our sexual and spiritual being and our identity lest it be stripped away? How long will we be robbed of ourselves and left for dead in a church and world hungering for wholeness? How long, God, how long?

Gracious God, you taught us to value the law of love; we must love our neighbor as we love ourselves. Yet we find it so hard to love ourselves when we have been shamed and stripped of our true birthright as women made in your image. In the parable of the good Samaritan we discover the amazing truth that our neighbor is anyone who needs us, most of all our own selves. The Samaritan is the one who stops, who sees, and who brings to wholeness the wounded one.

Our faith need not be a self-sacrificing or self-denying one but a self-recognizing and self-renewing expression of our humanness and need for one another.

Let us recall this affirmation as we go about our day:

*I am healed by the God of love who lifts me up and sees me as
I am. Amen.*

Anne M. Ierardi

October 5

The Witness of Life

*I call heaven and earth to witness against you today
that I have set before you life and death, blessings and
curses. Choose life so that you and your descendants
may live.* Deuteronomy 30:19

The year was 1980. I was suffering with low back pain, which
caused me to have great difficulty walking. Eventually, I could
barely put one foot in front of the other. After a week of tests,
doctors confirmed that I was suffering from polymyositis, a
sometimes fatal disease that causes the muscles to deteriorate. My
doctor said the bad news was that I had a *long row to hoe,* but the
good news was that the disease is treatable.

Since I grew up on a small farm, I knew what the term *long
row to hoe* meant and understood that I would be in the hospital
for quite awhile. I was scared. I knew I had God, my faith, a loving
family, and many caring friends. My condition grew progres-
sively worse. Finally, all the strength left my body except for my
fingertips. With a lot of struggle, I continued to brush my teeth
and feed myself. This was a time of great challenge, which I
considered to be a gift in my life in spite of physical pain and
emotional suffering.

Because of my faith in God, and in myself, together with the
constant support of family and friends, hope and life were my
focus rather than fear and death. I loved life and was not ready to
die. I accepted my limitations and decided I was willing to risk
living and loving with no guarantee of ever walking again. I
prayed a lot, kept the faith, and always believed that I would walk
again. I trusted God to be fully present, giving me strength to
endure and overcome. The only guarantee I had was the assurance
that there is fullness in living. I took the risk and chose life.

After four months of physical and occupational therapy, I

began to see signs of improvement. I attempted to walk on my forty-second birthday. At first I was unstable and nervous, but I persisted and learned to walk again. I was hospitalized for seven months, seven days, and seven hours. Physical therapy continued for two years; with each day, I grew stronger. Although I lost 20 percent of my muscle strength, the disease is now in remission, and the only difficulty I have is walking up stairs.

Each of us has her own burden. My burden is my body. Today, I am living with lupus, a baffling disorder of the immune system that virtually causes the body to turn on itself. Lupus is an incurable disease, but like polymyositis is treatable. For this, I give thanks and continue to choose life on a daily basis.

Gracious God, healer of body and soul, for all your blessings and gifts I give thanks. Amen.

Ressie Mae Bass

October 6

Love Yourself

You shall love your neighbor as yourself.
Matthew 22:39

This quote from Scripture is well known and referred to over and over by people of faith. We tend to focus on the first part of the sentence: to love your neighbor. We all know that this is very important, and we want to do things that will show people how much we care about others.

I remember when I was in college I was surprised by a comment made by the pastor of the church I was attending. He observed that I did a lot for other people but wondered if I really liked myself. He said that if I didn't, I would burn out trying to help others.

The second part of this Scripture is important for us. For many people today, especially women, it may be the most important thing for us to hear: If we do not love ourselves, we cannot love our neighbors.

Our actions often show how little we care about ourselves. If we abuse our bodies through drugs, eating disorders, or poor health habits, we are showing that we do not like ourselves. When we neglect ourselves and do not make our needs known, we are showing we do not care for ourselves. If we do not recognize when we need rest or *time out*, we will burn out and have nothing to offer. It is as we take care of ourselves and learn to love ourselves for who we are that we are able to know what it means to love others. We can be of the most help to others if we have taken care of ourselves.

Giver of life and love, help us to accept ourselves and know that we are lovable. As we know love, let us show that love to others as well. Amen.

Nelda Rhoades Clarke

October 7

Attitudes

Finally, beloved, whatever is true, whatever is honorable, whatever is just, whatever is pure, whatever is pleasing, whatever is commendable, if there is anything worthy of praise, think about these things.

Philippians 4:8

These words of Paul are on a plaque hanging on the wall in my home. Years ago I gave the plaque to my husband because he always looked for something good in everyone and in every situation. His positive attitude promoted trust and security.

Our attitudes have a profound effect upon our well-being. We all know people who have the attitude that nothing good ever happens to them; when something good does happen, they say yes, but . . . We know also persons who are bitter because of something that happened in the past. This bitterness colors all they do.

Paul tells us to place in our minds thoughts that are
true
      honorable
         just
            pure
               pleasing
                   commendable
                    excellent
                      praiseworthy!

Paul goes on to say that it is not enough to think good thoughts. We must *Keep on doing the things that you have learned and received and heard and seen in me, and the God of peace will be with you.*

What we place in our minds and hearts affects our attitudes and our actions. Let us be careful to look for something *good* in everyone and in every situation, and to rejoice in how often we find it.

God of truth, honor, justice, and purity, you who are worthy of all our praise, give us grateful hearts with positive, loving, and caring attitudes. Amen.

Sara Starnes Shingler

October 8

A Womyn's Meditation

The circle of White-haired Grandmothers formed a society of peace whose purpose was the upholding of the only law the Creator gave when the world was formed: You shall be in good relationship with all things and all beings in the Circle of Life.[1]

Womyn know the way of peace with all things on earth. They are the peacekeepers, peacemakers, peace upholders. In ancient matriarchal societies, there was no want—the world was revered for its abundance. Nothing was wasted or defiled—it was law.

Womyn know deep in their hearts that they are connected to all things. When harm is done to the earth or its creatures, it is done to all. Womyn grieve now in this time of great shattering, competing, raping, power-over struggling. We rise above our sorrow to create a vision for returning to balance, for preserving the future viability of the planet.

We plant, picket, protest, parent, promote, persevere, plead, persuade, praise, promise, procure, prevent, patch, and (em)power.

Take note of how you live in right relationship. Count the ways. Individual peaceful acts transform, transcend, and transport minds.

Gracious Giver of knowledge, may I remember that I am part of the Circle of Life. I will be mindful of walking gently on the good earth today. Amen.

Ann Audgerie

Free in the Lord

Now the Lord is the Spirit, and where the Spirit of the Lord is, there is freedom.   *2 Corinthians 3:17*

How many times have we boxed ourselves in with thoughts and memories of the past? How many times have we allowed them to consume our minds and to hold us back from doing what we need to do? Every day we make our spirits prisoners of our bodies, especially when we want to dwell on our past pains and hurts. The past can hold us back. It can keep us from experiencing the peace that comes from realizing our freedom of spirit. An awareness of our freedom empowers us in all circumstances. Jesus spoke of freedom of spirit when he said, *Know the truth, and the truth will make you free.* Spiritual freedom comes forth as faith that can move mountains of challenge in our lives—faith that allows us to rise above every limiting thought, habit, or action with joy and enthusiasm. Today we can choose to break the hold past hurts have over our spirits and to go forward with faith, strength, and serenity. Our freedom is a gift that can neither be given nor taken away by others, a gift that only God can give.

God of all being, transform our past and bless our present and our future with the priceless gift of freedom. Amen.

Tweedy Sombrero

Wholeness Is Centering Your Life

Keep your heart with all vigilance, for from it flow the
springs of life. Proverbs 4:23

This verse stands in my memory since my early youth. I can still see it written in the firm and clear handwriting of my mother. I had received my first autograph book for my twelfth birthday. I had wanted one for so long! This one was precious; the soft, navy leather covers were held with a brooch that opened with a small key to a rainbow of pastel-colored pages. I gave my mother the very first one. There she wrote this verse, which has since became central to my journey.

I remember that even at that early age, when anything related to the heart was interpreted as being synonymous with romantic love, I perceived something larger than that in what my mother wrote. I believe the Spanish translation is stronger in its meaning. A literal translation would go, "Above everything that it is to be kept and preserved as precious, preserve your heart, because it is from the heart that life springs forth."

Being raised in a Quaker family helped me, little by little, to understand the dimensions of the proverb. Who you are does not depend on your degrees, titles, rank, popularity, or wealth. Who you are depends on who you are inside yourself. Miguel de Unamuno, the great Spanish philosopher, explains this very well in his article "Adentro" ("Inside"). It is so easy to fool ourselves with the external appearances. It so easy to be broken by criticism, judgments, and other people's expectations of us. Only when one is able to center oneself can one pursue dreams, give and take, succeed and fail, cry and laugh, and still be whole.

Generous Provider of all good gifts, when I forgot to hold on to my heart, I got lost. When I tried to be everything to everybody, deep wounds were inflicted in my inside. When I looked back and found no one, looked forward and saw only a big blank, you forced me to look inside and, wonder of wonders, I found myself again and again and again. I am whole! Help me to preserve my wholeness and gracias Señor.

Yolanda Pupo-Ortiz

Green Shouts

For I have no pleasure in the death of anyone, says the
LORD GOD. Turn, then, and live.   Ezekiel 18:32b

Go, green, grow.
Burst out seed,
Dance your roots
Deep into earth.
Slurp up water, soil.
Sprout stalk, up, up.
Greet with green shout
Hello, welcome, amen.
Receive my breath,
Toss me yours in exchange.
Pop up, primordial promise.
Reach, stretch, imbibe this sun.
Make green, sing green,
Uncurl, pristine miracle.
Declare the ancient song,
You, delicate tendril.

Creating God, leader of cheer for the seed within us that insists,
I will be: As we fingertip newborn leaves, let us graze the
contagion of miracle and carry your song. Amen.

Dallas A. Brauninger

Time With God

It always comes back to the same necessity: go deep
enough and there is a bedrock of truth, however hard.[2]

I begin each day by writing three pages in longhand in a spiral
notebook. It takes about half an hour. If I skip a day, I really miss
it. I write whatever comes into my head. I try to keep the pen
moving and not worry about grammar or style. In three years of
writing in the morning, only once have I drawn a complete blank.

I was reduced to writing down the names of vegetables in alphabetical order.

I write this way for two reasons. The first is that it provides me with a kind of companionship that is always available. It used to be that if I wanted to talk something over with a friend, I would call around, get only answering machines, and be very frustrated. Now a listening friend is never any farther away than a notebook and fountain pen.

The other reason I write is that it keeps me from getting stuck. It keeps the internal conversation about my life going. I can take time to celebrate the joys and pleasures in my life. I tend to be more aware of personal issues and concerns because I write. If I complain about the same thing day after day, eventually I do something about it.

After I write, I go for a brisk half-hour walk. Writing and walking now form the core of my spiritual practice. They help to keep me healthy in my body and soul.

O God who knows all about me, help me find ways each day to be still and to listen to my own inner voices. Make sense of the deepest, truest longings of my soul. Amen.

Jeanette Stokes

October 13

The Still Small Voice

He said, "Go out and stand on the mountain before the LORD, for the LORD is about to pass by." Now there was a great wind, so strong that it was splitting mountains and breaking rocks in pieces before the LORD, but the LORD was not in the wind; and after the wind an earthquake, but the LORD was not in the earthquake; and after the earthquake a fire, but the LORD was not in the fire; and after the fire a sound of sheer silence.   *1 Kings 19:11-12*

Be still, and know that I am God!   *Psalm 46:10*

And the one who was seated on the throne said, "See, I am making all things new."   *Revelation 21:5*

This morning as I sit in meditation and listen to the quiet, gentle rain, I think about the still small voice of God. It is so easy to see God in thunderstorms, lightning, and powerful rain storms. But the God that is in the gentle, quiet rain is the form that is less showy, hardly noticed, and yet most nurturing to the ground that harbors new life. Often God speaks to us gently, if we are still enough to hear. God may speak through our feelings—compassion for another human being; or through our minds—an insight that makes sense out of a difficult situation; or through our souls—intuition that prompts a phone call to a grateful acquaintance; or through our bodies—a discomfort that reminds us we have not taken care of ourselves properly. God is speaking, and we are free to listen or to stay too busy to hear or heed.

When we do hear and then heed God's voice, we realize that the ground of our being is nurtured and refreshed and healed. Furthermore, new life springs forth. *Behold, I make all things new.* Even what we may have thought was old, unchangeable, or unredeemable may yield to God's prompting and to our response in faith. Miracles still happen when we listen to that still small voice.

God who art perfect love, help me to be still, so that I may hear your voice when it speaks quietly. Amen.

M. L. Henderson

October 14

Inner Healing

Let anyone with ears listen!   Matthew 13:9

The healing parables of Jesus have oftentimes seemed unhelpful to health-wounded people, as they have been interpreted to them. The presence of illness is real. Encountering the life-giving Christ is far more complex than being healed by a *magic zap.*

Often it has been implied that the point of Jesus' miracles was that anyone who had enough faith and trust could be healed. Jesus would erase all traces of illness, effecting a complete *cure.* I believe, rather, the point Jesus was making is that the power of the Spirit can enable resiliency and survival that transcend the limitations of the body and create an affirmation of being loved, not abandoned, by God.

Perhaps we have a prime example of this in the story of the bent-over woman. In the gospel story we read, "Woman, you are set free from your infirmity, . . . and immediately she straightened up" (Luke 13:12-13, NIV). Most of us have read this to mean that she stood up and was no longer bent over. But if you read the story closely, you see this as her essential problem: she had a spirit of infirmity eighteen years (v.11, KJV).

What occurred at healing? Maybe she still looked like the same old bent-over woman, but her spirit was redeemed, as was her resolve to survive humanly. Perhaps she was *standing up on the inside.*

The parables of Jesus speak of the healings but rarely follow those *healed* to see what happens to them and whether, in fact, those healed by God's grace become the *wounded healers* themselves.

People who embody catastrophic illness, whatever it is, may not have an option of being healed outwardly, at least not in an instant with all signs of their infirmity disappearing. Recovery is a long struggle for many, if there is to be recovery at all. The inner life, however, needs resurrection every day if people are to live powerfully in the faith.

The same is true of the sick places in our society. They need resurrection power so that they may be transformed into pulsing signs of hope.

Health and wholeness encompass not only able-bodiedness but also able-spiritedness. This is what we seek from our reading of the healing parables of Jesus.

Where are your *bent-over places* where you need Jesus to help you *stand up on the inside,* personally and in your community?

God of mystery and resurrection, break us out of all our tombs of illness—individual and social—that we, with your great Spirit, might be born again to ourselves and might be witness to your healing power in the world. Amen.

Valerie E. Russell

A Good Bargain

*For those who want to save their life will lose it, and
those who lose their life for my sake will find it.*
                                        Matthew 16:25

My life was a mess. I had just moved from one coast to the
other. I had given up a job that was fulfilling. I was now adapting
to a new role as helper for my spouse. But nothing seemed to be
working. I was lonely and depressed.

One day I was visiting with a friend and sharing my despair. I
had sought her help because she seemed to have her life together.
She told me her story about a time in her life when she felt the
way I was feeling.

"What changed for you?" I asked.

"I recognized that I had an addiction and that I needed a group
to help me find healing for it."

As she explained her process, I found myself bordering on
panic. I didn't want to give up my addictions. I didn't want to
sacrifice parts of my life that gave me comfort—even if the
comfort was false and destructive. When my friend had finished
telling me her story, I voiced my reservations.

"I can't face the fact that I have to give up so much more than
I already have. It seems that I'll have nothing left. I keep thinking
that there must be an easier way. How do you stand it?"

"It's true," she replied, "that I had to give up my addiction, but
what I received in return was so much more valuable. I got my
life back—and I got it back in Technicolor instead of black and
white!"

My friend had just reframed the whole idea of sacrifice from
one of giving up to one of gaining back. Since that day, my life
has changed so much that it's barely possible for me to remember
the despair and helplessness of that time. In giving up my addictions to God, I made room in my life for new challenges and
opportunities.

More than getting my life back, I found new life—colorful,
exciting, fulfilling new life. Giving up addictions in exchange for
new life. I call that a good bargain!

Giver of every good and perfect gift, please help me to care for myself in a way that will bring glory and honor to you. Amen.

Carol Spargo Pierskalla

October 16

Walking with God

But the Lord answered her, "Martha, Martha, you are worried and distracted by many things; there is need of only one thing."   Luke 10:41-42

Anger seems to have become our national pastime. People are calling ours *the age of rage.* Where do these strong feelings come from? In her book, *Anger,* Shannon Rainey states that the difference between righteous and unrighteous anger begins with the source; that is, not just what triggers our rage, but what lies underneath this powerful emotion. She lists four internal sources of anger. (1) *Violated Convictions.* We all have a God-given awareness of truth and justice, a sense of right and wrong. In Luke 15, the elder brother was convinced that his father's gracious reception of his wayward brother was unfair, so he refused to join the banquet. (2) *Unmet Desires.* When we desire something and don't get it, we become frustrated. Martha worked diligently while Mary sat at Jesus' feet (Luke 10). Martha didn't just want Mary's help; deep down she wanted Jesus' attention and appreciation. When she didn't get what she wanted, she felt justified in demanding that Jesus fix the situation at once. (3) *Feelings of personal assault.* We all want to feel safe, loved, appreciated, and respected. When our sense of personal safety and worth is threatened, we experience fear and hurt. Martha made a mistake. She was focused on herself. Without sitting at the feet of Jesus, we lose sight of what service is about. (4) *Rebellion against God: our root problem.* We want God to make things *fair.* We expect God to *fix things.* We may feel that God doesn't care when he doesn't come to our rescue exactly as we want him to. Anger can be a catalyst for spiritual growth. Understanding and evaluating the source of our anger can lead us to deeper repentance. Reflecting on the source can enhance our intimacy with God and help us see ourselves as we really are. We need to learn to control and transform our anger into praise. Nothing cures anger like the wonder of the grace of God. He longs to hear the cry of our soul—however angry, desperate, or rebellious—so that he can embrace us and quiet us with his holy love.

Heavenly Father, the injustice in the world makes me angry. I become worried and distracted, and I lose my focus. Help me to love you with all my heart, soul, and mind; to love others even as you love me. Amen.

Betty Susi

October 17

Clear Vision

That very Spirit intercedes with sighs too deep for words.   Romans 8:26b

For the first time in my adult life, I have access to a garden plot in my backyard. This small clearing had been tended years ago, but when I moved in, I noticed that several years of neglect had invited in the poison ivy and various tall, hay-fever-inducing weeds. I made a mental note to borrow garden tools in the near future and clear that space. I always have been drawn to what is living and green; suddenly, I was being invited to cocreate a future of flowering color and earth-fruits in my own backyard.

Four months later, I thought again about the small plot of land on the east side of my yard. Autumn had arrived; I had done nothing in the gardening department. Already bulb-planting season was upon me, and it was time to take time for the garden.

A strange phenomenon takes place whenever I intentionally carve out space away from work demands, lists of domestic tasks, preparation time for upcoming events, concern about health issues, phone-call fielding, and driving the superhighways. This phenomenon occurred when I lived in an apartment and tended to plants, but I have discovered a greater depth to it while I am outdoors.

You see, I stop thinking. The ground of my being clears and empties.

When my brain stops and my body engages in slow, life-giving work, I find a place of stillness and deep completeness. The weeds of my existence disappear for awhile. In such a rare space, the soul and Spirit connect in sighs too deep for words. This connection becomes transformed into living, wordless prayer—living as prayer.

Deep Holy Well of nourishment, grant us depth of presence connected wholly with you in the different spaces of our lives. Amen.

Lisa Withrow

October 18

A Clean and Complete Heart

Create in me a clean [complete] heart, O God, and put a new and right spirit within me.   Psalm 51:10

Cardiologists, as well as other physicians and technicians, use the electrocardiogram (EKG) to look for indicators that determine the health or duress of the heart. The EKG measures the electrical activity of the heart, which reflects its muscular or mechanical activity. The electrical and muscular activity of the heart is a cause-and-effect process. The electricity in the heart causes the muscles or the ventricles of the heart to function.

One condition that EKGs may indicate is a disorder called electrical mechanical dissociation (EMD). In EMD, the heart may appear normal, but in reality, it doesn't work. The heart, in this case, doesn't work because it's not *plugged in*. There is a *short* of sorts in the electrical system that causes the heart to simply lie suspended in the chest cavity. This condition is inconsistent with sustaining life.

A spiritual EMD may be apparent at times in our personal and corporate activity in our relationship with God. Who we are externally—our muscular structure and even our infrastructure—may appear normal. Everything looks like it's in place, but despite external appearances, we may be unplugged. The Spirit of God is the *electrical* activity that enlivens *the body*. One danger is giving so much attention to musculature, structure, and cosmetics that we forget to put the plug in.

Another understanding of the word *cleanse* is completion. The psalmist states with confidence that God cleanses or completes us. When God has cleansed or completed us, we shall be in his presence. But meanwhile we have the greater blessing of knowing that we are *plugged in,* for we shall see God in our lives and ministries. Blessed are the pure (complete) in heart, for they shall see God.

God, help us move beyond what we appear to be. May our hearts beat toward completion, so we may see you, and others see you in us. Amen.

Cheryl F. Dudley

October 19

Watchcare

Then Job answered: "I have heard many such things; miserable comforters are ye all."   Job 16:1-2

Through my work in hospice, I have come to understand that Job's visitors did a great job of grief care until they opened their mouths. Then all went downhill.

I have learned that in the dark night of the soul, what is needed is companionship, not answers. But companionship is the hardest thing to give! To place oneself in companionship with someone who is suffering is to face the awful with the courage to merely attend. In the garden, Christ asked his disciples to sit with him while he prayed. They fell asleep.

It is difficult to give the gift of *watching with* (I call it *watch-care)*. It is an unnamed sacred space and a sacrament to simply listen in the face of suffering. There is always the temptation to figure it out, to try to make sense of the experience. But this is a mystery beyond the ability of simple answers to comfort. Suffering is not a puzzle that can be understood simply. Not punishment or judgment, it is nevertheless awful. We like quick answers, to know what, why, believing that this will open the door to making *it* go away.

The good news is that in providing comfort one does not need to have the answers to unanswerable questions; the bad news is that it is far harder to resist quick fixes in the face of such suffering. Our work is to *sit with.*

Healer of the sick, help me give others the gift of presence, while helping me trust enough to say I don't know. Amen.

Anne H. Brady

October 20

Loving Our Neighbors

"The second is this, 'You shall love your neighbor as yourself.'"   Mark 12:31a

The familiar command of Scripture to love your neighbor as you love yourself is often defined as the Golden Rule: *Do unto others as you would have them do unto you.* In the United States, we have been reared to believe in the efficacy of this rule of conduct. Had we been reared in China, we would have learned a similar maxim stated in the negative: *Do not do unto others what you do not want others to do to you.*

Native Americans emphasized a different principle, that of learning to walk in another's moccasins. This emphasis on empathy, feeling with another, can move us beyond the Golden Rule to what has sometimes been called the Platinum Rule: *Do unto others as they would be done to.*

An emphasis on equality and on treating others in the way we want to be treated is not always productive of health and wholeness. Just as one does not give equal amounts of water and sunlight to a cactus, an African violet, and a philodendron, so persons need to be recognized as having unique needs. Some respond, for example, to being singled out for praise; others are embarrassed by it.

Responding with equity, not equality, and with empathy, rather than the Golden Rule, shows a love of our neighbor that recognizes and values individual difference.

Heavenly Wisdom, grant us the wisdom to love our neighbors as they wish to be loved, respecting that their wishes may be different from our own. Amen.

Elizabeth V. McDowell

Contact with God

The LORD GOD has given me the tongue of a teacher,
that I may know how to sustain the weary with a word.
Isaiah 50:4a

My daily reprieve from extreme worry, doubt, and fear is directly related to my conscious contact with God. Without it, I drift from sea to sea. It is a rock that stabilizes me and pushes me through both calm and stormy seas.

Winds may blow, yet my sail remains steady. The sun will wrest its light from night, and once again I can see more clearly.

When the winds start to blow again, my faith may wander. I have lost the strength to furl my sail, and again I feel lost at sea. Then in the distance the rock appears, but then vanishes once more.

I become weary of reaching out again and again. Yet the tide continues to move in and out, and I find the strength to wade through those currents that pull and push me away; finally I am once again in God's steady, calming waters at sea.

Ruler of all people on earth, when I am tired and empty, help me to find solace and comfort in the assurance that you are always by my side and will never abandon me. Amen.
Mary Ann Overcash-Austin

Wholeness Is Balancing Your Life

But Martha was distracted by her many tasks; so she came to him and asked, 'Lord, do you not care that my sister has left me to do all the work by myself? Tell her then to help me.'
Luke 10:40

I have been very critical of Martha because I am so much like her. As much as I like to be quiet in order to pray, read, meditate, and write, I find myself being a doer. I cannot sit down to read a book until I know that the day's requirements have been met: dishes washed, reports submitted, letters answered, calls returned, and so on.

It is in the middle of all of this activity that I refute Martha the most. Life cannot be a series of deadlines to meet, no matter how important those meetings and other engagements may be. The rush-rush without a time to think and, more importantly, without a time not to think but to empty myself to let the Spirit of God totally guide my most inner feelings and thoughts can only lead to spiritual desolation and physical fatigue and exhaustion.

Those are the times that I can push myself from the desk and from the calendar to be more like Mary. And then my soul is refreshed—so refreshed. "How can I forget this glorious feeling so soon?" I asked myself. "How can I allow myself to be pushed backed again and again to the rush-rush and to the never-ending goal of having everything done?"

But I do because you see, I am also critical of Mary. From the distance I remember a time in my own life, when I was very young, that I tried to be like Mary all the time. I'll never forget the day when I came out of that: the shame I felt when I realized that while I was having a wonderful time praying and singing, others had been working hard with the hurts of my country at war.

So you see, I am attracted to this Bible passage because I am in it. I have been both Martha and Mary. It has been this struggle of being one or the other that has led me to realize that wholeness is being both, not being Martha all the time, not Mary, but both. Being Martha and Mary is being able to balance out life, and that is what wholeness is.

Thank you, God, for your presence and help in the struggle of my life. How good was your push when I tried to be Martha all the time. How important your reminder when I, disregarding others, tried to be totally Mary and nothing else. It is still difficult, but if I hold on to you, I know I will remember to be whole: time to pray in order to do, time to do in order to go back to reflect and pray. Amen.

Yolanda Pupo-Ortiz

Dreams

An angel of the Lord appeared to Joseph in a dream.
Matthew 2:13a

As I put my four-year-old daughter to sleep, she was worried that bad dreams would come to her in the night. I rubbed her back and told her a story about the *dreammaker*, whom God had appointed to make sure that all people in the world would have good dreams at night. I described this dreammaker making his rounds, planting happy thoughts in the minds of sleeping girls and boys, women and men. These beautiful dreams would help them to sleep peacefully and wake up feeling good about life. These dreams would be about good things to eat, fun places to visit, and people who love us, I told Rachel.

As I shared this story, tears came to my own eyes. I thought of the times in life when it seems there are only dreams to sustain us because reality is so painful and offers little reason for hope. I was touched to realize that children as well as adults need God's voice of comfort and encouragement that comes through angel's dreams.

In the space of only ten verses from Matthew 2, Joseph had three dreams that prepared him to take Mary and Jesus into Egypt to protect the newborn child from Herod's wrath. Dreams can alert us, warn us, sustain us, and guide us. But this happens only when we truly listen to our dreams.

All of us need good dreams, especially in times of difficulty, and all of us have a responsibility to plant these dreams in those who are vulnerable and growing in faith. Like children, our minds are often frightened and long to hope. Who will keep our dreams alive and see that they come true? If we practice prayer and meditation, times of silence, and attention to God's Word in Scripture, the dreams will come. They will flow into us and become part of us. God will touch us and renew us, speaking to us even in the midst of healing slumber.

God of all compassion, thanks for sweet angels, who helped my Rachel and all of us enjoy a peaceful night. Amen.

Julie Ruth Harley

And Again I Say Rejoice

*The light of the eyes rejoices the heart, and good news
refreshes the body.*   Proverbs 15:30

I worked with five-year-olds one summer at a day camp in
Philadelphia. I loved working with that age!

Along with the day camp, every Wednesday evening we held
a neighborhood club and sometimes would have seventy-five kids
attend. One particular evening, two other adults and I were in
charge of games. We had just led two other age groups in games
and were just about gamed out. Exhaustion was setting in. However, we still had the five-year-olds, and in my mind they required
the most energy. It was their turn to come into the gym. For them,
games were the absolutely best part of the evening. They could
play Duck, Duck, Goose for hours and not get tired.

During the shift change, which by the way we learned very
quickly had to be well-organized and ordered, the five-year-olds
marched into the gym as the older group walked out. They were
instructed to wait in line in the balcony that overlooked the gym.
When they all arrived, I looked up from the gymnasium floor and
saw their little heads peeking over the railing and their little
radiant eyes looking down at me. What a sight to behold! The light
of their eyes and the smiles on their faces truly did rejoice my
heart and gave me the energy to make it through the rest of the
evening.

As the summer continued, it was these looks from the neighborhood children that provided me with the sustenance to make
it through. Amidst the poverty and violence, I found hope in the
light and the sparkle of their eyes.

*God of light and darkness, thank you for sending people into
my life who rejoice my heart. Help me also to be one who rejoices
the hearts of others. Amen.*

                                        Tammy L. Martens

Who Me? That's Ridiculous!

Now Sarah said, "God has brought laughter for me;
everyone who hears will laugh with me."

Genesis 21:6

I am always amused at the story of Sarah and how she laughed when told she would bear a child at the age of ninety-nine years! *Ha, Ha! That's ridiculous, impossible! I can't do that! I'm too old!* We often react the same way: I'm too old, too young, sick, tired, stressed out, handicapped by this and that—on and on the list grows!

The apostle Paul was frustrated with his "thorn in the flesh" and three times asked the Lord to take it away so that he might be better equipped for ministry. But God firmly replied, "My grace is sufficient for you, for [my] power is made perfect in weakness" (2 Corinthians 12:9).

It is easy to dwell on our limitations. Our self-esteem falls low, we shut God out, and we look for meaning and purpose in life by feeling sorry for ourselves. We are most aware of our aches and pains. God says, "Stop! Listen! Hear me! I love you just the way you are! Plug into the power I can give you, to live, love, and serve me, in any circumstance. Do what you can do!"

What a gift to receive! Nothing is too small to be a part of God's loving will for us: a smile, a thank-you for help received, a letter to someone who needs a friend, a joyful kiss, or loving thoughts sent in prayer to an ever faithful God. Let God into your life that you might always be a blessing to others.

God who art perfect love, let me be open to the wonderful ways you work in my life. Amen.

Rebecca J. Dobson

Soft as the Rock

*And I tell you, you are Peter, and on this rock I will
build my church.*   Matthew 16:18a

I look at my soft hands, uncalloused, contemplate
the pebbles I can grasp to build Christ's church.
Widow's mites, these hands, but also bearers of perfume
to lavish, like the Magdalene, upon his toughened feet.
Lamp bearers, too, my hands, to light the Master's path,
dispel the darkness, lead a stranger to the light.
They sweep and clean, my hands, and gather mustard seed
like coin, and fold in secret prayer and praise.
Servants of the Lord, these hands perform upbuilding acts
of love when Spirit-led, and joined with yours.

*Take our hands, gracious God; consecrate and ordain them to
your purposes in the name of Jesus. Amen.*

Peggy L. Shriver

Salt of the Earth

*You are like salt for everyone on earth. But if salt no
longer tastes like salt, how can it make food salty? All
it is good for is to be thrown out and walked on.*
Matthew 5:13

Salt is a purifying, preserving agent. In the Roman world it symbolized purity. Jesus compared believers to salt, demonstrating the influence of their lives in preserving and bringing purity to the world. Salt was also used as a form of money. Due to its great value as a basic staple, Roman soldiers were often paid with salt. That is the basis of the word "salary." As a flavoring, salt is sprinkled over food. Having no distinct flavor of its own, it enhances the flavor that is already in the food. As believers, we must sprinkle ourselves onto the world to make a difference in it.

I worked as a hospital nurse for forty years. Since my retirement, I have been searching for opportunities to sprinkle salt in these times. I recently became a volunteer at a local hospital in the emergency room. I also take blood pressures at a local shopping mall and have had the opportunity to sprinkle salt as people come by with their many needs or just to talk about their problems.

Lord God, thank you for the joy of serving you each day and for the power to overcome our complacency and to reach out to those in need. Amen.

Rosetta C. Dudley-Tilghman

October 28

Praises Go Up

For it was you who formed my inward parts; you knit me together in my mother's womb.   Psalm 139:13

My friend Miriam's cancer had been in remission for many months. But then the dreaded disease returned and settled throughout her spine and her skull. It was terrifying to hear the diagnosis. The evidence was displayed in the X rays of her body. The following days and weeks were intense. Treatments began immediately. Prayers also began and continued without ceasing. No one knew how long the cancer cells could be contained. At this advanced stage of the cancer's growth and development, few of the doctors and nurses were optimistic. The unspoken thoughts and fears were that it was a matter of time for cancer to take over her body and to claim her life.

Miriam had been a nurse. She understood very well what cancer is, how it grows, and how hard it is to stop. But that knowledge did not take away her hope, her faith, or her courage. She took all of the prescribed treatments and medicine. But her health and strength came from beyond the knowledge and prescriptions of the medical authorities. They came from within. They seemed to come from the powerful life force within her that is generated by prayer and by the concern and care of those with whom she is in community.

One friend brought her a cassette tape of Christian songs that includes "Rock Me Gentle." She listened to the tape often, and this song drew her to Psalm 139. She read and prayed it over and over. In it she found tremendous comfort and assurance that God knows her and her body intimately; God holds her close and never lets her be alone. Ever present, loving God was with her throughout the darkest, most fearsome, and most painful days.

Verses 19-22 helped her to focus all of her anger and energy against the destructive cancer cells that were the enemies of her God-given, life-giving body. The final two verses led her to plead with God to open her mind and heart to a new self-awareness. She needed to know if there was anything else keeping her from fullness of life; anything within her being that was in need of change. Having prayed earnestly through the ancient psalm, she entrusted her life to the giver of life. Gradually her hope and health were both strengthened.

O God of all time and space, let me fully know your life, peace and strength throughout my whole being. Amen.

Linda Scherzinger

October 29

All-Wise God

God's foolishness is wiser than human wisdom, and God's weakness is stronger than human strength.
1 Corinthians 1:25

Often we take ourselves too seriously, thinking that we can fix all that is wrong with this world. Those of us who grew up with the Protestant work ethic never learned how to play. I think somewhere along the line we were told that God worked hard six days a week and rested on the seventh. We should do the same, although we also had worship inserted as something to do on the seventh. Repayment for this lifestyle is hypertension, strokes, and heart attacks.

When I look at God's work, I am truly amazed at what God created. I am awed by the beauty of the earth. Then I come to the birds and animals. I believe that is where God had fun and maybe even played. In addition to many beautiful creatures, however, there are some truly odd-looking ones. Look at the aardvark, duck-billed platypus, or sea horse to see a variety of mismatched animal parts stuck together. And what about that horse with striped pajamas, the zebra! There are animals with uneven legs that look as if they might have been switched around. The hyena has front legs that are longer than the back ones, and the kangaroo has front legs shorter than the back. Of course the kangaroo also has a pocket for its babies and they hop and box. A giraffe has legs and neck proportionately longer than its body, and do those huge eyes really belong on that head? Then there are those animals that are huge but don't really fit their skin, like the elephant, rhinoceros, and manatee. The elephant has an overgrown nose, and the manatee looks as if its nose might have matched its face at one time but is now boxed in, and the rhino has a horn sticking right up in the middle. Maybe the next time that you feel stressed out, you should visit the zoo or look through a big picture book of animals. How can you help but laugh?

Lord of all creation, remind us that you are master planner, artist, and creator. Remind us that no matter how hard we try we cannot outdo you or outknow you. You know us and have known us from the moment of our creation. You know even the number of hairs on our heads and the number of days of our lives. Help us to not take ourselves so seriously that we overlook the joys of life and the humorous things that you created. Amen.

Jacqueline Sullivan

October 30

Where Is Your Goodness?

The LORD is good to all; [God] has compassion on all [God] has made.   Psalm 145:9 (NIV)

Creator,
A seizure?
We came to greet Mom, our first time since she moved.
Instead news of a grand mal seizure greeted us.
I didn't know this, too, could be a part of Alzheimer's devastation.
Where is your goodness?

The pastor of her church prayed for those in the nursing home, asking for joy and peace.

Can Mom experience joy through all the medication? Perhaps as she sleeps.

Where is your goodness?

I am grateful that Mom's clothes and body are clean.

I am thankful that Dad's visits seem to comfort her.

Where is your goodness?

I believe Mom will know it in death.

Can she feel it now? Oh, I hope so.

Have we come to embody Your goodness in forms that Mom can see, touch, and hear?

Help us extend your compassion through our eyes, hands, and mouths.

Please, God, pull up a bucket full of courage from our well of faith.

God, each of us longs for wholeness. May you grace those we love with your encouraging presence today. We ask it in the name of Jesus, who showed us what wholeness might act like. Amen.

Jill Kimberly Hartwell Geoffrion

October 31

All the Days of My Life

I lift up my eyes to the hills—from where will my help come? My help comes from the LORD, who made heaven and earth.   *Psalm 121:1-2*

I'm now eighty-seven years old. The hardest time in my life was during World War II. As an American citizen, I had been evacuated from a mission school in Japan to another in the Philippines because of threatening war clouds. Hardly had we arrived at Silliman University when suddenly Pearl Harbor was bombed, followed by the bombing of Manila.

After six months of living at the mission school, we were captured and then interned, first on the campus and then taken by barge to the other side of Negros Island. Six months later we were taken to the large internment camp at Santo Tomas University in Manila.

It was a small city behind walls, and we experienced diminishing contact with the outside world. There we were in crowded conditions with inadequate food, wondering how long it would last. Many people griped all the time, blaming the United States government for not getting them back home before war broke out. They felt that surely the government leaders would have known that war was inevitable.

But there were those of us who knew that *my help comes from Yahweh who made heaven and earth. Yahweh guards you from harm and protects your lives. Yahweh protects your coming and going now and for always.*

Truly those of us who had a strong faith in God had an inner strength to face the difficulties. We had a *hope* that kept us going with confidence in the future. At first we thought that the United States Army and Navy would be back in three months. We didn't know how little was left of Pearl Harbor. *Surely God restores my soul* was one thought that kept us going as we bore the delays that extended those three months into three years.

Finally on February 7, 1945, the First Cavalry came in overland through Leyte and liberated us. We finally had good Army food to nourish our starving bodies. Truly *God prepared a table before me in the presence of mine enemies*, even as we endured being under siege for several days. Finally Manila fell, and then Corregidor. We were overjoyed and relieved when United States ships came into Manila Bay and took us home at last.

Yahweh, thank you for guarding us from harm and protecting our lives, now and always. Amen.

Nannie Hereford

November

Refreshing Spirit

*He leads me beside the still waters; he restoreth my
soul.*   *Psalm 23:2-3*

Howard Thurman in his essay *"Reservoir or Canal"* suggests
that we have three lifestyle choices—a canal, a reservoir, or a
swamp.

A canal channels water from one place to another. A reservoir
holds water for future use. A swamp has an inlet but no outlet—life
becomes stale and dies.

Fifty years on a busy canal! Friends of many races and cultures.
Responsibilities that stretched the imagination and tested the
ability to learn new skills, develop extensive networks, and meet
the challenges involved in building bridges between people. A
husband, three children, six grandchildren, and two great-grand-
children. All made life exciting and fulfilling. Life was great on
a speedboat in a fast moving canal.

Then life changed. My husband's serious illness brought that
canal travel to a stop, almost.

Was it going to be reservoir time or swamp time?

A discovery! During all of those years a small raft had been
carrying water to the reservoir. Strong family relationships, supportive friends, a caring church family, and rich memories were
all there and ready. Still waters. Quiet time. Restoring time.

Back in the canal. The speedboat is gone. Now it's two in a
canoe with one paddle. New happy memories are being made.
Life is lived each day as creatively and as fully as possible.

No swamp for us!

*Power that brings healing to the sick, help us live each day with
the acceptance of change. Help us make happy memories. Amen.*

Hazel M. Boltwood

Feelings

God created feelings. To achieve and nurture emotional health, we must accept our feelings and those of others.

I have vague, painful memories of shopping when my children were young. If they begged for something, I would say, "You know you can't have that, so don't start begging." Or, "If you start crying here and make a scene, you can go home without buying anything."

Recently I went into a bookstore with three of my grandchildren. "You can each choose one book to buy," I told them. "It has to be something from the table of children's sale books or a paperback book because I can't spend too much today."

The children looked at books, trying to decide. Five-year-old Kevin sat on the floor looking longingly at a toy and book beautifully packaged together—priced at thirty dollars. He finally looked up and asked, "Grandma, do you know why I'm going to cry?" "I think so, Kevin," I replied. "I think you really want that toy, but you know I won't buy it."

"I am going to cry," he persisted. His older sister came to offer assistance, but he pushed her away. "It's okay, Barb," I told her. "Kevin is sad right now because he wants that toy and can't have it. But he will be all right in a few minutes and will find something that he can have and will like." In a moment, Kevin got up and walked away. By the time he reached the end of the aisle, he was cheerful again, ready to find a book Grandma would buy for him.

We feel more whole, acceptable, and loved when people acknowledge and accept our feelings. We also feel better about ourselves and others when we speak and act in love, accepting others and their feelings.

Am I afraid to deal with the disappointment of another because it touches disappointments in my life? Do I react—rather than respond—to another's anger because it taps into my own unresolved anger?

Creator God, help me to acknowledge and accept the emotions with which you created us. Let us respond to others with love. Amen.

Wilda K. W. (Wendy) Morris

The Gift of Dying

I came that they may have life, and have it abundantly.
John 10:10b

The doctors said her cancer was inoperable and untreatable. It was time, they said, to acknowledge that the end was near—maybe a month, maybe two. *Enjoy what time you have left. Eat what you like. Live life to the fullest.* She did.

She gathered her friends and the few family members she had. Her closest friends, who had lived with her most of her life, called in other friends. They came in twos and threes from far and near. Some came from overseas.

The staff watched as they came. They would stay in her hospital room for hours telling stories. We came to know her through the tales they all told. The laughter echoed down the hall as they remembered the white-water rafting trip in Australia, climbing the mountain in Africa, and the time in New York City. And there were remembrances of the children she taught, the bright motivated ones and the frustrating angry ones. Her life unfolded before our eyes and she became not just a patient, but a soul who had lived life fully and on her own terms.

We shed tears with the friends as they said good-bye and left. With her passing, we lost a friend also. But she gave us a gift that will always be with us: the gift of learning how to die. She held her own wake and got to live life twice, once in the living and once in the telling. How joyous she was, how gracious and loving!

Loving God, help me to live life fully today. Let me be aware of the preciousness of each moment and remember to share your love and friendship with all those I meet today. Amen.

Nan Jenkins

Simply Be

Beloved, I pray that all may go well with you and that you may be in good health, just as it is well with your soul.   *3 John 1:2*

So much of our lives is tied to how well we are tending to our souls. We can, and often do, spend our days exercising our bodies or our minds. We neglect, to God's dismay and to our wounding, that which is at the very heart of our being—our souls. A way to remedy this is to pause, however briefly, in each day to reach within ourselves until we feel deep within a signal that we are moving into the very center of our being.

In that place, reach out with your hands, your eyes, your senses, your heart. Begin to feel the mystery of God in your life without trying to explain it or to define it. Simply be. If it helps, close your eyes, find a quiet place, or stand amidst the bustle and tugs of the day. Whatever you do, center down so that you may feel the presence of God within you.

As women who seek faith, it is important to take time each day for a soul check. As women who have full lives, it is crucial to take time to touch the Spirit. As women who seek meaning, fight loneliness, work hard, question injustice, it is urgent that we take time for ourselves. We need to allow all the emotions—the joys, the sorrows, the anger, the fears, the ecstasy—to have their way with us in a time of resting with our souls in the hands of a loving God. Our paths to health and wholeness come when we take time to truly be in and with our bodies, our minds, and our souls. We cannot reject or neglect one and have a truly centered life that embraces the challenges and delights that come our way.

As you go about your day, take some time to center into your soul. Give God's voice and your ear time to covenant once again.

Holy Spirit of our lives, lift us up into you so that we may rest once again in your loving care. Wrap us in a love that never lets us go. Guide us onward into the joys of your Spirit. Amen.

Emilie M. Townes

Love Your Neighbor

*"'You shall love the Lord your God'... 'You shall love
your neighbor as yourself.'"*   Matthew 22:37-39

We live, it seems, in an age of narcissism, a *me first* era. The
mythological figure who stared adoringly and unmovingly at his
own reflection in the water until he became rooted beside the
stream that was his mirror is both ancient and contemporary. We
may know that figure as parent, sibling, friend, or self. Such
persons modify the biblical injunction into "you shall love your
neighbor as an extension of yourself"; and with that modification
all that is joyous and freeing about the act of loving evaporates
like water on a hot hearth. We become prisoners of those who *love*
us in that way, chained by the expectation that we be like them,
be only what they want us to be, or become what they were not
able to become themselves. So bound, we cannot be who we are.
So we apologize, become angry, feel guilty, try to be what we are
not, fail, become depressed, and apologize again. Or we manage,
barely, to *pass* as what we are supposed to be, feeling like
impostors or impersonators, empty within though apparently
effective without. Alternatively, we make the same demand on
those we attempt to love, becoming frustrated, angry, impatient,
or insulted if they do not conform to our ideas of who they should
be or become.

Many of us puzzle over the idea of loving our neighbors as
ourselves. It is hard to know real love of self if we have little sense
of the God-given self we are. Our true self is not the one who must
be what someone else is or was or wishes, but the one who is known
through a love that is unmerited and freely given, and carries no
expectation. We have too little experience with freely given love,
but usually we can find such a model somewhere in our histories.
Finding it, we can trace our way back to the divine love from
which it springs. In so doing, we finally become free persons, no
longer slaves to another's demands. We can freely love ourselves.

*Giver of all life, may I find my life in the love you give to all.
And finding my life, may I love it. Loving it, may I love others
without asking that they be what I want them to be. Amen.*

Janel Cariño

Jesus' Woman

*Then [Jesus] said to her, "For saying that, you may
go—the demon has left your daughter." Mark 7:29*

It is amazing how often in the Gospels Jesus is confronted,
challenged, and argued with by women. Confident women, feisty
women, desperate women. In a day when women were not
supposed to approach, let alone address, let alone contend with
any man, Jesus apparently found himself face to face with an
inordinate number of stand-up women.

His first miracle was prompted by a woman. At a wedding in
Cana, his mother points out that the wine is down to the dregs. He
tells her, rather snappishly, that it's none of their business and
furthermore, that his time hasn't come, presumably to initiate his
public ministry. Neither argumentative nor cowed, his mother
simply tells the servants to do his bidding. Jesus turns water into
more wine. Ready or not, he is launched!

At a well in Samaria, an outcast woman takes him on in
wordplay and theological debate. A hemorrhaging woman—unclean! unclean!—has the effrontery to grab his cloak. A Syro-
Phoenician mother deflects his initial rejection and with
stubbornness and wit wins his blessing: "For saying that, you may
go—the demon has left your daughter."

In a circle of women we are discussing Jesus's casting out a
demon from the mute demoniac. One of us observes, "I think I
have had a kind of demon keeping me mute. I think it is time for
it to be cast out. It is time to find my voice." The Jesus of Scripture
will welcome that!

*Jesus, may we approach you boldly and celebrate our friend-
ship with you. Amen.*

Penny Sarvis

Do Not Be Anxious

*Therefore I tell you, do not worry about your life, what
you shall eat or what you shall drink, or about your
body, what you will wear. Is not life more than food,
and the body more than clothing?   Matthew 6:25*

Women have been socialized to be anxious about the daily
routine. We're often anxious about basic needs because we are
the ones most responsible for satisfying them—for ourselves and
for our families.

Additionally, modern life has greatly expanded the food, drink,
and clothing list mentioned in Matthew. To do our job well,
society tells us, we must keep a home that is neat, clean, and
decorated in the latest style. We must keep track of and provide
transportation for the people in our lives to a myriad of appointments: dentists, doctors, gymnastics, soccer practice, basketball
games, music lessons—the list can seem endless—plus read to
the children every night! And, for an increasing number of us, we
do this while holding a part- or full-time job in the marketplace.
When women are overburdened, it is difficult not to turn even
freely chosen responsibilities into the abnormal apprehension,
fear, and self-doubt that define anxiety.

Today many women are working to reject the *supermom* myth.
We are finding ways to share family responsibilities more equi-
tably with spouses, children, other adult family members, and
friends. We are scrutinizing and rejecting responsibilities that do
not fit our individual values. And we are arranging our days to
include some perspective-developing connective time with
Mother Earth—to dig in her fragrant soil, to walk through her
enveloping breezes, and to *consider the lilies of her fields.*

*Help me look to you, loving Earth Mother, for the nourishing
calm I need to carry me through my busy day. Fold me in your
arms and strengthen my spirit. Amen.*

Barbara Klatt

Claiming God's Healing Power

*Jesus said, "Someone touched me; I know that power
has gone out from me." Then the woman, seeing that
she could not go unnoticed, came trembling and fell at
his feet. In the presence of all the people, she told why
she had touched him and how she had been instantly
healed. Then he said to her, "Daughter, your faith has
healed you. Go in peace."   Luke 8:46-48 (NIV)*

When I worked for a women's health clinic fifteen years ago,
I learned an important lesson about women taking an active role
in their own healing. Coming from the nursing profession I had
been wrongly taught that patients needed doctors to heal them,
with nurses serving as their assistants. The health industry has
relied on the unequal power equation in which patients are to be
"done to" and not "in partnership with." To keep this unhealthy
power over others alive, we are taught that the medical professionals are the experts and that the patients are helpless victims
of disease. I have noticed also a parallel tendency for some to
believe that ministers are the experts of God and only through
them can the laity understand God and live a spiritual life. Both
of these attitudes are wrong, wrong, wrong.

Working with women in nonhierarchical models of equal
power and leadership, I began to integrate into my job this
understanding that we ourselves are the experts of our own bodies,
minds, souls and that in partnership with doctors, therapists, and
ministers we all seek health and wholeness. This partnership is
not concerned with giving away power and submitting to the care
of someone else but with using God's power to discern needs and
to seek wholeness.

The story of the woman whose bleeding had not stopped (Luke
8:43-48) is a very powerful one for me and for every woman I
know. She and Jesus broke the taboo that has imprisoned women
in feeling shame about menstruation, a normal and healthy function of the female body. Taking action for herself, she claimed
God's power, and her faith brought healing.

I love working for women's ministries because I can keep the
focus on what is healthy for me, and in doing so I peel away

centuries of untruths and learn new, healing ways of being with myself, God, and others. Just like the woman who reached out and touched the hem of Jesus, we too can reach for God's truth and healing power.

Compassionate God, we reach out to you for the healing we need. Give us the will and wisdom to actively participate in our own healing, even as we are led by faith to kneel at the feet of Jesus and receive your power. Amen.

Ann Smith

November 9

The Exodus

"Say therefore to the Israelites, 'I am the LORD, and I will free you from the burdens of the Egyptians and deliver you from slavery to them. . . . You shall know that I am the LORD your God, who has freed you from the burdens of the Egyptians.'"　　Exodus 6:6-7

God's call, I was convinced, would be as certain as a burning bush or a pillar of fire. I wanted to be led as clearly in the way I was to go as the departing Israelites had been.

Where I ended up instead was the doctor's office. Aches and pains, recurring exhaustion and respiratory problems, all were sapping me. I wanted them to go away. I wanted to be healed, to be healthy.

I came to dread the ring of my office phone, knowing it might be a certain client who was increasingly hard to work with. My energies were falling; rest was more alluring than starting many projects. My eyes searched eagerly for that burning bush.

But my ears were missing God's own voice in my body, a voice growing louder and louder the longer I ignored it. Every exhausted sigh, every muscle twinge, every tensing when the phone rang, was speaking directly to me. That holy, caring voice was saying, "Whatever your call is, Beth, this ain't it!"

God said the same to Moses, grieving over Israel's painful slavery and saying that whatever their destiny was to be, "This ain't it!" The start of their restoration was first for them to come out of whatever it was that was destroying them.

Jesus looked at a disabled man who had lain by the pool at Bethesda for decades, at a woman whose life had brought her disdain, at a tax professional of dubious ethics, at a man with myriad psychological problems, and he saw what they could be. Whatever the possibilities in their lives, his vision of wholeness for them started with knowing, "This ain't it."

While God's voice came from flames in a bush for Moses, sometimes for us it comes from the burning pains in our own bodies and psyches, a physical message that there is some *this ain't it* in our lives. Possibly we are being called out into some kind of exodus—the start of a passage to wholeness.

Indwelling Spirit, I will listen to you when you speak to me in my very own body. I am deeply grateful not only for amazing healing processes you've built into this body of mine but also how it carries very personal, silent messages from you. Amen.

Beth Resler Walters

November 10

Works of Charity

Now in Joppa there was a disciple whose name was Tabitha, which in Greek is Dorcas. She was devoted to good works and acts of charity.   Acts 9:36

Tabitha is not well known. Yet I admire her. From her we can recapture some of the wholeness that Jesus brought to earth.

Her story is sketchy. She is a disciple who lived in Joppa. Her name was Tabitha, or in Greek, Dorcas. She was devoted to good works and acts of charity. Today much of the charity work of congregations is spearheaded and done by women. I can imagine Tabitha standing beside these women directing the work as she likely did in those earlier years in Joppa.

When she became ill and died, two men from the church in Joppa went to nearby Lydda to find Peter. Such attention suggests that she was well loved and respected, and occupied a position of leadership.

Because Peter dropped what he was doing and went with them, Peter must have thought highly of her, too. Peter prayed for her and then called on her to get up. Her eyes opened. Seeing Peter, she sat up. He helped her up, and showed her, alive, to the people gathered outside. *Imagine the kind of work an already revered woman, now raised from the dead,* would do. Her life after the event is unknown. This conceivably has more to do with who wrote Scripture and who selected the canonized texts, than with the kind of work she would have done in the rest of her life.

In my own journey to wholeness, gaining an understanding of the women who lived in the days of Jesus and in the early church is important. Emphasis has been given to the ministry and acts of the male disciples and apostles. Yet clues have survived about the women. By taking off patriarchal filters, we can begin seeing and celebrating the richness which is there.

Tabitha is worth celebrating. As I learn to celebrate women from the past, I learn to celebrate the women in the present. I learn to celebrate myself.

God of life, plant within us a desire to reclaim, know, and celebrate the women disciples, past and present, who are faithful to the gospel of Jesus Christ. Help us to celebrate ourselves as creatures created in the image of God, empowered by Christ. Amen.

Julia D. Shreve

November 11

Creative Birth

Create in me a clean heart, O God, and put a new and right spirit within me.　　　　　*Psalm 51:10*

I was feeling sophisticated and accomplished that morning at the picture-framing shop. I was there to sign some original craft work before it was framed. My new dress, a brown and black tiny check, gathered slightly at the bodice and hanging in nice comfortable folds almost to my ankles, looked good.

As I waited, a woman in the shop asked me when it was due. "What?" I replied. "Your baby," she said. I thought I recovered quite quickly, responding, "No, there's no baby; that's just fat!"

My questioner was embarrassed, but if only she could have

known the irony of her question: I had undergone a hysterectomy at the age of thirty-three. Endometriosis had taken its toll; after five surgeries, years of infertility treatments, and day after day of pain, I made the final decision to have a hysterectomy, ending all hopes of giving birth.

It was a difficult decision, and one I essentially had to make on my own. After all, it was my body, and I was the one who would have to live with the results. And now, nine years later, I still live with the decision. Most days I don't even think about it, but there are other times . . . seeing a newborn actually takes my breath away . . . a baby shower makes me sad . . . a bulletin announcement inviting families to light advent candles makes me livid . . . churches focusing on families, families, families make me resentful . . . and knowing I'll never be called mom sometimes makes me want to scream: Why not me? Why did you allow this to happen? Why can't I experience the wonder and miracle of creation? Yes, sometimes I am still angry at God.

Then the irony of the comment in the framer's shop becomes even more apparent. Over and over, my gift of creativity has been affirmed. Creation comes in many forms: craft work, leading a women's group, designing programs, developing relationships, maundering, making people laugh, teaching. These are all things I give birth to: things that I can say I have given the world. But only because, over and over, the Lord creates within me a clean heart, removing the pain, hurt, and resentment, and replacing it with the assurance that my God has plans for *me*, other than being a mother! These plans include affirming other child-free women that we are whole, complete, beloved, and capable of creation, in the eyes of the Lord. And so should we be in the eyes of our churches, our circles of families and friends, and in our own eyes.

God of the spirits of all flesh, I thank you for placing your hand upon me, for the love and peace I have in you, knowing that you chose me as your daughter, and that you guide and direct each and every moment and experience of my life. Let me rest, yet live, in that assurance. Amen.

Beverly Burns Erskine

The Pine

Therefore lift your drooping hands and strengthen your weak knees, and make straight paths for your feet, so that what is lame may not be put out of joint, but rather be healed.   *Hebrews 12:12-13*

The sound of water tumbling twenty feet over the rocks was music to my ears on the hot day. I sat below the falls with my feet in the icy cold water as long as I could endure it, soaking up the restorative powers of Mother Nature in such a setting. The youth who had hiked with me were laughing and shrieking as they played in the water. What a glorious day! As I was taking all this in, a tall tree across the stream caught my eye. By its size I could tell the pine tree had spent many years on the bank and had some precarious experiences. Thankfully, there were no names carved in its bark, but the top of the tree was dead and shriveled, curled over with cones still attached. Yet the bottom of the trunk looked healthy. A branch that had been growing horizontally had tilted upward toward the sunlight, becoming a surrogate top. What a symbol of living! Most of us are born healthy and strong. Then the storms of life come and something vital to us dies. Our dreams turn into nightmares. Although the dead part is long remembered and stays part of us, through God's love, new life of a different sort springs forth, one we never imagined but one we embrace with faith. In the wilderness were visible cornerstones of our faith: life, death, resurrection. Alleluia!

Loving and gracious God, give me strength and endurance to face the difficulties in life and to endure hardships while celebrating all that you have done for me. Amen.

Belva Trask Duncan

The Power of Love

*And now faith, hope, and love abide, these three; and
the greatest of these is love.   1 Corinthians 13:13*

He had been ill for nine years with the relentless cancer that
wouldn't let go of his body. He had refused to give in, journeying
as far as his Airstream trailer and his chemotherapy would let him.
As was his custom, he went to church on the last Sunday of his
life. On Tuesday he breathed his last breath and went to be with
his Maker, who had been his guide and support—the Lord of his
life.

With my father's death, I began to search for the meaning of
his life and, by association, the meaning of my life. Why are we
here? What matters? Is this just a meaningless exercise in getting
dressed each morning, going to work, having a bit of fun, saying
nice things, suffering some, and dying? The religious platitudes
and God-language of the church was 'insufficient. What is life
really all about?

The answer came as I read through the letters I received from
the children he had taught in elementary school—all grown now.
With every word, I saw the love he shared. I felt his love for me.
I realized that as long as anyone who was loved by him was still
alive to pass on that love to someone else, then the important part
of my dad still lived.

Love—the important thing. It's the Shema, the Great Commandment, Paul's chapter to the Corinthians. It had been there in
the church all along. But now I knew, really knew, the depth of its
importance and value. It's all that matters in the long run.

*God of love, help me to love you more each day and share your
love with each person that I meet today. Amen.*

Nan Jenkins

My Refuge

Hear my cry, O God; listen to my prayer. From the end of the earth I call to you, when my heart is faint. Lead me to the rock that is higher than I; for you are my refuge, a strong tower against the enemy.
Psalm 61:1-2

Our daughter knew that she was to be home for supper at 5:30. I was worried because she was late. When she arrived, she looked sad, and we asked why she was late. It turned out that her friend Susie had broken her doll. "Did you help her fix it?" I inquired. "No, I helped her cry." There come those times in each of our lives when the tumultuous world around us seems overpowering and we no longer have the strength to go on. We need someone to cry with us.

I had just turned my life completely over to God, at the age of forty-five, when I was diagnosed with multiple sclerosis. I called my daughter to tell her the diagnosis, and she cried with me.

Ten years have elapsed since I thought the world was closing in around me, and I have learned that I am not facing my disability alone. *I have MS; MS does not have me.* There are ten guidelines I use to face the challenges of each day. (1) Concentrate on your abilities rather than your disabilities. (2) Take one day at a time—direct your energy toward solving today's problems. (3) Adjust your goals to realistic levels so you will be able to reach them. (4) Enlarge your scope of values to include qualities other than physical prowess. (5) Measure your success by what it is possible for you to accomplish. (6) Avoid dwelling on your problems—keeping them bottled up can lead to an explosion. (7) Keep as active as you can. (8) Be able to ask for and accept help when necessary, but don't demand it. (9) Remember you must accept yourself before you can expect others to accept you. (10) Do your best and let God do the rest.

What are you waiting for? In the past ten years God has opened doors I did not think were possible—inspirational speaking, serving on city, state, and regional boards, traveling to the Orient, leading Bible studies, and writing, among other things. With God my disability has enabled me, not disqualified me.

God is looking for people through whom he can do the impossible. What a pity that we plan only what we can do by ourselves.

Guardian of our lives, help us to remember that nothing is going to happen to us that you are not aware of. Amen.

Marlys L. Kroon

November 15

Clutter and Clarity

On this mountain the LORD of hosts will make for all peoples a feast of rich food, a feast of well-aged wines, of rich food filled with marrow, of well-aged wines strained clear. Isaiah 25:6

One summer I discovered my mother-in-law frantically cleaning out her dresser drawers. When I asked her what she was doing, she said she had discovered a lump in her breast. "I wanted to make sure if I died that things were in order," she told me. More than one woman feels threatened by the lack of order in her life. More than one of us feel that if we could just keep our houses from drowning us that maybe we could be well.

God promises wellness to us in many ways—and surely one is the wellness of aged wine strained clear. One form of wellness, whether we have discovered a lump or not, is living on the other side of clutter, in a place called clarity.

I find the clutterless life a rarity at home. When I travel, though, I seem to be able to live into a more free space. Probably that is why I see travel as being so healthy for a woman.

I spend a lot of time in religious retreat centers, and I spend a fair amount of time in motels as well. The little cubicles compete with the king-sized beds, not only in physical lodging but in spiritual lodging also. Retreat centers are simple, sparse, uncluttered. Hotel rooms are cold, neat, impersonal. One has all I need; the other has more than I need. The former has ivory soap; the latter has little bottles of lotions and shampoo. One is cheap; the other expensive. One is low stress on the environment; the other high stress.

In hotels I always owe more at the end. Each phone call is

tabulated the way ancients tabulated sins. In retreat centers I leave often full enough of heart to want to leave an additional contribution. In the one I encounter rudeness often. In the other, hospitality exceeds my desire for it. The art in hotels is generic; the art in the other is very particular, very populist, very definite—made with real hands. I am encouraged in retreat houses to walk in well-stationed gardens. In the other I am encouraged to drive a car. One way of life blends into the other; I go from one to the other. I also know which one I prefer.

I like living well, by which I mean uncluttered, well strained to clearness. God promises this kind of wellness. Someday I long to know it at home as well as away. Heaven? Certainly then. But maybe even now.

Refuge of those who put their trust in you, strain me to clarity. Amen.

Donna Schaper

November 16

Open Invitation

Martha, Martha, you are worried and distracted by many things; there is need of only one thing. Mary has chosen the better part, which will not be taken away from her.   Luke 10:41-42

In the early months of our marriage we would get together on Friday night with one or two other couples from church. We would share a potluck supper and then play cards or board games. Occasionally we took in a movie or went ice skating. As enjoyable as those evenings were, I came to detest them for one simple reason. At some point in the evening the women always ended up in the kitchen while the guys were in the living room. And while they talked of jobs, and politics, and the church, and the arts, in the kitchen conversation always came back to recipes, hair, and babies. I longed to be in the living room where the real world was being discussed, but in those days gender kept me trapped in the kitchen.

In the familiar story of the sisters in Bethany, we see Martha bustling back and forth setting the table and refilling wine glasses.

Occasionally she catches snatches of the conversation. She'd love to sit down and listen, but there are pots to be tended. When she finally bursts angrily into the living room—towel over one shoulder, hands on her hips, a string of damp hair dangling between her eyes—her words tell me that above all she wants to join the party. She doesn't care if Mary comes to the kitchen. They would probably just get into a fight, given Martha's mood. No, Martha wants to be part of the conversation in the living room, but she can't give herself permission to do that. She cannot step out of her self-chosen and socially reinforced role of hostess. She has become isolated and trapped in her kitchen.

Martha becomes a caricature of our time. We are a busy, busy people. But often under that busyness is a restlessness. There is this vague sense that something is missing. Life is supposed to have meaning and purpose, but we can't quite pin that down in the spin of exhausting days. So we redouble our efforts and get even busier with the things in our lives. We take on activities; we change jobs; we move often; we trade cars every couple of years; we change our hairstyles. Nothing seems to satisfy for very long, and the meaning that life is supposed to have escapes us. We work long and hard in our beautifully decorated kitchens, but we can't get over the feeling that life is better in the living room. Out there the real meaning of life is to be found.

Martha was guided by the conventions of her society, while Mary was guided by an inner voice and took her place where only men had been before. Martha was guided by what she assumed the needs of Jesus were, Mary listened till she found the need that Jesus had to share the journey with a trusted friend. I suppose verse 42 can be read as a rebuke. I prefer to see it as an *invitation*. An invitation to Martha to put away her preconceived ideas about what Jesus needed and about what she needed to be doing. It is an invitation to get out of the kitchen and join life in the living room. The end of the story isn't given to us. Usually that means we are to complete it in our own lives. Can you be open to what Jesus needs from you right now, even if that is rapt attention? Can you set aside your busyness to stop and listen as Jesus pours out his concerns for the world? Is there a kitchen you need to abandon?

Giver of every good and perfect gift, continue to come into our lives as a guest and give us the grace to welcome you with open ears and open hearts. Amen.

Lynn Vahle

ʼNothing to ʼDo with ʼMe

[Jesus] said to him, "Do you want to be made well?"...
"Stand up, take your mat and walk."   John 5:6-8

The man had lain paralyzed for thirty-eight years. Thirty-eight years, almost as long as I've been alive. Surely this story has nothing to do with me!

A new day dawns, and here I am. Okay, I'm going to eat better, exercise, spend time in daily devotion. Yet here I lie, wanting thirty minutes more rest before I grab a chocolate-covered doughnut on the way out the door, dreading the day that lies ahead.

What will make me stand up and take responsibility for my life and my health? Perhaps this story has more to do with me than I thought. Jesus asked the man if he wanted to be made well. Do I? Do I really want the benefits of a healthy life? Only a yes allows me to hear Jesus clearly: Stand up. Stretch your muscles. Walk around the block. Eat fresh fruit. Start the day thankfully.

Health is not just the absence of disease. It includes participation in life to its fullest—physically, emotionally, and spiritually. Do I expect God to bail me out after a life of irresponsibility? Just because I haven't lain paralyzed by a pool for thirty-eight years, do I assume I am not debilitated by my life habits? Yes, I need to hear Jesus' words: "Stand up and walk."

Struggling, I stand up on the cold floor, pull on my sweats and sneakers, and head out in the chill dawn air. I return invigorated by blood coursing through my veins. I give thanks for this new day.

Jesus, you know I can be lazy. Continue to urge me to stand up and walk, to care for my body that houses your Spirit, and to listen to your Spirit within me. Amen.

Adele ʼK. ʼWilcox

Casseroles or Committees?

For surely I know the plans I have for you. . . . when
you call upon me and come and pray to me, I will hear
you. When you search for me, you will find me; if you
seek me with all your heart.   *Jeremiah 29:11-13*

When I was asked to serve as president of American Baptist Women's Ministries, my response was an oft repeated, "Who me?" I had all the excuses you could think of, and I used them. During my deliberations the above verse was sent to me from three different women in different parts of the country. Finally I said yes. But the doubts continued as I began to serve and became involved in preparing agendas, planning meetings, and serving on the ABC general board.

My frustrations began to surface in conversation with a friend. Just that week I had been busy preparing for the executive committee meeting. Three of my friends had deaths in their families. Frantically I tried to prepare casseroles and be available to those friends. It is times like these that I want to get off the committees and bake casseroles or visit the sick. It seems I am so busy I don't have time for *real* ministry.

My friend listened to me and gave me some sound advice. Later she sent me a letter that comes out and restores my perspective whenever things get hectic. Let me share part of that letter with you:

> Now let's talk about casseroles. I don't have much time for casseroles either. You are right that even though the crazy things we do, do not always feel like ministry, they are. Even so, when someone we love is hurting, it is time to get off the merry-go-round and go make a casserole. In the midst of preparing agendas, chairing board meetings, and writing articles we also occasionally need to stop and bake a casserole.
>
> The trick is that whatever we are doing we should not feel guilty. Writing agendas is ministry and so is baking casseroles. God doesn't want us to feel guilty when we are doing ministry. It is all ministry.

Remember the joy while on the journey. What is stealing your joy? Is it other people or any number of things? Sometimes we think we should be somewhere else doing something else—like baking casseroles. The trick is to live where we are in the joy.

So get on with it. Don't look back, or even too far ahead. Just tell God, I'll do what you want me to do today. And I believe that you won't ask me to do anything that I can't do or delegate.

Strength of those who labor, I do believe that you have plans for me. Let me always be open to the leading of your Spirit and to doing ministry where you have placed me at this time. Help me to know when to plan for committees and when you want me to make casseroles. Thank you for the hope! Amen.

Evon Laubenstein

November 19

Faith Prevails

How long, O LORD? Will you forget me forever? How long will you hide your face from me? How long must I bear pain in my soul? . . . But I trusted in your steadfast love; my heart shall rejoice in your salvation.
Psalm 13:1-5

They were a couple with four children who lived in our daughter's neighborhood. The wife never looked happy, but the husband seemed friendly and cheerful.

The woman's mother attended our church and occasionally brought the grandchildren to church school. She mentioned the unhappy environment in the home. The husband had a terrible temper and would often beat the wife and the children.

Law enforcement officers were frequently called to intervene in abusive situations, but nothing was ever done about them. Finally, the woman escaped with three of the children, but the oldest child, a boy, had taken the school bus home before the mother could get to him.

A couple sheltered the family, and friends from the church provided clothing and personal items. After a while, we were distressed to learn that she had decided to return to her husband. She wanted all of her children and said that she would endure more beatings in the hope that the next time she escaped it would be with all four of them. Her only fear was that he might kill her before she could carry out her plan.

On her return, the husband promptly burned all of her new clothing. In a few weeks he moved the family to Montana.

Justice was swift and sure in the new state. The first time he beat his wife, he was sent to jail. Her long-sought freedom was finally a reality. She and her children had escaped their tormentor.

Eternal Friend, thank you for your steadfast love and mercy. Thank you for deliverance from those who would make life a trial and a burden. Give us the ability to offer justice and compassion to all with whom we associate. Amen.

Ruth T. Bosserman

November 20

Humor

A cheerful heart is a good medicine, but a downcast spirit dries up the bones.   *Proverbs 17:22*

This proverb observes that a cheerful heart is good for us. In recent times scientists have studied the effects of laughter and humor. They have learned that laughter can produce enough cardiovascular stimulation to raise and then lower pulse rate and blood pressure. Other findings have demonstrated a release of stress and anxiety, relief of pain, and beneficial muscular exercise. The most recent studies are indicating that laughter may help the body's immune system.

Common sense has told us that laughter is the best medicine for a long time. But somewhere along the way many of us have buried our sense of humor. It is said that children laugh four hundred times a day, while adults average fifteen laughs a day. Maybe we have dampened our ability to see the funny side of life because as we grew up, we heard messages such as *Quit giggling! Act your age! Wipe that grin off your face!*

Humor is not just telling jokes and funny stories. Rather, it is a lighthearted approach to troublesome times. Humor helps put things into a positive perspective. I have learned that the need for humor is no laughing matter—we really must take this business of lighthearted living seriously, loosen up, be a child again, find joy for ourselves, and share it with others.

During fifty years as a registered nurse and forty-eight years of marriage, with the joys and stresses of raising four wonderful children, I have been strengthened by faith, love, and laughter.

God of all emotions, of all experiences, help us to balance our lives with joy in the midst of sorrow, humor in times of apparent hopelessness, and laughter in facing our problems. Amen.

Mable Doris Gooden

November 21

Quiet Trust

O LORD, my heart is not lifted up, my eyes are not raised too high; I do not occupy myself with things too great and marvelous for me. But I have calmed and quieted my soul, like a weaned child with its mother; my soul is like the weaned child that is with me.

Psalm 131:1-2

I gave birth to a child this year. And so I have learned that even those things that are the most natural can be a struggle. The first few weeks of breast-feeding were far from those serene Madonna and Child images I'd picked up in art history class and filed away in my fantasy life under *M*. The means of fulfillment was an exercise in frustration for both of us. Peter's efforts were frenzied and frantic, his head searching and striking in all directions. It was as if he were trying too hard to take control, to be in charge, to make it happen. The very thing he sought couldn't have been any closer, and yet unable to be still before the source, he couldn't feed on what he needed.

If being still and focused is difficult for a hungry newborn, it is more than a slight challenge for those of us who have seen more of life and have come to know its demands, its needs, its injustices. We tend to come before God with our agendas—all the things we want and need God to do to make things right. Even the best causes and intentions can distract us. With our eyes not raised too high, and our minds not occupied with too much, we need to come with humility of heart—the humility of one who knows she is a child of God and that God is ever near and ever ready to feed our hungry souls.

Source of all things and Sustainer of each one, we thank you for your ever present love. Calm and quiet us before you so that we can receive what you seek to give us. Draw us near and feed us with your truth, that we might be strengthened to live your will in this world. Amen.

Jennifer P. Warren

November 22

Hemmed In

Susanna sighed deeply, and said, "I am hemmed in on every side. For if I do this thing, it is death for me; and if I do not, I shall not escape your hands. I choose not to do it and to fall into your hands, rather than sin in the sight of Yahweh."   Susanna 22-23

It is an all-too-familiar story. Sexually harassed, Susanna must now decide. Will she succumb to the elders' sexual advances? Or will she stand against them, knowing that she, the victim, will be made the culprit? What will she do?

Like the mother who chooses welfare over a minimum-wage job because she cannot afford child care, Susanna is hemmed in. Like the woman who continues to live with an abusive spouse, dependent upon his income, she is hemmed in. Like the woman who forgoes a mammogram, since her insurance does not cover *unnecessary* procedures; like the young corporate attorney who tolerates sexual advances from her boss, hoping to break the glass ceiling; like the pastor who is forced to accept the lower compensation of a small church because the larger congregations refuse to consider a woman, she is hemmed in.

Women have become accustomed to being *hemmed in*. We have been sexually, economically, physically, psychologically, racially, and spiritually battered. But the greater tragedy is that our battering has too often come from our sisters. Ours is a time to lift one another up, rather than tear one another down.

There is hope in Susanna's story. The hope is not that Daniel gallantly comes to her rescue. No, the hope is that Susanna was courageous enough to take a righteous stand despite the consequences. And God responded to her courage with justice.

Sisters, God is calling us to a courageous faith. God is calling us to join the struggle for one another in the fight for justice. God is empowering us to make a difference. May our daughters and our granddaughters read the story of Susanna and fail to understand what it means to be *hemmed in*.

Liberating God, lead us out of bondage into freedom. Look graciously upon our efforts at sisterhood so we might unify our strength in the quest for justice. Hear our prayer not only for ourselves, but for our little sisters. Amen.

Annell George-McLawhorn

November 23

There Is Hope

And you will have confidence, because there is hope; you will be protected and take your rest in safety. You will lie down, with no one to make you afraid.
Job 11:18-19a

In Job 10:1 we read words that tell us how Job was feeling: "I loathe my life; . . . I will speak in the bitterness of my soul." Job had lost everything! His family, his possessions, his health. Have you ever felt despair like that? Have you ever felt that God has abandoned you or that he is punishing you?

In chapter 11, Zophar, one of his friends, tries to encourage him. This is the message he gives to Job. It is a promise to us, as well. Our Lord is the Lord of hope. Like Job's friend, we can be ambassadors of hope to those who are in despair. We can give hope to one another, nurture and love to one another. Hope is a gift we can give to each other when life pushes us down. We can face each day because we know that God's presence is with us. We are secure because there is hope; we can rest in safety because he is our protection and our eternal hope. "Be strong, and let your heart take courage, all you who wait for the LORD" (Psalm 31:24).

Radiant and Glorious God, there may be times in my life when I feel hopeless and afraid. You have promised to be with me always. Help me to remember this promise and to put my hope in you. Amen.

Donna Authelet

November 24

Friendship

Some friends play at friendship, but a true friend sticks closer than one's nearest kin.   Proverbs 18:24

What is it that pushed me toward health and wholeness? More than anything, it is my friends. Most of us, women particularly, recognize the value of friendship—but you would never know it from reading theology. It is one relationship that is seldom treated in seminary texts or in pastoral-counseling courses, or in sermons. Friendship reveals a great deal about ourselves, each other, the nature of community, and our relationships with God—but it simply doesn't exist as a theological category. While friendship was important in Greek and Roman civilizations, it has never been a central concern of Christian thought. How did this happen?

Ours is a world in which work is dominant, and we identify ourselves in terms of what we have done, not who our friends are. Real friendship requires time, which is at a premium for all of us. There are also some reasons that are more deeply rooted in the way we understand relationships and values. Ethics, as we have understood it in recent times, has been concerned primarily with our obligations, not with the many choices we make about how we will live. Thus friendship, a personal bond entered freely and without obligation, has been unable to find a place in ethics.

There is another specifically theological reason, and we find it most clearly articulated in the Sermon on the Mount, where Jesus challenges his followers to love their enemies. He says, "For if you love those who love you, what reward do you have? Even the tax collectors do that!" (Matthew 5:46). We should not underestimate how deeply rooted in Christian thought is this preference for *agape* love, which is nonpreferential and not necessarily reciprocated, and how deeply it has influenced our belief that somehow *philia,* love which is preferential, chosen, and mutual, has come to be considered inferior. We need to make honored space in our theology and ethics for the very particular bond of friendship, while at the same time acknowledging that the introduction of *agape* has been a unique contribution of Christianity that has increased the quantity of charity and grace in the world.

We need to take friendships more seriously, to vest them with meaning—but our culture doesn't help us do this. We need to begin to sacramentalize friendship, to give it the attention and reverence it deserves.

Friendship, with its features of choice and mutuality, cannot be the whole truth about love. Underlying it and sustaining it must be the self-giving spirit of *agape.* But only an impoverished theological vision could deny friendship an important place in God's scheme of things.

We address you as Friend, one with whom we have a voluntary relationship maintained with love. Teach us reverence for our friends, for whom we give your our heartfelt thanks. Amen.

Peggy Halsey

November 25

Open My Eyes[1]

Beloved, since God loved us so much, we also ought to love one another.　　　　　*1 John 4:11*

She was the most cantankerous lady I knew. She had opinions about everything—most of them negative. She didn't like the church. She didn't like the way people mowed the church lawn. She didn't like the pastor. And now I was about to subject myself to several minutes of her complaining.

I got lost twice in the hallways looking for her apartment. I told myself it would be all right to give up and go home, but I came across the door before I could turn around. She was glad to see me and thanked me for the book that I brought. Then she invited me to sit down in what might have been a dining room. Stuff was piled everywhere so it was hard to tell.

"These are some magazines I've been going through looking for crafts," she explained as I moved them off a chair. "I think making crafts is a waste of energy, but some of the ladies from church spend so much of their time creating things to sell at the bazaar each Christmas that they run out of ideas. It's up to me to find something new for them to do."

As I sat there listening, I noticed some beautiful wood carvings in a glass case. There were large ones, small ones, abstract carvings, people, and animals. On one shelf by itself was an incredibly beautiful nativity scene. "Did you make these?" I asked, unable to believe in the possibility.

"No, one of my students made them. They came to me when he died."

I could not imagine her as a teacher. One of her students had a great deal of difficulty learning and was unable to hold a job that could provide for his needs. But she had been there to encourage him, and he responded to her direction. Eventually he moved to a facility where he was cared for. When he sent her a Christmas card, she responded by returning the greeting, inquiring about his welfare, and reminding him of her faith in his abilities.

Years passed. One day a messenger arrived with a box. When she opened it, she found the wood carvings and a letter from the home where the man had been living. He had recently passed away, leaving no next of kin. The staff found the carvings and the cards with her return address and decided to send the art to her.

I sat with tears in my eyes as she told this story. She was looking at the carvings as she finished her story. "I told him he was a special person. I told him he could do things no other person could do. I told him he could make a difference in this world. He should have listened to me." Her voice got quieter. "I was right."

I left the apartment and walked to my car. I had a talk with God on the way and apologized for all the things I had said and felt about this woman. How could I have failed to notice this little spark in an otherwise angry woman?

God of all knowledge, open my eyes that I might see. Amen.
Marge Nelson

'That I Might See

*Seek the LORD while he may be found, call upon him
while he is near.*   Isaiah 55:6

Early in my art school experience, I found my class in life drawing to be particularly frustrating. Repeatedly, my teacher would say as she reviewed my drawings, "Priscilla, you are not seeing." Not seeing? What was I missing? I could draw the human figure. What was I not seeing? I had the prescription changed for my eyeglasses. Same feedback. I still was not *seeing*. Come year's end, my teacher proclaimed that my drawings revealed that I was beginning to see. Wonderful. What had changed? I didn't have a clue.

Two more years of drawing classes followed. I did my best drawings using a beautiful Chinese paintbrush and watercolor paint. As I was drawing one spring afternoon, I had a most strange sensation that my drawings were flowing out of my paintbrush, not out of me. It was as though the brush had a life of its own. One amazing drawing after another flowed from my brush. I felt a deep peacefulness, at one with my work, meditative, and free of self-consciousness. After three years, I had stopped trying so hard to draw. *And I was truly seeing and drawing.* At the end of the class, I asked my teacher to comment on my drawings. He said that he had not wanted to even speak to me, dare he interrupt the miracle that he was witnessing. But as soon as we began to analyze my process of creating, I felt afraid. I had let go of control in my drawing, and the results were astounding. As we talked, I felt myself clam up inside, self-consciousness returning. I had experienced a taste of the deep freedom of creativity, and it filled me with awe.

The process of drawing and the process of prayer share much in common. Both involve letting go and allowing someone else to take over and guide our hand or our heart. Both involve letting go of our self-consciousness as a way of *seeing* the sacred around us or within us. Both require the courage to be still, to persist, and to be open to the holy, not knowing what will happen to us when we do. Both are gifts of God that open our eyes and souls to truly *see.*

Creative Spirit, your ways are a constant surprise, unexpected gifts that help us to see and then live anew. Free us to let go to receive you. Amen.

Priscilla Dreyman

Simple Gift

I am hard pressed between the two: my desire is to depart and be with Christ, for that is far better; but to remain in the flesh is more necessary for you.
Philippians 1:23

"Don't let her die in pieces," I prayed. My mother had developed a gangrenous toe that seemed like one burden too many. Arthritis had already confined her to a wheelchair, and she had lost her sight. The doctor was reluctant to remove the toe because he wasn't sure how much more they would have to remove; circulation was very bad in both legs.

As I prayed, I began to realize that if ever there had been a person who could handle such afflictions with grace and courage, a person who could be a wonderful witness to the encompassing love of God, it was my mother. She has a gift of joy that bubbles out over people around her.

I still pray that when the time comes, she will cross over peacefully into the life everlasting. But I have come to accept her ministry through these days.

My mother finds challenge and satisfaction in memorizing Scripture so that she can participate in leading her women's group at church. She types letters to people who need her special encouragement. She can't see what she is typing, but as long as her hands are positioned correctly on the keys, it works out pretty well. She listens to books on tape and is eager to learn. She rejoices that when she could see, she learned all the verses of many hymns. (As a child I thought she knew all the verses to all hymns!) Now she sings with enthusiasm, though I must admit she isn't very fond of those of us who write new words to old tunes. I tell her to sing the *right* words and not to worry about anyone else.

She has taught me a lot about simple gifts. On very bright, sunny days she can see just a little bit. If there is a red rose, she sees a blur of red. If I am wearing a brightly colored blouse, she sees the color and rejoices. We have fun with it and laugh and thank God for surprises.

The power of the Spirit in this woman doesn't take away all her afflictions, but it does give her the opportunity to touch lives in the living out of her faith.

By the way, the toe got better. The doctor couldn't figure it out.

Loving God, thank you for the simple demonstration of faith. Amen.

Susan Gillies

November 28

Welcome Places

When you give a banquet, invite the poor, the crippled, the lame, and the blind. And you will be blessed.

Luke 14:13-14a

When I was growing up, we regularly spent holidays at my aunt's home. She was a single woman who chose to live in a culturally, ethnically, and economically diverse inner-city neighborhood near her work. For me, the days spent in her home were wonderfully different from my usual suburban surroundings. Around her table gathered a diverse group of friends and acquaintances—each of us finding a *welcome place* at her table.

The wonder of the gatherings was not the food (the pies were not homemade), but the people and the conversation that took place as we lingered at the table. I heard stories of lives that had begun in distant places and of struggles against barriers that were absent from my life. The poor and the outcast became present at the table. Although ideas were exchanged and debated, commitment to love and justice for others was evident and affirmed. At times, perceptions of my immature world were turned upside down. In hindsight, it was as if the teachings of my Sunday school Scripture lessons were brought to life around the table: understandings of who is to be a part of the family of God.

Who sits at our tables? When we gather to sit around the table of our places of work, home, church, and neighborhood, how do we enlarge the places? It is in creating *welcome places* to speak, to listen, and to receive each other that God's family, a community of faith, will grow. Commitment is strengthened and lives empowered and made whole.

Our gracious God, help us to create welcome for all, that there might be many places at our tables. Strengthen us to acknowledge your grace—to hear others' stories—so that love and justice become present in the relationships of our lives. Amen.

Julie Tulloch

November 29

The Fence

Who have been chosen and destined by God the Father and sanctified by the Spirit to be obedient to Jesus Christ and to be sprinkled with his blood: May grace and peace be yours in abundance.   *1 Peter 1:2b*

The Fence

I built a fence around my heart,
It seemed somehow safer at the start.
I built a fence round my mind,
The time to think I could not find.
I built a fence around my hands,
To get involved I could not stand.
I built a fence around my feet,
I wanted only to retreat.
Then Jesus came my soul to bare.
The fence is down, at last I care!
The fence is down, at last I care!

Jesus, thank you so much for coming into our hearts and lives and changing us to please you. We know without your guidance and direction it is so easy to build a fence around our lives and not get involved for you. Show each of us the way you want us to live, and we truly will take down the fences that keep us from you. Amen.

Jacqueline Sullivan

November Gray

*[God] made the storm be still, and the waves of the sea
were hushed.*   *Psalm 107:29*

Our struggle to overcome life's hurts surprises us when, after
the hard work, we notice one day, mysteriously and unobtrusively,
we have turned toward life.

I was surprised—
After wearing always-gray school clothes
Trimmed at best with white,
Ribboned once with a straggle of red at the wrists.
"Gray," she had said, "so you won't stand out."
So later, when her granddaughter was born,
She spoke the words again over the phone.
"Your niece is really quite homely," she said.
"No baby's ever ugly," I said.
By then, I had learned to cradle another newborn
In my arms, the infant I once was,
Still crying to be held.
I wore no gray again, until now,
Gray hair beams its compliment to these wrinkles
And I am surprised
To find my face in the mirror
And see nothing ugly.

*God of compassion, how you do give us the alleluia of grace
to reconcile us with ourselves! Amen.*

Dallas A. Brauninger

December

Contentment

I have learned to be content with whatever I have.
Philippians 4:11

After spending some time in an Anglican monastery in Cambridge, Massachusetts, I decided that I had much to learn about being content with whatever I have. I hope that confession is good for the soul because this is my confession.

For years, it seems that my life has been filled with the desire to have more stuff. For whatever reason, I never seemed to grow tired of shopping not only for others but also for myself. I found myself *stockpiling* linen, toiletries, cards, books, clothes, paper goods, whatever I thought would be necessary for somebody's existence. I could not pass a sale ad without making a list of all the things that I considered to be *must buy* items. Especially because they were on sale!

But while I was taking classes at the seminary this summer, I realized how little time I was using for shopping. I was so occupied with reading, writing, and studying that I had little time for routine grocery shopping. I actually lost interest in the *sale ads* and found that even when I really needed to go to a store I debated with myself about the need to go!

While I am sure that I have not lost my desire to shop, I feel less excited about the prospect of entering a mall or going near a store, other than bookstores and grocery stores. I am striving to be disciplined as I make lists and purchase only those things on my list. For I learned that I am not any happier with more things. In fact, I actually felt spiritually more at peace when I had fewer distractions. I know that my pattern of acquiring will not be broken easily. But I also believe that my life is already richly blessed, and "more stuff" becomes irrelevant.

O God, how excellent is your name! Please help me to know that simple does not just mean less; it actually gives a greater quality to life. Contentment will come to me as I let go of this world's possessions and live with that which is most important—the love of your Son Jesus. Amen.

Cecelia M. Long

And Just in Passing, Say . . .

*Then people came out to see what had happened, and
when they came to Jesus, they found the man from
whom the demons had gone sitting at the feet of Jesus,
clothed and in his right mind. . . . Jesus sent him away,
saying, "Return to your home, and declare how much
God has done for you."* Luke 8:35, 38-39

Girl children listen
  resisting the naming,
Looking for ways
  to be truly themselves.
Girl children listen
  resisting the shaping,
Fleeing from life plans
  not really their own.
Putting away
  even talents and giftings,
Shutting off feelings
  that might overwhelm.
Fighting the
  stereotypical oughtness.
Walled into living
  a part of life.

Girl children listen
  too young to count the cost,
Giving fear's legions
  a heart-hold within.
Girl children listen
  and in their rebellion
saneness in safety,
  find numbness instead.
Cocooned then in niceness,
  escaping the power,
of a girl-child naming
  whose fit was too tight.
Until, like the Gerasene,
  there was a freeing,
God's gift of new cloaking,
  mind fully alive.

*Loving God, help us to recognize the demons we carry and to
let you free us to live in our right minds. Amen.*

Carolyn Hall Felger

Inner Light

The LORD is my light and my salvation; whom shall I
fear?   *Psalm 27:1a*

As the season of short days and long nights creeps on, this child of the South, now living in the North, thinks a lot about the sun. Memories flood back of shirtsleeve Christmas mornings so bright that the glare blinded us as we rushed outside to play with the new toys that Santa Claus had brought us.

Now the light outside my window is pale, reflected off snow and ice. I brood in the gathering darkness. I am not alone in my mood, for in this season the whole earth is leaning toward the light.

We make many ceremonies. The winter solstice is celebrated with a feast of candles to mark the return of the sun. Christmas trees decked with twinkling lights and tinsel appear in many windows. Explosions of color lift the darkness of country roads as unabashed enthusiasts outline entire houses and their surrounding trees and shrubs in strings of lights. In some places, fear of persecution requires—or simply the Spirit dictates—that this yearning for light be confined to a single taper burning in the depth of a church crypt.

There are many seekers of light: the Jewish mystic yearning for the Holy, the Buddhist searching for Enlightenment, the Christian pilgrim awed by the glory of the angels as they point toward Bethlehem, the Quaker's patient waiting for the coming of the Inner Light.

What is the nature of the light we seek? Is it self-actualization? Greater knowledge and understanding? I confess I do not know, but I believe it is more. What I do know is that light is not possible without darkness. One comes on the cusp of the other. What is knowledge and truth unless the pain and struggle that produce it lead to wisdom and compassion? What is self-actualization if it is divorced from concern for justice and the community?

Seeking the light, I am led to the liberating love of God. It is a love that freely chose to come into the world in darkness in total vulnerability, as a newborn child. It will stay with us forever.

True and only Light, give us grace to see you in our brightest days and our darkest nights and to know you as close as our own breath. Amen.

Peggy Billings

December 4

Sparkling Light

I will turn the darkness before them into light, the rough places into level ground. Isaiah 42:16b

Meditation, prayer, and visual imaging are acknowledged today by most medical professionals as legitimate tools in the storehouse of practices to be employed for healing. They stand alongside medical protocols and healthy lifestyle behaviors, each sending powerful messages of *Heal! Be well! Live!* to the body. There is ample evidence that both the body and the spirit respond, and health resurges.

My cancer diagnosis came during Advent. I was in a large city that lit up the skyline each night with fairy lights—outlining buildings, trees and houses, yards. All those bright sparkling lights were achingly beautiful against the darkness.

When my chemotherapy began, I was advised to visualize the chemicals doing their job in my body. I was told that some people find the image of warriors going to battle helpful; others are amused and energized by the image of little pac men running around inside, gobbling up the cancerous cells. However, neither of those worked for me. I discovered my own personal imagery in the Christmas lights all around me. The nurse told me that the three drugs used in my treatment were each a different color: one was red, one yellow, and one clear. In my mind's eye, I saw each one as a colored light; I pictured thousands of sparkling fairy lights coursing through my body, lighting up the dark places where the cancer cells were lurking. I felt *lit up,* and stronger for it. It energizes me today to remember.

My Advent meditation gave the image deeper meaning for me: *The light shines in the darkness, and the darkness did not overcome it* (John 1:5).

My imaging corrected the tendency to focus on darkness, common with a cancer diagnosis. Perhaps it is unavoidable. When you first understand what has happened to you, you are plunged into despair that is accompanied by long, dark nights, bereft of sleep. But the light of each new day does appear—predictably, inevitably. God's promise to turn the darkness into light becomes a beacon of hope.

The healing power of light became a sustaining metaphor in my quest for wellness. A water colorist knows that you must have darks in order to see the lights; a photographer understands that contrasts in light and dark are essential for focus. I live with the knowledge that there is a lurking darkness in my body, but I know that God's sparkling airy lights are there as well.

Holy God, may the healing power of your light sustain me all my days. Amen.

Marguerite Mackay

December 5

God's Spirit

For God did not give us a spirit of cowardice, but rather a spirit of power and of love and of self-discipline.   2 Timothy 1:7

There's a saying on a poster that I have in my office: "There are times in life when persons have to rush off in pursuit of hopefulness." We are living in such times, difficult times for our society, and especially difficult for women, children, and youth. Programs, support, and *safety nets* in place for decades are being challenged and dismantled. These are times when hopefulness is indeed in short supply in our collective human spirit. Under these circumstances, individuals working for justice and compassion can be stricken with a sense of futility, frustration, and depression. Sometimes, after I have given workshops on the prevention of harassment and abuse, I leave feeling absolutely ineffective. The day you are reading this page may be such a day for you. On such days, our best efforts should be devoted to *rushing off in pursuit of hopefulness.*

On such days, it occurs to me that hopelessness in my spirit leads inevitably to illness in my temper and my body. Health and a sense of wholeness seem out of reach as I rush through mail, computer files, lobbying schedules, and client appointments.

It's exactly on such days, in this self-centered, mean-spirited decade, that the Scripture reminds me of God's gift of a healthy spirit, not a spirit of cowardice or timidity, but of power and love and a sound mind. The spaces of our lives, as a nation and as individuals, need the healing power of a *sound mind* more than ever. Take a moment today to remind yourself of the gift of God's spirit of power, love, and a sound mind. Your health and your ministry depend on it.

Gracious, gift-giving God, surround me in the healing power and love of your Spirit today. Refresh me with a sound mind and a hopeful heart. Amen.

Pat Callbeck Harper

December 6

Rejoice in the Lord

Rejoice in the Lord always; again I will say, Rejoice. Let your gentleness be known to everyone. The Lord is near. Do not worry about anything, but in everything by prayer and supplication with thanksgiving let your requests be made known to God. And the peace of God, which surpasses all understanding, will guard your hearts and minds in Christ Jesus.   Philippians 4:4-7

The wonderful feeling of peace and joy in one's heart and mind are significant contributors to being healthy in mind, body, and spirit. For many that peace and joy are hard to find. Often the key factor is the word "worry"—worry about what was done, worry about what was not done, and worry about what will be done tomorrow.

Paul seems to say that the first step to the peace and joy that God gives is rejoicing. To rejoice with someone means to be glad with that person. To rejoice in the Lord requires making personal contact with God to develop a continuous relationship.

Everyone has worries—worries about our work, worries about our home, worries about our school. Worries can be found anywhere. Worries keep our hearts and minds from reaching up to God and reaching out to others. Worries rob our lives of peace and joy. Just wanting to stop worrying is not enough. We must fill the *worry space* with something else. Paul tells us to turn our worries into prayer, rejoicing in the Lord, reaching out to others in tenderness, humbly praying with gratitude. And the *worry space* in your life will be filled with the peace of God in your heart and mind.

God of all comfort, fill our hearts and minds with your perfect peace and joy. Amen.

Sara Starnes Shingler

December 7

Jesus Is My Dance Teacher

He said, "Do not weep; for she is not dead but sleeping." And they laughed at him, knowing that she was dead. But he took her by the hand and called out, "Child, get up!" Her spirit returned, and she got up at once.   Luke 8:52-55

I lettered a sign and hung it over my desk: "Jesus is my dance teacher." It helps me lighten up. It came to me as an image in meditation: Jesus approaching me, reaching out his hand, drawing me to my feet, inviting me into a graceful, twirling, rhythmic dance with him—a divine remedy to the grim, clenched-jaw drivenness I often get into with work.

The Christ-Spirit is lively and playful. It calls the inner child to awaken, even when others (and we ourselves) may be convinced that she is dead. Christ believes in her, knows her potential liveliness, and reaches out to connect with her, energizing her and drawing her forth.

The story of Jesus healing the woman with the twelve-year hemorrhage is curiously inserted in the middle of the story of Jesus' bringing the little girl back to life. Jesus is on his way to the home of the child when the bleeding woman comes up behind him and boldly touches the hem of his garment. The woman is forced to tell her woundedness and witness to her healing in public. Then she is tenderly affirmed: "Daughter, your faith has made you well" (Luke 8:48).

There is profound truth in the interweaving of these two stories, perhaps known best to those who are surviving and healing from incest and sexual abuse. The wounding of our reproductive self numbs or *deadens* our inner child. The tremendous courage required to reach out, as the bleeding woman did, for help and to speak our terrible truth, as the healer made her do, is healing and leads to reestablishing loving relationships. (He addressed her as "Daughter.") It is also part of the path *on the way* to waking up and bringing to life our inner child from her deathlike sleep!

Life-Spirit that was in Jesus, thank you for making us whole. You extend a hand to connect with and energize the life forces deep within us women. You lift us to our feet and lead us into the dance of life. Amen.

Noel Koestline

December 8

Healing Tears

> *You have kept count of my tossings; put my tears in your bottle. Are they not in your record?* Psalm 56:8

I have a small blue glass vessel that was made by Palestinian glassblowers in Hebron, Israel. It is a vessel for collecting tears, a replica of the ancient tear glasses. It reminds me that God sees my tears and my sadness, my pain and my struggles.

Tears are an avenue of healing. I don't like to cry—my sinuses get clogged up; my head hurts. The tears, the crying, the healing all hurt. But I heard one time that a person who has been deeply wounded must cry for one hundred hours in order to heal the wound. (It's probably like the *seventy-times-seven rule* on forgiveness. What it means is that one has to cry a whole lot of tears to heal a deep hurt.) Whenever I cry, I count off some more minutes toward my ultimate healing.

It's not a comfortable thing to heal. When there is a cut or a break on one's body, one stage of the healing of the tissues is pain. Perhaps it is the pain of nerves knitting back together, of tissue rebinding itself to bone. The pain of emotional or spiritual healing happens when the torn, bruised places within us are woven back together. There is hurt in that process, but the result of that hurt is wholeness, healing. What was broken becomes a place of great strength. My own woundedness becomes my source of wisdom, my well of compassion.

Great Healer of body and soul, remind us that the tears, the pain, the anger, and the sadness are your gifts to us for healing. That when we cry, shout, or sigh, we are held by the Compassionate One who keeps count of our tossings, who puts our tears in her bottle. Amen.

Beth A. Richardson

December 9

Weary to the Core

Spirit Creative, give us light, lifting the raveled mists of night; Touch Thou our dust with spirit hand and make us souls that understand.[1]

I was weary to the core. Pastoring three rural churches in towns where one tragedy followed the next, I moved numbly from crisis to crisis, with no time for personal grief. My ability to set healthy boundaries between my life and the needs of others evaporated. I felt a call to silence and a sense of urgency to be using my hands to create—what, I did not know. I recalled the voice, long submerged, of my nine-year-old self proclaiming that I would be an artist when I grew up. At age thirty-seven, I finally heard my own voice and went to art school, anticipating creative bliss and monastic solitude. Instead, I found hard work, relentless confrontation, and complete rebirth and healing.

Christine Woelfle, my sculpture teacher, challenged me early on. I said to her, "I'm interested in exploring art and liberation." Her response stopped me short. "That's funny," she said over her shoulder, "I thought that was a redundancy." Weeks later, I carved a writhing sculpture that I thought was quite dramatic. The class responded with a group yawn. Christine said, "Priscilla, you are too concerned that your pieces of art have meaning. Let the meaning that is inside of yourself into your work, and then it will have meaning." Her words threw me into a panic. I did not know how to express what was deepest within myself.

Three years later, I was diagnosed with a problem requiring surgery. I did healing meditations and found the walls of protection within myself beginning to crumble. One day, my inner self would no longer be silent. My own voice poured out of me into a painting of all the people I had known who had died. The painting was vivid in color. As I painted, the lump in my throat grew and exploded; I finally cried for all of those beloved folks for whom I had never grieved. Then I stood up straight, enormously relieved. I felt healed. I felt free. Art and liberation did go hand in hand. And my artwork was filled with meaning.

Spirit Creative, you give us the gifts of art and creativity—gifts of the Spirit that bring new life and healing, new hope and new beginnings. Using these gifts, O loving Creator, help us discover and express our most authentic selves. Amen.

Priscilla Dreyman

December 10

Walking with the Lord

I will tell you what I have learned myself. For me, a long five or six mile walk helps. And one must go alone and every day.[2]

For many years I have practiced the habit of going for a half-hour walk in the morning. In recent years I've added writing to my morning routine. First, I write for half an hour; then I walk. Walking seems to be the exercise I am willing to do. When the weather is bad, sometimes I do low-impact aerobics with a videotape, but that is so boring. It is the same instructor and the same music every time. Walking is never boring.

Even though I walk the same route every day, it is always different. The light, shadows, trees, and people are always different.

I notice the changing of the seasons. Sometimes it is so hot and humid I think I may have to swim home. Other times the air feels like silk against my skin. And other times it is so cold it takes a full ten minutes for my hands to warm up when I get back inside.

I began walking for the pure exercise of it. Brenda Ueland, in *If You Want to Write,* points out the virtue of long walks. She says that when she goes for a long walk, a walk that is a little too long, her imagination works better. Some days I walk with a friend and we talk. Other days I go alone. When I walk alone, my mind begins to clear. It is like meditation.

In the last year or so I have begun to run just a little. I run about fifty paces three or four times during my walk, just to make my heart beat faster.

Walking is good for my body and for my soul. It is inexpensive and requires very little equipment. I can do it almost anywhere.

Gracious God, you created us, and you sustain our bodies and our spirits. May we know you in the movement of our own limbs, in the beating of our hearts, and in the air we breathe. And may we give you thanks. Amen.

Jeanette Stokes

December 11

Healing from Greed

All who believed were together and had all things in common; they would sell their possessions and goods and distribute the proceeds to all, as any had need.
Act 2:44-45

Here is a moment in Christian history that is often overlooked. The very first Christians were true literalists. They took Jesus at his word and began to live his teachings.

Most people today would describe this as a utopian outburst based on unrealistic expectations. But it does show that people can function with the common good in mind rather than the survival of the few. People have the capacity to overcome greed.

This country is desperate for healing from greed. We live in fear of not having enough while consuming many times more than most of humanity, but making ourselves feel guilty and powerless before the forces driving such greed is not the answer. We need to have a very clear idea what our real needs are. With more and more women and families ending up homeless, it is not helpful or realistic to have women give away their livelihood in order to avoid greed.

What we need to overcome greed is assurance. We have God's assurance that our needs will be met, but in Acts needs were cared for through belief and action. Christians formed networks and communities to provide assurance and the distribution of resources to people according to their need.

Today churches coordinate their giving to help those in poverty, but little attention is given to the security needs of members who have more than enough. Wealthy members continue to hoard for *a rainy day* while letting too many people get washed down the drain.

This is not a casual undertaking. It would require a highly organized plan based on love, trust, and good documentation. The Acts community of the next millennium must not be a power broker, but an empowering broker that nurtures the lives of all God's family.

Loving and freeing God, heal us of our insecurities that leave us in the grip of greed. Free our imaginations to dream of ways to share our resources so that more of your children can live the fullness of life promised by Christ Jesus. Amen.

J. Ann Craig

A Spiritual Journey of Infertility

For the LORD will comfort Zion; he will comfort all her
waste places, and will make her wilderness like Eden,
her desert like the garden of the LORD; joy and
gladness will be found in her, thanksgiving and the
voice of song.   *Isaiah 51:3*

Five years had passed since the hopeful time when my husband and I began trying to become pregnant. Our expectations ran high; we were ready to become parents. Months passed, then years, as our prayers for a child went unanswered. As time went on, doubts grew in me about God. Infertility felt like a cruel sentence, pronounced each month, driving me ever closer to despair.

During that time my prayer life was a litany of anger and defiance in the face of a punishing God. My childhood faith tradition and role models had led me to believe that my worth as a woman was wrapped up in the role of motherhood. I had not been encouraged to pursue a career or further education. My scripted plan had been seriously interrupted, and now I was blaming God.

Slowly, gently, God pursued me and would not allow me to live a lie. Gradually, through the caring of true friends, counselors, and the Holy Spirit, I became aware that my desire to be a mother had become an all-consuming idol. There was no room in my life for the God who had borne me and had carried me from the womb (Isaiah 46:3). Eventually it began to dawn on me that the important thing was not that my prayer be answered. My relationship with the God I questioned and blamed was at stake.

The pain of infertility became the labor pains of the birth of my new self. After seven years of struggle I was able to embrace God's love and accept myself as Sharon, precious to God.

Through a remarkable healing prayer service I did experience physical healing that year. I became pregnant the month following that service, but then miscarried. We adopted our son Christopher, and by the time he was three and a half years old, we had two more children, homemade. I do not believe that I was ready to become a mother until God had pursued me to the utmost. Through the spiritual journey of infertility, God carried me to term and gave birth to me.

God of unchangeable power, you hear our prayers and give us ourselves, formed in the dark but safe in the womb of your love. Comfort all sisters who tarry there until the appointed birth day. Amen.

Sharon A. Buttry

December 13

Forgive One Another

Then Peter came and said to him, "Lord, if another member of the church sins against me, how often should I forgive? As many as seven times?" Jesus said to him, "Not seven times, but, I tell you, seventy-seven times."　　　　　*Matthew 18:21-22*

Blessed are you when people revile you and persecute you and utter all kinds of evil against you falsely on my account.　　　　　*Matthew 5:11*

A wise woman once told me, "Forgive those who have harmed you a little and those who have harmed you a lot." What an odd way to put it. Everyone knows that all religions emphasize for-giveness; Jesus said, "Forgive seventy times seven." So what's the big deal! Yet the idea continues to haunt me. I remember a favorite teacher who told me that when she became serious about her spiritual life, she went back to the beginning of her life and identified everyone she had ever had a cross thought about. In her mind she crawled with them to an altar of light, asking for forgiveness from them and then asking for forgiveness from herself for herself. Since then she practices this daily—with the cross clerk, the impatient driver.

As much as I slide away from this idea, thinking I have already forgiven my enemies, it continues to come back. *Forgive those who have hurt you a little* (the one who didn't speak or didn't invite you somewhere or overcharged you). I was recently re-minded once again of the importance of continuous forgiveness upon reading a note supposedly written from the *other side* in which a nun told her friend, "Work on the forgiveness piece because one minute after death, you have the same problems and you still have to work on them in this new plane." This concept was emphasized a day or two later when I heard the saying, "Any failure that engenders unforgiveness in you is your failure." Unforgiveness in you is simply your opportunity to reapply the Holy Spirit. So let the ones you can't forgive come before your mind one by one, for they are waiting to be forgiven by you. As they arise, confess to them that you have failed to allow the love of the Holy Spirit to operate through you and that you are learning to do this. You will not suffer on their behalf, and they therefore need not suffer on yours.

God of all compassion, today I surrender to your presence that I may forgive those whom I think have hurt me—a little or a lot. So the next time I pray the Lord's Prayer, forgive me my sins; as I forgive those who have sinned against me, it will be done not half-heartedly but with the power of the loving Holy Spirit flowing freely. Amen.

Judith Eastman

December 14

Happiness

Happy are those whose way is blameless, who walk in the law of the LORD.   Psalm 119:1

It happened again. I've just attended the wedding of a very young woman who married expecting to find complete and total happiness in her new husband. She truly expects that he will always make her happy.

Too many times I've known women who are waiting to be taken away by a knight in shining armor to their own private Camelot. They are waiting for someone to come along and make them whole. They are wasting their time!

Happiness does not depend on someone else. It depends on you and on your relationship with God. You must consciously ask God to change you from the inside out, to take away the negative feelings about yourself, and to fill you with his love and his attitude. When you are truly happy with yourself through God the Father, you won't need to be looking for that perfect someone who will make you happy forever. He will be living in your heart!

Lord God, maker of us all, help us to realize that true happiness that lasts a lifetime comes from only you. Amen.

Bonnie Scherer

December 15

Miracle Year

Has anything so great as this ever happened or has its like ever been heard of?   *Deuteronomy 4:32*

During graduate school, I worked as a teaching assistant with first-year divinity students. The professor with whom I worked loved challenging the students' understanding of miracles. Her teaching may be summed up as follows: when told to your grandchildren, a well-timed coincidence has become a miracle. By signs and wonders, by a mighty hand and an outstretched arm, God had taken one nation from the midst of another, and the grandchildren of that nation called those wonders "miracles." Perhaps by their standards a thundering volcano, some drops of dew in the desert, and edible insect residue were miracles. But how do such things stand up against a walk in space or a baboon heart pumping in a human chest?

Sometimes the great achievements of humankind shadow the great acts of God. It might take a well-timed coincidence to remind us to take to heart that the Lord is God in heaven above and on the earth beneath (Deuteronomy 4:39).

While I pray daily for a cure for HIV so that my five-year-godson Reggie might live to be one hundred, a client insists on paying what is to me a huge advance to secure my services for later in the year. I pay two semesters' worth of overdue school fees, reinstate myself, and keep my school loans from coming due while I write my dissertation. It doesn't save the world, but it saves me. When I tell Reggie's children about this year, the miracle of the money for school will be a standout. Which year will feature the miracle of the cure for HIV? "The LORD is a merciful God who will neither abandon nor destroy us" (Deuteronomy 4:31).

I pray that I will be grateful for all acts of God, tiny and great, disguised as well-timed coincidences and as great human achievements. Amen.

Mona Bagasao

December 16

Transformed

So we do not lose heart. Even though our outer nature is wasting away, our inner nature is being renewed day by day. For this slight momentary affliction is preparing us for an eternal weight of glory beyond all measure.   *2 Corinthians 4:16-18*

When I was a college student studying nursing some thirty years ago, I was struck by the way our physical lives and health become a parable for understanding our spiritual lives and spiritual health. That which is tangible to our senses helps us to understand the intangible reality. We need air to breathe physically. We need prayer to breathe spiritually. We need food to feed our bodies; we need Scripture to feed our souls. We need friends to nurture us emotionally; we need the Holy Spirit to nurture us spiritually. However, there is a major difference. Our physical bodies, no matter how much care and attention we pay to them, eventually begin to wear out and death comes.

On the other hand, our spiritual lives keep on growing eternally. Therefore, a very important principle of life for me became to seek a balance in that which makes life whole. We are not to be deceived into thinking that our physical life is all there is. We are to be transformed in our thinking so that spiritual health, in the final analysis, becomes our most important goal. We are the temples of the Holy Spirit and need to live our physical, emotional, and spiritual lives to God's glory. A quote from Teilhard de Chardin puts it into perspective for me: *We are spiritual beings having a human experience, not a physical being having a spiritual experience.*

Creator and Preserver of all humankind, teach us to live so that whether in life or in death we may praise and glorify you, loving you with all our hearts and souls, and strength and mind, and our neighbors as ourselves. Amen.

Norma S. Mengel

December 17

God Rested

And on the seventh day God finished the work that he had done, and he rested on the seventh day from all the work that he had done.　　　　*Genesis 2:2-3*

Do you ever feel that your work is finished? Too many of us suffer from the tyranny of the urgent to the neglect of the truly important. We have to keep on keeping on for the sake of getting the job done, oblivious to the fact that we are finite creatures in a world of infinite need, creatures who will never rest if we have to postpone rest for the completion of work. Too much about the pace of our work lives belies our words that attest to trust in God.

At a hectic time in my life a Jewish group invited me to travel to Israel with them. I had been living an impossible schedule that eliminated soul-restoring activities. I became bone-weary with an exhaustion out of which nothing good can come. Banished from my routines were times to walk on the beach or read a good book or sit quietly with a friend. The day I boarded the airplane for the flight to Israel I had to badger a doctor for an antibiotic to fight an illness taking advantage of my condition. At first the doctor called me a pig-headed fool and said that he would not become complicit in my self-destructive behavior by medicating me so that I could keep on running. After considerable argument, however, he yielded and prescribed and I took off.

On Friday evening in Israel the group met at the western wall, then gathered for dinner at a hotel. *Shabbat* began with candles and prayers and an explanation of this weekly observance of sabbath as a requisite part of the ordered rhythm of the good life to which God invites us.

The joy of that table's hospitality was like springs in the desert to my thirsty soul: delicious food and beautiful flowers, a glass of wine and good conversation, but most of all the soul-satisfying peace of resting in the space set apart from all our doing just to be. As the meal progressed, I turned to the group's leader and asked, "Hershey, can I be a Jew?" May God help me never to forget what I learned that evening in Israel, that we who walk in the way of Jesus Christ also need to take time, just as he let the work go, and let our lives be renewed.

Gracious God, for sabbath time we pray, and for the courage just to be in spite of all that we might do. Restore our souls and teach us to trust that it is your job to restore the world, ours to do only as much of that project as you ask and no more. We pray in the name of Jesus Christ who never took on all the needs around him, but who finished the work that you gave him to do. Amen.

Kate Penfield

December 18

Weary Soul

My soul is weary with sorrow; strengthen me according to your word.   *Psalm 119:28 (NIV)*

Have you ever felt so tired, burdened, or depressed that you weren't sure you could hang on? God has created us as physical, emotional, and spiritual beings. These aspects are all woven together as a single strand, and when one strand becomes frayed, the whole cord is affected.

The psalmist was weary with sorrow and asked to be strengthened by God's Word. Why is it so difficult to go to God's Word for our strength? Why do we want to find it ourselves? God must get impatient with me because I'm so slow to learn. There have been several incidents in my life that brought me to the edge, and my soul was weary with sorrow. Let me share just one of those times with you.

It was 1960, we had two children, and I was trying to finish my college education. My goal was set and I was on the way to completion. But much to my surprise, I became pregnant. This was not a good time; it did not fit into my schedule to have another baby. I felt resentment and perhaps a little bit angry with this interruption to my life.

In the third month of my pregnancy I lost that baby, and *my soul became weary with sorrow.* What followed were days, weeks, and months of guilt that caused deep depression. There were days when I could not leave the house or answer the phone.

When I was forced to be with other people, I managed to function to a degree that my condition was not too evident. My husband tried to help me, tried to get me to seek help, but I refused. There wasn't anything wrong with me! There are many times I wonder how he managed to live through this time. I'm sure his *soul was weary with sorrow,* also. He had to go to work each day, come home in the evening, and take care of the house and the children.

One day, I was at the end of my rope, and I flung myself across the bed and cried out, "Lord, you're going to have to help me. I can't do it by myself." Jesus said, "Come to me you who are weary and heavy laden." God heard my prayer. As my body shook with the sobs of release, the sorrow was removed and God's Word strengthened my soul, mind, and body.

I'm continuing to learn this lesson. God has shown me that I can receive help through the Spirit and through caring family and friends. I don't have to do it by myself.

God of all compassion, thank you for the assurance that you are with me, even when my soul is weary with sorrow. Your peace is with me in the daily struggles of life. Amen.

Evon Laubenstein

Our Insufficiency, God's Abundance

I am the gate. Whoever enters by me will be saved, and will come in and go out and find pasture. The thief comes only to steal and kill and destroy. I came that they may have life, and have it abundantly.
                                        John 10:9-10

"Worship helps some. Friends help some. But it's God I need and I don't know where to find him." Those words were written to a friend twenty years ago when my life caved in and I was in a pit of despair and depression. In my early forties, when I had three children still at home, my beloved husband died, leaving an insolvent business. Not knowing who I was apart from him, I was like an empty body walking around with no one inside. I had few resources to cope with the tasks that lay ahead. Every direction I looked seemed to cry out, *Not enough! Insufficient!* I certainly had no experience of the *abundant life* promised by Christ.

Yet today, I can attest to the truth of John's Gospel: those who enter will find pasture and life in all its fullness. I now know from experience that to the extent I receive and internalize the profound love God has for me (us), to that extent I am able to become healed and whole, fully alive.

Looking back, what made the difference? There were many people and events and books that helped with my intense search for God, and I discovered the spiritual disciplines that open us Godward. But the practice that helped most vividly was balancing my *searching* mode with being still and allowing God to love me. It happened through daily quiet times as I visualized that love as a golden shower pouring over me, or a warm light flooding around and through me. It happened at Communion as I ate the broken bread, representing this ultimate love. It touched me in singing hymns, and while writing dialogues with God in a journal. It came gradually over many years, but there has been a paradigm shift from *not enough-ness* to *enough and to spare*, from scarcity to

Paradoxically, as I live out of the abundance, I have been freed to want a simpler lifestyle so that others may have enough. I'm free to let go of some ego demands for attention or affirmation, for *being heard*, and can now better attend to and *hear* those around me who need it. God's abundance has taught me who I am, and it has freed me from the tyranny of what others may think. Now I try to live each day from that inner place where deep meets deep, where the ever-flowing stream sustains and directs my life. I'm not finished yet, and certainly am not completely whole, but the process of healing is well begun, and I trust the One whose abundance keeps pouring over me in fresh and surprising ways. When I become willing to bear *the beams of love*, it never fails me, for God's love never runs out—it is enough, and to spare.

God of all sufficiency, help me to risk bearing the beams of your love, and to live out of your abundance rather than out of my insufficiency. Amen.

Ann W. Young

December 20

Potential for Joy

There is no creation that does not have a radiance . . .
All creation is gifted with the ecstasy of God's light.[3]

I love this thought! With this image of God's presence, I look at everything differently: every child, man, woman, dog, tree, and ocean comes alive when I see the spark of God's radiance within. It is not only the divine light I see—I see the *ecstasy* of God's light as well! This means that I can see the potential for joy in the heart of every living thing.

I need this perception of God's presence. So often I see only the suffering in the faces of the children I work so hard to protect from abuse. I look into the eyes of their parents and see only shame and the rage of helplessness. How can they love their children well, no matter how much they want to, when they have never been loved well themselves? So often my vision of humanity is focused on the frustrated and violent behavior I see in families all around me. I forget to look deeper into their wounded hearts for the hidden spark of light.

Where is God's light? How deep must we probe to find its presence? How many layers of scar tissue must we peel away before we find its smoldering flame? How much cold must we suffer before someone blows gently to rekindle the warmth of this inner fire?

This is my faith in the face of too much evidence to the contrary: we are born with this radiance, and it can never be fully extinguished. Healing is always possible. I believe this because I have seen the miracles that love can create. With others, I have held the survivors of abuse in my arms while they wept, releasing torrents of pain, releasing years of shame. And then I have watched the light come back into their eyes as they opened them gently, carefully, to the loving recognition in all of the eyes around them. The light of acceptance. The light of unconditional love. The light of God.

The ecstasy part of life will come, too. God has promised us not only healing, but joy! As God kindles the divine flame within us, our ability to actually enjoy life catches on like a fire in our souls. Soon enough, we dance like flames of ecstasy. We sing like a chorus of fiery angels. We die like a spark of light rejoining the eternal radiance at the heart of all things.

Source of all power, help us to believe that the ecstasy part will come. For you have promised us not only healing, but joy! Amen.

Susan Savell

December 21

Who Are the Blessed of Today?

Blessed are you who are poor, for yours is the kingdom of God. Blessed are you who are hungry now, for you will be filled. Blessed are you who weep now, for you will laugh. Blessed are you when people hate you, and when they exclude you, revile you, and defame you on account of the Son of Man.   Luke 6:20-22

Often discussion of the Beatitudes centers on exactly who is to be blessed in each individual phrase. The phrasing in Luke 6 differs slightly from that in Matthew 5. This is an interesting discussion but may deter us from the overarching concept that is being presented. If one looks at the lists of those who are blessed, the theme is that those who are blessed are those who are seen as weak by society, who choose right instead of might. Whether it is the poor or the poor in spirit, those who are blessed are weak in the eyes of the world.

A challenge to understanding this passage for today is to think about who the weak are today in the eyes of society. Might it be those who are abused, those who do not see their own self-worth, those who do not put others down, those who dare to tell the truth, those who take responsibility for their actions, or those who dare to reach out and care for others? Who would you include in such a list of those who are blessed today?

When you look at a list of those who are blessed, is your first thought to see how you fit into that list? Do you seek assurance that you are one of the blessed? Do you think about how you can help others realize they are blessed? How can you be a blessing to others?

God of all, help us see those who are in need today. Show us how to reach out and help them feel blessed. May we be instruments of your blessing in our world today. Amen.

Nelda Rhoades Clarke

December 22

Answered Prayer

For the world and time are the dance of the Lord in emptiness. The silence of the spheres is the music of a wedding feast. The more we persist in misunderstanding the phenomena of life, the more we analyze them out into strange finalities and complex purposes of our own, the more we involve ourselves in sadness, absurdity and despair. But it does not matter much, because no despair of ours can alter the reality of things, or stain the joy of the cosmic dance which is always there.[4]

We have just been told that one of our three-year-old identical twins has a severe hearing loss—maybe progressive. What a shock to learn something that we had all dreaded since their traumatic birth. Our daughter had almost died of toxemia immediately following delivery. Nothing went right. She was dying as each part of her worn-out body shut down. The tiny babes became bionic infants, wired to monitors at every pulse and orifice. One had been stillborn for twelve minutes before making a tiny struggling cry after all the attendants had given up hope of life. For two weeks our world kept vigil. Parishioners knelt at the chapel altar, taking turns by day and by night. Friends called from distant shores to offer love and prayers, souls as diverse as the church in their natures and theologies, but for all that, united in a true *communion of saints.*

Our diligent prayers for survival and healing were answered. Our daughter recovered slowly, tentatively, but finally completely returned to wholeness. The little girls grew, inseparably, adorably, hilariously—and apparently free from our fear that maybe one of them had been physically compromised at birth. So it was unexpected and shocking to learn about Emily's inability to hear certain sounds. Hearing aids, speech therapy, counseling, were inevitable.

But once again, the spiritual power of God's presence came down upon each of us. Their daddy said, "We are so fortunate. We didn't know at their birth if they would ever walk, much less talk or hear!" Others disbelieved the diagnosis, and others were encouraging about the great advances in aural medicine. The older children had only one fear—that the kids in school would laugh and avoid her. And some well-meaning Christians said words of comfort like "God never gives you more than you can handle or this suffering will only make you stronger or it could be so much worse."

But the God who is holding our twins and ourselves is always weeping with us over the pain we endure, always creating and recreating new life, new healing, new spiritual power.

Refuge of those who put their trust in you, hold us in your embrace, in sickness and in health, in this life and in resurrected joy in the next. Amen.

Nancy Grandfield

Stand Up for Jesus

*When [Jesus] laid his hands on her, immediately she
stood up straight and began praising God.*

Luke 13:13

Jesus was teaching in one of the synagogues on the sabbath when
a woman approached him who had been suffering from an illness
for eighteen years. She was bent over and could not stand up straight.
The Scripture says that Jesus saw her and then he called her to him
and said to her, "Woman, you are set free from your ailment" (v.12).
Then the Scripture says that he laid his hands on her and immediately she was made straight, and then she glorified God.

Each one of us is like this woman. Each of us suffers from a
lifelong spiritual illness that keeps us separated from God. Our
illnesses may have many different symptoms. We may be fearful.
We may be arrogant. We may abuse drugs, alcohol, food, money,
or other substances. We may resist praying and spending time
alone with God. Our dependency may be on things or on other
people instead of God.

But like Jesus, God sees us. God sees us as we are. God knows
our weaknesses better than we do. And like Jesus, God calls us to
come. If we come, we, too, can be cured from our infirmities. We
only need to come and ask God to cure us from our disease.

Our whole lives can be a process of renewal. Each time we
come to God openly, like peeling back the layers of an onion, God
can remove our infirmities and renew us.

The good news is that it is through our infirmities that we can
glorify God. As we see how God is able to work miracles in our
lives and in the lives of those we love, we are drawn closer to God,
as the woman was to Jesus. Freed from our infirmities, we are
able to stand up and praise God.

What has you bent over this day? In what areas of your life do
you need renewal? Know that today you can approach your living
Lord and ask to be renewed. Your God is able to restore you to
perfect health.

*Great Physician, you know my every weakness. Help me to
stand up straight, so I may glorify you. Amen.*

Mary L. Mild

To Be Free

Let us strip off anything that slows us down or holds us back, and especially those sins that wrap themselves so tightly around our feet and trip us up, and let us run with patience the particular race that God has set before us.   *Hebrews 12:1 (TLB)*

As part of a prescribed exercise program for an injured shoulder, I attached weights to my one arm. The purpose was to increase the resistance, thereby making the prescribed exercises more difficult to accomplish. After months of diligent adherence to the prescribed program, I regained full range of motion of my arm and shoulder and was able to set aside the weights and resume normal activities. Many times, as I faithfully carried out my routine several times a day, I thought about the above Scripture verse and looked forward to the day that I could lay aside the strapped-on weight.

At times, each of us carries around physical or emotional weights that result from myriad circumstances, including health, employment, or finances. It is very easy to get sidetracked as we deal with our daily responsibilities and challenges. We need to spend time in prayer, meditation, and fellowship with other Christians in order to continue on the path that God has set before us.

God of steadfastness and encouragement, help us to cast all of our cares on you, for you care for us. Amen.

Marilyn O. Harris

ᴡomen ᴡays

*"I will surely return to you in due season, and your
wife Sarah shall have a son." And Sarah was listening
at the tent entrance behind him. Now Abraham and
Sarah were old, advanced in age; it had ceased to be
with Sarah after the manner of women. So Sarah
laughed to herself.* Genesis 18:10-12

My mother is soft and smells of morning coffee and Pond's
cold cream. She wears her eighty-four years with determination
and a wicked sense of humor. Her heavy dark brown hair has only
recently begun to show faint traces of gray; it is done to her
specification each Thursday afternoon. Her life has a predictable
rhythm to it, Royal Neighbors on Tuesday, Ladies Circle on
Wednesday, to town for errands on Thursday, Bingo on Friday
with the senior citizens. We talk on the phone each Saturday
morning.

The rhythm suits her, though she willingly throws out all her
usual patterns to go on vacation with us in our woods or visit her
brother in Madison or my sister in St. Louis.

Two old women, living millennia apart but sharing the secret
and wisdom of age. Sarah laughed to herself, and my mother
laughs too. They laugh at the absurdity of turning back the pages
of the calendar when, at last, the years are feeling comfortable.
The years are wearing well. "Just when I was getting the hang of
being old, I'm supposed to have a baby?" Maybe that's what Sarah
was thinking. In terms of being old women, not much has changed
over the millennia that separate Sarah and my mother. The world
still doesn't value women who have grown old. The most interesting thing about Sarah is that God has intervened in her life, has
bypassed the natural processes of life, and has allowed her to
become pregnant and bear a child.

We live in a technological age that experiments with post-
menopausal pregnancy, rather than adopting a mature attitude
toward aging. There is a time for bearing children, and there is a
time for bearing vision and hope and life for the larger world,
beyond our families. Women of age offer these gifts to the world.
The wise old woman knows how to name what is important,

knows how to pray and weep and worry for those she loves, and understands that she is part of the larger circle of life.

Wise old women are women of calm hearts and resilient spirits. They are like the doilies that adorn my mother's dressers, circles of lace. But make no mistake, circles of lace are strong, made up of many threads woven together, interconnected, each piece touching and depending on the others.

Ageless God, you have bound us in the gift of time. Help us not only to accept the limits that aging imposes but also to embrace the new gifts and opportunities that being wise old women can bring. Impart to us understanding of our foremothers, who go before us, and help us to build families and communities that honor and respect those who grow old, even as we live in a world that does not. Amen.

Kay Ward

December 26

Only Believe

And without faith it is impossible to please God, for whoever would approach him must believe that he exists and that he rewards those who seek him.
Hebrews 11:6

'Twas the night before Christmas . . . We'd been up for a family get-together and had returned home late. It was 11 o'clock. My two grandsons had been told to run upstairs and go to sleep—fast.

The younger of the two, a nine-year-old, sidled up to his father and said, "I *really* want a crane!" Then up the stairs he went, knowing that in the morning a crane would be under the tree for him. It was!

As a child, I believed anything and everything my parents, sisters, teachers, or neighbors said. If my mother said she was going to *throw me into the middle of next year* (obviously for some small infraction), I believed her.

I knew there was a bogeyman! My sisters even described him. I knew Santa Claus saw everything I did, bad or good, and my gifts were based on my behavior. I *believed* in my elders. They spoke the truth!

When Jesus said in Mark 10:15 that anyone who does not welcome the kingdom of God like a little child will never enter it, I wonder if he intended for us to return to the faith we had as children.

My parents showed me the way to faith. When Dad had a problem or a case that created some uncertainties, he'd go to his office—his closet—to seek comfort in prayer. Mother, on the other hand, sought solace in her garden. My closet is my car.

When I pray, as I did when cancer was first diagnosed, and now, I knew my prayers had been answered. I had not the least bit of doubt. Like my grandson, I knew it was a done deal. Today my faith has never faltered, and each day I thank the Good Lord that I am healed!

Generous Provider of all good gifts, thank you for the gift of faith modeled by my parents, whose very lives strengthened my beliefs. Amen.

Juanita Locker Ivie

December 27

Here I Am

When the LORD saw that he had turned aside to see, God called to him out of the bush, "Moses, Moses!" And he said, "Here I am."   *Exodus 3:4*

A very dangerous hymn is printed in the pages of our Presbyterian hymnals; perhaps you've sung it. The name of these perilous stanzas is "Here I Am, Lord." When we sang it two Sundays ago, two things happened. The first was that one of the sopranos said, as we disrobed, "That's such a lovely hymn." I answered, "Yes, but it's dangerous." She looked at me in great surprise, so I explained, "Every time I sing it, I get a new job," meaning that another door in my life always seems to open up, another opportunity to grow or give service in a new way. My life seems so full all the time that I wonder how I'll adjust to more doors opening.

This particular Sunday was the ordination of new elders and

deacons, following which we sang this hymn. I just knew something would happen. That week, the pastor called and asked if I would preach the next Sunday while she was on vacation. Another door, one that I have entered only once before and that I approach a little nervously. Will I find an appropriate theme, will God speak through me to someone, will I be adequate? And then there are all those little details to remember, like where to stand at which times, and when to pray, and when to take the offering. But having sung "Here I Am, Lord" once again, how could I say no?

This hymn was almost a theme for a church women's conference I attended last summer. Our focus was on hospitality to the stranger. Sure enough, after singing this hymn several times, I was not home from the conference for two days before an opportunity came to help three strangers in our community who had car trouble.

Watch the words we sing and pray; don't take them lightly. Heartfelt singing of "Here I Am, Lord" will bring new opportunities, new purpose, and new excitement to your life.

Mysterious and powerful God, let me respond to your calls to me with an open heart and an open mind. I do not need to know the results; I just need to feel close to you in my life. Amen.

Cathie Burdick

December 28

Hearing God

Where were you when I laid the foundation of the earth? Tell me, if you have understanding. . . . Have you entered the storehouses of the snow, or have you seen the storehouses of the hail, which I have reserved for the time of trouble. . . . From whose womb did the ice come forth, and who has given birth to the hoarfrost of heaven? The waters become hard like stone, and the face of the deep is frozen.
Job 38:4, 22-23a, 29-30

Snow and ice. Ice and snow. Freezing temperatures. No business as usual. Stores, offices, churches closed. Meetings canceled. Events postponed. Travel delayed. Plans changed. Schedules upset.

Indeed, as God asked Job, "Who is this that darkens counsel . . . without knowledge?" If there is only one thing I learned from the thirty-inch snowfall we received in Philadelphia, it is that I am not in control. Not of everything. Maybe not at all. Maybe never. The Blizzard of '96 reminded me that much as I like to be in charge and like to be competent, there is still a lot that escapes my control. The weather, for example. I may make plans and set schedules, but ultimately, I am not in control; God is.

During the blizzard, I had to relax. My priorities became groceries, meals, warmth, clear paths, and shoveling. For a week, I was not focused on work, professional tasks, or career-related issues. For seven days, I concentrated on family, relationships, quantity and quality time, leisure activities, and a power greater than I.

It is God who is in control, not you and not I. Something as truly awesome as a blizzard puts it in perspective for me. I do not control very much, not much at all. God is in control—of blizzards and of *principalities and powers* and of me and my life.

Our faith is based on belief in the God of power and on trust in the God of mercy. Our God is with us in blizzards and walks with us—even through the snow.

Giver of every good and perfect gift, thank you for reminding me of your power. Thank you too for being gentle and loving as well. Help me be less concerned with my own control and more focused on doing your will, now and always. Amen.

Janet K. Hess

December 29

Offering Support

And what does the LORD require of you but to do justice, and to love kindness, and to walk humbly with your God?　　　　　　　　　　*Micah 6:8*

We had just visited a *maquiladora* located across the river from El Paso in the Mexican city of Juarez. I was deeply dismayed at seeing so many teenagers who were working for four to five dollars a day. They had left school to trade their lives for a cheap job and thereby faced a life of abject poverty. Thousands of families had come from other areas, hoping to find a better life.

In the colonia where they now lived, cardboard and sheet-metal shacks reached as far as we could see. There was no grass, no trees, no electricity, and only an occasional faucet.

Some of the people were there to greet us. It was obvious that many of them had never seen a dentist and doubtful that they had ever felt satisfied after they finished a meal. They greeted us with warm smiles and then told us of their hopes and dreams. We were standing beside a small concrete building that belonged to the state. The dream of these people was to buy this building and use it for a day-care center. It would be a place where the children would be safe and would start to learn before they began school.

I asked them what it was that they wanted the most. Their reply was that their children would be educated so that their lives and their children's lives would be better and that their children would be prepared to make decisions about what would happen to them. These people wanted wholeness for their children even as you and I do.

Great God, you have called us to be your people and through Jesus the Christ have given us the understanding that we are whole persons in your sight. Help us to be just. Help us to help those who have been marginalized by injustice to become the whole persons that God intends them to be. Amen.

Sally Graham Ernst

December 30

Where Do I Turn?

Wait for the LORD; be strong, and let your heart take courage; wait for the LORD! Psalm 27:14

It comes as no surprise to you, I am sure, that men and women are very different. We were created by God to be different and to complement one another. One major difference between them is their source of self-esteem. Men derive much of their self-worth from their careers and work, while women derive much of their esteem from their relationships. When children enter the picture, moms are tremendously concerned about their children and how their children are doing in this world.

Parenting is a tough job; that is a given. Special needs children present an even bigger challenge. As the mom of one of those children, I have met many amazing moms who give unselfishly to their families. I can think of moms who have blessed my life and enriched it greatly with their stories and sharing about the special children who have been entrusted to them. Children with challenges, some great and some less severe, all nevertheless painful to parents who hoped for the perfect child (Downs syndrome children, diabetic children, blind children, A.D.H.D. children, bipolar children, to name only a very few). Although we see their problems and disabilities, God sees their perfect souls. God knows that they were created perfect.

All moms and dads have difficult days. I know some of your pain, your tears, your confusion, your discouragement, and your desire some days to throw in the towel! Those times can continue for days, months, and even years. I want to encourage you to continuously seek God's wisdom and direction for your child. Your life may not be *normal*, but God has a plan for you and your family. God makes no mistakes and chose you to parent the child you are struggling with! Over the years, many persons have offered me advice regarding my precious son, but only God has the wisdom to advise me correctly. Many times during my son's school years, I have felt pulled in different directions. Everyone has an opinion regarding his difficulties. Even the most skilled professionals have opposing opinions. We, as his parents, often have differing opinions. But only God knows exactly what our children need. So where do I turn and whom do I go to? Where can I go but to the Lord!

God of all wisdom and knowledge, thank you for creating us in your image. Remind us that when we look upon other people that we are seeing you. Amen.

Brenda Marinaro

Homecoming

But now, Lord, what do I look for? My hope is in
you.   *Psalm 39:7 (NIV)*

Hope,
A friend just called and asked me to pray for her daughter who
    is in labor.
My first thought surrounds the baby whose passage has begun.
A moment later I envision the strong mother exuding joy and
    raising the child to her breast.
Hope,
After a month of being surround by decay and threats of death
    I welcome the promise of new life.
Like a sunflower I have embodied both deep darkness and
    bright light.
Now I am ready to harvest from my center the seeds which
    hold abundant possibilities.
Hope,
Recently I have named so many hopes that relate to comple-
    tions.
This unborn child reminds me that endings are also beginnings.
What I embrace this morning is Your presence.
Hope,
You are the hope inside all my other desires.
I dream my visions for the future with You.
And I ask, "What do You want to do together?"
Hope,
Which dreams do You pray for me?
What in me needs to bravely push its way into a new phase of
    existence?
Will I, like a mother, take the new life I meet and instinctively
    and joyfully nurture it?
Hope,
Oh, beautiful Hope,
Oh, fragrant Hope,
I long for You even though You are with me and within me.

Hope, for all that is ready to be born, we pray . . . Amen.
                    Jill Kimberly Hartwell Geoffrion

Contributors

Laura Alden is director of communications for National Ministries, American Baptist Churches in the U.S.A., and is the author of twenty-two children's books.

Joyce Anderegg is an active United Methodist who lives in Maryville, Tennessee.

Gloria E. Applegate is a retired registered nurse who formerly lived on a ranch but has now moved and adjusted to city life.

Ann Audgerie is a member of the feminist class of First Baptist Church, Granville, Ohio.

Donna Authelet, from Vallejo, California, is a Bible study and workshop leader. Her interests include oil painting, crafts, music, and reading.

Mona Bagasao is a musician and Doctor of Philosophy candidate in Hebrew Bible at Vanderbilt University.

Linda Bales is a United Methodist from Dayton, Ohio, who constantly searches for the meaning of life.

Ressie Mae Bass is a member of the national staff of the United Methodist Women's Division with responsibility for membership and organizational development.

Lavon Bayler is minister to the churches and pastors of the Fox Valley Association, Illinois Conference, United Church of Christ; a wife; a mother; and a grandmother. She has also written six books of worship resources published by Pilgrim Press and United Church Press.

Holly Vincent Bean serves on the staff of the Ministers and Missionaries Benefit Board of the American Baptist Churches in the U.S.A.

Siegrid Belden is the mother of two adult children and serves as economic justice director with National Ministries of the American Baptist Churches in the U.S.A.

Peggy Billings has served as a missionary to Korea and as a national church program executive; she is now retired and lives on a farm in upstate New York.

Betty Blue is a 1947 graduate of the Baptist Missionary Training School and lives in Milwaukee with her husband, Fred.

Carolyn Stahl Bohler is the Emma Sanborn Tousant Professor of Pastoral Theology and Counseling at United Theological Seminary, Dayton, Ohio; the author of several books including *Opening to God, Guided Imagery Meditations on Scripture*, 1996; and the mother of a twelve-year-old girl and the daughter of her eighty-three-year-old mother.

Hazel M. Boltwood is an American Baptist woman whose professional and volunteer life has been in interracial and intercultural ministries.

Ruth T. Bosserman is a local-church worship ministry chair and choir director.

Katherine Halsey Bostrom is a United Methodist clergywoman in South Carolina.

Anne H. Brady is a hospice director.

Kolya M. Braun works for the Women's Division of the United Methodist Church on issues of children, youth, and family advocacy, while she balances her involvement in her local church as a Sunday school teacher for children, which gives her great joy.

Dallas A. Brauninger, in her twenty-fifth year as a United Church of Christ minister, now sings her special ministry of writing using a computer doubly adapted with speech output and input to accommodate blindness and overturn changes due to juvenile rheumatoid arthritis.

Frances Breton, Minister of Mission Support for American Baptists of Ohio, and her daughter, Sherry Brumford, may have been the first mother and daughter in the history of any denomination to be ordained in the same service. During the editing of this book, Fran has been recovering nicely from her brain tumor surgery.

Julia D. Brodie is a member of the feminist class at First Baptist Church of Granville, Ohio, and a psychologist who especially values her work with women.

Jackie Bryant is a Southern Baptist and currently serves as the state affiliate leader of the Arkansas Parents as Teachers program.

Sally Mitchell Bucklee, a grandparent, retiree, and consultant to nonprofit and religious systems, has been a leader at every level of the Episcopal Church and currently serves on its national executive council.

Cathie Burdick is a woman of many interests who tries to enter each door that opens in her life by enjoying new experiences and learning new lessons.

Karolyn Holm Burkett is a member of the feminist class at the First Baptist Church, Granville, Ohio, and is a teacher of English and a searcher after women's spirituality.

Sharon A. Buttry recently completed a Master of Divinity/Master of Social Work degree and ordination in the American Baptist Church. She is executive director of Friendship House in Detroit, Michigan.

Barbara E. Campbell recently retired after many years on the staff of the Women's Division, United Methodist Church.

Janel Cariño is a psychiatrist in private practice in West Caldwell, New Jersey.

Dosia Carlson, a semiretired United Church of Christ clergywoman living in Phoenix, Arizona, leads conferences and workshops often focused on her specialty, older adult ministries. Writing hymns is a treasured activity for Dosia, who, until moving to Phoenix in 1974, was on the religion faculty at The Defiance College, Defiance, Ohio.

Joy Carol, director of international programs of Christian Children's Fund, is the United States Convener of the Forum on Vietnam, Cambodia, and Laos and a board member of the Vietnamese Memorial Association. In November 1993, she underwent surgery for a brain tumor and is now completely healed.

Carolyn Carpenter lives in Charlotte, North Carolina, and is a corporate trainer for a healthcare system. She enjoys reading, fun times with friends, and Bible study.

Cathy Carpenter has been doing interim ministry in western New York for several years and tends wounded churches.

Mary Cartledge-Hayes is a United Methodist pastor and the author of *To Love Delilah: Claiming the Women of the Bible.*

Jan Chartier is an ordained American Baptist woman in ministry who serves in a team ministry with her husband, Myron.

Kathryn Choy-Wong is an area minister, covering forty-four churches, and minister of public ministries for American Baptist Churches of the West in northern California and Nevada. She is a wife, a mother, a Christian Disciple, and an observer of human life.

Amelia Chua is a pastor fascinated by the spiritual journeys of individuals and communities. She attended the Non-Governmental Forum on Women in Beijing, China, in August 1995.

Kathleen Clark coordinates the work of Church and Community Ministries for the United Methodist Church.

Nelda Rhoades Clarke is executive director of the Emma Norton Residence, a National Mission Institute of the United Methodist Church, and a Church of the Brethren clergywoman.

Melanie Cooper is a registered nurse, just beginning a career in nursing at her small rural community hospital and school system in western Kansas. She is active in her rural church along with her husband, Kevin, and three children.

Kristen Corselius is a missionary in the United Methodist Church who works at Mary Elizabeth Inn in San Francisco.

Carol Q. Cosby works in ministries for women by women in the Office of Disciples Women, Homeland Ministries, Disciples of Christ.

Alice Cotabish worked for over forty years as a church secretary and after retirement continued with volunteer activities with the church, meals-on-wheels, and the Cleveland Sight Center.

J. Ann Craig is executive secretary for spiritual and theological development for the United Methodist Women's Division.

Sheryl Cross is a parish nurse of Deaconess Health System and an active member of Immanuel United Church of Christ in Ferguson, Minnesota.

Rhonda Cushman has served American Baptist churches in Colorado, New York, Rhode Island, and Pennsylvania. She and her husband, David, are the parents of two teenagers, April and Mike.

Ginna Minasian Dalton resides in Richmond, Virginia, and follows her call as a Christian education consultant primarily in the field of pluralism. She has served on committees of the National Council of Churches and the United Church of Christ.

Sara J. Davis is executive director, Spiritual Renewal Ministries, and a United Methodist spiritual director and retreat leader.

Debbie Deane is an ordained minister of the American Baptist Churches in the U.S.A. with a ministry focus in spiritual formation who has experienced the woundedness and healing of child sexual abuse and breast cancer and is now learning to live with chronic fatigue immune defiency sydrome.

Rebecca J. Dobson is a writer, teacher, and violinist who lives in Windsor, Connecticut.

Priscilla Dreyman is a United Methodist minister and director of Spiral Arts, a ministry of outreach and healing through the arts in Portland, Maine.

Cheryl F. Dudley works as a denominational executive for American Baptist Churches in the U.S.A., National Ministries. She is a home missionary, ordained minister, womanist, poet, and most recently a gardener and nurturer of flowering plants.

Rosetta C. Dudley-Tilghman is a retired registered nurse and wife, mother, grandmother, and community volunteer.

Belva Trask Duncan is pastor of a United Church of Christ in Maquoketta, Iowa. She is currently enrolled in the doctor of ministry program in preaching through the Chicago Association of Theological Schools. Also, she has hiked numerous fourteen-thousand-foot peaks, rim to rim, in the Grand Canyon and hopes to hike the Appalachian Trail.

Judith Eastman is a clinical social worker in Chapel Hill, North Carolina.

Connie Le Elgan belongs to the Reorganized Church of Jesus Christ of the Latter Day Saints and is an administrative assistant at the church world headquarters in Independence, Missouri.

Sally Graham Ernst, past president of the Women's Division of the United Methodist Church, is a member of its Commission on the Status and Role of Women.

Beverly Burns Erskine lives in Swarthmore, Pennsylvania, and spends her free time developing her skills in Scherenschnitte (paper cutting), weaving, writing, and creative dieting.

Melbalenia D. Evans graduated from Howard University School of Divinity in 1993 and was ordained a United Church of Christ minister in 1994 at Trinity United Church of Christ, in Chicago, Illinois, by Dr. Jeremiah A. Wright Jr. and the Chicago Metropolitan Association of the Illinois Conference.

Cindy Farmer is an ordained deacon in the United Methodist Church and a student at Vanderbilt Divinity School.

Carolyn Hall Felger is a Presbyterian elder, cancer survivor, caregiver, wife, mother, grandmother, and thankful eleventh-hour worker in God's vineyard, who is writing again after forty-five years of trying to avoid it.

Mary Jo Ferreira is the spouse of a retired pastor and a past member of the National American Baptist Women Ministries Board and American Baptist General Board.

Velma McGee Ferrell's renewed goal is to combine family, campus ministry, faith community, personal growth, and leisure into a healthy and contributing lifestyle.

Shirley Ferrill is program associate with METRO, the United Methodist Urban Ministries in San Diego district, where for fifteen years she has been working with women's issues, emergency services, and volunteers.

Julie Fewster is a perennial gardener and the associate pastor at the First Baptist Church in West Hartford, Connecticut.

Allene M. Ford is a deaconess and Christian educator who lives in Houston, Texas.

Lynn Forsberg holds a Master of Divinity degree and is currently working as a counselor with adolescents and children in Pennsylvania.

Patricia A. Fraser is the campus minister and director of the American Baptist Student Foundation at Michigan State University. She resides in East Lansing with her husband, Tom, and two children, Jonathan and Emily.

Karen F. Freberg is a Reorganized Church of Jesus Christ of the Latter Day Saints pastor in Loveland, Ohio.

Eugenia Gamble is a Presbyterian Church (USA) minister who can't write anything in one page.

Peggy L. T. Garrison is a United Methodist minister who teaches pastoral care, has a therapy practice, and plays with computers.

Elaine Gasser, retired after forty-plus years as national staff of the Evangelical United Brethren and United Methodist Churches, lives in Maryville, Tennessee.

Jill Kimberly Hartwell Geoffrion is a poet-theologian, student of Christian spiritualities and women's studies, mother, partner, friend, ordained American Baptist pastor, and dreamer. She writes to help create the church she longs for.

Annell George-McLawhorn is a full-time mother of two preschoolers, who currently serves in two part-time ministries: as pastor of a small Disciples of

Christ congregation and regional staff minister to the women of the Christian Church (Disciples of Christ) in North Carolina.

Susan Gillies is deputy executive director of National Ministries, American Baptist Churches in the U.S.A.

Gay Gilliland-Mallo is an ordained minister in the United Church of Christ. She has spent the last fifteen years working with children who have disabilities or terminal illness and who have experienced abuse and neglect.

Mable Doris Gooden is an education specialist working with Healthsouth Rehab Institute of Tucson, Arizona.

Nancy Grandfield has been blessed with a loving husband for fifty years, two splendid children, four perfect grandchildren, loyal and kind friends, and an unbounding enthusiasm for practically everything. Her happiest moments are when she is with her family, standing in awe of their wondrous graces and gifts.

Katherine Griffis likes to watch deplaning passengers at the airport in Colorado Springs—which is not at all dingy and out of the way. Katherine tills the ground in Colorado Springs, Colorado.

Pam Gurley has specialized in ministry to senior adults in the local church.

Miriam Z. Gutiérrez is president of American Baptist Women Ministries in Puerto Rico and a seminary student.

Betsy L. Halsey is a United Methodist clergywoman in the Baltimore Washington Conference.

Peggy Halsey directs the Office of Ministries with Women and Families of the United Methodist Board of Global Ministries.

Elly Haney is a scholar and an activist currently writing a book on a feminist perspective of a post-Christendom Christianity.

Ann Leslie Hanson is a native Montanan. She has worked for the United Church of Christ for twelve years as a program administrator. She loves working with youth, mentoring younger women, and howling at the moon with her women friends.

Julie Ruth Harley is vice president of ministry and mission at Lifelink in Bensenville, Illinois, and she continues to be amazed by the transformation that has resulted from her deepened spiritual life.

Pat Callbeck Harper lives in Helena, Montana, and is a national consultant/trainer in education and employment equity.

Maria Harris is the author of *Dance of the Spirit* and *Jubilee Time: Celebrating Women, Spirit, and the Advent of Age.*

Marilyn D. Harris is a registered nurse of forty years, the director of hospital-based home health and hospice programs, and is active in local church and community.

Abigail Hastings is a writer living in New York City.

Cynthia G. Haynes has two adult children, lives with her husband in Overland Park, Kansas, where she is a mental health nurse and a freelance writer, and is presently participating in a minister of health/parish nurse program at St. Luke's Hospital in Kansas City.

Nancy T. Heimer has been living in London, England, for the past five years developing an interim ministry program for the United Reformed Church after nineteen years as director of leader development for Women of the Christian Church (Disciples of Christ).

M. L. Henderson is a geriatric nurse practitioner with a special interest in end-of-life decision making; and a clinical assistant professor of nursing at the University of North Carolina School of Nursing, Chapel Hill, North Carolina. She has a Master of Divinity from Yale University and a Doctor of Ministry from Southeastern Baptist Theological Seminary.

Nannie Hereford, a Presbyterian missionary for forty years, was born in Japan of missionary parents. She worked in Japan, but lived with other missionaries in an internment camp in the Philippines during World War II. As a respected activist, she received a Jefferson award during her first retirement in Nashville for leadership in serving the needs of women and children in the community.

Janet K. Hess is a former secondary school English teacher, copastor of a Philadelphia congregation, vice president of the Metropolitan Christian Council of Philadelphia, and delegate to both the Northeastern Jurisdictional and World Methodist conferences.

Jan Hoffman is a Quaker who currently serves as clerk of Quakers Uniting in Publications and clerk of the Committee on Ministry and Counsel of New England Yearly Meeting. She also speaks and leads workshops in the United States and abroad.

Theressa Hoover is the former staff head of the Women's Division of the United Methodist Church. She is retired and lives in Fayetteville, Arkansas.

Ann Marie Hunter is a United Methodist pastor, the director of Boston Justice Ministries (which organizes churches and communities against domestic violence), and the mother of two small children.

Anne M. Ierardi is a pastoral counselor at Healthsigns Center on Cape Cod and an interim parish minister. She loves the arts, especially painting.

Juanita Locker Ivie is a retired deaconess and diaconal minister in the United Methodist Church.

Nan Jenkins is a pastor and hospital chaplain, as well as a mom and grandmother, who enjoys surfing the Internet.

Nancy Johns is a trained psychologist and a child and family development specialist. She is currently consulting with a community health education program on the outskirts of Sao Paulo, Brazil, for the American Friends Service Committee (Quaker).

Norma R. Jones is an ordained minister of the Presbyterian Church (USA) and serves as professor and chaplain at Alcorn State University in Mississippi, the oldest black land-grant university in the United States.

Jane Kamp has served the church in many capacities—as Christian education director, lay preacher, worship leader, and musician. She now works for the United Way and lives in Philadelphia with her husband and two children.

Carole Jeanne Kane is a caregiver learning to nurture herself and a world traveler learning to journey within.

Deborah Kapp is an assistant professor of ministry at McCormick Theological Seminary in Chicago.

Gini King worked for ten years with the Connecticut conference, United Church of Christ, as area minister and minister of Christian education and youth; the biblical Miriam was her companion and spiritual guide. Presently she is director of continuing education, Bangor Theological Seminary. Now that Gini is living on a sandy beach in Maine, the wise woman Huldah, who interprets the meaning of God's will, has entered her life as her spiritual sister.

Ellen Kirby is the director of Brooklyn Green Bridge, the community horticulture program of the Brooklyn Botanic Garden, Brooklyn, N.Y., and previously was on the national staff of the United Methodist Church.

Sharon Kirkpatrick is a Reorganized Church of Jesus Christ of the Latter Day Saints minister and a dean of nursing who directs village health-care projects in developing countries.

Barbara Klatt teaches elementary school, reads, gardens, and has two grown sons. She remembers how chaotic life could be when her sons were still at home. She is a member of the feminist class of First Baptist Church, Granville, Ohio.

Noel Koestline pastors a United Methodist church on Long Island, New York, and has served as a spiritual guide and retreat leader, a hospital chaplain, and a missionary in Peru.

Margaret Kornfeld is an ordained American Baptist minister and pastoral psychotherapist practicing in New York City where she also teaches at Union Theological Seminary and at the Blanton-Peale Graduate Institutes.

Virginia Kreyer, cerebral palsied since birth, is an ordained minister of the United Church of Christ. She has helped make churches aware of the ministry to and with persons with disabilities.

Marlys L. Kroon: "I have it all—I am a wife, mother of three and grandmother of two, bookstore manager, inspirational speaker and singer, community volunteer, church worker, interdenominational Bible study leader, international traveler. And I have multiple sclerosis. My disability has not become a stumbling block but a measuring rod by which I can evaluate the most effective use of my God-given abilities."

Sharon Kutz-Mellem is the former managing editor of *The Disability Rag* and is comoderator of Presbyterians for Disabilities Concerns, a committee of the Presbyterian Health, Education, and Welfare Association (PCUSA).

Dorothy Lairmore is ordained in the United Church of Christ and on staff in Jefferson City, Minnesota.

Evon Laubenstein is executive president of American Baptist Women's Ministries.

Grace T. Lawrence is pastor of First Baptist Church, Lykens, Pennsylvania, as well as a clown minister who witnesses faithfully to the journey to joy *through it all.*

Ruth M. Lawson is executive secretary for the Office of Community Developers and the Office of Black Ministries of the General Board of Global Ministries, United Methodist Church.

Lois LaFon has been a registered nurse for thirty-four years, twenty-two of them in neonatal intensive care. She is a mother of two, a grandmother, and an elder in her local congregation.

Millie Leuenberger is the pastoral administrator (lay pastor) of two Roman Catholic churches in scenic northeast Iowa.

Kae Lewis is executive director of Mary Elizabeth Inn Women's Residence in San Francisco, a national mission project related to the United Methodist Church.

Cecelia M. Long is a member of Sherman United Methodist Church, a candidate for diaconal ministry, and general secretariat of the General Commission on the Status and Role of Women for the United Methodist Church, Evanston, Illinois.

Berlinda A. Love serves on the executive board of Trenton Ecumenical Area Ministry and on the executive committee of the Capital Association of American Baptist Churches of New Jersey.

Mary B. Lovett is a Master of Divinity student at Eastern Baptist Theological Seminary, graduating in 1997, and is assistant editor of this book.

Rose MacDermott is the justice, peace, and earthcare director for her religious congregation. She coordinates the Bernardine Center in Chester, Pennsylvania.

Marguerite Mackay is a school librarian in St. Croix, U.S. Virgin Islands.

Brenda Marinaro is a secretary for the West Virginia Baptist Convention and is an avid participant in a Total Triumph program at North Parkersburg Baptist Church, her home church.

Tammy L. Martens is a Quaker by conviction who pastors a small, programmed Friends meeting in rural Wisconsin.

Denise R. Mason is the student associate pastor at People's Congregational United Church of Christ in Washington, D.C., and completed her seminary studies at Howard University School of Divinity.

Maureen Matthews is a nurse who cofounded the Older Consultation Service in Stanford, Connecticut.

Cynthia A. Maybeck serves as pastor of Bethany Christian United Parish in Worcester, Maryland.

Dolores E. Lee McCabe is assistant professor of social justice and counseling and assistant to the provost for multicultural concerns at Eastern College.

Leah E. McCarter is an editorial associate in the Office of Communications for the American Baptist Churches in the U.S.A.

Carol McCollough, with her husband, Charles, leads marriage enrichment events. They live in Hopewell, New Jersey, and have three children and one grandson.

Gay Holthaus McCormick is a founding member of a United Church of Christ conference task force on issues of disability and accessibility and serves as a resource person to churches that need to make accessibility modifications.

Elizabeth V. McDowell has a special interest in intercultural communication through the arts and education. Formerly a college professor, she now directs a community arts center in the Adirondack Mountains.

Karla McGray began her body and soul event in earnest in her early forties while toting her toddler children around and now speaks on *The Spirituality of Menopause.*

Norma S. Mengel is a beloved child of God, made in God's image, and diaconal servant as associate for program, Council for Health and Human Service Ministries. Her mission is to be an instrument in advancing the healing and service ministry of Jesus Christ.

Mary L. Mild is the director of the American Baptist Personnel Services and the managing editor of this book. She is also the editor of *Songs of Miriam* and *Worthy of the Gospel.*

Kathleen A. Moore is a retired nurse, an active wife, mother, grandmother, and American Baptist woman.

Wilda K. W. (Wendy) Morris is the coordinator of Shalom Education, an ecumenical organization that provides educational experiences and curricular resources on peace and justice issues.

Anabel Moseley is a farm wife and mother who finds sharing vegetables, perennials, and woods lore, as well as working in all levels of church activities, rewarding and rejuvenating.

Jo Ellen Murphy is an employment-challenged 1995 graduate of Christian Theological Seminary, where she received her Master of Arts in Church Music degree. She began a new part-time organist position at East Tenth Street United Methodist Church in Indianapolis, Indiana, in 1996.

Dorothea Murray is a Presbyterian elder who is active in Democratic politics as an expression of her faith in God.

Kathie Murtey is a deputy public guardian. She is employed by county government and appointed by the court to be responsible for the well-being of mentally ill adults. She is also a storyteller.

Marge Nelson works with children's ministries in the Reorganized Church of Jesus Christ of Latter Day Saints.

Joey Noble has had breast cancer and lives daily with insulin-dependent diabetes. Jeremiah's words have encouraged her to live toward the future with hope.

Tilda Norberg is a United Methodist minister, a teacher, and a psychotherapist in Staten Island, New York.

Carolyn Henninger Oehler is executive director of the Scarritt-Bennett Center, a continuing education center in Nashville, Tennessee. She is a candidate for the Doctor of Philosophy degree at Garrett-Evangelical Theological Seminary/Northwestern University.

Elizabeth Okayama was coordinator of Ecumenical Women's Center from 1981 to 1988 and is assistant general secretary for episcopal services, General Council on Finance and Administration, United Methodist Church, from 1988 to present.

Meg Oliver is a member of Immanuel United Church of Christ of Catonsville, Maryland. She is married with two sons and has just completed her first year of law school.

Sally Olsen is a graduate student in clinical psychology at the University of South Dakota.

Mary Ann Overcash-Austin is a forty-year-old wife and mother of two children. In the last year she has lost her father and an uncle to cancer. She writes in loving memory of them.

Amanda Palmer lives and writes in the forest outside Flagstaff, Arizona.

Kate Penfield is executive director of the Ministers Council of the American Baptist Churches in the U.S.A. and the mother of five grown children.

Lois Pew, of San Juan Capistrano, California, is a retired teacher, minister's spouse, music director, and full-time grandmother.

Carol Spargo Pierskalla served as director for Aging: Today and Tomorrow for National Ministries, ABC/USA, from 1984 to 1993. She is currently a writer and the author of *Rehearsal for Retirement.*

Nina H. Pohl is a freelance editor and writer who been married for forty-seven years. She is a Midwesterner by birth and nature, but a Californian by climatic choice.

Neta Lindsay Pringle is pastor of Concord Presbyterian Church in Wilmington, Delaware, and an avid gardener.

Kristy Arnesen Pullen is associate publisher for Judson Press of the American Baptist Churches, U.S.A., an active member of her local congregation, and a contented wife and mother.

Yolanda Pupo-Ortiz is a United Methodist clergywoman in the Baltimore-Washington Conference. She is on the staff of the General Commission on Religion and Race.

Rebeca M. Radillo is pastor and chaplain of the Waterloo United Methodist Church and the Waterloo Village. She is also a pastoral psychotherapist and a doctoral candidate.

Donnis Reese is pastor of First Baptist Church of Ferndale, Michigan.

Mary Rehmann, C.H.M., is an attorney who helps poor people obtain health care by representing them in disability proceedings.

Gail Anderson Ricciuti is co-pastor of the Downtown United Presbyterian Church in Rochester, New York, and co-author of *Birthings and Blessings: Liberating Worship Services for Inclusive Communities,* volumes 1-2.

Beth A. Richardson is a United Methodist diaconal minister and assistant editor of *alive now!* magazine.

Marie Roberts is a Presbyterian clergywoman with a parish ministry and a private practice in Christian yoga, meditation, and wellness.

Patricia J. Rumer, formerly general director of Church Women United, is working as a consultant on issues of equality for women.

Valerie E. Russell is executive director of the Office for Church in Society in the United Church of Christ.

Penny Sarvis is a United Church of Christ minister who works for San Francisco Network Ministries. Part of the time she serves as chaplain at Mary Elizabeth Inn, a Methodist residence for women in transition.

Dorothy Savage, a Roman Catholic, is the director of Ministries in Christian Education for the National Council of Churches.

Susan Savell is a United Church of Christ minister serving women, children, and families as the executive director of the Maine Association of Child Abuse and Neglect Councils, a statewide prevention organization that provides leadership for the Healthy Families Maine Initiative.

Susan L. Scavo is a preacher's kid, pastor's wife for over 40 years, and mother of three. She has been employed for over 20 years as a licensed professional counselor.

Donna Schaper is associate conference minister for the Massachusetts conference, United Church of Christ. She is mother of three children who are being educated in both American and Jewish traditions.

Bonnie Scherer, a former registered nurse, is a children's author who has written and published two children's books.

Linda Scherzinger is a lay pastoral minister with the United Church of Canada in Cape Breton, Nova Scotia.

Nancy Hastings Sehested is a Baptist preacher, teacher, and storyteller who loves to hike high mountain trails.

Karyn Shadbolt is director of pastoral care at Long Beach Memorial Medical Center.

Sara Starnes Shingler is a director of the Women's Division of the United Methodist Board of Global Ministries from Spartanburg, South Carolina.

Julia D. Shreve, ELCA clergy, serves as chaplain with Lincoln Lutheran of Racine, Wisconsin. She works at the Becker Shoop Center with Alzheimer's and other dementia residents. In 1990 she received the Granger Westberg Award for Pastoral Care.

Peggy L. Shriver is staff associate for professional church leadership, National Council of Churches, and author of *Pinches of Salt, Spiritual Seasonings*, a book of original poetry published in 1990 by Westminster/John Knox Press.

Ann Smith is director of Women in Mission and Ministry, The Episcopal Church.

Patricia A. Smith is a United Methodist diaconal minister and social worker in Dallas, Texas.

Tweedy Sombrero is the pastor of United Methodist Native American Ministries in Phoenix, Arizona.

Liz Lopez Spence is a United Methodist clergywoman in Odessa, Texas.

Francine Stark is a member of Morgan Park Baptist Church in the ABC of Metro Chicago region, is married with four children, and is a seminary student working toward a Master of Divinity degree.

Jeanette Stokes, an ordained Presbyterian minister, writes and paints in Durham, North Carolina. After seventeen years as the founder and director of the Resource Center for Women and Ministry in the South, she is presently reinventing herself.

Jacqueline Sullivan is a chaplain at Monroe Community Hospital in Rochester, New York.

Betty Susi, a homemaker of forty years, mother of five, and grandmother of ten, longs to be a woman who walks with God.

Carol Franklin Sutton is a preacher's kid, a preacher's wife and a preacher, and is the executive director of the American Baptist Women Ministries.

Debra Sutton is director of adult education for the Board of Educational Ministries, American Baptist Churches in the U.S.A.

Jean Anne Swope is a Presbyterian minister who finds sabbath rest among the white pines and birches of the Adirondack Mountains of New York State, where she lives with her husband and ascribed family.

Barbara Ricks Thompson is general secretary of General Commission on Religion and Race for the United Methodist Church in Washington, D.C.

D. Elaine Tiller, executive director of community ministries, Baptist Senior Adult Ministries, works with senior adults from eighty-five congregations in the

Washington metropolitan area and enables them to minister in their congregations and communities.

Jean DeGraff Tischler has lived with a serious form of cancer for the past two years. She dreams of being a model to other cancer patients and hopes to become a certified Christian educator.

Emilie M. Townes, an American Baptist clergywoman, is associate professor of Christian ethics at Saint Paul School of Theology in Kansas City, Missouri, and the editor of *A Troubling in My Soul: Womanist Perspectives on Evil and Suffering* and the author of *Womanist Justice, Womanist Hope* and *In a Blaze of Glory: Womanist Spirituality as Social Witness.*

Jean Triplett is twenty-three months in remission and counting.

Julie Tulloch is executive staff for leadership education, Women's Division, General Board of Global Ministries in the United Methodist Church.

Yolanda Turner is a psychotherapist in private practice, a wife, and the mother of two boys.

Deborah Ulrich is a musician and serves as a diaconal minister in the United Methodist Church.

Jackie Underwood is a member of the feminist class of First Baptist Church, Granville, Ohio. She is also a family physician and mother of two daughters and one son.

Lynn Vahle is interim pastor at New Hope Presbyterian Church in Castle Rock, Colorado. After raising three sons and enduring about twenty years of night nursing, she saw the light of day, returned to school, and completed requirements for ordained ministry in the Presbyterian Church, USA.

Greta Wagner is an ordained American Baptist minister who serves as chaplain at St. Rita's Medical Center, Lima, Ohio, with specialty areas in cancer services and intensive care.

Beth Resler Walters is a mother, a professional writer focusing on health issues, and a faith-development and retreat leader in Charlotte, North Carolina.

Audrey Ward is a pastor in the California-Nevada conference of the United Methodist Church.

Kay Ward is a Moravian pastor, a religious educator, and currently the director of continuing education at Moravian Theological Seminary in Bethlehem, Pennsylvania.

Jennifer P. Warren has served as pastor in Presbyterian congregations in Delaware and Maryland, and since April 28, 1995, as mother to Peter Mack Warren Olson.

Adele K. Wilcox, a United Methodist clergywoman, is director of Migrations, a retreat and consulting center in north central Pennsylvania.

Peg Shelton Williamson's experience with chronic illness in family and parishioners led her to explore spiritual sources of healing.

Lisa Withrow, author of *Seasons of Prayer*, facilitates pastoral care groups for women and teaches worship while serving a United Methodist congregation in Ohio. Earlier in life, she was an environmental biologist.

Juanita Bass Wright, a United Methodist clergywoman, is currently serving as superintendent of the Clarksville District in Tennessee.

Betty Wright-Riggins is the head of school at Cornerstone Christian Academy. She recently completed the Master of Divinity degree at Eastern Baptist Theological Seminary in Philadelphia, Pennsylvania.

Ann W. Young is a Presbyterian minister and psychotherapist who leads retreats on spiritual formation and growth and volunteers in an AIDS ministry in Little Rock, Arkansas. Her current challenge is balancing her calling as a contemplative living in hermitage with an active life of ministry in the world.

Diane Bonner Zarowin is a chaplain in Staten Island, New York.

Penny Ziemer is the grateful mother of two healthy daughters, serves as minister of spiritual enrichment at First Christian Church, Goldsboro, North Carolina, and teaches religion at Mt. Olive College in North Carolina.

Notes

March

1. "Be Not Afraid," © 1975, 1978, Robert J. Dufford, SJ and New Dawn Music, 5536 NE Hassalo, Portland, OR 97213. All rights reserved. Used with permission. From the songbook, *Earthen Vessels*, published by North American Liturgy Resources, 10802 N. 23rd Avenue, Phoenix, Arizona 85029.

2. Ntazake Shange, *Sassafras, Cypress & Indigo*, Journal Entry 298 (New York: St. Martin's, 1982).

3. Susanna Wesley, mother of John Wesley, founder of Methodism.

4. Tillie Olsen, *Silences* (New York: Delacorte/Seymour Lawrence, 1978).

5. Ralph Waldo Emerson, "Self Reliance," in The Essays-First Series.

6. Storyteller's creed, author unknown.

April

1. Per-Olof Sjogren, *The Jesus Prayer* (Philadelphia: Fortress Press, 1975), 31.

2. Gabriele Uhlein, O.S.F., *Meditations with Hildegard of Bingen* (Santa Fe, N.Mex.: Bear, 1983).

3. Edith Wharton in *The Quotable Woman* (Philadelphia: Running Press, 1991), 131.

May

1. Marc Gellman, *Does God Have a Big Toe?* (San Francisco: HarperCollins Child Books, 1989).

2. Attributed to Eleanor Roosevelt.

3. From the song "His Eye Is on the Sparrow" by Civilla D. Martin.

June

1. Miriam Therese Winter, *Woman Wisdom* (New York: Crossroad, 1991).

2. Brenda Ueland, *If You Want to Write* (St. Paul, Minn.: Graywolf, 1987), 179.

3. Gary Dorsey, *Congregation* (New York: Viking, 1995), 381.

July

1. Anne Morrow Lindbergh, *Gift from the Sea* (New York: Pantheon, 1975).

2. Kahlil Gibran, *The Prophet.*

3. *Hospice Newsletter*, anonymous.

August

1. Carol Saline, *Sisters*, photographs by Sharon J. Wohlmuth (Philadelphia: Running Press, 1994), 13.

September

1. Chellis Glendinning.

2. May Sarton, in "The Family of Women: Growing toward the Light," *MS* Magazine 1982.

3. Jeannette Winterson, *Oranges Are Not the Only Fruit* (Madison, Ala.: Pandora Press, 1985), 160.

October

1. Brook Medicine Eagle, *Buffalo Woman Comes Singing: The Spirit Song of a Rainbow Medicine Woman* (New York: Ballantine, 1991).

2. May Sarton, quoted in *The Artist's Way* by Julia Cameron with Mark Bryan (New York: G. P. Putnam's Sons, 1992), 15.

November

1. Adapted from "Love Them As We Find Them," by Marge Nelson, *Restoration Witness*, November/December 1996, 28-29. Used with permission of Herald Publishing House, 3225 South Noland, Independence, MO 64055.

December

1. From the hymn, "Spirit of Life in This New Dawn" by Earl Marlatt.

2. Brenda Ueland, *If You Want to Write* (St. Paul, Minn.: Graywolf, 1987), 42.

3. Hildegard of Bingen.

4. Thomas Merton.